READING THE QUR'AN

ZIAUDDIN SARDAR

Reading the Qur'an

*The Contemporary Relevance of the
Sacred Text of Islam*

OXFORD
UNIVERSITY PRESS

OXFORD
UNIVERSITY PRESS

Oxford University Press, Inc., publishes works that further
Oxford University's objective of excellence
in research, scholarship, and education.

Oxford   New York
Auckland   Cape Town   Dar es Salaam   Hong Kong   Karachi
Kuala Lumpur   Madrid   Melbourne   Mexico City   Nairobi
New Delhi   Shanghai   Taipei   Toronto

With offices in
Argentina   Austria   Brazil   Chile   Czech Republic   France   Greece
Guatemala   Hungary   Italy   Japan   Poland   Portugal   Singapore
South Korea   Switzerland   Thailand   Turkey   Ukraine   Vietnam

First published in the United Kingdom by C. Hurst & Co. (Publishers) Ltd., 2010
Published by Oxford University Press, Inc.
198 Madison Avenue, New York, New York 10016

www.oup.com

Oxford is a registered trademark of Oxford University Press

Library of Congress Cataloging-in-Publication Data
Sardar, Ziauddin.
Reading the Qur'an : the contemporary relevance of the sacred text of
Islam / Ziauddin Sardar.
p. cm.
Includes bibliographical references and index.
ISBN 978-0-19-983674-1
1. Koran—Criticism, interpretation, etc.
2. Koran—Appreciation.   3. Koran—Reading.   I. Title.
BP130.4.S376 2011
297.1'226—dc22   2011008721

9 8 7 6 5 4 3 2 1

Printed in the United States of America
on acid-free paper

CONTENTS

CONTENTS

PART THREE: THEMES AND CONCEPTS

PART FOUR: CONTEMPORARY TOPICS

CONTENTS

Read! In the name of your Lord who created:
He created man from a clinging form.
Read! Your Lord is the most Bountiful One
Who taught by [means of] the pen, who taught man what he did not know

The Qur'an: 96:1–5 (M A S Abdel Haleem translation)

I would think that, of all the books in this first list ... the crucial work is the Koran.
Whether for its aesthetic and spiritual power or the influence it will have on all our
futures, ignorance of the Koran is foolish and increasingly dangerous.

Harold Bloom, *The Wester n Canon: The Books and Schools of the Ages*, Harcourt
Brace and Company, New York, 1994, p531

PREFACE

Reading the Qur'an grew out of my 'Blogging the Qur'an' project for the British newspaper, *The Guardian*. The book retains some of the distinctive features of the blogs: the concern with contemporary relevance, the emphasis on various contexts, including the context of the society and conditions in which the Qur'an was revealed, varied contexts by which readers through history have read and interpreted the text, all accompanied by a critique derived from my own engagement with the text and its meanings. I have also kept the conversational tone of the blogs.

But, of course, a book is not a blog. By their very nature, blogs tends to be short, punchy, and often, hurried. The book expands the content quite extensively, with an emphasis on a more discursive and reflective analysis. The commentary on al-Fatiha and al-Baqara, the first and the longest chapters in the Qur'an, have been considerably reworked. It was also necessary to fill some of the obvious gaps in the blogs with new subjects and topics. The blogs, written during 2008, and aimed at Muslims and non-Muslims alike, are interactive and include comments and questions posed by Guardian editors and readers, my answers and rejoinders, and responses to my responses. Readers interested in this vigorous, and sometimes heated, discussion will have to refer to the blogs themselves, available at http://blogs.guardian.co.uk/quran/. Here, they will find a more systematic, more elaborate, more wide-ranging, calm and collective, but I hope just as lively, discourse on Islam's Sacred Text. The journey that began with 'Blogging the Qur'an' continues, the destination remains the same – developing an understanding of the text for our own time – but the mode of travel has definitely changed.

I owe a debt of gratitude to all those who participated in the blog. Thanks are due to Georgina Henry, who commissioned the blog, Madeleine Bunting who posed the initial questions, Andrew Brown and Brian Whitaker, who jumped in with their interventions, and Theresa Malone and David Shariatmadari who sorted out the nuts and bolts of the whole process. Numerous bloggers contributed to the discussion and provided valuable insights, but I can only mention a few: Yayha Birt, Samia Rahman, Bill Sylvester, D Pavett, Richard Kimber, Noor Al-Yaqeen, Shamim Miah, Jonathan Close, Rosalinda, Kashif Shahzada, Sakeena, Abdullah Al-Hasan, Theo Hobson, Khokhar976, jammyfool, solocontrotutti, MiskatonicUniversity, thinkbreath and Dr Jazz. My apologies to those who have been left out – you all made me think anew!

A number of friends furnished useful comments on the whole blog, and hence provided helpful suggestions for the book. I am particularly grateful to Farid Esack, Bruce Lawrence and M A Abdel Haleem, who, in their various ways, I regard as my teachers. Manazir Ahsan gave invaluable support by providing me with a host of classical and modern texts on the Qur'an; and Ehsan Masood was always there with his comments and suggestions and an odd reference or two to neglected books. Finally, my heartfelt and fulsome thanks to my friend and collaborator Merryl Wyn Davies: you are always there with your trenchant criticism, your insistence on rewriting everything I have written, and your invaluable help and support. Where would I be without you (don't answer that!)?

PROLOGUE

We live in troubled times, in a dangerous and destabilised world. At the heart of present conflicts and perceived future threats stands a book. The book is the Qur'an, the Sacred Text of Islam. How people read the Qur'an and what is read as the Qur'an are not necessarily the same thing. Yet the distinction is fundamental to how people think, feel and react to the problems afflicting the world today. Whether Muslim or non Muslim, understanding what is involved in reading the Qur'an, how it has been read in history and the ways in which people derive meaning from its message, makes a significant contribution to contemporary debates, controversy and doubt.

Even though it is one of the most read books of all time, what the Qur'an actually says is shrouded in veils of assumptions and received opinions. Other people's readings of the Qur'an present considerable obstacles between the text and today's readers whether they are Muslim or non Muslim. The problems of how to approach and make sense of the text are common to Muslim and non Muslim and have existed almost since the original revelation of the Qur'an. What has been read into its meaning often seems to count for more than what the text itself expressly states.

Among believers the Qur'an is invoked to support directly contradictory meanings: a majority insist it is a book of peace; extremists use it to argue that it legitimises their recourse to mass murder. And on both sides of the divide there is no consensus on how the majority of the text, accepted as governing a total way of life, could, should, or ought to be applied to the whole gamut of actual dilemmas of contemporary Muslim society or global human problems.

For non believers the Qur'an presents a host of baffling conundrums. It is not a linear text, it does not replicate conventions familiar from reading the Bible. Yet the Bible is the inescapable source of comparison and contrast employed to evaluate how to read and what is read into its words. No book divides opinion as passionately. No book more urgently needs to be read with greater clarity.

There is a need, I would argue, for Muslims and non-Muslims alike, to approach the text with fresh eyes. For non-Muslims there is a need to make an effort to see what is so special about the Qur'an that convinces Muslims to regulate their lives according to its teachings, what motivates and generates passion, how the Qur'an shapes their thought and behaviour. And for Muslims the corresponding need is to understand the ways in which it inspired earlier generations to reach the zenith of civilisation, and to distinguish the possible and potential shades of meaning from the various interpretations that have accumulated over the centuries. However, the greatest challenge for both Muslims and non-Muslims is to read the Qur'an on its own terms, to engage with its text unencumbered by prejudices and preconceived ideas, to free their minds as far as humanly possible from what we have been told to understand and encounter its words anew.

This is what I have tried to do in this book. I have attempted to read the Qur'an to uncover what the text communicates to me. *Reading the Qur'an* is not an argument for or against any particular school of thought or tendency. It is a product of a personal journey, my own engagement with the text of the Qur'an. While I stress the importance of reading the Qur'an *personally* this necessitates an exploration of what is required to make a text readable. However, the personal, one man's reading, inevitably is connected to the process of how other people have read and responded to the same words, now and in history. So this book seeks to identify and reflect on how my reading emerges from and is distinct from the nuances, biases, dogmas, pieties and hostile criticisms I have imbibed and am aware of in all I have ever read about the Qur'an. I attempt to demystify the very act of reading by exploring the various contexts that are essential parts of how readers engage with a sacred text.

I am not a special reader. Indeed, I have no qualms in admitting that I am not the most qualified person to talk about the Qur'an, let alone offer my own particular reading of the text and its meaning. I am not a Hafiz, or an Imam, or an *Alim* – a religious scholar trained for years in a religious seminary. Although on certain bad days, I do imagine myself as a Muslim thinker of some repute. Worse: I don't even speak Arabic.

However, most readers of the Qur'an are in the same position as me. Not all of us can devote most of our lives to learning classical Arabic or become Qur'anic scholars. But that does not deprive us of our right to read the Qur'an with all our shortcomings and gaps in knowledge. I, like most people, Muslims and non-Muslims alike, read the Qur'an in translation. Here there is a basic distinction to be made between reciting the Arabic words of the Qur'an and reading with comprehension which is only possible with a translation in one's own native language. This is not ideal; but it is not unusual nor is it a major drawback. Even modern Arabic speakers– and these constitute less than four-fifths of the Muslim population of the world - do not find it easy to grasp the meaning of its verses. Native Arabic speakers may have an advantage in pronouncing its words correctly, but they are in the same boat as everyone else when it comes to struggling to discover the meaning and contemporary relevance of the words and verses of the Qur'an. They have to use classical and modern commentaries to enhance their understanding. For Muslims, Arabs and non-Arabs alike, the challenge of understanding the Qur'an, and making sense of it for our times, is formidable. For non-Muslims the task is even greater. The point is we all, whatever our state of knowledge and station in life, have to struggle with the Sacred Book.

I write as Every Muslim; as an individual trying to understand what the Qur'an means to me in the twenty-first Century. I believe that every Muslim is duty bound to accept responsibility for making this effort. I contend that one can have only an interpretative relationship with a text, particularly when that text is regarded as eternal. By this I mean that readers can only strive to do their best to arrive at conviction in their tentative, contextual and timebound understanding of the text. The eternal and infinite are not qualities of human knowledge, understanding or experience. By definition, not all the scholarship of all the ages, individual and/or collective, can ever be an absolute and permanently fixed reading of the divine word. To accept the Qur'an as eternal means acknowledging that there is always more to the text than our partial intellect will comprehend and to begin one's reading from that premise with humility. The interpretive relationship begins with personal and individual reading but that does not undermine or obliterate collective consequences. The personal and individual are the necessary precursor and inclusive of a perspective on communal obligations and responsibilities. Everyone who claims to be a Muslim must struggle with the meaning of the Qur'an. There is no 'get out' clause, no escape. This responsibility is not fulfilled by merely reciting its words; or by being told by other, more qualified people, what it means and should mean. It is something we need to discover for ourselves.

The Sacred Text of Islam was revealed over a period of 23 years, from 610 to 632 AD; it marks the beginning of Islam. It is the Book which defines all

Muslims: they are people who believe its text is the Word of God recorded exactly as revealed to the Prophet Muhammad. The Qur'an is an inescapable presence in the daily life of Muslims: passages are recited during the five daily prayers while people read the whole text frequently throughout their lives.

However, the message of the Qur'an is not directed exclusively to those who believe. The Qur'an addresses all humanity, in particular 'people who think'. It describes itself as a book of guidance for all humanity, even though many of its verses specifically address 'those who believe'. It admonishes those who believe blindly; and asks it readers, again and again, to observe, reflect, question. In other words it is a book that demands critical thought of all readers. It is a book about relationships, concerned to establish the relationship between God and all created things including all humanity. While it devotes considerable space to delineating the attributes of God, the power and majesty of the divine that is beyond human comprehension, the Qur'an stresses throughout that knowledge and reason are as important and valid as faith itself in apprehending and understanding God.

The message of the Qur'an is not easy to grasp. It is quite simply unlike any other 'book' having no conventional beginning or end. At first sight, it is full of repetitions, seems to imply internal contradictions and appears to have its own logic. This is why non-Muslims readers are often baffled. They expect it to resemble the Bible. The Qur'an does contain many Biblical stories, relating incidents in the lives of 25 Prophets also mentioned in the Bible, such as Prophets Moses, Abraham, Jesus, Noah and Lot. Yet reference to these Biblical Prophets is not found in a single place. Their stories occur in fragments and recur, introducing and focusing on different details at various points throughout the entire book. But the comparison ends there. The Qur'an, unlike the Bible, has no narrative structure: the few stories it relates are not exhaustive factual recitals but assume a familiarity with detail and focus on drawing a particular insight or moral from the sparse details specifically referred to; it has surprisingly few commandments; its verses are not arranged in chronological order according to the sequence in which they were revealed. All this makes the Qur'an much more difficult to read in English, or indeed in any other translation, than most conventional texts.

The Qur'an uses a heightened form of Arabic, language of great beauty with the power to move listeners. This Qur'anic Arabic has a particular structure: it locks every word with every other in the text and places it in a precise location in the whole text. This interlocking language is seen by Muslims as a proof of the Qur'an's Divine origins; it also makes the text easy to memorise. Millions of people around the world, known as *hafiz*, have committed the entire Qur'an to memory. They carry it, as the Muslim tradition says, in 'their heart'. But there is a profound irony here: memorising the Qur'an is not the same as reading, interpreting or understanding. Reading involves a struggle with words and meanings.

To genuinely struggle with words and meanings requires something more. Recitation and memorising are tools of preservation; they ensure the continuity of the original text as the enduring basis for a personal interpretive relationship with scripture. To make that relationship meaningful the preserved and remembered words have to be comprehended through the language of one's conventional understanding. Only through the medium of one's own language can there be a critical engagement with the text that can uncover its significance for the circumstances of one's daily life. Translations can be good and bad, they can hide as much as they reveal. While reading the Qur'an through translation, I have tried to unravel the multiple shades of meaning in some of its key terms and phrases. The overall emphasis is on finding contemporary relevance. What does the Qur'an say to our times, what guidance it provides for contemporary problems, how it seeks to promote a life of virtue and righteousness – these are questions uppermost in my reading.

Yet, I begin with the assumption that in translation both Muslims and non-Muslims can gain a basic appreciation of the Qur'an and its message, without any specialised knowledge. All one needs is an eagerness to know and learn, working with the assistance of a range of readily available resources, some humility and patience, and the Qur'an opens up. Of course, each reader will examine the text through his or her own experience, asking questions that seem pertinent to them. Asking questions, I believe, is particularly relevant here: the Qur'an responds, I discovered, to questioning, which is my main methodology in this endeavour. Obviously, as a Muslim, I bring particular understandings and experience to my reading of the text but I also ask questions that a believer would perhaps not ask and which are uppermost in the minds of non-Muslim readers. By asking significant questions, acknowledging my own experiences and concerns to other readers, debating them aloud for myself and the readers, it becomes possible to consider what each passage means *on an individual level* here and now. Making the text accessible through a process of personal questioning, I hope, offers new insight on possible and potential meanings that provide a stimulus for more informed debate on current issues and concerned differences of opinion. The Quran, like all religious scriptures, has many layers of meaning and this book attempts to uncover these multiple layers. Making evident these multiple layers and considering how and in what ways they have been, are or could be relevant to different audiences enables readers to consider for themselves the contemporary relevance of the text. *Reading the Qur'an* is an invitation to readers to make up their own minds about the content and meaning of this sacred text.

Muslims have been wrestling with the meaning of the words of the Qur'an since the inception of Islam. Traditionally, the Qur'an has been interpreted verse by verse; classical scholars would start with the first verse and continue all the way to the last, explaining the meaning and significance of each. Classical commentators, such as al-Razi (964–930 AD), ibn Arabi (1165–1240) and ibn Kathir (1301–1373) followed this methodology as do contemporary commentaries, such as those of Syed Qutb (1906–1966) and Abu Ala Mawdudi (1903–1979), the ideological leader of Muslim Brotherhood and the founder of Jamaat-e-Islam respectively. Syed Qutb often provides long, discursive passages that analyse each verse in considerable detail. But verse-by-verse exegesis has its limits. It can, for example, lead to literalism. Moreover, as the noted Muslim scholar, Fazlur Rahman (1911–1988), suggests 'by the very nature of their procedure they cannot yield insight into the cohesive outlook on the universe and life which the Qur'an undoubted possesses' [1]. The practice of verse-by-verse has led to the practice of citing specific verses to justify certain positions, no matter how far these positions may be from the overall spirit of the Qur'an. It is a particular favourite of the fire and brimstone brigade who reduce the Qur'an to a checklist of do's and don'ts. I have never believed that a single method can tell us all there is to know about a phenomenon, let alone such a complex and multilayered text as the Qur'an. Here, as elsewhere, I opt for multiple methods.

I identify, combine and explore various methodologies and approaches in my reading of the Qur'an. Even in the section where I attempt to provide an approximation of the verse-by-verse technique, in deference to tradition, I consciously employ a number of old and new methods, from contextual analysis to hermeneutics, from literary theory to semiotics, to tease out new meaning and appreciation of the Qur'anic text. By combining multiple methods and approaches, I hope to alert myself, and hence the reader, to different levels of meaning and interpretation of the text – how it has been classically read, how it can be read differently, and how it might be read today.

Classical commentaries emphasise two types of context. First, the context within the Qur'an: what the Sacred Text has to say about a subject in different places. Here the most common example is the Qur'an's prohibition of alcohol.

First, we are told not drink while praying, then the Qur'an says alcohol has both good and bad properties but its bad effects often outweigh the good. Finally, it asks the Muslim community not to drink at all. In this contextual analysis, traditionally, the last verse is accepted as the final injunction while the previous ones are said to be abrogated and therefore can be ignored.

The second context is provided by the life of the Prophet. The Prophet Muhammad was not only the recipient of the revelation, but the revelation itself is a commentary on his life. So, the interpretation of its verses, many of which are addressed directly to the Prophet, has to be seen in the context of what was happening to the Prophet. Verses that apply specifically to the household of the Prophet Mohammad, for example, may or may not have universal connotations. Whether such verses have implications for other times must be an act of interpretation, ideally the work of reason, reflection and questioning rather than a literal incitement.

I add two further contexts to those used in classical commentary: the context of history and the context of our time. It is these additions which perhaps make my reading different from others. The Qur'an is an eternal text – that its words are valid for all time and place is a basic Muslim belief. But it is also a text revealed in history, a history whose context - social conditions, norms and customs, political structures – it could not ignore. Indeed, the Qur'an acknowledges that it was revealed during a particular history with particular circumstances. While it is not a narrative history, it uses the history of the time of the Prophet as a commentary on the meaning and implications of human history. It questions the history of other peoples and places to illuminate and point to a deeper understanding of both spiritual and material truth. So, I argue that many of its verses, such as those on women and crime and punishment, should be read in this context; and understood in terms of their spirit rather than specific injunctions.

Moreover, we as human beings can only engage with the Qur'an, and interpret it, according to our own contemporary understanding. It has to make sense to us as ordinary mortals here and now; it has to have significance for us in the light of our needs and requirements in contemporary times; it has to guide us through the moral, ethical and spiritual dilemmas of our time. So, the context of our time is equally important for its interpretation. Thus, we have to approach the Qur'an from the perspective of how morality, on such issues for example as gay rights and environmental concerns, has evolved in our own time; and engage with the text in the light of our changing circumstances. My insistence on the context of our time actually inverts the traditional understanding of the Qur'an: most Muslims believe that morality ends with the Qur'an; I, on the other hand, argue that the Qur'an marks the beginning of morality. The morality of the Qur'an is not the end point of human thought and evolution. If that was the case then human evolution would have no meaning and history would really have ended. Rather, it marks the beginning of ethics and morality from which and upon which reflection depends and genuine progress is possible.

A Qur'an relevant to all time and place also means no interpretation of the Qur'an can be eternal; it can only be limited and time bound – something that I argued in my, now forgotten book, *The Future of Muslim Civilisation* several decades ago [2]. The twelfth century Muslim theologian and philosopher, al-Ghazzali, who is perhaps one of the most misunderstood classical Muslim thinker, argued that the Qur'an was open to as many interpretations as there are drops of water in the ocean. 'O you who recite a lengthy portion of the Qur'an', he wrote, 'Do you not know that the Qur'an is like an ocean? Do you not have a duty to sail into the endless ocean of its meanings? Dive into the ocean's depths so that you may become wealthy by gaining its rubies and pearls. Why do you persist in remaining on the shore, satisfied with the manifest?' [3]. To go beyond the 'manifest meanings', we need to interpret the Qur'an again and again. My thesis is that the Qur'an has to be reinterpreted from epoch to epoch, generation to generation. The natural corollary of this thesis is that it is legitimate for Muslims to reject, enhance, go beyond and differ significantly from the interpretations of earlier times.

Reading the Qur'an is divided into four parts. Part One provides an Overview, discussing the style, nature and structure of the Qur'an, how the Qur'an has been read and interpreted conventionally, problems and strengths of translations, and the burning question: who has the authority to interpret the Qur'an?

Part Two, 'By Way of Tradition', provides a commentary on chapter 1, Al-Fatiha, which is regarded as the summary of the Qur'an, and chapter 2, Al-Baqara, the longest chapter in the Qur'an. Al-Baqara actually provides a compendium, or précis, of the themes and concepts of Qur'anic teaching from basic beliefs such as heaven and hell and good and evil, fundamental Islamic practices such as prayer, fasting and hajj, basic legal injunctions on social relations, equality, women's rights, war and peace, and pluralism. In this section while I acknowledge the conventional method of verse by verse exegesis in the need to highlight specific verses I give much greater emphasis to identifying groups of verses, sometimes a mere handful sometimes long passages, as being interlinked by overarching themes and subject matter. Looking at what seem to me to be self selecting sections is where I find a new perspective on verses I have previously read innumerable times. Balancing the 'atoms' of the verse by verse tradition with the broader focus on theme and subject matter I find uncovers the connective tissue of the text, it maintains a consistent appreciation of a coherent interlinked whole and uncovers an inner logic which suggests the rationale for what at first sight appear to be disparate and unrelated references. Read in this way each section opens new perceptions which positively encourage and require me to question and reflect on the contemporary relevance of Qur'anic teachings.

Part Three focuses on major themes of the Qur'an and identifies some key concepts used in the text. This is the kind of approach that some reformists – and many postmodern Muslims – like to take. This part looks at the Qur'an as a whole, an integrated text, and explores what the Qur'an has to say about truth and plurality, humanity and community, individual and society, reason and knowledge, rights and duties, nature and environment, ethics and morality, reading and writing and other similar issues. These themes are not normally addressed individually in conventional commentaries.

Part Four deals with issues and topics of contemporary times – from the Shariah (Islamic Law) to suicide bombing, politics and democracy, sex and homosexuality, science and evolution, to freedom of expression and the veil. Here verses from various parts of the Qur'an are brought together to explore the position of the Qur'an and its possible and potential meaning in relation to some of the pressing issues of our time.

I hope the reader will have as much pleasure and intellectual stimulation in exploring the Qur'an with me as I did. Most of all I hope this book convinces readers that the tools are readily available for the Qur'an to be read by anyone without the need for specialised knowledge. The Sacred Text of Islam requires effort and is not easy. Yet it speaks to us today and everyone can avail themselves of the tools that common sense and basic reasonableness require to make its language and message meaningful. You are not going to get anything out of the Book that shapes the outlook of a quarter of humanity if you approach it with a hostile intent – except, perhaps, a convoluted justification of your own prejudices and phobias. Equally, applying ninth century exegesis and answers to twenty-first century circumstances not only defies the spirit of inquiry and debate the Qur'an commends to its readers, it can result in customs and actions that violate the ethos and meaning of Qur'anic teachings and beliefs. Love of the self and one's own self-righteous positions, dogmatic or liberal, religious or secular, can only be a barrier to a serious engagement with the Qur'an. The Sacred Text demands an open mind and a modicum of effort. It does not provide us with ready made answers. But it does guide us, if we are willing, towards a fresh understanding and appreciation of our eternal ethical and moral dilemmas and what it means to be human.

To be human, by definition, is to be imperfect. Any reading of the Qur'an will bound to have imperfections, mistakes, misinterpretation, misrepresentations, and, in my particular case, tendency to berate the self-righteous of all shades and colour. Following on the footsteps of the great twelfth century Andalusian philosopher, ibn Rushd, I repeat after him: 'God knows every single letter, and perhaps God will accept my excuse and forgive my stumbling in His bounty, generosity, munificence and excellence – there is no God but He! [4]'.

Part One

OVERVIEW

1

THE QUR'AN AND ME

I grew up reading the Qur'an on my mother's lap. It's an experience I share with most Muslim children. It's usual, once children are about four or five, for mothers to start reading the Qur'an and getting the child to repeat the words, again and again, till the Arabic sounds become familiar and can be recited from memory. And so it is that our connection to the Qur'an is infused with associations of the warmest and most enduring of human bonds. The Qur'an enters our lives as an integral part of home and domesticity, the environment in which we become aware of ourselves as a person. Outside the home five times a day throughout the Muslim world we hear the *muadhin's* call to prayer: 'come to *falah*' (well-being, felicity), he urges, while indoors mothers teach the most familiar and basic words which constitute prayer. Actually, I started reading the Qur'an a little late—when I was pushing six. In those days, we lived in a small town on the Pakistani side of the Punjab. After dinner every Thursday evening, my mother would shout '*Sipara* time'. I would stop playing, run to her, jump on her lap and put my left arm around her neck. She would open a slim, well read and rather torn booklet, and start reading: Bismillah ir-Rahman ir-Rahim: In the name of God, the Beneficent, the Merciful. I remember how she would pronounce each word distinctly and separately. I would repeat each word after her, and then she'd have me repeat them again to make sure I pronounced each one correctly.

A *Sipara* contains a section of the Qur'an. The word 'Qur'an' means reading; and the Holy Book is often described as 'The Noble Reading'. To make it easier to read, it is divided into thirty sections known in Arabic as *juz*'. *Sipara* is the Urdu equivalent, sometimes shortened simply to *para*. Reading one *para* a day,

3

you can complete a recitation of the whole Qur'an in a month. This comes in handy during the fasting month of Ramadan; then the whole Qur'an is read, one section each evening, to vast gatherings at special congregational prayer sessions. The particular emphasis on reading the Qur'an during Ramadan is in recognition that this was the month when the first words of the Qur'an were revealed to the Prophet Muhammad.

Children begin their reading at the end. So I started with the 30th *Sipara*. It contains short chapters, or *suras*, some just a few verses long, all rather easy to commit to memory. When I had memorised most of the chapters in this *Sipara*, and it was time to tackle the longer *suras*, my mother decided to send me to the *madrasa*, or religious school, in the local mosque. It is vaguely equivalent to going to Sunday School, but with rather more emphasis on the school since the curriculum is set and the same everywhere: learning to read the Qur'an. Most mosques have a *madrasa* attached to them; and I suppose my *madrasa* was like a *madrasa* in any mosque, anywhere in the world. It was a small, darkly lit room. Children would arrive at an appointed time, in my case after midday Friday prayers. On arriving we'd all perform the obligatory ablution, mastering the ritual of carefully washing hands, forearms, head and feet to cleanse ourselves of the dust and grime of the mundane and prepare ourselves for the encounter with the Sacred Text. Then we'd all take our places on small stools behind a long, narrow table. The Imam sat on a chair in front of us, waving a long stick. By the age of seven or eight, children are expected to know the words, having mastered the letters and sounds of the Arabic alphabet, and thus be able to read the Qur'an themselves. We would be instructed to open our *Sipara* on a specific page—and start reading aloud. The Imam would listen, somehow able to pay attention to each child. If someone got the pronunciation of a word wrong, or made some other mistake, down would come the stick. I don't remember anyone actually being hit; the punishment seemed to land on the table. But I do remember how the rapid-fire swish and thwack frightened all of us.

I wasn't enthusiastic about my *madrasa* lessons, which lasted about an hour. They lacked the loving touch of my mother. But I loved what happened frequently after lessons. The classes were not graded, even though everyone from the locality came, so all ages and stages mixed in the harmonics, or to an untrained ear the cacophony, of reading aloud their personal assignment of different parts of the Qur'an. Someone in the class would always be about to reach the completion of the whole Qur'an. When they did, their family would celebrate with a general and generous distribution of sweetmeats: you know, things like *gulab jaman*, *ras malai*, and my all-time favourite, *barfi*. I'd gorge myself and always got to take a plateful home. On certain occasions a particularly notable student would have managed to memorise the whole Qur'an. They would be honoured with the title '*hafidh*'; and then their family's joy would know no bounds. There would be *barfi* by the truckload!

Of course, the classes I attended were for boys. But exactly the same classes with the same curriculum and system were held for girls, or how else would there be mothers ready and able to teach their children? After the *madrasa* comes the chasm. The awful difference in attitudes to and provision of education for women in many Muslim countries never ceases to outrage me.

My *madrasa* lessons did not last long. When I was nine, my family moved to Clapton Pond in Hackney. In the early sixties, there were few mosques in London. There was no chance of me going to a *madrasa*. So back I went to my mother—but her lap was now occupied by my younger sister. Besides, she expected me to read the Qur'an by myself; not surprising, since I had reached the end of the 29th *para*. My mother now said I should start from the beginning again, with the 30th *para*. But this time she was insistent that I read the words with meaning.

For Muslims, the Qur'an is the Word of God. In fact, that's how we define a Muslim: someone who accepts the Divine origins of the Noble Reading. To read the Qur'an is to see and hear the very words of God. This is why we read it in its original form: in Arabic, just as it was revealed to and then recited by Prophet Muhammad. Translations may convey meaning, but all translations are at best approximations, and therefore definitely not the actual words of God. As such, they do not amount to prayer or worship, which in Islam consists largely of reading the Qur'an. When my mother was taking me through my first *Sipara*, it was nothing like her reading me a bedtime story, which she sometimes did—mostly short, Urdu versions of *Arabian Nights*. When my mother taught me to read the Qur'an it was an act of worship and prayer. She was, in fact, teaching me how to pray—or rather, exactly what to recite as the basis of the five daily prayers.

Even before I started to read the Qur'an with meaning, I had a personal emotional connection to the Sacred Book. I felt a deep love for the text; it grew naturally from the experience of learning with my mother and how she taught me to read. The Glorious Qur'an, as far as she was concerned, was all about love: Love of God, Love of His Words. It was a deep, all-pervasive, unconditional love—like that of a mother for her son. I also felt reverence for the Qur'an. This came from watching how my mother herself approached the

Qur'an: with total respect and humility. And I felt fear. Somehow, reading the Qur'an always invoked the memory of the *madrasa* and the Imam Sahib with his long, bamboo stick. Swish! Later, I rationalised this fear as the apprehension of actually encountering the Majesty of God. Once you know the significance of the Qur'an, then you know that each time you open the Book or hear its words, right then and there, in the here and now, you are receiving the direct Word of God without intermediary. So trepidation, and more than a hint of caution, are no bad thing; and a large dose of humility is certainly needed, or just plain fear—fear of misunderstanding or misinterpreting His Word.

My emotional connection became more complex once I started to read the Qur'an with meaning. Now, I had to engage my mind: an inquiring, restless mind busily engaged in the process of being shaped by educational experiences and systems radically different to those honed in the *madrasa*. I was beginning to learn that reason makes its own demands. In London, the ritual of reading the Qur'an in our household changed. Both my parents worked from Monday to Friday. So Qur'an reading took place on Saturday mornings. Sundays were devoted by my mother to more profane ritual: she went, without fail, to the local fleapit to watch the latest offering from Bollywood [1].

Every Saturday I would sit in front of my mother and read out some selected verses. She would then explain their meaning in Urdu, with the aid of a translation. I would then read out the English translation of the same verses. Then, we would chat; and totally disagree.

My first problem was with the Urdu translation. Urdu is an exquisite, beautiful and poetic language. It is suffused with Arabic words. That's why those, like me, who read Urdu find it easy to read Arabic. (We simply read Arabic as though it was written in Urdu!) But I found Urdu translations of the Qur'an to be rather ugly; worse, the Urdu translation was often at odds with the English translation. The same verse sometimes conveyed quite different meanings when read in Urdu and English translations. Reading the Qur'an, I quickly realised, is one thing, but understanding it quite another.

Most of my life since adolescence has been a struggle with the meanings of the verses of the Qur'an. During my university years, when I was active in various student Islamic bodies, I joined a study group, or *Usra*. Each member took turns to host our sessions; we studied the Qur'an systematically, with the aid of a number of classical and contemporary commentaries, under the guidance of a well-known scholar. I was also involved, during this time, in the Federation of Students' Islamic Societies (FOSIS) and *The Muslim*, its monthly magazine [2]. In 1968, *The Muslim* began serialising a translation of Sayyid Qutb's *In the*

Shade of the Qur'an, a massive, multi-volume commentary by one of the leading ideologues of the Muslim Brotherhood. I approached each instalment with expectation and a little thrill. Qutb (1906–66), who was a literary critic, wrote his commentary with style and panache; and I devoured it with relish and enthusiasm. He provided assurance for a believer, and his command of the scope and sweep of Muslim history, culture and civilisation gave one pride in the achievements of Muslims. However, Qutb was nothing if not a man of total conviction. There was a certainty in his commentary that I could not share.

In particular, I had problems with Qutb's insistence that sometimes it is necessary to dispense with reason when reading the Qur'an. He throws scorn at what he described as 'the rational school'. The rational school, he claimed, 'had gone too far' in demanding 'rational explanation for all which may be unacceptable to it'. It shows, he thunders, 'clearly a strong desire to reduce the greater number of miracles to only the more familiar of Allah's natural laws rather than the supernatural' [3]. Now, I must confess that I have always had problems with miracles and continue to do so. But I have no difficulty in accepting the limits of human reason. Neither would I argue with Qubt's declaration that 'Allah's will and power are absolute, limitless'. But how, I wondered, could one make sense of what the Qur'an says without making full use of one's reason, however limited, in every and each situation? Is God's will not amenable to interrogation by human reason? How, without recourse to reason, are we to check harsh, arbitrary and absurd interpretations of the Qur'an? Are we supposed to read the Qur'an, and engage with the Absolute and the Limitless, without enquiring how and why? And, equally important: is it reasonable to presume one can have an absolute understanding, as Qutb's own commentary seems to imply, of the Absolute?

The consequences of not using reason, fully and unhindered, in one's reading of the Qur'an became evident when, on a visit to Pakistan, I went back to my old *madrasa*. It had not changed much, except for one thing. I could see that it had become a much more regimented and violent environment. The Qur'an classes were being led by three Mullahs who were beating the children mercilessly for every mistake, however insignificant. One could see the fear in the eyes of children who were endlessly repeating the same verse of the Qur'an again and again, while their teachers tried to ensure that they pronounced every word correctly. This was not about inspiring the love of a Sacred Text. It was about instilling the fear of God by brutal means. Later on, when I visited other larger *madrasas*, which were more like colleges, I found them to be puritan, authoritarian and hierarchical institutions. Young men grew and lived within their four walls, in poverty, without family, recreation or any form of amusement, eating and studying in an environment which to all intents and purposes resembled nothing so much as a medieval monastery. Here, the Qur'an was used not for meditation and inner reflection, questioning and thought, but as a tool of oppression. Bearded students, in their trademark loose-fitting, knee-length tunic (*kurta*) and baggy pants (*pyjamas*), quoted the Qur'an or traditions of the Prophet like automatons to justify everything from their 'Islamic dress' and beards to their xenophobia and self-righteousness. It was not just that these students, and their teachers, had accepted the so-called 'miracle' verses of the Qur'an unquestionably; they accepted everything without question and use of reason. Irrationality, obscurantism and dogma ruled every aspect of their lives.

In these *madrasas*, not just the Qur'an but everything is learned by rote and taught as the final, unquestionable word. 'The texts used are redundant and at times impenetrable', writes Ebrahim Moosa. Born in Cape Town, South Africa and now Director of the Center for Islamic Studies at Duke University, Moosa travelled to India in his youth to undergo a traditional Islamic education. Of his studies at two of the Muslim world's premier *madrasas* he writes: 'Inertia has turned the texts and syllabus into inviolable monuments to the past. The result is that the students are poorly prepared and lack confidence to engage the tradition critically to meet the needs of a changing world. At its worst the system recycles intellectual mediocrity as piety'. His education made him 'self-righteous' about the 'Islamic dress code' and 'the superiority of the interpretations of madrasa authorities' [4].

Just a few years ago I watched a documentary made by a group of Nigerian friends to defend the reputation of traditional *madrasas* in their country. Nigeria is plagued by religious tension that often boils into bloody conflict. The film was intended to demystify and explain how this system of education works. They wanted to show that, rather than bringing together a collection of ragamuffin youths who become a danger to the surrounding community, the *madrasas* are the only form of education open to poor Muslims who often travelled long distances from their home to study free of charge. The film dwelt on the familiar scenes of sessions of rote learning of the Qur'an and students learning to write the text on the elegant traditional wooden boards that are particularly fine examples of Hausa craftsmanship—and a source of income for the students. After watching the programme I turned to one of the sponsors who happened to be a leading educationalist, indeed a person responsible for training teachers in the modern school system of Nigeria: 'Is that how you would recommend a syllabus to be operated in your schools?' I asked. If a Nigerian face could have turned ashen, it would have. It was as if my friend had suddenly crashed with great force into a brick wall. Even as a professional educationalist it had never before occurred to him to question the content and form of *madrasa* education. Tradition was to be defended, subtly and efficiently, with all the skills of modern communication. Quite simply, it was never to be questioned.

As my career developed, I attended innumerable conferences of Muslim scholars, visited many Muslim countries, and met many people who argued about the meanings of the Sacred Text. The more I learned of Muslims' intellectual history and thought about the differences and distinctions, as well as similarities, between classical and modern scholars, the more I had to struggle with what Muslims throughout their history have made of the Qur'an. In Saudi Arabia, where I lived for almost five years, I spent some time at Mecca University and visited the university in Medina. You could hardly move a few yards without someone quoting the Qur'an at you. But the quotations were not meant to be discussed or explored: they were used explicitly to force you to behave in a certain way or accept certain unjust laws or unreasonable positions, or to shut you up. The Qur'an had become a stick frequently used for ensuring conformity and suppressing dissenting views. It was all so far removed from the Qur'an I had known during my childhood.

It was not just that different people were finding different meanings in the Qur'an, and interpreting it in different ways—some I could hardly agree with. It was also that some were finding things that went totally against my own conscience: justification for misogyny, validation for hatred of others, an obsession with dress, facial furniture and mindless ritual, oppressive laws, rules of running modern states, arguments for superiority of certain classes and individuals, even the discoveries of science (from electricity and relativity to geology). All of this I found deeply troubling. And I was particularly perturbed by the sight of protesters waving the Qur'an and shouting obnoxious, hate-fuelled and incendiary slogans. It was as though for many Muslims the Qur'an was as closed as their minds, an ornament on which to project all one's prejudices and paranoia. I shared the thoughts of Urdu poet Mahir-ul-Qadri (1907–78), who has the Qur'an lamenting:

> As an ornament do they adorn me,
> Yet they keep me, and sometimes kiss me,
> In their celebrations they recite me,

In disputes they swear by me,
On shelves do they securely keep me,
Till another celebration or dispute, when they need me,
Yes, they read me and memorise me,
Yet only an ornament am I,
My message lies neglected, my treasures untouched,
The field lies bare, where blossomed once true glory,
Wrong is the treatment that I receive,
So much to give have I, but none is there to perceive. [5]

Every Muslim can reel out a string of commonly held attributes about the Qur'an. It is Divine. It is Eternal. It is timeless, its words unchanged, it is ever present. It is unique, perfect, a literary miracle. It is complete, universal, the very proof of the existence of God. It is the Final Word of God. Yet, it seems to me, they forget an obvious fact: sacred texts, by their very nature, are complex, multi-layered, allegorical, metaphorical and an embodiment of pluralistic meanings. A Divine Text does not yield a divine meaning: the meaning attributed to it can only be the product of human understanding. A timeless book has meaning only in time. It can only speak to us in our own time and circumstances. Our understanding of 'the Final Word of God' cannot be final. It can only be transitory and limited by our own abilities and understanding. It gives us intimations of the divine, the mind of God, but by definition, however perfectable we may think humankind is, we are not and cannot be the mind of God. Absolute understanding, absolute certainty, infallible knowledge—these are not attributes of humanity; our lot is wrestling with our all too evident limitations. Therefore, the 'Word of God' is not beyond question: only through questioning the text can we tease out possible answers to our moral dilemmas. This is precisely why one of the most insistent commands in the Qur'an is to think and reflect. The struggle to understand and interpret Scripture is perpetual. The Qur'an does not change, but the circumstances of human life, the potential of our thought and action, the social, economic, technological, environmental and political conditions of our times are ever changing. As well as requiring us to think, the words of the Qur'an also imply movement: the religious life, it tells us, is not about standing still, but always striving to make our life, our society, the entire world around us a better place for everyone, all of God's creation without exception. And that means we have to keep on asking what the Sacred Text can, should or ought to mean, and how it could or should apply in the circumstances of today.

The Sacred Text of Islam has no significance for us outside our own time. The significance and meaning of the verses of the Qur'an have to be rediscovered by each generation in the context of its own time. Things change, contexts change, and old meanings, the customs born of old interpretations, far from liberating you can actually suffocate you; or worse, can be turned into means to oppress or oppose other people, whether fellow Muslims or not.

I have come to see the Qur'an as a text that simultaneously promotes thinking and doing. It is a dynamic text whose relevance and implications for our time we have yet to discover fully. It is a text that demands us to stand up for justice and equity irrespective of circumstances. It is a text that seeks change not through revolution but through renovation and evolution of human thought and action. It is a text that urges communities constantly to scrutinise themselves and guard against all forms of inhumanity. It is a text that polishes the souls of individuals so that their humanity can shine.

The Qur'an does not yield its meaning without a struggle with its text. To see the significance of an allegory or metaphor, to separate the truth from the simile, the eternal from the transient, the universal from the local, one has to struggle with words and concepts, contexts and interconnections, and the structure and style of the Qur'an. This is not an easy or a quick task. It requires effort and patience. But reading the Qur'an, as I discovered, can be very rewarding. It surpassed all my expectations.

2

STYLE AND STRUCTURE

Expectations tend to condition our reactions. Think of the hype involved in adverts for the latest film releases: they string together some of the best bits, so that we expect fireworks throughout. But the edited highlights bear little relation to the whole, which turns out to be a damp squib. The result is not just disappointment but a sense of being cheated of our justified expectations. So, before we start our exploration of the Qur'an, let me say some words of caution by way of conditioning your expectations.

Clearly Muslims and non-Muslims approach the Qur'an with different expectations. The distinction is significant. The definition of a Muslim is a person who believes the Qur'an to be the direct word of God as communicated to the Prophet Muhammad. Therefore, Muslims approach the Qur'an with an implicit acceptance of its style and nature. It would be inconceivable to start with the question 'Why isn't God telling me a simple story with a beginning, a middle and an end?' This is not to suggest that Muslims should not question; it is merely to point out that our questions start from a different point. For example, Muslims normally would not raise the question of authorship of the Sacred Text; they start with the assumption that it is God who is speaking to us through the Qur'an. Moreover, they regard both the structure and the style of the Qur'an as a part of its Divine origins. So the questions that Muslims would ask are focused on the meaning and understanding we should take from the nature and style of our Holy Book.

Non-Muslims would naturally question the Divine origins of the Qur'an. They may ascribe its authorship to Muhammad. They may raise other questions about its authenticity, its origins and its contents. They would approach the

Qur'an with the Torah and Bible in mind; and get very perplexed because the Qur'an is not like that at all. The Torah and the Old Testament begin with God's creation of the universe and all it contains, and then proceed with a straightforward history of the people of Israel and their prophets. The New Testament begins with the Gospels, which give a number of chronological accounts of the life of Jesus as the central narrative thread through which his teachings are presented, and then turns to the development of early Christianity. The Qur'an provides neither a chronology of God's revelations to humanity nor a linear narrative of the life and times of Prophet Muhammad. Non-Muslims thus find its style not just confusing but incomprehensible.

Whatever questions arise about the Qur'an, and however coherent or confusing we find its content, there are a couple of things both Muslims and non-Muslims can agree on. As a book that shapes the lives and outlook of a quarter of mankind, what the Qur'an says, the meanings we find in its pages, its contemporary relevance, are important for all of us. In an interconnected, globalised world, we are all going to be affected, directly or indirectly, by how the Qur'an is read by the majority of Muslims. And we can all agree that the structure and style of the Qur'an is complex. It defies expectations of being a simple story, and therefore raises questions about how and why it is structured as it is, and what we should understand from this arrangement.

The Qur'an is definitely not a chronological text. For example, the first verses revealed to the Prophet Muhammad are not at the beginning but are found in the 96th chapter of the Qur'an (96:1–5). The last revelation comes in the 3rd verse of the 5th (5:3) of the Qur'an's 114 chapters, or *suras*. Moreover, the Qur'an does not deal with its subjects in one place but in several places, dropping them suddenly and then picking them up later in the text. It says one thing on one subject in one place, and something different on the same subject elsewhere. All of this makes it difficult to make sense of the Qur'an.

Sound plays a very important part in the structure of the Qur'an. Before it was a written text, the Qur'an existed as sound; this is why it is often compared to an epic poem. But I like to think of it in terms of a musical symphony. Just as the melodic themes in a symphony may be repeated, so the verses in the Qur'an are frequently repeated. Just as misplaced notes may play havoc with the whole symphony, so a misreading of the Qur'an throws the whole text out of sync. This is why Muslims pay so much attention to the correct reading of the Qur'an.

We know that Prophet Muhammad, like most of his community in Mecca, was illiterate. His response to the first word of revelation, '*Iqra*' ('Read'), was

'I cannot'. But an illiterate community is skilled in the oral tradition, the ability to commit words to memory. Muhammad repeated each revelation to his growing circle of followers, who committed the words to memory. He recited the growing body of the Qur'an in prayers, which is how the characteristic form of Muslim prayer developed. The Qur'an uses a heightened form of Arabic, unlike any other Arabic text in its language and use of language. The language of the Qur'an stretched the oral traditions of the society, but also utilised its conventions in its strong sound and metrical forms, which enabled the growing community of believers to assimilate and memorise the words. Even to this day, millions of Muslims continue to commit the entire Qur'an to memory. Listening to Qur'an recitation is a popular art form, one in which the entire audience would be aware of any mistake that disturbed the sound structure as much as it would the meaning of what is being recited.

However, even though the Qur'an was revealed orally, and it was memorised by the Prophet and his followers, it is also a written text. The Qur'an refers to itself as *kitab*, or book, that is something that is designed to be written and bound together as a single volume. Indeed, making a written record of the verses of the Qur'an as they were revealed was common practice amongst the literate companions of the Prophet. There were also a number of scribes specially commissioned to write down the revealed verses who worked with Muhammad to arrange these written texts in the proper order. According to Muslim historians, Prophet Muhammad himself arranged the verses, as they were revealed, in the final structure, often instructing his scribes to 'place this verse (or these verses) in the *sura* where such-and-such is mentioned'. But the Prophet died before he could bind all the chapters of the Qur'an into a written master volume.

The years after the death of Prophet Muhammad saw a rapid expansion of the Muslim community far beyond the confines of Arabia. Where Muslims went, they took the Qur'an with them, both in oral and written form. But it became clear that textual variations were beginning to appear in different parts of what was becoming the Muslim world. Both the first two caliphs, Abu Bakr (r. 632–4) and Umar (r. 634–44), the immediate successors of Muhammad, wanted a single authorised version to be produced. But it was Othman (r. 644–56), the third Caliph, who took decisive action. He established a committee of twelve companions of the Prophet and gave them the responsibility for assembling an authoritative text to be written down exactly as the Prophet had recited it. This committee comprised people who had learned the recitation of Qur'an from the Prophet, as well as the scribes who had compiled written texts under his guidance. They consulted with many more of those still living who had heard the Prophet and committed the Qur'an to memory. The product of the committee's work is the text called Othman's *mushaf*, or codex, completed by 652 and distributed throughout the Muslim world.

There are, as one would expect, lots of scholarly disputes about exactly how the final text was produced [6]. Slight differences exist between Muslim scholars; Western scholars have a wide range of views and differences, some even suggesting that the Qur'an was compiled over 200 years after the death of the Prophet [7]. But these differences of opinion and scholarly concerns do not, and cannot, change the reality that Muslims regard Othman's *mushaf* as the standard, authoritative and final text of the Qur'an. It is the Qur'an as known to all Muslims today.

The Qur'an was revealed piecemeal, over a period of twenty-three years, from 610 to 632. The Prophet received his first revelations when he was in Mecca, where he stayed for another thirteen years. The *suras* revealed during this period are known as Meccan Suras. We can divide the Meccan period of the Prophet's life into two phases. During the first phase, which lasts about five years, the Prophet had only a handful of followers. He preached in secret to those who clustered around him. The verses revealed during this period—short, replete with rhyme and assonance—are concerned with the inner substance of faith, worship and spiritual pursuits; they deal with such subjects as the attributes of God, the nature of monotheism, accountability and judgement in the Hereafter, issues of justice, human virtues and the importance of good conduct. This is followed by a period of eight years during which the Prophet openly and actively propagated his message and faced a hostile reception from the Quraysh, the dominant tribe of Mecca. He and his followers were persecuted, some were ostracised, some forced to flee to Abyssinia, and some were tortured and killed. Faced with stubborn and violent opposition, the Prophet had little option but to be patient, persevere with his preaching, and continue to repeat the essentials of his message, again and again, from different perspectives and viewpoints, and with different examples relating the historic experience of the Arabs themselves. Repetition and reiteration are thus most prevalent in the verses revealed during this period. When life in Mecca became unbearable, in the year 622 the Prophet migrated to the city of Medina, where he was welcomed. The nature and style of the revelation thus changes once again.

The Prophet lived in Medina till his death, some ten years after the *hijra*, or migration. The *suras* revealed in Medina are known, naturally, as Medinan Suras. It is the *hijra* and not the beginning of Muhammad's prophetic mission which is taken as the beginning of the Islamic calendar. The dating of the events of Muslim history commences from 622, often written as years AH (*Anno Hegirae*), because the migration marks a seminal shift. During his time in Medina, the Prophet was busy establishing a community with the necessary social order and the basic instruments of governance. He had become the leader of a substantial and growing community, eager to put the basic principles of Islam they had learned into practice. But his enemies in Mecca had still to be curbed, relations had to be established with non-Muslim communities in Medina and elsewhere, and his followers encouraged to lead the good life. So the tenor, style and content of revelation changes in Medina. The Medinan Suras tend to deal with issues of communal law (marriage, divorce and inheritance), bonds within the community (between parents and children, young and old, men and women), relations between different communities (particularly Jews and Christian), conflict and peace building.

There are eighty-five Meccan and twenty-nine Medinan Suras. However, the non-linear structure of the Qur'an is such that many *suras* contain passages from both periods. The longer Medinan Suras are found at the beginning of the Qur'an; the shorter Meccan Suras tend to be towards the end of the Sacred Text. A *sura* is said to be Meccan if its early verses were revealed in Mecca, even if it contains many verses revealed in Medina; and vice versa. The distinction between the Meccan and Medinan Suras could be described as a journey from 'why', the ultimate nature of faith and worship, to the 'how', the translation of faith into a form of living that is the practice of religion. The arrangement of the Qur'an with the Medinan Suras coming first puts this journey the other way round, moving from how to why. The presence of both Meccan and Medinan verses in many *suras* suggests that 'why' and 'how' are not discrete poles: both are necessary and interwoven in complex relationships across the whole gamut of existence; that we are forever journeying between these two dynamics to find the proper balance.

Muslims see the structure of the Qur'an as a sign of its Divine nature. It is considered a mechanism for developing a deeper understanding of the Qur'an. This explains why this aspect of the Qur'an has received serious attention from Muslim scholars. Structures of individual chapters, pairs of chapters and groups of chapters have been explored in detail. Indeed, some Muslim scholars have even suggested that the Qur'an has other levels of structural organisation. For example, the noted Pakistani scholar Amin Ahsan Islahi (1904–97) suggests that the chapters of the Qur'an can be arranged in seven groups, each group containing Meccan verses followed by Medinan verses. This additional structural layer, Islahi argues, has thematic significance and is important for developing fresh interpretations of the Qur'an [8].

But for non-Muslims the structure of the Qur'an, with its non-chronological order, non-linear arrangement, non-narrative organisation, can be a major source of confusion. The bewilderment is well articulated by the protagonist of Margaret Drabble's *A Natural Curiosity* [9]. After reading a rather bad translation of the Qur'an, he asks his wife: 'How can you understand the minds of people who don't respect *sequence*?' 'I am sure there must be *some* kind of sequence', she replies. But, of course, it is not necessary for texts or, as the French philosopher Michel Foucault would have said, 'things' to have order as understood by the West to have meaning and significance. The barrier to understanding is not in the text but in the expectations and assumptions that there is only one possible normality, just one way of thinking and knowing about the world and that anything which deviates from this norm must by definition be both inferior and wrong-headed. It is the failure of a monocultural imagination.

Equally problematic is the question of who is actually speaking in the Qur'an. The speaker is God. But, as some of my non-Muslims friends have told me, they are often confused why the speaker changes from the first person singular ('I') to the first person plural ('we') to the third person singular ('He'). For Muslim readers this is not a problem; they know that it is the voice of God who can refer to him/herself however he/she chooses. But for non-Muslim readers, and certain Western scholars, these changes are a barrier to making sense of the text. Some Western thinkers believe that 'We' refers to angels, 'I' to the Prophet Muhammad, and 'He' to either an angel or the Prophet when talking about God. Others have suggested that the Prophet 'slipped up' and used these different 'voices' by mistake—and that, as he was revealing his text over time, he simply forgot what he had said a year or two ago. But we need not pay much attention to these suggestions. A close examination actually reveals a simple pattern.

'We' is used in passages where God's majesty, might and magnificence are being shown. These verses are intended to generate awe and wonder at God's majesty. 'He' is used in passages where particular phenomena are being described. These verses are meant to inculcate belief in and worship of one God. The 'I' is used in specific circumstances: when, for example, intimacy is implied, often at a crucial moment in history where Muslims face trial and tribulation: 'When you begged your Lord for help, He answered you, "I will reinforce you with a thousand angels in succession"' (8:9). These words are intimate and there is a promise of protection from God. Other specific circumstances include when judgement is made, where the third (more impersonal tone) changes to the first person; or when an oath is being made, 'I swear', the first person singular is used and then changes to the plural form to illustrate God's magnificence and power. It is worth noting that the Qur'an never has 'Oh Thou Muhammad', only 'Oh Thou'. The significance of this, as Neil Robinson [10] has pointed out, is that the message is not limited in time and space. 'Thou' could be anyone—and anyone can be addressed by God.

While appreciating the problems that the style and structure of the Qur'an produce for non-Muslims, the point I would like to make is that the Qur'an has its own logic. This is not the binary, Aristotelian logic we are all familiar with—which, by the way, was re-introduced to the West by Muslims—but a different, multi-fold, one could say higher form of logic, which reveals itself in different forms the more one struggles and engages with the Qur'an. Thus, if you are looking for 'sequence' in the Qur'an, you would be disappointed. However, if you were looking for lessons, then one form of the logic that determines the structure of the Qur'an will reveal itself.

The Qur'an says it is a guidance, a teaching. And what is the first principle of pedagogy? Whatever the subject, you begin with the basics, then in later years you return to particular topics and acquire more information and insight. Education is the process of gaining a deeper, more profound understanding. The structure of the Qur'an unfolds similarly, I can say from my own experiences, as a series of lessons. This makes sense on a number of levels. Episodic lessons are much easier to assimilate, especially for its initial audience in a largely illiterate community, who would be helped by the sound and metrical properties of the language in which the Qur'an is expressed. Then over time the lessons became more complex, with additional ideas being introduced and inserted in already known passages. But, as we all know, not all lessons can be mastered easily, or are learned when they should be learned, so they have to be repeated. Hence we find the frequent repetition of certain lessons and principles in the Qur'an. Moreover, certain subjects are taught during early years in such simplified versions that they do not tell the whole story [11]. In later years, these lessons have to be overhauled to introduce and deal with complexity. This is why certain verses in the Qur'an, revealed earlier, seem to contradict other verses which were revealed later. The contradiction is in fact an accommodation of complexity to generate a broader picture.

The Qur'an teaches through the use of a diversity of material. Apart from the Prophet Muhammad and his community, it refers to stories from the lives of previous prophets, such as Musa (Moses), Ibrahim (Abraham), Nuh (Noah) and Lot as well as Isa (Jesus), familiar from the Torah and Bible. It frequently refers to history and the rise and fall of empires. It refers to the creation of the universe and uses examples from the natural world. It employs parables, metaphors and allegories to explain both moral principles and things beyond direct human experience. And it concerns itself with the practicalities of how a society should reform and organise itself internally and in its relations with other people to advance in ethical behaviour and righteousness. But it does not treat these themes as one-off lessons. The Qur'an returns to these themes a number of times, on each occasion adding some new information or insight or offering a slightly different perspective to provide new food for thought and deeper understanding.

Learning involves a great deal of thinking. And the Qur'an constantly urges its readers to think, ponder and reflect. But it is asking for much more than a conventional, one-dimensional process of cause and effect or sequential analysis. It is suggesting that we should reflect on our perspective which can hide certain views, make far-off things appear close and complex things appear simple. Thinking requires synthesis as well as reduction. When the Qur'an urges its readers to seek understanding, it is not simply the understanding of the world around us. It is also the understanding of our inner world of feeling and experience, love and emotion, self and the soul. When the Qur'an asks us to look at the cosmos and reflect, it is suggesting we look at the interconnection of things, how everything is connected to everything else. In modern parlance, the Qur'an is asking us to think 'outside the box' and beyond binary logic. Indeed, the very structure and style of the Qur'an, I find, insistently points to necessary relationships, to the need to think of things not in separate compartments but as involved and integrated with each other. We are being guided towards a multidimensional rather than a one-dimensional approach to all aspects of life. But equally, I never cease to be amazed at how easily and readily Muslims reduce this complexity to a simplistic list of dos and don'ts.

The Qur'an does not ask me to accept anything passively; rather it invites me to engage actively in a process of questioning and reasoning. It is the only way, I think, of approaching and interpreting the Qur'an in our time, here and now.

3

APPROACH AND INTERPRETATIONS

On one level, the Qur'an is an easy book to read. Most pious Muslims read it every day as a devotional exercise. But devotional reading, while a form of prayer, does not take us very far in understanding what we read. Overemphasis on devotion can also lead to a rather simplistic position on the Qur'an. As Mona Siddiqui notes in *How to Read the Qur'an*, most Muslims believe that the Qur'an is 'a closed book which one can only read, recite and obey' [12]. But obedience requires knowing what kind of society the Qur'an seeks, appreciating the distinction between the universal and particular, and understanding how a society adjusts and maintains its basic outlook in the face of rapid social, cultural and environmental changes. The power and guidance of the Qur'an, as Siddiqui notes, emerges when it is read and interpreted in the light of new and changing situations. But reading the Qur'an from the viewpoint of changing situations is rare indeed. On the whole, traditional interpretations of the Qur'an pay little attention to changes in society.

A complex text, particularly one that is seen as eternal, can be interpreted in a number of different ways. Not surprisingly, Muslims have approached and interpreted the Qur'an from a host of different perspectives: theological, devotional, literary, literal, legal, allegorical, rhetorical, mystical or philosophical as well as from purely sectarian outlooks. Western scholars have approached the Sacred Text critically, sympathetically, caustically, and sometimes with the intention of undermining it. The South African Muslim scholar Farid Esack has proposed an interesting topology of different approaches [13]. He suggests that the Qur'an is seen and approached as a female body of exquisite beauty. In most cultures the female body is seen as a passive object, a subject of the

21

male gaze. The Qur'an too is often read as though it was a passive text; and most of its interpreters are men.

In general, Esack says, Muslim scholars approach the Qur'an as their beloved. There is the uncritical lover who totally loses himself in the text. Mystical interpretations of the Qur'an, such as those of the great Andalusian mystic ibn al-Arabi (1165–1240) and Turkish Sufi Jalaluddin Rumi (1207–73), would fit this category. The scholarly lover wants to tell the whole world why his beloved is the most sublime. Confessional interpreters, old and new, fall in this group. Examples would include the classical commentary of Jalal al-Din al-Suyuti (d. 1505) and the contemporary exegesis of Abul Ala Mawdudi (1903–79), the founder of the Jamat-e-Islami. The critical lover seeks commitment and is willing to ask difficult questions about his relationship with his beloved. Here, Pakistani thinker Fazlur Rahman (1911–88) and the French linguistic philosopher Mohammed Arkoun (b. 1928–) fit the bill. The lovers also have friends who take a keen interest in their relationship. These are Western scholars, such as Montgomery Watt (1909–2006) and Kenneth Cragg (1913–), who accept the general contours of the Muslim approach to the Qur'an and study it as received scripture. Where there is a female body there are bound to be voyeurs. So we have a string of other scholars who are openly hostile to the Qur'an and everything it stands for.

I would say that I am the argumentative lover. I think the Qur'an should be approached through questions and arguments. That's what the text itself demands. The Qur'an is full of questions: 'How can you worship something other than God?', 'How did this happen?', 'Have you considered?', 'Have you heard?', 'What are they asking about?' And it is jam-packed with debate—particularly in the longer *suras*. Clearly, God loves a good argument. Perhaps the most important question to consider is: what is the Qur'an asking us to do *now*? The potential answers would lead to numerous arguments. Given that Muslims see the Qur'an as a living, dynamic entity—which is what Esack argues beyond his analogy—it is not an argument that could be settled once and for all. It is an ongoing debate whose contours change with changing circumstances.

New circumstances would raise a host of new questions, all of them leading to new arguments. But the Qur'an does not give definite, yes or no, answers to our questions. It provides certain principles, the essentials of a moral and ethical framework, allegory and metaphors that hint at direction as a guide to discovering viable solutions. Beyond question, not everything is settled and laid out in the Qur'an. It is up to the reader to wrestle with the text and find the answers.

Yet, today there are Muslims who advocate, or allow themselves to be convinced by, a literal reading of the Qur'an; worse, they insist that this literalism contains all the answers necessary to live in the twenty-first century. This belief is not just limited to narrow-minded circles and particular strains of thought. It is also a common position of most intellectuals who support various strands of the 'Islamic movements' as well as various conservative and traditionalist brands of Islam. If all the answers to the questions of our changing world were readily available in the Qur'an, Muslim societies would be a beacon of progress and would not be in their current dire positions. If all was as clear as daylight, there would not be so many sects and so many different, contradictory and divergent views within Islam. If literalism is all that we require, there would be no reason for the emergence of the vast body of intellectual work accumulated over the centuries devoted to the interpretation of the Qur'an.

In fact, the Qur'an had to be interpreted immediately after the death of the Prophet Muhammad. He was succeeded by four men known and accepted by all Muslims as the Rightly Guided Caliphs. Abu Bakr (632–4), Umar (634–44), Uthman (644–56) and Ali (656–61) had all learned the Qur'an directly from the Prophet, had listened to him teaching, explaining and deciding matters for the community. And yet when they became leaders they found many questions on which they were unsure of the exact meaning and import of what the Qur'an said, or how to apply and implement its teaching in a changing and expanding society and hence what decision to take. It became their practice to call upon other companions and ask for their opinion, understanding and interpretation. The need for interpretation increased with the second generation of Muslims, who included diverse populations of non-Arabs. Political conflict, sectarian divisions, and the expansion of Islam to Iraq, Persia and Egypt, all led to the need for and development of Qur'anic interpretation. By the beginning of the ninth century, interpretation, or *tafsir*, had been established as a fully-fledged discipline with its own principles, methods and knowledge base (*Usul al-Tafsir*).

On the basis of this scholarship, distinctions were made between the contextual, what was specific to the particular time and place of revelation, and the general principles of the Qur'an's message which were eternal, timeless and relevant in any place or circumstance. A set of procedures was established for reasoning by analogy from the specific to the general. One specific discipline that emerged from the outset of Muslim history was the dating and study of the circumstances in which each verse of the Qur'an was revealed. It was agreed that to understand the questions as well as the meaning of the Qur'an it was necessary to know as much as possible about when and why a particular verse was revealed. Despite a disciplinary core on which most scholars agreed, differences of opinion on issues of interpretation were common.

One particular procedure that emerged for settling differences of opinion among scholars was consensus. Consensus, or *ijma'*, was seen as the best way to arrive at decisions. Now, consensus is an agreement arrived at after debate among a diversity of opinions, and by definition it is an act of interpretation arrived at by a community, whether all believers or a select group of learned scholars. To accept consensus does not necessarily preclude differences in emphasis and application. But relying too heavily on the consensus of learned opinion can mean relegating the ongoing dynamic effort to reason with the meaning of the Qur'an. In which case, those who rely on the received consensus of ancient scholars are effectively saying that the timeless and eternal became fixed and unchanging many centuries ago, no matter what changes have happened since. It also means that interpretation based on the opinion of a select group of ordinary, though often gifted, scholars has a monopoly on understanding the Qur'an. I think this is not a tenable position.

However, my problem is not with the basic principles of exegesis developed by classical commentators. I think they are as important today as they have ever been, largely because they are eminently reasonable, indeed, prescient of just the kind of methodology necessary in any age for sound scholarship. Contemporary interpretations that take change into account have to start with these principles.

First, the guiding principle accepted by traditional scholars was that the Qur'an is an integrated text. Not only is it complete and applicable for all time, but it is internally consistent and the whole of the Book must be considered to arrive at a sound understanding. Another way of saying this is that the message of the Qur'an is concerned to establish the right relationships between different things to achieve the best possible end here and hereafter. So each verse in the Qur'an is connected to every other verse and has to be seen in the spirit of the whole text.

Second, the main source for the interpretation of the Qur'an is the Qur'an itself. This is a natural corollary of the first principle. Thus, when a word or a particular verse of the Qur'an can be clarified or interpreted by another, then recourse to an external source becomes superfluous.

Third, the most important source of understanding and interpretation outside the Qur'an is the life of the Prophet Muhammad. The Prophet was not only the recipient of revelation but embodied the revelation in the way he lived. As such, his *Sunna*, life, practice and custom, are a living commentary on the Qur'an. So, the interpretation of its verses, many of which address the Prophet directly, has to be based on and seen in the context of what was happening to the Prophet.

Fourth, the early scholars accepted local custom in widely differing parts of the Muslim World as valid sources of interpretation and application of Qur'anic principles. This point is almost totally neglected nowadays, but in my opinion it is an important principle. It means that all human activity and ideas need to be tested against the coherent standard of Qur'anic principle. When this is done, many customs, many forms of organisation of human activity, many ways of thinking and acting, can fulfil or comply with Qur'anic principles. In other words, there is more than one way to be a good Muslim; ultimately Islam is not a brand name that belongs exclusively to Muslims. It is equally possible for Muslims to behave in unIslamic ways as it is for non-Muslims to behave Islamicly!

Classical commentaries, or *tafsir*, were based on these principles. Their basic methodology was to go through the Qur'an systematically, verse by verse, bringing together all that is known and relevant to interpreting the individual verse. Each verse was subjected to a series of questions: Was it, or the *sura* of which it was a part, revealed in Mecca or Medina? What prompted its revelation? What was happening at the time of its revelation in the life of the Prophet Muhammad? Are there specific traditions of the Prophet related to this verse? What are its particular grammatical features? Why is there repetition of words or phrases? Does the verse continue to have a legal implication, or has it been abrogated? Renowned commentators such as al Tabari (838–923), who produced one of the earliest commentaries, and Fakhruddin Razi (1149–1209), start from the first verse and continue all the way to the last, interrogating each verse with these and other similar questions. Their explanations rely largely on one part of the Qur'an to explain another part, and, quite extensively, on the traditions of the Prophet. Contemporary traditionalist commentators such as Sayyid Qutb and Abul Ala Mawdudi follow the traditional encyclopaedic verse-by-verse method, while infusing their commentaries with ideological fervour.

We owe a great deal to classical commentaries. They are rightly seen as a literary genre providing the exegesis of the Qur'an within well defined parameters and boundaries of knowledge. By bringing out the style and idiom of the Qur'an, its literal and metaphorical use of language, the traditional commentaries have played a vital role in increasing our understanding of the Qur'an. I find it particularly stimulating to look at how a group of classical commentators, from varied backgrounds and schools of thought, interpret the same verse. The exercise has become much easier nowadays with the availability of anthologies of classical commentaries. Mahmoud Ayoub's *The Qur'an and Its Interpreters* [14], for example, enables one to compare the commentaries of thirteen classical authors, including ibn Kathir, ibn Arabi, al-Tabari, as well as, surprisingly, the twentieth-century *tafsir* of Sayyid Qutb. The more recent *An Anthology of Qur'anic Commentaries* [15] brings together twenty commentators, classical works of Sunni, Shia, Ismaeli, Sufi and rationalist scholars, as well as more recent commentaries of Mohammad Abduh (1849–1905), Rashid Rida (1865–1935) and Abul Ala Mawdudi. These anthologies are a rich storehouse of interpretation; and they have a great deal to teach us on spiritual matters. But I find the argumentative nature of the Qur'an tends to get lost in traditional commentaries. Where arguments do come into play they tend to be arguments from authority and obscurantist theology, which are not always based on thought and reason. The evidence sometimes put forward to justify particular positions defies every kind of logic. And the language, to be honest, leaves me cold.

But, my personal difficulties apart, there are serious problems with the classical verse-by-verse interpretation of the Qur'an. There is the obvious problem that focusing on the meaning of individual verses inevitably leads both Muslims and non-Muslims to believe that it is the only proper way to interpret the Qur'an. Notice how often Muslims brandish just one verse of the Qur'an as if it is an answer to everything in and of itself or, even worse, a justification for the unjustifiable. Non-Muslims also pick up particular verses from the Qur'an to prove that Islam does not come up to their standards. A good example is the famous verse, used by fictional as well as real terrorists, to justify violence. In films such as *Rules of Engagement*, for example, the terrorists claim that the Qur'an commands Muslims to kill 'the infidel' Americans, their allies, including civilians, and plunder their possessions. This message is repeated in a string of films such as *True Lies*, *Executive Action* and *The Siege*, going right back to *Khartoum* [16]. Real terrorists, including Osama bin Laden [17] and al-Qaeda operatives, also quote this verse to justify their nefarious actions. The same is true of the Taliban and other fundamentalist groups, in Britain and abroad. The verse they cite reads: 'We will put terror into the hearts of the unbelievers. They serve other gods for whom no sanction has been revealed. Hell shall be their home.' (3:149). Now, how are we to communicate to these people that the apparent meaning attributed to this verse could not be further from the true spirit of the Qur'an? The verse in fact addresses the Prophet himself. It was revealed during the battle of Uhud (625) when the small and ill-equipped army of the Prophet faced a much larger and well-equipped enemy. He was concerned about the outcome of the battle. The Qur'an reassures him and promises that the enemy will be terrified by the Prophet's unprofessional army. Seen in its context, it is not a general instruction to all Muslims, but a commentary on what was happening at that time. However, this background is lost on those who think, and have been brought up to think, that the normal way to read and discover meaning in the Qur'an is simply to pluck verses out of context.

The Pakistani-American scholar Fazlur Rahman dubbed this approach as 'atomistic'. It was responsible, he argued, for the widespread tendency towards literalism. The verse-by-verse commentaries, he wrote, 'do not yield an effective *"Weltanschauung"* that is cohesive and meaningful for life as a whole' [18]. That, I believe, is a crucial problem. While Muslims insist that they live by the Qur'an, they often exist in a fragmented, atomised world where ethics and morality are disconnected from their daily lives as well as their social and legal concerns. There is little awareness, let alone appreciation, of the worldview that the Qur'an seeks to foster.

Rahman also argues that it is not good enough simply to look at the life of Prophet Muhammad for interpretation. We need to go beyond the *Sunna* and see the role played by the social and historical conditions of Mecca and Medina. 'The Qur'an is like the tip of an iceberg', he writes, 'nine-tenths of which is submerged under the water of history and only one-tenth of which is visible. No one who has attempted to understand the Qur'an seriously can deny that much of the Qur'an presupposes a knowledge of the historical situation to which its statements provide solution, comments and responses.' Thus, meaningful interpretation should involve examination of 'the customs, institutions and general way of life' of Arabia during the time of the revelation. In a similar vein, Abdullah Saeed argues that knowing the social and cultural conditions of the Prophet's Arabia is essential for understanding why the Qur'an allowed certain provisions, such as polygamy, in the seventh-century Hijaz which have no relevance in contemporary times.

There is one final point. Whatever the merits of classical commentaries, they tell us little about the relevance of the Qur'an to our own time. Traditional methodology, as Saeed argues so cogently, cannot cope with the enormous challenges of contemporary times. Neither is a sensible commentary on the Qur'an possible without taking the needs and requirements of our times into consideration. As human beings, we can only engage with the Qur'an, and interpret it, according to our own contemporary understanding. It has to make sense to us as ordinary mortals here and now; it has to have significance for us in the light of our needs and requirements in current times; it has to guide us through the moral, ethical and spiritual dilemmas of today. So, the context of our time is equally important for its interpretation. Thus, we have to approach the Qur'an from the perspective of how morality on, for example, such issues as gender equality and environmental concerns has evolved in our own time, and engage with the text in the light of our changing circumstances.

The Qur'an provides the essential basics of morality on which we have to build and expand in ever widening horizons. That is exactly what exploring the Qur'an in a contemporary context is all about. For many Muslims this prospect raises a whole series of concerns that have been inculcated by history. Islam has increasingly become a redoubt to be defended by conservative and preservative traditionalism. Further, defining and observing in practice an idealised traditionalism offers religion as a badge of identity, a supposedly inherited persona in the face of depersonalising mass society. By relying on classical commentators, inherited opinion has elevated the original community, the Medina state of the Prophet Muhammad, to that of a timeless ideal. Clearly the Qur'an was revealed, preached, and its precepts applied to address the imperfections of the time and place of Prophet Muhammad. The reformative programme, the process of becoming Muslim, worked upon the specifics of the social, cultural, economic and political norms of sixth-century Arabia. But how is it sensible to equate Islam with keeping consonant with what are supposedly the norms and problems of the sixth century in the twenty-first century, which has more than enough problems of its own? The answer many Muslims give is that traditionalism is a bulwark against redefining religion according to our own needs and desires, allowing the exigencies of our time and place to tailor religion rather than the other way around. To substantiate this argument, one would have to be very sure that the circumstances and cultural context of classical interpreters who devised so much of what is termed 'traditional' were not similarly influenced. And the evidence of careful study shows that, however much one can appreciate the reasonableness of the principles they established in application, in the synthesis of interpretation they produced they were people of their own time and place. So, far from traditionalism getting us to a pure, unsullied practice of original religion good for all time, what is defended as 'Islamic tradition' is redolent of the minds, social, cultural and intellectual predilections and proclivities of various times and places in Muslim history.

Tradition is made by many hands. It is a work of both thought and action. And tradition can be remade, can become a matter of doing differently by applying the same principles and exercising the same discretion as previous generations of Muslims. The acid test is not how closely we resemble our ancestors, but how well we apply the moral and ethical principles of religion to problems of our own day to achieve a better outcome for not just our own community but the whole of humanity and the world in which we coexist.

This also means that no interpretation of the Qur'an is itself absolute and forever. All interpretation is limited and time-bound. The meaning of the Qur'an is not fixed, even though it is universal. While some Muslims see classical commentaries as written in stone, the suggestion itself is not new. All generations stand in the same interpretive relationship to the Qur'an. The inspiration and interpretations we draw from the Qur'an constantly return us to the Divine source to think and reflect and be prepared to do things differently, to change and be changed, to remain consistent to the meaning of the eternal message of the Qur'an.

For me, this is the most profound and dynamic of all outlooks with which to approach and interpret the Qur'an. It calls for rational, considered thought and interrogation not of appearances but of the deeper implications and meaning of how human beings think and act within and between all the diversity of our cultures, histories, languages and beliefs. It requires just as intense scrutiny of the traditions and customs we inherit as Muslim history and norms as of those of non-Muslim society. Most of all it places all humanity in an interconnected world in the same position, just as the Qur'an itself argues. And therefore it ought to focus our attention on the challenge the Qur'an places before a diverse world: to find ways to cooperate and work together to make the world a better place, more just and equitable for everyone, since everyone and everything is equally part of God's creation, and all of us will be judged on how we have lived our life.

Seeking the contemporary relevance of the Qur'an requires, to some extent, going against tradition. However, standing against traditional interpretations that have shaped the outlook of Muslims for centuries, and have acquired a sacred/eternal aura, is not easy. Traditionalists of all varieties, scholars as well as ordinary Muslims, regard challenges to classical authorities with particular hostility. And that antagonism begins with a basic question: what authority do you have to speak about, let alone interpret, the Qur'an?

4

QUESTIONS OF AUTHORITY

Who should comment on and interpret the Qur'an? This seems like an innocuous question. The straightforward answer is that all those who read the Qur'an should be able to comment on its content and offer an understanding, however simple, of its verses. Reading is always an interpretative act; so those who read the Qur'an are also simultaneously interpreting it, at least for themselves if not others. But reading, and hence interpretation, is not just an act of engagement, an attempt at understanding and comprehension, but also an exercise in authority and power.

In Muslim history and tradition, that power has been the sole preserve of a particular class of people. The prerogative of interpreting the Qur'an has been limited to those with 'legitimate' authority: those who have been schooled in various Qur'anic sciences, who have followed the traditional disciplines and curriculum, and have reached the position of an *'alim*, or a recognisable religious scholar. These scholars also served as the custodians of a long, cherished tradition that provided a continuous connection with the historical narrative of Islam as a fixed, unchanging dogma, law and morality—an additional source of their power and prestige. I believe this tradition turned the Qur'an, the fundamental source of moral guidance for all Muslims, into a closed book for the vast majority of believers; and had serious consequences for the evolution of Muslim thought and culture.

There are two basic points to be made here: one about the *ulama*, the so-called religious scholars with 'legitimate authority'; and one about the vast majority of ordinary Muslims.

It is a standard boast of many Muslims that Islam has no priestly hierarchy. The Qur'an does not sanction a particular class of people, such as Christian priests, who are ordained to minister Divine worship, administer the sacrament, give absolution, forgive sins, and otherwise act as intermediary between God and humans. This is the theory; but in reality this is both an untenable and a deceitful position—a deceit that Muslims have been perpetuating for centuries. For the *ulama* are de facto priests of Islam and act as such; indeed, they even dress as a priestly class. By reserving the right of interpreting the Qur'an, they act as intermediaries between the Word of God and the ordinary believer. Worse: in some cases, the interpretation of the *ulama* of a particular school, for example the Hanafi School of Thought, is actually placed at par with the Qur'an itself. So the *ulama* have the same authority as the Qur'an and speak with the voice of God. We thus find ourselves in a situation where the text of the Qur'an and its interpretation are collapsed into a single discourse; criticism of the *ulama* and their interpretation then becomes criticism of the text of the Qur'an itself, and any attempt at new interpretation automatically becomes a violation of the Sacred Book. Total domination—of the Qur'an, its interpretation and religious knowledge—is thus clearly and cleverly maintained.

Authority in the traditional framework is often acquired through the strict practice of working backwards. What this means is that the interpretations of the scholars of previous generations are read systematically going right back to original interpreters of the Qur'an during the classical period of Islam. This is supposed to provide historic continuity as well as legitimacy for the current crop of guardians of interpretation. But it also repeats all the mistakes of history, undermines criticism, and retains the ethos and morality of medieval times. This is why so many interpretations of the Qur'an, including many 'modern' ones, appear so archaic and out of sync with contemporary issues and concerns.

To maintain their domination of who could interpret the Qur'an and how it can be read, the *ulama* used a number of tactics. They reduced the Qur'anic concept of *'ilm*, which refers to all kinds of knowledge, to mean only religious knowledge; and then went on to suggest that those with religious knowledge are superior to those who did not have this knowledge. They reduced the Islamic concept of *ijma'*, which means consensus of all people, to mean only the consensus of a few privileged religious scholars—and, through a long and arduous process, closed the 'gates of *ijtihad*', or new interpretation. Indeed, during the fifteenth century, the religious scholars even stopped the spread of printing in the Muslim world. For centuries, printing was prohibited in Muslim societies because religious scholars feared that copies of the Qur'an would become commonplace, leading to the Muslim masses not just reading but interpreting the Holy Text [21]. The consequences of these developments have been nothing short of catastrophic for Muslim societies.

For ordinary Muslims too, the hegemony of the *ulama* has been devastating. The believer is reduced to an empty vessel into which religious knowledge is poured, to be accepted unquestioningly. We are simply told what the Qur'an says or means. We can present questions to warranted scholars and follow the answers given. To challenge the traditional opinions of this elite body is not only presumptuous, but also an indication of a weakness of faith, creed and belief and nefarious intentions, since without their special educational preparation no sensible thought or understanding is possible. Hence, most Muslims actually fear engaging with the Qur'an directly, thinking they lack the basic qualifications, and would therefore make serious errors of judgement and interpretation. If they read the Qur'an at all, they read it with utmost caution and a mountain of classical commentaries, or through the eyes of a contemporary but classically trained scholar, with their own minds and critical faculties firmly in check. Thus, concerned, thinking and dedicated Muslims are disenfranchised from engaging in earnest and reasoned debate with the Qur'an.

Traditionally, individuals face two specific barriers to direct engagement with the Qur'an. The first is 'specialised knowledge' which, according to the religious dons, is a prerequisite for opening and reading the sacred text. Much of this knowledge relies heavily on memory. It requires one to know where, when and why verses of the Qur'an were revealed, be familiar with classical commentaries, have instant recall of over 2,000 traditions of the Prophet Muhammad, and be able to quote generously from the canonical books of Islamic law and jurisprudence. Now, it is probably a good idea to have this background if you wish to undertake a painstakingly scholarly exegesis of the Qur'an. But if the Qur'an is meant for everyone, ordinary mortals as well as the experts, then why would one, or indeed everyone, need umpteen qualifications to engage with the Word of God?

This formidable specialist barrier was created during a period when books were scarce, memory played an important part in learning, and general education was not widespread. In contemporary times it is not so important for you to have committed thousands of sayings of the Prophet Muhammad to memory, or to have learned the canonical legal text by rote. They are easily available in print, digital form and online: if one needs to refer to them they can be accessed easily. Indeed, there are even specialist software products, such as *Al Alim*, that provide most of the background material one may need, leaving the mind free to think about the text itself. There is, however, one aspect of the traditional requirement that I do think is rather important: knowledge of when and why particular verses were revealed, the context of the revelation. This is where the struggle that I mentioned earlier comes in: one does need to put in a little effort, to do some research, to discover the context. But it is not a fearsome task; it is something that any educated person can do.

The second barrier is Arabic. The conventional requirement is that one must have a command of the Arabic language as well as its grammar, phonetics, semantics, syntax and history and evolution; in fact, be a complete master of Arabic linguistics! The curriculum of traditional religious seminaries (*madrasas*) gives so much importance to Arabic language and grammar that young children are force-fed (and not infrequently brutalised) with classical formulae and rules, in a process that is based almost exclusively on rote learning. Not surprisingly, many Muslims have an in-built phobia of Arabic and see it as a major impediment to approaching the Qur'an.

Clearly, it would be a good idea to have a solid background in Arabic if you wish to pursue scholarly endeavours. But here is a self-evident truth: knowing Arabic does not necessarily mean that one could, or would, understand the Qur'an better. To begin with, the Arabic of the Qur'an is not the Arabic spoken in some eighty different dialects in the Arab world today. These dialects vary considerably; just because they are written with the same script does not mean that they say the same thing. Mandarin and Cantonese are both Chinese, but they are two different languages; Korean and Japanese are written in the same script and sound similar, but they are not the same language. Just because someone speaks Arabic does not necessarily mean they understand the Qur'an. Indeed, classical Arabic may not be of much help. His total command of classical Arabic, and mastery of traditional disciplines and Qur'anic sciences, did not prevent the late Grand Mufti of Saudi Arabia, Sheikh Bin Baz, from claiming that, according to the Qur'an, man could not land on the moon, football is evil and women (who are hardly human) should not be allowed to drive! Perhaps it is unfair to single out Bin Baz: the Muslim world is full of scholars, many graduates of such prestigious institutions as Al-Azhar in Cairo, Mecca and Medina universities, and Darul Uloom Deoband, India, who appear to know all there is to know about Arabic and yet have a truncated, not to say violent, understanding of the message of the Qur'an.

What about the vast majority of Muslims who do not speak Arabic? Arabic-speaking people constitute less than a quarter of the global Muslim population. If having Arabic is a prerequisite for reading the Qur'an, then God has been rather unjust to all those who do not have Arabic. Yet the Qur'an itself tells us that it is irrelevant whether one speaks Arabic or not: 'if we had made it a foreign Qur'an, they would have said: "if only its verses were clear! What? Foreign speech to an Arab?" Say it is guidance and healing for those who have faith...' (41:44). In other words, it is a text open to all, whether or not they speak Arabic. But speaking Arabic is not an advantage either: 'We know very well what they say: "It is a man who teaches him" but the language of the person they allude to is foreign, while the revelation is in clear Arabic' (16:103). Here, the Qur'an is saying to the Arabs that they are illiterate in the language of the Qur'an, even though they may speak Arabic.

The 'clear Arabic' of the Qur'an, I believe, is open to all: specialists and scholars as well as non-experts and ordinary folk. It does require one to struggle with the specific words, a vocabulary of less than 600 different and distinct words, terms and concepts, of the Qur'an. But discovering their meaning, seeing what they signified when they were first revealed, how they have been interpreted in history, and what their significance could be today, is part of the intellectual fun of engaging with the Qur'an.

So, I would argue that on the whole one does not need any prerequisite qualification to engage with the text of the Qur'an. Neither do we need the permission of a cleric, nor to have the authority of specialised knowledge. Indeed, I believe the barriers created by traditional scholars to be the most serious problem facing Muslims today and for the future. It disenfranchises concerned, thinking, dedicated Muslims from engaging in earnest and reasoned debate with the Qur'an, while it leaves a stultified, closed system of education unchecked, producing obscurantist scholars who have little knowledge of the complexity and problems of the modern world. A class of scholars, who value received outmoded opinion, exist in hermetically sealed religious and cultural capsules, and can spout little more than slogans that are dangerously obsolete. To follow the dictates of such an elite is to deny any possibility of change and evolution. The great challenge of contemporary times is for Muslims to be liberated from their clutches.

However, it would be beneficial to approach the Qur'an with an open mind; or, to paraphrase Abdul Hasan Ali Nadwi (1913–99), with a desire to learn, a dissatisfaction and discontent with the current conditions, a longing for positive change and a passion to improve the situation of humanity [22]. A complex text such as the Qur'an requires patience, and reveals and unfolds itself with multiple readings, diligent scrutiny and continuous and constant contemplation. The reader is invited by the Sacred Text itself to reflect and meditate on its contents: 'Will they not contemplate the Qur'an?' (47:24); and 'Will they not think about this Qur'an?' (4:82). Answers can only be found if questions are asked; and different readers, no doubt, will ask different questions of the text.

But the questions themselves change over time. Old questions lose their significance, new questions acquire urgency. I suspect that the question whether the Qur'an was created or has always existed, which occupied the minds of classical scholars for centuries, is not of much significance in a world of climate change, deep social inequalities, gender bias, chauvinism, terrorism in the name of religion and radical evil. On the whole, traditional exegesis has seldom asked questions outside the proscribed boundary of orthodoxy: what we could call the 'unthought' of Islam. Part of the problem, as Farid Esack points out, was the inability of the traditional scholarship to deal with any forms of Otherness, either within the Muslim community or outside it. But dealing with Otherness, and being at ease with profound pluralism, is a major issue for contemporary times and raises all variety of questions. Does the Qur'an really consign all non-believers to hell? Are Muslims commanded to fight non-Muslims perpetually? Does the Qur'an really divide the inhabitants of globe into believers and non-believers? All these are questions a non-Muslim reader may legitimately ask.

And Muslims from various backgrounds, who bring their own social and cultural experience to the text, would ask questions that are more pertinent to their personal lives. Is the Qur'an a patriarchal text (as some Muslim feminists, including Asma Barlas, Fatmia Mernissi and Amina Wadud, have asked)? Is the Qur'an explicitly homophobic (as some gay and lesbian Muslims, including Scott Siraj ak-Haqq Kugle and Irshad Manji, have inquired)? What does the Qur'an have to say about the environment? What would constitute the 'authentic' meaning of the Qur'an in contemporary times? Given that we bring our own perspectives to our readings, and every reader will approach the Qur'an from his or her own context, is it possible to speak of an interpretation that is applicable to the whole world? And is it possible to be truly imaginative in our reading and interpretation of the Qur'an?

Such an open and questioning approach to the Qur'an would no doubt be looked on with suspicion, if not hostility, by some. It would certainly not please traditional scholars, who would regard opening up the text to all, whatever their background and state of knowledge, as a direct challenge to their dominant position—a position that has been defended, throughout history, with the rhetoric of fire and brimstone. Indeed, it would confirm their worst suspicions: not just that different interpretations of the Qur'an are possible, but these could lead to different forms of Islam and different ways of being Muslim; a splendid thing, in my opinion.

It is necessary to ask different questions, and hence to confront the dominant mode of thought and interpretation, for another very specific reason: not to do so would be tantamount to being complacent in perpetuating oppressive readings of the Qur'an. Meaning and interpretation are always tentative, time-bound and frequently biased. Their significance can only be realised through contention and debate involving all elements of society. Rather than being told what the Qur'an says, what is the interpretation of its verses, and what it requires one to do and not do, concerned Muslims everywhere need to get back to their religious duty of reading and actively interpreting the Qur'an for themselves. To some extent, as this book itself demonstrates, Muslim thinkers, writers, academics and intellectuals are beginning to reclaim their interpretative rights. This is happening, as Barlas notes, in proportion 'to attempts by some Muslim states and clerics to keep Muslims from reading' [23]. Opening up readings and interpretations of the Qur'an would no doubt also open up democratic, alternative potentials within Muslim countries themselves. This struggle for inclusive, pluralistic possibilities begins with the translations of the Qur'an.

5

LIMITS OF TRANSLATIONS

For the vast majority of people, Muslims and non-Muslims alike, the Qur'an is only accessible in translation. But translations have been a source of controversy throughout Muslim history. The need and desire for translations arose as soon as Islam spread beyond the Arabian peninsula, where the growing number of new converts to the faith did not speak Arabic. Two related questions came to the fore. Was it permissible to translate the Arabic Qur'an into another language? And was it lawful to recite the translation during prayer?

The first person to address the issue was Imam Abu Hanifa (699–765), the great jurist and founder of the Hanafi School of Thought. Of Persian origins, Abu Hanifa declared that it was permissible both to translate the Qur'an into Persian and read the Persian version during prayer. He argued that the Qur'an is simply the meaning of the revealed Arabic text, and this meaning does not change if rendered into a different language. Indeed, from the death of the Prophet Muhammad in 632 to the days of Abu Hanifa, translations of parts of the Qur'an into the languages of new converts to Islam were permitted and widely used.

But the practice did not last. The founders of the three other dominant Schools of Thought—Imam Malik (711–795), Imam As-Shafi (767–820) and Imam Hanbal (780–855)—vehemently disagreed with Abu Hanifa. Imam Malik thought that it was reprehensible for a non-Arab even to make an oath by God in a language other than Arabic. Hanbali jurists argued that the inimitability of the Qur'an was based not just in the meaning of the words but also the unique structure, the sounds and the rhyme and rhythm of the text. As it was humanly impossible to capture this, translations could not be permitted.

As-Shafi, a pure Arab, argued that the Qur'an was revealed in the language of Muhammad's own people to the exclusion of the tongues of non-Arabs; therefore, people who did not have Arabic were duty-bound to learn the glorious language of the Qur'an.

The majority consensus became the dominant position. But the controversy continued, as it was challenged, from time to time, by scholars and jurists within the dominant tradition. A seventeenth-century jurist, for example, used the same argument as As-Shafi to reach the opposite conclusion: 'if you argue that the Messenger of God was not sent to Arabs alone but to all mankind who speak different languages', he writes, 'so that if the Arabs could not make any plea (of ignorance) others could, then I would say this: Either (the revelation) could be sent in all the tongues or in one of them. But there was no need for it to be revealed in all languages, since translations make up for that...(and could be used) to transmit it and spread it... to explain... (it) to non-Arab nations...' [24]

More recently, a famous *fatwa* against translations was issued by the Syrian jurist Rashid Rida, in 1908 [25]. Concerned with an imminent Turkish translation of the Qur'an, Rida's *fatwa* identified three major problems with translating the Qur'an: a translation reflects the understanding of one person; metaphoric verses could be rendered literally and thus lead to confusion; and a translation cannot reproduce the diction, rhyme and structure of the Qur'an and would therefore deprive the reader of these benefits. This is why, Rida argues, it is essential for all Muslims to learn Arabic, the only gateway to understanding the true message and meaning of the Qur'an, the life of Prophet Muhammad and the history of Islam.

We cannot really dispute the fact that a translation, as Mohammad Marmaduke Pickthall (1875–1936) notes, 'is not the Glorious Qur'an, that inimitable symphony, the very sound of which moves men to tears and ecstasy' [26]. As such, during daily prayers, where blessings of God are being sought, nothing but the original text will do. In prayer, as some Muslim scholars have rightly argued, the true Majesty of God can be invoked only with His own words. Equally, we have to acknowledge that there are serious problems with translating the Qur'an associated with its style, non-linear order, specific lattice structure, and perhaps the most difficult, if not impossible, problem of conveying its intricate, rich and varied rhythms which, to use the words of A. J. Arberry (1905–69), 'constitute the Qur'an's undeniable claim to rank amongst the greatest literary masterpieces of mankind' [27]. However, does that mean that no attempts should be made to translate it? Or that translations per se are unnecessary and irrelevant, as Rashid Rida and so many other theologians and jurists, have suggested? Even when it is difficult, or indeed impossible, to render all that makes the Qur'an unique in another language, would not a good translation communicate something of the meaning and essence of the Qur'an, thereby making it easy for non-Arabs to understand its message? Why such vehemence against translations?

There are four basic reasons why the traditional scholars were strongly anti-translation. The first is related to the perception of the alleged superiority of the Arabic language. Yet, as A. L. Tibawi (1910–81) notes, the classical scholars had no acquaintance with other languages, apart from Persian, to pass such a judgement. 'They all seem so charmed at the undoubted versatility of Arabic, that they took the matter for granted and gave little or no evidence in support of their assertion' [28]. It is analogous, perhaps, to the belief that the famously monoglot English maintain about 'the language of Shakespeare', which they sought to spread around the globe in the colonial era. There is in fact no evidence to suggest that Arabic—or indeed English—is in any way superior to any other language, even though the Qur'an is revealed in Arabic. All languages have their unique features and qualities and their strengths and weaknesses. Moreover, it would be an odd God who, having established diversity and citing different languages and people as one of His signs in the Qur'an, then proceeded to defy it by requiring that He can only be understood in a single language.

The second reason is well articulated by Mahmoud Ayoub: 'the ideal cherished by those who oppose the translation of the Qur'an is that of unity among all Muslim nations under the banner of one faith and one language. The natural way to bring others to Islam, they believe, is to urge those who wish to know Islam to learn the Arabic language' [29]. Whatever the ideal, reality says otherwise. Having a common language has never united the Arabs in history or in contemporary times. Indeed, the distinguishing feature of the Arab world is its perpetual and stark disunity. In contrast, despite a range of different languages and ethnicities, Europe has been able to come together as an economic and political community: the European Union. An Islam that can only be understood through a single language is not only diminished but has a limited future: monochromatic understanding and outlooks are as doomed as monocultures in nature.

The third reason is that a translation, however good or flawed, presents an interpretation of the Qur'an, as suggested by the title of Arthur J. Arberry's famous translation: *The Koran Interpreted*. It conveys the understanding of the translator(s), an attempt to provide one possible meaning of a complex, multilayered text. Or, as Rashid Rida says, it is actually a *tafsir*, a commentary and an exegesis. So, a translator is unwittingly stepping in the footsteps of those—the traditional scholars—who see themselves as the only ones with requisite knowledge and legitimate authority to write *tafsir* and interpret the Qur'an. For the traditional scholars, the Qur'an is not just a Sacred Text; it is also a secret book, and they are the sole key to unlocking its secret. No wonder they are so vehemently against translations.

Finally, there is the suggestion that translations could, deliberately and consciously, subvert the meaning of the Qur'an. A translation can be used to present a distorted view of Islam and project and represent Muslims in the colours of darkness [30]. Indeed, for centuries Muslims have harboured the suspicion that translations have been used by Christian missionaries to destroy Islam. This perception does have some basis in reality [31].

Some of the earliest English translations were undertaken with precisely this aim. One of the first translations to appear in English was *The Alcoran of Mahomet* by Alexander Ross, published in 1649. Based on a French translation, the subtitle made its aim clear: 'newly Englished, for the satisfaction of all that desire to look into the Turkish vanities'. In a note to Christian readers, Ross explains his purpose further: 'I thought good to bring it to their colours, that so viewing thine enemies in their full body thou must the better prepare to encounter...his Alcoran' [32]. A more scholarly translation was produced by George Sale in 1734; entitled *The Koran: Commonly called the Alkoran of Mohammed*, its main purpose was to serve as a weapon in 'the conversion of Mohmmedans'. Sale was generous enough to suggest that 'For how criminal soever Mohammed may have been in imposing a fake religion on mankind, the praises due to his real virtues ought not to be denied him' [33]. But this munificence did not prevent Sale from committing a few offences himself, including mistranslation, omitting part of some verses, and generally berating the structure, logic and rationality of the Sacred Text, which provided, he claimed, clear evidence that the Qur'an was the work of several authors.

Subsequent translators decided to do away with the problematic structure of the Qur'an altogether and totally rearrange it in some sort of chronological order. J. M. Rodwell, Rector of St. Ethelberga, London, was the first to come up with a rough chronological order for his translation, *The Koran*, published in 1861. But Rodwell continued the Western tradition of both subverting the text and using it as an instrument for missionary activities. He thought Muhammad was a crafty, self-deceiving person predisposed to morbid and fantastic hallucinations. A more thorough rearrangement was attempted by Richard Bell (1876–1952), a noted Scottish Orientalist, as is evident from the title of his translation: *The Qur'an translated with a critical rearrangement of the Surahs*, published in Edinburgh during 1937–9. Bell found 'evidence of revisions and alterations' in the Qur'an [34] but his reorganisation does little for the translation. He thought Muhammad was a good poet, indeed a special one as his poetry covered the themes of religion and righteousness, but could not understand why poetry required repetition. Repetition within the Qur'an, he argued, was a mistake produced by inserting some verses where they did not belong.

But playing havoc with the structure of the Qur'an was not enough. More recent translations have been a bit more subtle, using a number of devices, ranging from omission, distortion and mistranslation, to project the Qur'an as a violent and sexist text. The best example is N. J. Dawood's *The Koran*, which first appeared in 1956 as a 'Penguin classic', and has since gone through a dozen editions. Dawood's chapter headings themselves point to a deliberate approach. For some reason the opening chapter of the Qur'an universally rendered by other translations simply as 'The Opening' is converted to the far more obscure though equivalent 'the Exordium'. The title for chapter 39 (*Az-Zumar*) becomes 'the Hordes', suggesting barbarian mobs, while it is more commonly translated as 'The Crowd' or 'The Groups'. Chapter 96 is translated as 'Clots of Blood'; the word used here, '*Alaq*', is in fact singular and literally means that which clings, and refers to the embryo as it attaches to the wall of the uterus. Most Muslim translators simply call the chapter 'the Clot'; what is intended to convey the idea of birth Dawood projects as a notion of death. *Al-Saff*, chapter 61, he translates as 'Battle Array'; it actually means 'the Ranks' or 'Solid Lines'.

Often Dawood mistranslates a single word in a verse to give it totally the opposite meaning. In 2:217, for example, we read: 'idolatry is worse than carnage'. The word translated as 'idolatry' is '*fitna*', which actually means sedition or oppression. Dawood's translation conveys the notion that the Qur'an will put up with carnage but not idolatry. In fact, the Qur'an is making sedition and oppression a crime greater than murder. The verse should read: 'oppression is more awesome than killing'. Similarly, a word here and a word there are rendered in a specific way to suggest that the Qur'an is a sexist text. Thus, while the Qur'an asks humanity to serve God, Dawood changes that to Men, as in 2:21 which is translated as 'Men, serve your Lord'; it should be 'O People! Worship your Lord'. Similarly, 'Children of Adam' becomes 'Children of Allah'.

Spouses become virgins. Moreover, the translation uses rather obscurantist images throughout to give the impression that the Qur'an is full of demons and witches. For example, in 31:1, Dawood has God swearing 'by those who cast out demons', while most translators have rendered the same verse as 'Behold the revelations of the Wise Book' or 'wise Scripture'. In 113:4, Dawood has 'conjuring witches' while the verse actually refers to the evil of witchcraft. Where Dawood suggests God 'communed with Moses for forty nights', a rather odd thought for a monotheistic faith, most translators point out that God 'appointed for Moses forty nights'. While Dawood insists that the followers of Moses are 'made to drink the calf into their very hearts' (2:93), more sensible translators render the verse as 'they were made to imbibe the love of the calf in their hearts'. And so on. Not surprisingly, Dawood's translation has been a great source of discomfort for Muslims, who see it as a deliberate attempt to malign Islam. Dawood's translation is the one that most non-Muslims cite when they accuse the Qur'an or Islam or Muslims, often with great conviction, of having no option but to be fanatical, violent and depraved.

These translations had tremendous impact on the outlook of European thinkers and society. Constantin Volney (1757–1820), French philosopher and historian, found the Qur'an to be 'a tissue of vague, contradictory declamations, of ridiculous, dangerous precepts' [35]. The explorer Charles Doughty (1843–1926), whose *Travels in Arabia Deserta* was one of the most popular books of the late Victorian world, had limited Arabic and relied heavily on translations. The totally incomprehensible and trite Qur'an (which he always spelled as 'koran' with a lower case K), he wrote, had given the Arabs 'a barbarous fox-like understanding' of the world [36]. In *On Heroes and Hero-worship*, Thomas Carlyle (1795–1881) denounces the lies that missionaries, led by 'well-meaning zeal', have heaped on Muhammad. The Prophet is one of his grand heroes of humanity, a 'Great Man of him I will venture to assert that it is incredible he should have been other than true' [37]. Yet, after reading the translation by Sale ('our translation of it, by Sale, is known to be a very fair one'), he found the Qur'an to be 'a wearisome confused jumble, crude, incondite; endless iterations, long-windedness, entanglement, most crude, incondite; insupportable stupidity, in short!' 'Nothing', he declared, 'but a sense of duty could carry any European through the Koran' [38]. Across the channel, Voltaire (1694–1778) initially reached similar conclusions by reading Sale's translation. But further reading, and copious annotation, led him not only to revise his views but also, as Zaid Elmarsafy shows in *The Enlightenment Qur'an*, to use the Qur'an to shape some of the key features of the Enlightenment [39].

Of course, not all 'Orientalist' translations served a polemical, missionary or political purpose. Arberry's translation, which was first published in 1955, received high praise from Muslim scholars and critics for its approach and quality. For me, it is undoubtedly the most poetic: Arberry devises rhythmic patterns and sequence-groupings to echo the Arabic, and arranges his paragraphs 'as they form the original units of revelation'. Making an engaging translation does require some empathy with the text, and Arberry clearly had affection for the Qur'an, which in turn had a profound impact on him. Towards the end of his introduction, he gives a hint of what he was going through: 'the task was undertaken, not lightly, and carried to its conclusion at a time of great personal distress, through which it comforted and sustained the writer in a manner for which he will always be grateful. He therefore acknowledges his gratitude to whatever power or Power inspired the man and the Prophet who first recited these scriptures. I pray that this interpretation, poor echo though it is of the glorious original, may instruct, please and in some degree inspire those who read it' [40].

Despite the objection of religious scholars, and Rashid Rida's strong *fatwa*, the early twentieth century saw the emergence of a number of English translations by Muslim scholars. This was a refreshing shift, from translations that were, on the whole, hostile to the subject of their study, to an approach that took Muslim appreciation of their Sacred Text into account. The move was apparent in the titles that Muslim translators chose for their works: rather than use the old anglicised form 'Koran', Muslims adopted the new 'Qur'an', which is now accepted as the correct Arabic transliteration and pronunciation of the word.

The path was led by Mohammed Marmaduke Pickthall (1875–1936), a British novelist and journalist educated at Eton. A passionate man, he supported the Ottoman Empire and was an outspoken critic of Britain's involvement in Turkey. Pickthall, who embraced Islam in 1917 and went to India to work for the Nizam of Hyderabad, believed, 'like old-fashioned Sheykhs', that the Qur'an cannot be translated [41]. But he was persuaded by the Nizam, who also supported the venture, to accept the task. *The Meaning of the Glorious Koran*, subtitled 'an explanatory translation', came out in 1930. It is an accurate and faithful rendering in the language of the King James Bible.

Pickthall's translation was followed, four years later, by Abdullah Yusuf Ali's *The Holy Qur'an: Text, Translation and Commentary*. Born in Bombay, Yusuf Ali (1872–1953) belonged to a wealthy family of merchants. He studied English literature at the University of Leeds and travelled widely in Europe and

North America, promoting the Indian contribution to World War 1. On the whole, Ali provides us with a literalist translation, although he does lean towards mysticism in some of his interpretation and commentary. Given that Ali aspired to be a Victorian gentleman, it is not surprising that his translation has the flavour and spirit of the age. He died in London, alone and unrecognised [42].

Amongst the Muslims, both Pickthall and Yusuf Ali served as standard translations for much of the twentieth century. Both have gone through numerous editions, and have been published in different forms worldwide. However, towards the end of the millennium, when fundamentalism was on the ascendance, both translations became a battleground over the interpretation of the Qur'an and hence the meaning of Islam in contemporary times. Even though both translations are fairly orthodox, they are not conservative and dogmatic enough for certain Muslims.

So the revised editions of Pickthall expunge the old English pronouns 'thou', 'thy' and 'thine' and claim to be more readable and accessible. But in the process of editing 'ye olde' English, Pickthall's own opinions are radically changed to make him appear more narrow-minded and anti-rationalist. His sceptical approach to miracles has been replaced with conventional, conservative views. New explanatory notes highlight the 'correct' Islamic viewpoints; and where Pickthall admits that the meaning of certain allegorical verses are not clear to him, the editor now tells us exactly what the 'true' meaning of these verses are [43].

But it is Yusuf Ali, the more popular of the two, who has been subjected to what can only be described as a truly nefarious onslaught of revisions. Ali was a humble and cautious translator. 'In translating the text', he writes in the preface to the first edition, 'I have aired no views of my own, but followed the received commentator. Where they differ amongst themselves, I have had to choose what appears to me the most reasonable opinion from all points of view. Where I have departed from the literal translation in order to express the spirit of the original in English, I have explained the literal meaning in the notes' [44]. But Ali's literalism is not literal enough for some. In particular, his notes on miracles and eschatology have been a cause for concern by blinkered conservatives, as was his inclination towards mysticism.

So the revised editions of Ali [45]—brought out by Amana Publications, an American conservative publisher, and the Saudi Arabian religious propaganda organisation, 'The Presidency of Islamic Researches Call and Guidance'—set out to 'clear any misconceptions regarding the articles of faith, varying juristic opinions and thoughts not in conformity with the sound Islamic point of view' (p.viii). The 'sound Islamic point of view', or the Saudi Wahabi interpretation of Islam, cannot cope with allegory or metaphors and is inimically hostile to any view other than its own. Hence, Ali's appendices giving allegorical interpretation of the story of Joseph, a mystical interpretation of the Verse of light, and a symbolic explanation of the idea of heaven are ruthlessly cut. Ali was a Sunni, but he showed great respect towards the grandsons of the Prophet Muhammad, Imams Hussain and Hassan, both of whom are revered by the Shia. The revised edition deletes Ali's description of the two Imams. His constant references in the commentary to a Caliph or Imam to lead the Muslim world are a reflection of his time. I suspect that he was traumatised, like most Muslims at that time, by the recent collapse of the Ottoman Empire and the Caliphate. All references to a caliph or pious leader have been removed. His view that insurance is not a form of gambling if it is organised on an ethical basis and is a necessity in the modern business environment has been ditched, as is his note on usury. His symbolic explanation of Muslim prayer, his references to the mystical meaning of love, indeed anything that smells of allegory or metaphors has been ruthlessly expunged. And his views on jihad, sex in heaven, and resurrection are totally changed.

It took Yusuf Ali four years to produce his translation and commentary. The numerous committees at the 'Presidency' took ten years to do the revisions. So even the minutest deviation from the Saudi orthodoxy is cleansed. For example, commenting on the verse 'No reward I ask of you for this except the love of those near of kin' (42:23), Ali argues that 'the love of kindred may be extended to mean the love of our common humanity, for all mankind are brothers descended from Adam'. But this inclusive humanity is much too much for the Saudi orthodoxy, and has thus been deleted. In explaining 45:14, 'it is for Him to recompense (for good or ill) each people, according to what they have earned', Ali states that 'it is not right for private persons to take vengeance even for the cause of right and justice...Nor is it permissible even to a group of persons to arrogate to themselves the championship of the right....'. The editors of the revised version have done precisely this: arrogated to themselves the right to decide exactly what is and what is not right. So out goes the part of Ali's commentary that questions their authority.

The 'Presidency' thinks it is right not just to change Ali's commentary, remove his preface, delete his appendices, and modify his translation, but also to remove his name from the translation itself. We learn that this is in fact Yusuf Ali's translation from the one line mention to 'Ustad Yusuf Ali' in the preface to the revised edition. '*Ustad*', a title one gives to a low-ranking scholar, adds insult to injury, suggesting that Ali, despite his monumental achievement, did not have the qualification to be a fully-fledged Sheikh. Of course, Yusuf Ali has no comeback. But we should not hesitate to state clearly that these revisions are both dishonest and reprehensible. No one has the right to change Yusuf Ali's opinion; except the author himself.

While Muslims have constantly complained about distortions and falsification in Western translations, some of their own translations are not short on misrepresentations. A notable recent example is *Interpretation of the Meaning of the Noble Qur'an in the English Language* by Muhammad Taqi al-Din al-Hilali and Muhammad Muhsin Khan [46]. It comes complete with a certificate of approval from the late Grand Mufti of Saudi Arabia, Sheikh Bin Baz (who, let us remind ourselves, thought the earth was flat), and other prominent religious authorities in the Kingdom. Intended to replace Yusuf Ali, it has been distributed largely free and extensively through mosques, seminaries, religious organisations and Muslim bookshops throughout the Muslim world.

Subtitled 'a summarized version of At-Tabari, Al-Qurtubi and Ibn Khathir with comments from Sahih Al-Bukhari,' the translation ostensibly seeks to explain and interpret the Qur'an with the help of three classical commentaries and the traditions of the Prophet Muhammad. But the use of more puritanical and combative classical commentaries that saw the world largely in black and white terms, together with clever and selective deployment of the traditions of the Prophet, enables the authors to present the Qur'an as a rather aggressive, authoritarian and misogynous text in conformity with the Wahabi worldview. The rendering is awkward and stilted, dry and literalist in the extreme. Certain key terms are left in the original form and simply transliterated. The copious *Hadith* footnotes are quite incomprehensible to ordinary readers of English.

The aggressively puritanical tone is set right at the beginning with *al-Fatiha*, the opening chapter of the Qur'an. Thus, the verse 'Guide us to the straight path' is explained as the way of not just God and His Prophet but also 'pious preachers', that is the scholars and religious authorities of the Kingdom. 'The way of those who have earned Your Anger' means the Jews, and 'those who went astray' are the Christians! While no context is provided for the verse 'kill them wherever you find them' (2:191), an interesting twist is given to the second part of the verse. The key word here is *fitna*, which means social disruption or temptation to sin. Yusuf Ali translates this as 'tumult and oppression are worse than slaughter'; Pickthall as 'persecution is worse than slaughter'. But Al-Halali and Khan explain *fitna* as 'polytheism, to disbelieve after one has believed in Allah', suggesting that polytheists and apostates, by their very nature, have committed crimes that are on a higher plane than carnage; and hence they are legitimate targets for killing. So the next but one verse, 'fight them until there is no persecution' (2:193) becomes 'fight them until there is no more disbelief and worshipping of others along with Allah'. Similarly, *zalimun* (literally those who commit *zulm*, or injustice, i.e. the oppressors) in 29:14 become polytheists and disbelievers, suggesting that the very existence of non-Muslims is a form of injustice and oppression! In 33:59, where the Qur'an asks the Prophet to 'tell your wives, your daughters, and women believers to make their outer garments hang low over them so as to be recognised and not insulted', the Al-Halili and Khan translation has 'cloaks (veils) all over their bodies (i.e. screen themselves completely except the eyes or one eye to see the way)'. Similar interpolations throughout the text turn the Qur'an into a blueprint for replicating the xenophobic and misogynist Saudi society in every detail. No wonder so many Wahabi-inspired fanatics use the Qur'an to justify their nefarious activities. I would suggest that in many respects this is the Muslim counterpart of Dawood's translation; and in some respects it is even worse.

But it is not just the Saudis who seek to impose their own sectarian imprint on English translations of the Qur'an. Almost every Muslim sect and ideological camp has produced its own translation during the last few decades. So now we have Shia translations, Sufi translations, a translation that reflects the partialities of Turkish Islam, a feminist translation, 'The First American Version', translations by 'translation committees', and even a bizarre translation based on the absurd thesis that words of the Qur'an have magical numerical values.

Most of these translations are upfront about their specific outlooks. For example, the standard Shia translation, which has gone through several permutations, revisions and editions, declares its sectarian bias in the title: *The Holy Qur'an With English Translation of the Arabic Text and Commentary According to the Version of Holy Ahlul-Bait*. The translation is by Mir Ahmed Ali, an Indian scholar, but the commentary is provided by Ayatollah Mirza Mahdi Pooya Yazdi, a noted Iranian scholar with strong mystical leanings. As one would expect, it is strong on Shia doctrines and ritual observances. In particular, it tries to show that the Prophet appointed his cousin and son-in-law, Ali, and eleven others, as his successors, with full authority as religious and political leaders for the whole Muslim community—to be obeyed unquestioningly. As such, we read in the Introduction, 'Ali is the Foremost and Topmost One next only to the Holy Prophet in the thorough knowledge of inner and outer significance of every word, sentence, passage and part of chapter of the Qur'an in its revealed and pre-revealed form to which the Qur'an itself bears testimony...' [47]. It also tries to justify other Shia practices, such as glorification of martyrs and temporary marriage (*mut'a*). But the translation also denigrates companions of the Prophet revered by the Sunnis, throws scorn at Sunni beliefs and insists that Shi'ism is the correct, authentic and original Islam.

Both the standard Shia and Saudi translations use *Hadith*, the sayings of the Prophet, to argue for their particular, sometimes quite absurd and irrational, positions. In the appendix to *Qur'an: A Reformist Translation* we get a whole list of how 'authentic' *Hadith* have been used not just to justify sectarian positions, but also to promote the interests of a particular class, tribe or family, justify violence and misogyny, validate superstition, prohibit certain cultural products (such as music) and to suppress dissent. But the reform that this translation seeks is not so much social and cultural as rooted in numerology, a dubious practice of little value [48]. The translators, Edip Yuksel, Layth Saleh al-Shaiban and Martha Schulte-Nafey, are followers of Rashad Khalifa, an Egyptian American biochemist, who claimed in 1980 to have discovered a hidden mathematical code in the Qur'an: when you add the numerical equivalent of the verses of the Qur'an, they all add up to, or are multiples of, number 19 [49]. So impressed was Khalifa with his discovery that he began to describe himself as 'Rashad Khalifa PhD, Messenger of Allah'. Khalifa was murdered in 1990, but his legacy has continued unabated. Thus the function of this translation is to prove, by hook or by crook, that the magical number 19 is embedded in each and every verse of the Qur'an. There is a large worldwide Muslim movement of benighted imbeciles who swallow this nonsense.

It is quite evident that translations can sometimes create more problems than they seek to solve. Fortunately there are reliable translations that both Muslims and non-Muslims can use gainfully. *The Message of The Qur'an*, 'translated and explained' by Muhammad Asad (1900–92), is a superb example of a non-sectarian, rational, humane and straightforward rendering of the Qur'an. Asad was a scholar adventurer who, having converted from Judaism, travelled widely throughout the Muslim world, worked with various anti-colonial liberation movements and even served as the Pakistani ambassador to the United Nations. He was an accomplished scholar with an intimate knowledge of classical Arabic, *Hadith* (he also translated *Sahih Bukhari* [50]) and classical commentaries. His translation, published in 1980 from Gibraltar, where Asad lived during retirement, is not only eminently readable, faithful to the original text, but also erudite. His footnotes reveal his extensive knowledge of Muslim sources, Islamic law and culture as well as the Bible. He shows that both *Hadith* and classical commentaries can be used objectively to delineate the pluralistic and humane message of the Qur'an.

On the whole, Asad's views were quite orthodox (after all, he was a companion of King Abdel Aziz, the founder of Saudi Arabia, as we learn from his autobiography *The Road to Mecca* [51]), but this does not stop him from being critical. 'The great thinkers of the past', he writes in his foreword, approached their commentaries 'with their reason', and were 'fully aware of the element of relativity inherent in all human reasoning'. To disagree with them is not to show animosity but to imply that 'differences of opinion are the basis of all progress in human thinking and, therefore, a most potent factor in man's acquisition of knowledge' [52]. So Asad sometimes respectfully disagrees with the classical commentators. Moreover, he offers a more allegorical interpretation of some of the miracles mentioned in the Qur'an, disagrees with the conventional Muslim opinion on the story of Ibrahim's attempted sacrifice of his son, provides several interpretations of the term and concept of *jinn*, and rejects the orthodox line on the doctrine of abrogation (that some of the earlier verses of the Qur'an are superseded by later ones). All of which was enough for Saudi Arabia to ban Muhammad Asad, not just *The Message of The Qur'an* but also most of his books. But that is all the more reason for using and consulting Asad's translation. I must confess that I find Asad to be an enlightened and progressive scholar and adore his translation.

Two other excellent translations have appeared recently. Both carry the same title: *The Qur'an: A New Translation*. The first to appear, in Oxford World's Classics series, is by M. A. S. Abdel Haleem, a classically trained Egyptian scholar who is Professor of Islamic Studies at the School of African and Oriental Studies, University of London. The second, by Tarif Khalidi, a Palestinian scholar who is Professor of Islamic and Arabic Studies at the American University, Beirut, is in Penguin Classics (I suspect it is supposed to replace the old N. J. Dawood translation that Penguin peddled for decades). Both are published as trade books and should be widely and easily available. Together they provide a good illustration of just how different from each other translations of the Qur'an can be.

Abdel Haleem provides us with an accurate and highly readable translation. The complex grammar and structure of the Qur'an are transformed into smooth, contemporary English mercifully free from archaisms, anachronism and incoherence. Abdel Haleem uses a simple, but ingenious, device to solve a couple of crucial problems. The Qur'an often addresses different parties—for example, the Prophet, or the Community of Believers, or the hostile Meccan tribe of the Quraysh—and switches from one party to another in the same verse. Abdel Haleem makes it clear who is speaking or being addressed in parentheses. Parentheses are also used to provide context: for example, when the Qur'an says 'those who believed and emigrated', Abdel Haleem adds '[to Medina]', to show that it is emigration to Medina that is being described. Context is also emphasised in the brief summaries that appear at the beginning of each chapter. Although footnotes are kept to a bare minimum, they are judiciously used to explain geographical, historical and personal allusions. Abdel Haleem's emphasis on context, the connection of each verse to many, many others, and how different parts of the Qur'an explain each other, make this translation original and exceptionally useful. You do get an impression that you are reading a commentary on the life of Muhammad and an inkling of the social conditions in Mecca during the period of revelation: Abdel Haleem points out the cultural context of some verses, such as those relating to female witnesses. But he also conveys an appreciation that the teachings of the Qur'an are relevant, as he says in the introduction, to a world struggling with 'such universal issues as globalisation, the environment, combating terrorism and drugs, issues of medical ethics and feminism' [53].

There are, as always with any translation, some limitations. Despite the originality of the translation, Abdel Haleem is a bit too conventional and conservative. He adheres strictly to orthodox doctrines in the explanatory footnotes, which rely heavily on classical commentators, particularly the late-twelfth-century commentator Fakhr al-Din al-Razi. And he does not inspire a sense of poetic beauty.

Like Abdel Haleem, Khalidi is not interested in providing the context of the verses of the Qur'an. We therefore do not always know who the Qur'an is addressing at various junctures or who is speaking to whom in its internal dialogues. Neither is Khalidi all that concerned with providing some help to the reader: there are no footnotes or any explanation. Instead, Khalidi takes a rather unusual attitude to the Qur'an; it is 'a bearer of diverse interpretation', he says; and its ambiguities are deliberately designed to stimulate thinking. Let the reader be 'patient of interpretation' and read at will [54]. All that is needed is to approach the text with sympathy.

What Khalidi really wants is for the reader to enjoy the experience of reading the Qur'an. Of course, he wants to communicate the majesty of its language, the beauty of its style and the 'eternal present tense' of its grammar. But he aims higher: he also wants the reader to appreciate the unique structure of the Qur'an, how the language changes with the subject matter, how it swirls around and makes rhythmic connections. He wishes to show how each of the seven tropes of the Qur'an (command, prohibition, glad tidings, warnings, sermons, parables and narratives) register a change in the style of its language. It is a lofty ambition, but Khalidi pulls it off with some success.

The shifts in style are presented in two ways. Linguistically, Khalidi moves between literal translation, rendered in clear prose, to the use of heightened language, to deeply poetic renderings. Physically the layout of the passage changes, so each style looks different on the page. The narrative passages, or sections dealing with social and legislative affairs, appear in a prose format. The dramatic and metaphysical sections are arranged in poetic style. An example:

In likeness, they are like one who lit a fire. When the fire illuminated his surroundings, God extinguished their light and left them in darkness, unseeing,

Deaf.
Dumb.
Blind.
They do not repent. (2:17–18)

Khalidi also separates the dialogues and questions and answers that are the hallmark of some of the verses as separate paragraphs. So a great deal of the translation reads as conversations—'He said', 'They said'—that have occurred, are occurring and may yet occur in the future:

He shall say: 'How long did you remain on earth, in number of years?'
They will respond: 'We remained for a day or a part thereof. Ask those who count.'
He will say: 'You remained only a short while, if only you knew.' (23:112–14)

It is difficult to deny that this translation has a certain beauty and manages to capture a glimpse of the grandeur of the original. No doubt, Khalidi's poetic efforts will be compared with Arberry. I would suggest that Arberry has a slight edge. However, both Arberry and Khalidi's translations have a problem with numbering the verses. The verse numbers appear only sporadically, giving no indication of the specific beginning and ending of verses in between. Neither translation would help someone unfamiliar with the text if they wanted to check a reference to a specific verse; so the translations are not easy to navigate.

However, navigating translations is by no means easy, as I have tried to show. Since a single translation can be very misleading, it is best, I have found, to use more than one. However, to present my reading of the Qur'an, it is necessary to share with the reader my best approximation of the Qur'an as I understand its English translation. Therefore, in what follows I present my own synthesis of a number of English translations as the basis for the discussion of *al-Fatiha* and *Al-Baqara*. To produce this synthesis I used six translations: Arberry, Pickthall, Yusuf Ali, Asad, Haleem and Khalidi. I read each verse in each of these six translations and opted for the most lucid language, shorn of archaic form, that I could to convey the sense I had accumulated from them all. Each passage of this synthesised version is followed by a discussion of meaning, which incorporates discussion of the significance of the Arabic terms used and the subjects that are addressed in footnotes. By no stretch of the imagination is my rendition a new translation. It is, however, a sincere and serious effort to convey to the reader as accurately as possible the sense I apprehend in reading the Qur'an, the point from which I begin to engage with its meaning, to work out the contemporary relevance of the text. In synthesising this reading I have made personal choices. I have been hugely informed by having to wrestle with the differences and distinctions in the linguistic choices of some very notable scholars. Most of all, the process was an essential element of my personal quest. It helped to uncover new depths of meaning and implication in a text I have been familiar with since childhood. I cannot commend too highly to anyone interested in engaging with the Qur'an the practice of reading multiple translations in conjunction with one another. I would ask all readers not to stop and certainly not to be satisfied with my humble synthesis.

Part Two

BY WAY OF TRADITION

6

INTRODUCTION

When I was six, my mother began teaching me to read the Qur'an. I began, as is usual, at the end with the 30ᵗʰ *Sipara*, the last of the sections into which the Holy Book is divided for purposes of study and devotional reading. However, the short *suras* that comprise this *Sipara* were not the first words of the Sacred Text with which I became familiar. Like any Muslim, as I learned to understand speech I frequently heard the words that open all but one of the chapters of the Qur'an: *Bismillah ir-Rahman ir-Rahim*, In the name of God the Compassionate, the Merciful. This phrase is woven into the pattern of our daily life. It is a convention of common speech, used at the beginning of a whole variety of ordinary activities. In the same way I became familiar with the words of *al-Fatiha*, the first chapter of the Qur'an. The *al-Fatiha* is not only the basis of the five daily prayers Muslims offer; it is also recited on a host of occasions: individually at times of stress or trouble, or collectively to solemnise and give thanks at an innumerable variety of family and communal gatherings. Indeed, there are a plethora of phrases and sayings invoking God, such as *Inshallah* (God Willing) or *Alhamdullilah* (All praise or thanks is for God), which are conventional expressions frequently used in Muslim daily life. And daily life in a Muslim country is punctuated with the sound of the adhan, the call to prayer proclaimed from every mosque. It summons the faithful with repeated statements of the declaration of faith: 'There is no god but God and Muhammad is His Messenger.' The refrains of the Qur'an are embedded in the cultural norms, the traditions that define one's identity. As one grows up, by way of tradition in word and deed, one absorbs aspects of meaning derived from the Sacred Text before ever one formally encounters the text itself.

57

The traditional method of learning the Qur'an is and always has been repetition of recitation, designed to commit the text to memory. Familiarity and remembrance are not the same as reading; nor are custom and tradition, the conventional understandings one inherits and grows up amongst, the same as reasoning with the meaning and implications of the Sacred Text. Living with tradition is being socialised and conforming to the ways of one's elders, ways that have been formed from other people's interpretations of the Sacred Text. No human being can plumb the mind of God completely, nor devise rules and regulations based on scripture which cater to all the permutations, vicissitudes and needs of all time. Such omniscience is the preserve of the Divine. To claim that there is one definitive way to be Muslim and that that way has been settled for all time long ago in human history is to reduce the Qur'an to the narrowest of human reasoning. Holding to tradition promotes the stance of previous generations over the duties and responsibilities that should be the task of every generation. However well such reasoning served other times and places, it is legitimate and necessary to question how well it addresses the circumstances of the twenty-first century. Moreover, failure to consider its contemporary meaning is to deny the insistent message of the Sacred Text.

The troubling question for me as an individual, as well as for Muslims generally, is how to transcend tradition and find the meaning and implication of the Holy Book for our time and place. For many well educated Muslims of my acquaintance, the very idea of taking responsibility for reading the Qur'an and thinking afresh seems tantamount to renouncing the past, and somehow undermining their cherished identity which has been shaped by tradition. Moreover, how can one read afresh words that are so familiar? How can one think afresh about interpretations that have become second nature, because we have always been taught that is how things should be? Even worse, taking individual responsibility for reading and thinking afresh sounds, to many Muslims, remarkably like denying the claims of community and opening the flood gates of chaos that lie beyond established traditional consensus. Whatever their private qualms, standing four-square behind tradition and the authority of the traditionally educated preservers of traditional interpretation—the *imams*, the *maulvis* and the *ulama,* the learned—serves a desire for unity. It is supposed to demonstrate bonds of fellow feeling, brotherhood and sisterhood among and across the diversity of the world's Muslims. The most obvious outcome of such conformity is the common practice of invoking, and defending, an idealised Islam. Sadly, this idealised Islam is seldom to be found in reality. It is the frequently heard plaint: 'Ah yes, that is what Muslims are doing, but that is not the real Islam.' The defensive reflex on behalf of the ideal too often sounds like apologetics in the face of justified and justifiable criticism of what Muslims actually do in the name of their religion. Criticism and complaint come as much from Muslims as non-Muslims, though they are usually aired in entirely different domains and contexts; the essential point being that in so many instances that which is complained of, that which Muslims are actually doing, is precisely what they believe constitutes the requirements of following tradition, and therefore traditional interpretation.

My personal journey is an attempt to engage directly with the Qur'an. The objective is to search beyond the impasse of an idealised but unrealised understanding and discover how the Sacred Text speaks to the pressing concerns of my time and the predicaments of the world in which I live. The journey is a process of becoming aware, and sharing with the reader, how I find freshness in the words of the Qur'an. Equally, it necessitates awareness of tradition, the classical tradition of Qur'anic exegesis and interpretation. In this process I find one does not abandon tradition but comes to understand that it is neither as uniform nor as narrow as is usually presented. Both in reading the Qur'an and exploring the legacy of Muslim traditional scholarship, the key is to understand the context and distinguish between the general and the time-bound specifics. The distinction is between what relates to a particular person, place and time and the principle and methodology, the way of thinking and asking questions which is relevant far beyond a specific context. When the principles and some of the methodologies are released from the embalming crust of tradition and applied to contemporary circumstances, they generate different ways of achieving a purpose and meaning which are enduring.

To read the Qur'an afresh on this journey I have gone beyond merely reading different translations. The Qur'an is an Arabic text and I speak no Arabic. My languages of cognition, the languages in which I think, are Urdu and English. To approach the Qur'an in a way that makes sense to my reason, and therefore allows me to reason with the meaning of its words, translations are essential. Any translation, however, is but one person's approximation of the original. One translation is never enough. I have over the years read numerous translations. On this journey I have consulted a number of translations simultaneously: Arberry, Pickthall, Yusuf Ali, Asad, Haleem and Khalidi. Reading them against or in concert with each other inevitably raises questions. How are the same words rendered differently by different translators? Exploring the significance of these differences leads to reflections on the choices they made. The result is to confront an array of implications, possible and potential meaning. What had been conventional, traditional, familiar in this way becomes directly pertinent to one's own understanding, a matter not of faith and repetition but of deliberation and cautious reasoning. To discuss my interpretation of the verses, it seemed reasonable to present the reader with the sense I derived from reading these translations together. The text that appears before each section is my own conclusion from the translations I consulted. Arriving at this compound translation required serious rereading of the various translations, as well as detailed consulting of footnotes and thoughts of various commentaries, and also considering the derivations of particular words in the Arabic text. The compound I have arrived at would have been impossible without tradition, but is not in and of itself anywhere else in the tradition of Qur'anic translation.

I have applied this approach to the first two chapters of the Qur'an, *al-Fatiha* and *Al-Baqara*. The opening short *sura*, *al-Fatiha*, is known to Muslims as *Umm al Kitab*: 'Mother of the Book'. It is recited in each section of the five daily prayers, because it is a summation of God's message to mankind, a summary of the essence of the whole, the source from which all that follows flows. *Al-Baqara* is the longest of the chapters in the Holy Book, and as I read it closely it became evident that its wide range of subjects in fact serves as a precis of the Qur'an as a whole. It deals with topics which cover the entire gamut, from spiritual truths about the nature of God to mundane consideration of the duties and obligations of living a good life as part of a community. From paradise to drinking and gambling, from rules of marriage and inheritance to reflections on the history of religion, the themes in *Al-Baqara* recur and are taken up again throughout the Qur'an. To examine the two opening chapters therefore is the most direct way to establish a foundation for understanding the style and import of the Qur'an as a whole.

The classical tradition of interpreting the meaning of the Qur'an is to proceed verse by verse. Here I deviate from tradition. Commentaries that provide verse-by-verse analysis atomise the Sacred Text. They encourage the tendency to take individual verses out of the context of the Holy Book as an integrated whole. The search for connection and interrelationship between verses, the conditioning of one part by another, the search for a balanced understanding on the preponderance of evidence or the weight to be given one statement in the context of the whole, which is the essential character of an integrated text, recede into the background. On this journey I discovered something else: in struggling with several translations to produce what I hope is a clear and lucid sense of the text as I understand it in English, the verses quite clearly fell into delineated passages dealing with discrete topics. These are the units in which I present both my compounded translation and my discussion of the meaning I take from each passage.

Thinking about the meaning of these passages, questioning the interrelationship within and between their verses, led me to a deeper understanding of the logic behind the structure of the text. It challenged me and eventually led to a fresh encounter with the implications of the words of the Qur'an. This does not mean that I did not consider individual verses, even individual words, in detail; nor does it mean that I could ignore the assistance of the enormous repertoire of scholarship contained in classical and modern commentaries. I was engaged in a wrestle with words and meanings throughout, and sometimes had recourse to and relied upon the fruits of traditional scholarship. The result, however, was something I had not expected. I was frequently surprised by how forcefully themes of considerable contemporary relevance emerged directly from familiar pieces of text in ways I had not previously encountered or considered. What I have made of my engagement with the Qur'an is a personal reading, but one whose excitement and energy I hope the reader will share.

7

AL-FATIHA

ATTRIBUTES OF GOD

In the name of Allah, Most Gracious, Most Merciful.
1. Praise be to God, the Sustainer of the worlds;
2. Merciful to all, Compassionate to each;
3. Lord of the Day of Judgement.
4. You do we worship, and to You we call for aid.

To be a Muslim is to accept that the Qur'an is the direct word of God as revealed to the Prophet Muhammad. We are reminded of this at the beginning of all but one of the chapters of the Holy Book: each word read and recited is 'In the name of God', for we are saying God's own words. But who or what is God? Or rather, of what nature is the God who addresses humanity through the means of revelation to the man Muhammad? How are we to understand and respond to the purpose and intention of revelation? In providing us with answers to these questions, *al-Fatiha* establishes the basic meaning of religion.

Revelation is God's self-declaration to humanity. And the God who speaks to us in the Qur'an is awesome: the 'Sustainer of the worlds'. The word used here is *Rabb*, a complex term with multiple connotations. It contains the idea of having a proper claim to possession and consequently authority over something, while the essence of the relationship of the *Rabb* to what it possesses is nurturing, fostering and sustaining a thing from inception to its final completion. The 'Sustainer of the worlds' is therefore the source and possessor of all creation, a constant active presence nurturing all that exists. As the origin and sustainer of all creation, indeed all praise and thanks should be for God alone.

Clearly God who possesses such incredible creative power and authority is beyond the comprehension of humanity: 'no vision can grasp Him', as the Qur'an says elsewhere (6:103). And this realisation leads me to a number of points. First, classical commentators were agreed that in this opening chapter of the Qur'an the *Bismillah*, 'In the Name of God...', is actually part of *al-Fatiha* and should be regarded as its first verse. The familiar phraseology of the *Bismillah* recurs in what then is the third verse. So I have taken the opportunity to render this most familiar of phrases in a number of variants. To begin with I retain the word *Allah*. *Allah* is the Islamic term for God; literally the meaning of the Arabic is *The* God. The God who is addressing humanity is Infinite and Unique, He is the God of all creation, not merely a God for Muslims. I say He/*Allah*, but this is misleading, for the Divine whom 'no vision can grasp' is beyond gender and all our categories of anthropomorphic comparison, not to be likened to human form. Similarly, it is the limitations of our language that cause God to be referred to as He. It could as easily and appropriately be translated as She. In the Qur'an, God speaks sometimes in the first person singular ('I'), sometimes in the first person plural ('We') and sometimes in the third person singular ('He' or as it could be 'She'). If we concede to the traditional reflexes of normal speech and use 'He', it requires particular emphasis that it is our limitations which are being made evident.

God is the *Rabb*, the source, sustainer, true owner, the 'Lord of the worlds'. Some scholars translate *alamin*, the word for 'worlds', as Universe. I prefer the common translation 'worlds' because it emphasises the plurality of creation. God's creation comes in different forms: not just the conventional Muslim division of humans, angels and *jinn*, but also different races, cultures, religions and worldviews. Beyond the diversity of humanity there is the natural world, again in all its diversity of form, environments and eco-systems; and then there are worlds beyond our own terrestrial setting: the solar systems and galaxies of space, and of all these too, God is the Creator and Sustainer. This emphasis on plurality, especially in the sense that human diversity is an intentional and purposeful part of God's creation, is central to the message of the Qur'an (49:13).

How can humans possibly comprehend a being of such awesome capacities? Only God can reveal to us His nature. By tradition, scholars have assembled a list of 99 facets of His nature, known as the attributes of God, which are mentioned throughout the Qur'an. These 99 names of God are a popular subject for decorative calligraphy; their complex, interwoven designs are a common illustration in books and may be found as decorative pieces in Muslim homes.

It is usual to refer to these attributes God with capital letters: Infinite, Unique, Ever Present, Omniscient, the First and the Last. Of the 99 attributes, two are the most frequently mentioned and are repeated twice in *al-Fatiha*, the summation of the most essential things to learn and remember about religion. They are: *Rahman* and *Rahim*. Here I have given these terms in translation as 'Most Gracious, Most Merciful' and then as 'Merciful to all, Compassionate to each.' These translations, slightly different from the most common wording—the Beneficent, the Merciful—emphasise two cardinal points. First, God is incomparable in His Graciousness, Mercy, Compassion, Forgiveness and Beneficence: all of which senses are contained in the *Rahman*. And secondly, God dispenses His Mercy to all, every individual whosoever they may be, whatever their identity or faith or no faith. God is Compassionate to each according to their individual desserts, for each person is individually known to God. I prefer the translation 'Merciful to all, Compassionate to each' because it is a constant reminder of the vastness and yet particularity of the relationship of God to all creation. Also this translation echoes the sense of universality and plurality contained in the term *Rabb*, 'Sustainer of the worlds'.

Rahman and *Rahim* derive from the same root word, which is appropriate since we are to remember that God is One, yet multifaceted beyond our imagination. Muslim scholars have given great attention to the significance of these two words. *Rahman* has the meaning of a womb, as well as kinship, relationship, loving kindness, mercy and nourishing tenderness. What could be a more feminine attribute than a womb? It is the most ubiquitous reminder of the folly of thinking of God in simplistic gender terms. And the connotations coming from that derivation are indicative of the relationship of God to His creation. Essentially, the scholars see this term as defining what is inherent in God, the attribute of overflowing love and mercy from which all creation comes. Translating *Rahman* as 'Merciful to all' is the best way to indicate that all creation shares equally in this mercy, without regard to anything we do or ask, no matter who we are: believers or not, Muslims or followers of other faiths, or of no faith. God makes no distinctions, and is ever ready to forgive.

Rahim is seen as introducing an active connotation: it is the beneficence that has to be earned through good deeds. When we respond to God's guidance on how to live, endeavour to build a better world by putting into practice as much as we can understand and replicate of God's goodness and guidance, then we are rewarded and strengthened in our activities by God's beneficence. The good and bad may benefit equally from the fact that God is *Rahman*; but the fact that He is also *Rahim* means that His future beneficence is a function of His justice. God is 'Compassionate to each' according to our actions. Unjust deeds, such as tyranny or undue exploitation of natural resources, have consequences both in future time on earth and in the Hereafter.

Human existence is not merely in this world. God brings His creation to completion not in the here and now but the Hereafter. He is the 'Lord of the Day of Judgement'. Different people behave differently, their cultures and traditions vary. Yet all will have to account for their conduct on the Day of Judgement, when God will not be concealed, and it will become all too evident that God is the Absolute Master of all things. The moral challenge, the purpose of religion, then is common to all, the same in each case: to do good as much as one is able, no matter what one's culture or tradition. There will be a Day when all different worlds and each member of those worlds will return to their source, the Forgiving and Just Lord, to receive their individual share of reward and punishment.

Religion begins by appreciating the awe and wonder of the Infinite. Establishing our relationship to God inspires gratitude, humility and admiration. But how can we, finite created beings, express these sentiments? How can one appropriately praise the Infinite? Answer: in the words of the Infinite Himself. The whole of *al-Fatiha* is a prayer in which God teaches humanity how to praise Him.

Human existence begins and ends with God. Understanding the nature of God is the basis for getting our relationship with God right. Indeed, it is inherent in the Muslim worldview that only by knowing and acknowledging God in all aspects of our life can we truly know and fulfil ourselves as human beings. Praising God is the consequence of recognising His essential attributes and living accordingly. In seeking God's aid, we have to rely on mercy and compassion, so surely it is incumbent on each and every individual to reflect and demonstrate these qualities in all their actions, in all their relations with other people and the world in which we live. When we look around us at the state of the world, clearly, in too many cases, repeating the words of prayer is no substitute for listening to them and thinking about their meaning.

8

AL-FATIHA

'THE STRAIGHT PATH'

5. *Guide us to the straight way,*
6. *The path of those on whom Your grace abounds,*
7. *Not those on whom Your anger falls, nor those who go astray.*

Al-Fatiha begins with God's self declaration of His most significant attributes. It begins by focusing our attention on the wonder of God. Naturally if we appreciate God our response is to praise and worship Him. And from whom else should we seek aid and guidance? In particular, we pray to be guided towards the 'straight path', a way that will lead to success in this world and salvation in the Hereafter. Basically, we are asking God to illuminate both, the truth itself and the way to the truth.

But truth, as we all know, is not always easy to delineate. Islam itself is sometimes described as the 'Straight Path'. Like truth, Islam can be complex and open to a number of diverse interpretations. The 'straight path' can thus be defined in a number of different ways.

There is a sense in which any road we follow can be called a straight path, simply because, no matter how many twists and turns it takes, however many intersections it has, eventually it will get us to our destination. If we just keep going, somehow, by whatever route, we will inevitably arrive.

It is quite easy for this common understanding to become, in religious terms, the equivalent of just keeping on doing what people have always done. Follow in the footsteps of tradition, do what custom authorises, that's what the straight path has always been, so why argue or question? But I am less and less convinced that this can be the appropriate way to understand the meaning of the straight path.

So what exactly is this path, and where are we hoping to arrive? What we need is advice on how to arrive at our final destination, the Hereafter where all our deeds will be examined and judged. Therefore, the guidance has to be qualitative information, advice on how to travel rather than on where. We can have no doubt where we are going: we will all die.

Qur'anic terminology is full of metaphors and allusions to travel and movement. *Shari'a*, the term used for Islamic law, derives from a word signifying 'the way to a watering hole'. In the desert, water holes must be found among shifting sands, changing and often hazardous weather conditions; and to survive, one has to keep on finding and returning to the water hole.

So, for me, the movement towards this direction is perpetual and eternal: rather than a destination, the 'straight path' is a navigational tool by which to assess how one ought to travel. It serves as a lighthouse that guides vessels at sea, illuminates hazardous areas and highlights safe passages. What is 'straight' in the 'straight path' is the manner of travel, and not the road you see in front of you.

Our journey through life on our terrestrial abode, planet Earth, is a conceptual journey. The 'guidance' we need consists of how we should travel, for that is exactly what the Qur'an offers: the mindful travellers 'walk on earth in humbleness, pass their nights preparing themselves to make a rightful submission and take a rightful stand, spend their wealth on others, and are neither extravagant not stingy' [25:63–8]. They are 'proactively steadfast, truthful in word and action, ever submitting to the Commandments, keeping their wealth open for the society, and seeking protection early against any forthcoming challenge from the bottom of their hearts' [3:15–17]. En route, they 'turn away from evil and indecency' [12:24]; and establish prayer, fast during the month of Ramadan, pay *zakat* (what is due to the poor), and go, at least once in their life, on a pilgrimage to Mecca.

These moral references, a set of principles, help reorient our lives, and keep to or get back on the right track. It is a way of avoiding the path of those who have 'gone astray'. Surely the implication here is that, despite guidance from God, there is no infallible guarantee of doing right or keeping to the straight path. In itself this is not enough. Paths have inclination; and the 'straight path' is, as *sura* 90 tells us, a 'steep path'. It is a path of 'toil and trial', full of hazards and challenges: our constant struggles with the moral, material, social, cultural and political complexities of an ever and rapidly changing society. In which case the problem is not knowing there is a straight path, but working out how to locate it among all the multiple choices presented to us. The path, as a conceptual tool, is a way of making choices between good, better or best, bad, worse or worst ways of living on our journey through all the complexities of the time and circumstances in which we live.

Al-Fatiha ends with a reminder that we are neither the first nor the last people to have wrestled with how to live a good life. The Qur'an situates itself in history, among the successive generations of God's creation, all of which faced the same dilemmas. The Qur'an is not the first instance of revelation from God. All peoples that existed before the coming of the Qur'an received a 'warner': there were Prophets before Muhammad, each of whom brought the same core message of how to live a good life in worship of God. History records ample evidence of human frailty and failure. If we use the conceptual map, we can distinguish among and between the works of human history, and discern the bright spots from the looming mass of instances where peoples have spectacularly gone astray.

Whether we look to the past or think about our future, what we need are qualitative assessments that help us make more informed, better choices in the place we now are and according to the conditions prevailing. The best possible choice is to make regular returns to the watering hole, to use our intelligence to find a way back to the straight path.

The Egyptian scholar Shaykh Muhammad al-Ghazali (not to be confused with the great classical philosopher and theologian a-Ghazali, 1058–1111) considered the 'straight path' to be in fact 'a straight line', the shortest distance between two points. 'Whoever leads a straight and righteous life', he declares in his commentary on the Qur'an, 'will be on the right path to God, for that is the one and only sure way and direct way that leads to Him' [1]. This 'straight and righteous life' depends basically on following a list of dos and don'ts. I think this approach is simplistic and one-dimensional. It treats the world as flat. On a three-dimensional, spherical planet, a straight line is in fact a curve!

Sayyid Abul Ala Mawdudi sees the 'straight path' as 'a way which is absolutely true' [2], which begs the question: how would mere mortals get to this absolute truth? For the classical commentator Al-Qurtabi, the 'straight path' is a path 'which has no crookedness or deviation in it' [3]. Those who belong to the Shia branch of Islam have argued that 'the straight path' refers to Ali, the cousin of Prophet Muhammad and the fourth Caliph of Islam [4]. Through his personality and example, the true and straight path of Islam can be discovered. This is why the Shia venerate him.

Sufis, or Muslim mystics, have their own interpretation of the straight path. For Ibn Arabi (1165–1240), the Andalusian Sufi who is described by his followers as the 'Great Master' (*al-Shaykh al-Akbar*), the straight path is in fact the way towards the knowledge of spiritual and divine mysteries. In his mystical commentary on the Qur'an, ibn Arabi says that 'guide us to the straight path' means 'set us firmly upon right guidance and confirm us with rectitude in the way of unity, which is the way of him upon whom You bestowed the special favour of mercifulness, which is gnosis and love and the guidance of the divine essence' [5]. For the Sufis, the worlds we inhabit are nothing but shadows. The straight path takes us away from these 'perishing shadows' and leads directly to a union with God.

The straight path is thus not as straight and simple as it seems.

I would argue that the straight path is not self-evident to anyone in the complexities of contemporary life. Moreover, it is not a fixed path: it is not a priori given. It changes with changing circumstances; and reveals itself differently in different circumstances. It has to be constantly discovered and rediscovered. And, most definitely, following the straight path does not mean having a single answer which is invariably applicable.

Furthermore, there is and can be no guarantee that everyone will find the 'straight path'—not even the most pious believers. The true determination of how we have fared will be made in the Hereafter by the Lord of the Day of Judgement. All frail and fallible human beings can do is the best they are able, their best as a work of intelligence and diligence. Believers who pray for guidance are duty-bound to employ all of their God-given faculties to work as individuals and communities to reorient themselves in changing circumstances towards the desired path. That path is navigated with the aid of the Qur'an— which is where our efforts to gain guidance actually begin.

9

AL-BAQARA

THE QUR'AN AND DOUBT

1. *A.L.M.*
2. *This is the Book, wherein is no doubt, a guidance to the God conscious*
3. *Who believe in that which is beyond the reach of human perception, are steadfast in prayer, and spend of what We have provided them;*
4. *And who believe in the Revelation sent to you, and sent before your time, and know for certain there is an afterlife.*
5. *These are truly guided by their Lord, these are the ones who prosper.*
6. *As to those who reject Faith, it is the same to them whether you warn them or do not warn them; they will not believe.*
7. *God has set a seal on their hearts and on their hearing, and on their eyes is a veil; and there awaits them a mighty chastisement.*

Sura Al-Baqara, the longest chapter of the Qur'an, begins with a ringing self-declaration: 'This is the Book', and presents us with a summary of the purpose of the revelation that is the Qur'an. The origin of the Qur'an, that it is the direct word of God, is the foundation of faith and the most basic belief. The counterpoint of faith and belief is the freedom to believe or not believe. However, choice is not without responsibility: how and what we freely choose to believe has consequences, both in this life and the life to come. And right at the outset this first passage intimates two other vital issues: one is the distinction between doubt and the rejection of faith and belief; the second is the consistency and continuity of divine revelation as guidance for all humanity. The consequence of belief is accepting the guidance provided by revelation, which must be translated into practical action.

71

This is the Book, the Sacred Text, or Divine Writ—God's words; of this there should be no doubt. And its purpose is equally clear: it is 'a guidance' to those who are 'God conscious'. The word used, *muttaqi*, is often translated as God fearing. However, I prefer the translation 'God conscious'. This translation takes us to the derivation and root sense of *taqwa*: God consciousness, a central concept of Islam. What exactly does this mean? To the non-believer this is the hardest thing to explain, while for believers it is the most obvious and basic premise of faith. *Taqwa* is consciousness, an awareness of the certainty, reality and presence of God that is experienced intellectually, spiritually, emotionally. It is the realisation that, as the Qur'an says: God is nearer to us than our jugular vein, He knows and is constantly aware of all our actions, thoughts and motivations. The purpose of guidance is to teach humanity how to live out, or live up to, the implications of this consciousness in each and every moment of our lives. *Taqwa* may be the basis of faith, the certainty on which belief is founded, but the real challenge is to incorporate it into all our thoughts and actions. Consciousness is the faculty by which we think and reason, and inherent in the process is doubt.

Taqwa is the moment of insight, the lived experience of knowing something beyond ourselves. Making sense of that consciousness, understanding the nature of God and operating proper relationships based on this awareness, is the message of the Qur'an. Awareness, God consciousness, shapes how we perceive the world around us, the connections we understand and the practical means for applying this understanding to the questions of our daily life.

The opening verses of *Al-Baqara* then give a concise statement of the five consequences of *taqwa* that are the central themes running throughout the entire Qur'an. The five themes are: that God is the self-sufficient fount of all being; that the fact of God's existence as told by prophet after prophet is accessible to human intellect; that righteous living—and not merely believing—is the necessary complement of this intellectual perception; that bodily death will be followed by resurrection and judgement; that all who are truly conscious of their responsibility to God need have no fear.

What intrigues me is how, right at the outset, the straightforward declaration that this is God's Word recognises the human capacity to doubt. The Qur'an takes doubt seriously, and throughout the Book it recurs and appears in various guises. It is presented as a continuum which stretches from being an essential aid to belief all the way to a blinkered determination not to believe under any circumstances. Doubt is a function of our free will: we are free to accept or reject belief in God. Repeatedly, the Qur'an engages with various kinds of doubt, offering, as we shall find, arguments and strategies against which or by which to test our doubts; and thereby a rational process to arrive at conviction in the uniqueness of the Qur'an, the truth of its origin and the guidance it contains.

The Qur'an does not require its readers to stop or refrain from doubting. It repeatedly asks them to explore their doubts. It is far too simplistic to think that doubt refers only to the existence of God or the origin of the Qur'an. As we read we also have to explore, analyse and interrogate, as examples given later in this *sura* show, the meaning and implications as well as the applications of the guidance contained in God's word. There is thus absolutely no reason to feel intimidated. Doubt and certainty are not diametrically opposed conditions. Unless we reason with and through our doubts, we can have no confidence in our certainty. Certainty that is never questioned, that ignores or is not tested by doubt, can become prejudice, complacency, the blind following of tradition that undermines the meaning and spirit of the very guidance that should be applied to our daily circumstances in the conditions of the times in which we live.

It is *taqwa*, the reasoning consciousness, that leads to belief in 'the unseen', that which is beyond our physical and material perceptions. 'The unseen' is the conventional translation of *al ghayb*. Asad argues that this is erroneous, and I agree with his argument and follow him in using 'that which is beyond the reach of human perception'. Whichever translation one uses, the Qur'an's repeated use of this term is a reminder that there will always be matters that require an inductive jump, the proverbial 'leap of faith'. Those who are aware of God realise that human intellect has serious limitations. The Qur'an is lyrical about the potential of the human intellect. It is essential to the way we come to know God. Faith is not the antithesis of reason; true consciousness of God must be the work of both. And only when our intellect and reason are fully engaged will one appreciate how to live righteously. But intellect cannot provide answers to all our questions: such questions as 'what is the meaning of life?', 'what is the purpose of the universe?', 'what happens after death?', and in any case 'why do we have to die?' We can offer no definitive answers to matters that have no experiential, experimental, objective, observable tests. Here we rely on belief, as commitment and consequence of accepting the existence of God, who can create, do, knows and understands all. We can receive only intimations, through metaphor and simile, of what is Unseen and beyond human perception, as in the Qur'anic vision of paradise we shall soon encounter.

But belief in what is beyond the reach of human perception in itself is not good enough. Belief is not simply about consolation, self-fulfilment or personal salvation. To be meaningful it must be transformative: it must be lived, put into action as social, economic and political change to achieve justice, equity, dignity and improved well-being for all of humanity. This is a key message of the Qur'an.

The Qur'an makes consistent association between belief and 'establishing prayer', which is then linked to giving generously from what God has provided for us as individuals and communities. This is how Muslims should practise their consciousness of God. I see prayer as more than simply ritual worship. If the human intellect is a way of appreciating, becoming conscious of and understanding God, then it is also another way of worshipping Him. The Qur'an wants us to praise God by studying His signs: reflecting on nature, experimenting with the material world, promoting thought and learning. So, I see what God has provided in both concrete and abstract terms: wealth and property as well as knowledge and intellectual resources. Believers give generously of both varieties.

The Qur'an proclaims itself to be a distinctive revelation of God's word. However, those who accept the revelation given to Muhammad are not the first to receive God's message. History begins with God's revelation to the first prophet, Adam, and since then a succession of prophets have brought God's message to humankind. The Qur'an has a great deal to say about how people of faith should relate to one another. But it seems to me that Muslims have been and are as bad as anyone else in turning the commonality and continuity declared by the Qur'an into an exclusive and excluding identity. Once one accepts that all faiths and moral systems begin with or have common threads, then the basis exists for collaboration in putting faith in action. There is a shared rationale for finding the means to work together to make the world a better place, a place of peace and peaceful cohabitation based on transformative change. In a globalised world of increasing interconnection, there is no separately sustainable way of seeking, let alone establishing, justice, equity, dignity and well-being for all. The message from God is not and should not be a brand name, certainly not a 'holier than thou' arrogance that divides Muslim from Muslim, and all Muslims from members of other faiths. The history of continuity of God's message is part of the unity of God's creation.

All people, not merely the God conscious, will be resurrected and face God's judgement in the Hereafter. As the Qur'an tells us elsewhere, in the Hereafter differences and distinctions, the 'us' and 'them' divisions, the human constructs of interpretation we call our religions will be clarified. Theological disputes and the arcane doctrines manufactured by human interpretation, especially those that delve into things beyond human perception, will be exposed for what they are: human imaginings. God's judgement will concern not only what we believed but what we did, how we lived. All who lived well, who conducted their lives to the best of their ability consistent with consciousness of God and adherence to His guidance, will be rewarded. Again, various translations tease out the significance of God's rewards, whatever shape and form it takes. I prefer the phrase 'the ones who prosper' because we may prosper in a whole variety of diverse ways in all aspects of human existence. To flourish is to prosper; to be secure in respect and dignity, to be without want with access to equitable resources is to prosper; to have liberty and freedom to follow one's own conscience is to prosper.

The interplay between the phrases 'spend of what We have provided them' and 'the ones who prosper' indicates another point. A major characteristic of the Islamic worldview is that it is distributive. To spend is to distribute, to give of that which one possesses. The Qur'an is full of exhortation and regulation on the subject of distribution: what we have is for use and not mere accumulation or self-enjoyment. Other people have a claim on our resources, economic, intellectual and creative, social, cultural or emotional. People are not absolute, exclusive owners, as we shall see in more detail later when we consider the concept of *khalifah*, trusteeship. It is by distributing, putting to work, sharing the bounties that come our way that we 'prosper'. Ultimately the prosperity we earn by being distributive with our talents and possessions is God's pleasure and favour, the supreme reward.

What of those who do not believe? I think it is important to appreciate that this verse does not refer to those who simply doubt—for doubt may be resolved one day, in favour of or against belief. Most of *Al-Baqara* was revealed in Medina, soon after Prophet Muhammad's migration from Mecca. So, in the first instance, the unbelievers being addressed here are the enemies of the fledgling Muslim community who were bent not just on denying the message of the Qur'an but on persecution and eradication of those who had become Muslims. They are referred to in the past tense: as those who had conscious intent and deliberately resolved to deny the truth.

What about our own context? The world is full of doubters and atheists of all varieties—and quite a few have chosen to be my friends! For the Qur'an, and therefore for me, atheism itself is not a problem. We are free to choose: to believe or not to believe. But God consciousness is a commitment to a way of living that is or certainly should be dedicated to care for justice, equity, the dignity and well-being of all. Such concern can be found as much among people of no faith as among those who claim to believe. Indeed, some atheists may be better examples of righteousness in action than many a believer I can think of! In the here and now, practical concern for the state of the world and the condition of our fellow human beings provides a basis for collaboration. In the final analysis, it is God alone who knows all and will make the only judgement that matters. Or, to put it another way, who am I to judge? If non-believers share my concerns for making the world a better place, then let's get to it! There are more than enough horrors in the world, and far too many of them created because people stopped to argue and create animosities about matters on which God has left us free to choose, or matters which are in truth beyond human perception and therefore definitive human reason. For me it's not just a case of 'live and let live', although I certainly believe and uphold the principle; I'm for doing what is right by all people, irrespective of what they believe or don't believe, and working with anyone and everyone who shares my objectives for a better world.

But the movement away from God is also a journey. And in their journey, atheists can acquire, my friends included, certain problematic characteristics. They can, as the Qur'an tells us elsewhere, become arrogant (35:42–3, 39:59, 45:31) and insist that their path is the only true path and all else is irrational nonsense. They can become self-satisfied and engage in self-exaltation (27:14, 38:2), praising their own position sky high while denigrating, ridiculing or humiliating believers. They can, through political expediency or opportunism (35:42–3), try to privilege their own position in society. These and other similar characteristics gradually lead them to lose the ability to understand the very idea of religious truth. The 'sealing' of their hearts, as an act of God, is a product of the baggage they have picked up on their particular journey.

Of course, believers are not immune from these diseases.

Finally, we come to the first verse of this chapter which consists of three Arabic letters: A.L.M. (*Alif Lam Meem*) *Al-Baqara* is one of the 29 chapters of the Qur'an that begin just with alphabetical letters. The intention here, I think, is to arrest the attention of the reader. This is a poetic device. Apart from that, I find no convincing argument that anyone, and certainly not I, really know what the letters signify. There is no evidence of the Prophet himself referring to these letters. Muslims have interpreted them in various ways: some see them as abbreviations relating to God and his attributes, others argue that they illustrate the inimitable nature of the Qur'an, some others interpret them mystically, still others have read mathematical codes in them. I will simply echo the words of the classical thinkers and say: I know not. Only God knows.

10

AL-BAQARA

'THE HYPOCRITES'

8. *Of the people there are some who say: 'We believe in God and the Last Day'; but they are not true believers.*

9. *They would deceive God and those who believe, but they deceive none but themselves.*

10. *Sickness abides in their hearts and God increases their malady. A painful punishment awaits them because they are false (to themselves).*

11. *When it is said to them: 'Do not spread corruption in the land', they say: 'We are the only ones that put things right.'*

12. *Truly, it is they who are spreading corruption but they perceive it not.*

13. *And when it is said to them: 'Believe as the people believe', they answer: 'Should we believe as the weak and the ignorant believe?' Truly, it is they who are weak-minded, but they know it not.*

14. *When they meet those who believe, they say: 'We believe'; but when they are alone with their evil ones, they say: 'We are really with you: We (were) only jesting.'*

15. *God will requite them for their mockery, leaving them to wander blindly in their excess.*

16. *These are they that have bought error at the price of guidance: and their commerce has not profited them, and they are not right-guided.*

17. *The likeness of them is the likeness of one who kindles a fire; when it illuminated all around them, God took away their light and left them in utter darkness. So they could not see.*

18. *Deaf, dumb, and blind, they cannot turn back.*

19. *Or else like a rainstorm from the sky wherein is darkness, thunder and lightning: they press their fingers in their ears to keep out the thunder-clap, for fear of death. But God engulfs the rejecters of Faith!*

20. *The lightning all but snatches away their sight; whenever it lights their way they move forward; but when it grows dark they stand still. Had God willed, He would have taken away their hearing and sight; for God has power over all things.*

The concept of doubt and the freedom to accept or reject belief was introduced in the preceding passage. Now *Al-Baqara* turns to another condition of particular concern throughout the Qur'an: hypocrisy. It covers a range of actions of human behaviour that have familiar consequences with an incredibly contemporary ring. This passage defines the condition as a self-delusion whose judgement and resolution are a matter for God.

These verses have an historic context. In the first instance, they refer to those people of Medina during Prophet Muhammad's time who, while publicly professing adherence to Islam, privately reserved judgement about the Prophet and his message. They are addressed directly in these and other verses of the Qur'an. So, in the first instance God's displeasure is directed against them. However, I think these verses have great relevance today, not least in the way some believers use these and similar verses to justify their behaviour.

Hypocrisy, we are told, is both an attempt to deceive the community and to deceive God. It is, however, self-delusion, a 'sickness' that 'abides in their hearts' because hypocrites ultimately 'deceive none but themselves' because 'they are false to themselves'. The judgement of such people belongs to God.

The all too evident attraction of making religion a licence to denounce others is neither its purpose nor the right way to proceed. From declaring people as unbelievers, whether Muslim or non-Muslim, is a short step to finding others insufficiently rigorous in their belief and observance. It is all too evident in history and today that human beings spend far more time being judgemental about one another than attending to the transformative task that is the purpose of God's guidance. When it comes to fair weather, friends and fellow travellers, 'God will requite them for their mockery'. It is not a business for self-appointed human judges to take upon themselves.

What intrigues me most are the examples of hypocrisy enumerated. They are a very pertinent list of pitfalls. The hypocrites claim to be the only ones 'that put things right'. We are all too familiar with those who insist they alone know the right way, people who argue, quibble and nitpick about the fine distinctions of piety. For some, these fine details seem more important than fulfilling the transformative purpose of religion, the spending and using of our resources to make a better world. The matter mentioned here is 'spreading corruption in the land'. This is the central concern in the Qur'an, the contradiction of its purpose to guide humanity to the eradication of injustice, unfairness, all that leads to poverty, exclusion, suffering and division between people; all, in short, that contributes to tyranny and oppression in the widest sense. Those who claim they alone know 'what is to be done'—as Lenin said, in a different context—often have narrow, self-serving and self-protecting definitions which leave the basic structural inequities in place and fall far short of genuine transformative change.

From those who would like the environment protected but nevertheless are NIMBYs—not in my backyard—when it comes to taking action, or wealthy nations that talk a great line about free trade and aid to the neediest, yet continue to benefit from the operation of an unjust and inequitable global economic system, there is pause for thought here. There are many ways to be holier than thou about the substance of practical religion.

In the historic context, it is the nature of their belief which is highlighted. They do not believe like the 'others believe'—the bulk of the Muslim community. But the point is that they do have some sort of belief. They have, like all other Muslims, dipped their little finger in the Infinite Ocean of God's Mercy. For most Muslims, engagement with God leads, or should lead, to *taqwa*, which makes them cautious, watchful, humble and acutely aware of their social responsibility to the rest of humanity—the term incorporates all these meanings. However, 'hypocrites', who do not start out as hypocrites, travel in a different direction. They think that their appreciation of the Divine gives them a special dispensation: they not only understand God's Truth but actually embody it. It is in this sense they are trying to deceive God, though they themselves 'do not realise it'.

Then we come to people who, not to put too fine a point on it, relish elitism: those who disparage what 'the weak and ignorant believe', who regard the majority of believers as 'fools'. All this leads to the will to dominate: they seek nothing less than to impose their monolithic notions of truth on all others, leading to violence, strife and corruption. They are convinced that their actions are not only right but also that it is right to impose their own path on others, whatever the cost. When the consequences of their actions are pointed out to them, they simply declare: 'We are only putting things right.'

The purpose of God's guidance, again and again, is to strengthen the connections between people within and across all their divisions and differences. The 'weak' and 'ignorant' may be poor and uneducated, but they are as capable of *taqwa* and as valuable in God's sight as the highest and mightiest. What is called simple faith, firm conviction and commitment to doing right are the result of God consciousness, and this is open to all. If people are weak and ignorant in social terms, the problem is human injustice, the legacy of corruption which it is the purpose of religion to transform.

I think the bracketing of 'weak' and 'ignorant' is significant here. It is a reminder that it is not only intellectuals who have access to insights on faith, who are capable of understanding the meaning of God's guidance or demonstrating God consciousness. Intellectual elitism is to be guarded against as much as economic, social and political or indeed religious elitism. If there are differences in how people articulate their understanding, then the remedy surely ought to be working harder to achieve mutual comprehension, to work towards consensus and not to declare oneself above the lesser orders and their quaint lack of sophistication. The goodness people do is what matters. And doing good is not the exclusive preserve of any group, even intellectuals and the socially advantaged.

The third condition of hypocrisy is what would usually be seen as the most obvious example: saying one thing while meaning another. Hypocrites are people who publicly declare their faith while, in private or in certain company, they say: 'We were only jesting.' The phrase 'evil ones', literally in Arabic *shaya-tin*, satans, is taken by classical commentators to mean people 'who through their insolent persistence in evildoing have become like satans' [7]. So we can here imagine a whole variety of human behaviour and company in which it might be smart or self-serving to admit that one's public show of faith was 'only a jest', only what had to be done for form's sake, not to frighten the family or neighbours or social convention, but not to be taken seriously. Asad argues that the 'evil ones' can as easily be one's own personal demons: in private, looking down on the religious, or what one feels is done only for the sake of convention.

Whether by being holier than thou or elitist or conforming merely for the sake of convention, hypocrisy makes a mockery not of religion but of personal integrity. God will requite this mockery by 'leaving them to wander blindly in their excess'. So in whatever way hypocrisy is expressed, it is an excess, a self-indulgence as much as a self-delusion.

The Qur'an uses a number of metaphors to describe their situation. They seek the light, but when all is illuminated they become blind. They seek signs of an approaching storm, but when thunder strikes they put their fingers in their ears. The theme and metaphors are repeated in *sura* 63, 'The Hypocrites'. There we learn that simply declaring one's belief in God is meaningless. Believers should be judged by what they do here and now.

Now, I wouldn't dream of pointing a finger at anyone. But modern-day equivalents of the hypocrites are all around us. Just look at their actions.

The distant 'scenario' of the Hereafter is a function of what one does in this world. The emphasis is as much on the action of believers in this life as it is on the judgement on the Last Day. The point the Qur'an is making is that ends never justify bad means, and it is a great illusion for any person or group to think they posses all truth. The goal of a blissful existence in the Hereafter must be pursued with good actions, expressed in terms of what is truly human and humane in the world in which we live.

11

AL-BAQARA
PARADISE

21. *O humankind! Worship your Lord, who created you and those who came before you, so that you might remain conscious of Him,*

22. *Who has made the earth your couch, and the heavens your canopy; and sent down rain from the heavens, thereby producing fruits for your sustenance; then set not up any rivals to God when you know better.*

23. *And if you are in doubt as to what We have revealed from time to time to Our servant [Muhammad], then produce a single sura like it; and call your witnesses, apart from God, if what you say is true.*

24. *And if you cannot—and most certainly you cannot do it—then fear the Fire whose fuel is men and stones, which awaits all who deny the truth.*

25. *But give glad tidings to those who believe and do deeds of righteousness, that their portion is Gardens, graced with flowing streams. Whenever they are offered its fruits as sustenance they say: 'Why, this is what we were fed with before,' all alike in excellence is their provision. And there shall they have spouses pure; and there shall they abide forever.*

26. *God disdains not to use the similitude even of a gnat or else anything less than that. Those who believe know that it is truth from their Lord; but those who reject Faith say: 'What could God mean by this parable?' In this way God causes many to stray, just as God guides many to the right path; but none does He cause to go astray, except those who forsake (the path),*

27. *Those who break God's covenant after God had established it, who sunder what God has commanded to be joined, and spread corruption on earth: these shall be the losers.*

28. *How can you refuse to acknowledge God, seeing that you were lifeless and He gave you life, and that He will cause you to die and then will bring you again to life, then to Him you shall return?*

29. *It is He who hath created for you all that is on earth; and has applied His design to the heavens and fashioned them into seven heavens; and He alone has full knowledge of everything.*

In these verses for the first time we encounter the idea of paradise. With all that is alleged and claimed for Muslim visions of paradise in our day and age, we need to consider this passage carefully.

I have always loved the image of *janna* (literally 'the garden') in this passage, 'graced with flowing streams' and containing all the mouth-watering fruits one can imagine. It always puts me in mind of glorious summer days, enjoying a refreshing picnic in the most perfect garden with the best possible company; something better even than the holidays I always long for. And I have no doubt this image inspired the art of garden building. Wonderful examples of gardens grace traditional Muslim cities around the world. Interior courtyards of traditional houses have miniature gardens replete with the pleasing sound of fountains of running water. The idea of paradise inspired the detailed consideration of how this vision could be captured in this world as a reminder of the world to come. Religion, after all, is or should be the endeavour to make this earth as much of a paradise as possible.

This same vision of paradise is repeated elsewhere in the Qur'an with variations of phrasing. The rivers are such 'as time does not corrupt' (47:15): its fruits and shade will be everlasting (13:35). It will be a place of perpetual bliss, enjoying the fruits of our good deeds in the forgiveness of our Sustainer.

The vision of Paradise comes after the clear message that God has created a world capable of being a terrestrial paradise. It is a 'couch' under the canopy of the heavens, watered by rain that produces the 'fruits for your sustenance'. This earthly garden of God's creation should be cherished, nurtured and looked after in gratitude. And for all that we make of the bounty of the earth we should give thanks to its Maker, God Alone. I see this as a reminder that however learned, skilful and inventive humanity becomes in harnessing the resources of the earth, we are only employing the faculties and potential, the endowments given by our Creator. We use and manufacture but do not in the ultimate sense 'create'; we have responsibility to think carefully and prudentially whether we make a garden or a wasteland of the earth created for our benefit.

The Qur'an comes with 'glad tidings' to assure us of God's plan for this world and the Paradise to come. How can we be sure? We return again to the question of doubt. Here it is answered with a creative intellectual challenge.

Those who doubt the source of the words revealed to Muhammad are invited to 'produce a single *sura* like it'. The distinctive, sublime use of the Arabic language in the Qur'an, unlike any other Arabic text, makes it inimitable and is testimony to its authorship, to its being a work that in structure and scope is beyond human capability. The text itself, when examined, questioned by a doubting mind, leads to the conclusion that its origin is not human but a revelation of the divine. God is the ultimate guarantor of the uniqueness of His Word; what other witnesses could be found? In the final analysis, being conscious of God through faith and the use of our reason is the only witness on which we can rely.

The 'glad tidings', a phrase repeatedly used in the Qur'an to describe revelation, is to assure 'those who believe and do deeds of righteousness' that the completion of their existence in the Hereafter will be something far beyond any bounty and delight experienced on earth. It will be an unending perfection of everything we take to be necessary and delightful for true bliss. And in this state of perfection we will 'abide forever'.

But before I get carried away with thoughts of rest from my labours, there are a host of earthly complications to deal with. Are Muslims paradise obsessed? Is our particular promise of paradise really an incitement to mayhem and murder?

Hardly! Paradise has to be earned. It is not for those who spread corruption on the earth. And I have to admit I find it curious that, on the one hand, people find Muslims too focused on religion in this life, fanatical about wanting Islamic states and Islamic law; and then, on the other hand, consider us too paradise obsessed, determined to get away from this world too quickly and destructively, thereby bequeathing the task of state-building to those unscathed and left behind.

Muslims are no more paradise obsessed then members of any other religion. Have those making such claims never heard a Sunday sermon in a Christian church of any denomination? Certainly, they have not consulted any of the proliferating websites devoted to The Rapture, the doctrine of transport to paradise especially favoured by American evangelical Christian groups. And what about all those images of winged people sitting on clouds?

The Hereafter, for people of faith, is part of our true existence. This life is not all we are or will be. However, the completion of our existence, whether in paradise or hell, is beyond the reach of human perception. The Qur'an gives us a 'parable' using allegory and metaphor to intimate, by analogy to the things we know. We achieve a proper realisation of how to live by keeping the two parts of our existence, here and hereafter, in balance.

And what of the companions we will have in the supreme triumph (4:13) of attaining paradise? They will be our spouses pure. In this passage (2: 25) the term used is *azwaj*, plural of *zawj*, meaning spouse. In Arabic this word signifies either of the two components of a couple, that is the male as well as the female.

In four places in the Qur'an the word used for the companion is *Hur*, from which comes the much used term *houris*. The word has many connotations, variously interpreted as signifying pure and soulful. The most important point, however, is that once again the word can signify either a male or a female. And in the Qur'an no number is ever mentioned. So what of all the '72 virgins' that supposedly incite the activities of the paradise obsessed? What the Qur'an actually says is that all who enter Paradise will have life renewed (56:34). In the everlasting bliss of the eternal we will all, male and female, be restored to our pure state, i.e. virginal innocence. The only antidote to the misogyny marshalled by Muslims in their history is reading and understanding the equal opportunity words of the Book.

There is one crucial popular misconception to be borne in mind: Paradise is not self-selecting. It is not we, the individual believers, who determine or even can ever know which of us gets to Paradise. The decision is not ours. It belongs to God alone who knows everything, just as this passage concludes. Human presumption has a great deal to answer for, but the greatest must be the willingness to hand out or assume one has a 'straight to Paradise' ticket. To me it is the most irreligious affront of all, nothing more than usurping God for our own purposes.

Equally offensive is the abomination of thinking that by destroying what God has made sacred—human life—one automatically has a passport to Paradise. No sophistry or contortions of perverted human reasoning can make such a concept 'Islamic'. It stands in stark and unequivocal contradiction to everything the Qur'an has to teach. It is nothing but an indication of the debased level of religious knowledge and understanding that anyone who professes to be a Muslim could entertain or indulge such scurrilous notions. For all who know, the Qur'an is quite explicit that anyone seduced by the unsubtle logic of violence that leads to murder or suffering of innocent people faces a very different prospect from Paradise. The analogy of Paradise in this passage is balanced by the image of 'the Fire whose fuel is men and stones'. Those who break God's covenant after God has established it, who sunder what God has commanded to be joined, and spread corruption on earth: 'These shall be the losers.' And they will get just desserts quite different from the self-delusions they peddle to recruit those who fail to read and reason with the clear meaning of the Sacred Text.

The vision of Paradise is a similitude, a parable. This passage contains a clear warning that what is presented is an approximation, a way of suggesting something that is beyond human perception. It is not literal; it is an indication of the spirit of the thing, not a description of the thing itself, the truth of which we can never discover in this world. Yet, all religions have spent inordinate energy either insisting that the metaphor and allegorical are actual, or extensively defining and detailing what no human intellect can ever determine. I am ever ready to let the poetic vision of the Qur'an stimulate my imagination. However, the gladdest tidings I can imagine are the thought that my ideas are but a poor intimation of what awaits if I earn a place in Paradise.

The previous passage used the interplay between those who 'spend' and those who 'prosper'. Here there is the counterpoint that identifies those who are the losers. Who will be a loser: those 'who sunder what God has commanded to be joined, and spread corruption on earth'. We are about to consider a number of passages concerned with the diversity of human society and the coexistence of different faiths. The Qur'an is at pains to emphasise the commonality and continuity that underlie human social, cultural and religious differences. Yet man-made division, and our dedication to excluding and exclusive identities is a prime mover in spreading the corruption of violence, hatred and mutual distrust on earth. So if we have to spend and distribute to prosper, do we not also have to join together and promote co-existence to save ourselves from joining 'the losers'? And if to 'prosper' is to be understood as flourishing in the widest sense, then losing too has the widest connotations. What is lost is the humanity, the integrity, the very soul of those who violate God's covenant. They have deceived, deluded and lost themselves and their true purpose. In the final analysis there is no better riposte to the corruption that men of violence have made of the Qur'an's vision of Paradise.

12

AL-BAQARA

FALL AND EVIL

30. *And when your Lord said to the angels: 'I will create a vicegerent on earth', they said: 'Will You place therein one who will spread corruption and shed blood, whilst we hymn Your praise and glorify Your holy (name)?' God answered: 'I know that which you know not.'*

31. *And He taught Adam the names of all things; then showed them to the angels, and said: 'Tell me the names of these things if you are truthful.'*

32. *They said: 'Glory be to Thee! We have no knowledge except what You taught us. In truth, You are All Knowing, All Wise.'*

33. *He said: 'O Adam! Reveal to them their names.' When Adam revealed their names, God said: 'Did I not tell you that I know the secrets of heaven and earth, and I know what you make public and what you conceal?'*

34. *And behold, We said to the angels: 'Prostrate yourselves before Adam' and they all bowed down, save Iblis, who refused and gloried in his arrogance: and thus he became one of those who deny the truth.*

35. *We said: 'O Adam! Dwell you and your wife in the Garden; and eat of the bountiful things therein as you will; but do not approach this one tree, lest you become wrongdoers.'*

36. *Then Satan caused them to slip and thus brought about the loss of their erstwhile state. And so We said: 'Down with you, [and be henceforth] enemies unto one another; and on earth you shall have your abode and your livelihood for a while.'*

37. *Then Adam received words [of guidance] from his Lord and He relented towards him; for He is Oft-Returning, Most Merciful.*

38. *We said: 'Get down all from here; and when My guidance comes to you, whosoever follows My guidance need have no fear, neither shall they grieve.*

39. *'But those who are bent on denying the truth and giving the lie to Our messages, they are destined for the fire, and therein shall they abide.'*

It is appropriate, in light of the contemporary significance some Muslims ascribe to the parable of Paradise, that we move immediately to the subject of the fall from grace. The Qur'an's juxtaposition of the two subjects speaks directly to connections that have to be made here and now. Juxtaposition is a technique employed throughout the Qur'an: the connections we have to consider are not only between verses within a passage, but also how one passage is connected and helps one reflect more deeply on the meaning of another. Here we learn not only of the creation of humanity, of the faculties endowed on us in our creation; we are also reminded of the ease with which we can deny and debase our humanity. The parable of Adam and his wife is a conceptual account of our origin. Their fate, the fall from grace, is an ever present possibility for those who stray from the straight path of God's guidance and will not repent and reform.

The first thing to make clear is that this is not the Biblical story of Adam and Eve. So beware of similarities and differences from which flow big implications. The parable of Adam gives us a clear definition of the origin and purpose of human creation. However, Adam is identified not merely as the first man— but also the first prophet. His companion is simply referred to as his wife; she is not called Eve. Further, there is most definitely no suggestion that she is a subordinate creation; she is not fashioned after the fact and from Adam. Both are conceptual representatives of humanity, both are going to be the successors or inheritors of God on earth.

First God informs the angels He intends to add a new order to creation. So what are angels? They too are part of creation, they praise God and act in total obedience. We know the angel *Gibreel* (Gabriel) was the intermediary who brought God's Word to Muhammad. Beyond that I have no knowledge of angelic hosts and am quite content; although others may know better. If I can accept the need for quarks and the gluons of quantum theory and a string theory universe of umpteen dimensions, I can happily live with the concept of angels. This is not to say I am indifferent or uninterested. It is the case that even while wrestling for as intelligent a reading and understanding of the Qur'an as possible, I am ready to admit there remain things I do not comprehend. Such realisation is salutary. When I reach the limit of what I think I can comprehend, the only sensible option is to say so and leave the truth of what I do not know to God, not endlessly speculate on what is beyond my perception.

Understanding the purpose of this new order that God announces to the angels is a subject much more necessary to understand, and thankfully something I think I do comprehend. This new order takes a distinctive place within God's creation. God introduces humanity as *khalifa*. This is a central concept of Islam. The word is often translated, as I do here, as 'vice-regent', but it also has the sense and can be translated as 'trustee'. *Khalifa* includes the notion of succession, of one who succeeds another, or inherits. What we inherit is our place in God's created order. This whole passage deals with the limits and ongoing relationship with God that comes with being the *khalifa* or trustee of God.

Our inheritance is not outright ownership but a conditional trust: we have to discharge our trust responsibly with accountability to God. We will each have to answer for how we used this inheritance. We must answer for our own actions; we must answer for how we operated our relationships with our fellow human beings; we must answer for how we cared for and utilised the resources of the world in which we live. And, as the term implies, we live as part of succeeding generations of human beings and thus have responsibilities towards future generations. We are responsible for handing on the trust of this world in as good a state as possible for the use and benefit of those who come after us. The concept of *khalifa* relates directly to the distributive idea of the interplay between 'spend' and 'prosper' discussed previously. It is indicative of the way that passages of the Qur'an overlay, interact with and reinforce our understanding of the meaning and significance of words.

To be human is to have abilities: this is symbolised in God teaching Adam the 'names of all things'. The word for names (*ism*) is understood to mean the ability to define and distinguish between things, the essence of reasoning and conceptual thought. We are created with the capacity to be knowledgeable beings with the ability to learn. Learning and knowledge are by their very nature cumulative, so I take it as axiomatic that we have the potential as well as the responsibility to progress in understanding. To know the names is the basis of language. As the Qur'an makes clear (30:22, 49:13), the diversity of human languages, cultures and races and nations is part of the intention of creation. Therefore, whatever the language or cultures of our birth, the challenge is to employ these endowments, to use our abilities to make the best of our life on earth.

The angels are not entirely convinced; and who can blame them? Human beings will 'spread corruption' and 'shed blood' on earth, say the angels—well, they got that right. So the obvious point of God requiring the angels to bow to humanity, in the symbolic personages of Adam and his wife, is to emphasise that we have the capacity, the potential to do better. We can rise above angels in our good deeds.

The test presented to Adam and his wife is the practical demonstration of both human weakness and the better way. The couple are granted all they need to sustain a bountiful existence but they are given one limit, one 'do not', to observe. We learn more of the nature of this test when the Qur'an retells this incident (7:10–25; 20:115–27). Iblis, otherwise known as Satan, convinces them that the limit is unnecessary and against their interest. And by listening and being led by the arrogant and defiant angel, Adam and his wife lose the innocence in which they were created.

Both Adam and his spouse disobey God, but they did not commit an irredeemable sin. They made a slip. No special blame is placed on Adam's wife for leading him astray. No one feels ashamed of their nakedness. Both repent and both are forgiven. There are no bloodcurdling Old Testament curses from God about the pain of childbirth or the 'painful toil' of humanity. This is definitely not the drama of Christianity's 'Original Sin'.

Instead, the emphasis is placed on the nature of Iblis. His stock in trade is arrogance—the prime conceptual evil in Islam. It is arrogance, the Qur'an says, that can lead to the downfall of humanity. That is why we need to be humble; humility before God and His creation is the main virtue in Islam. And just as our relationship with God and God's guidance is ongoing, so is our relationship with Iblis, the temptation to be arrogant. Iblis is always with us in the form of hubris, the inclination to play God, and our myopia in not recognising that there are limits to our actions as well as our understanding. Arrogance is inimical to prudential reasoning, to accepting that for all we know and learn we also accumulate ignorance of the questions we do not ask, the risks we do not and cannot comprehend. In short, arrogance is what causes us to ignore our fallibilities.

After being led astray, falling from grace, humanity is forgiven. The conceptual parable of human creation is a precursor to our existence on this earth. The story of Adam and his wife is the prelude to terrestrial time and history. In this world Adam is the first prophet, the first to be given words of guidance from God. Human history begins with a message of God's guidance and the assurance that there will be a succession of prophets bringing God's Word to all people. For all who succeed Adam and his wife in the life of this world, there will be the selfsame challenge and reward.

Conceptually Adam and his wife serve to explain the origin and purpose of all humanity. All humans emerge from God's forgiveness. All are born pure.

The parable is not 'once upon a time' but a description in and for all time of the human condition.

The allegory of the fall from grace is actually a message of hope. Human beings will always be faced with the task of living responsibly, and will also have to beware of and confront the temptation of arrogant disregard. But those who live creatively and constructively according to God's guidance 'need have no fear and neither shall they grieve'. This phrase is repeated many times in the Qur'an, I find it immensely encouraging, a beautiful and consoling thought but one that, nevertheless, has to be earned.

While it is quite clear that this is not the Biblical story of Adam and Eve, its fate in Muslim scholarship has undermined the subtle conceptual distinctions the Qur'an presents. Muslim scholars through history have had recourse to the Biblical version to find a name for Mrs Adam: she has been dubbed Hawwa. And in their commentaries they have introduced a great deal of misogyny, by way of reasoning from the Biblical story and inveigling their own cultural conventions and predilections into their interpretations of the Qur'an. This legacy has been handed on to the fables, folk tales and prognostications of Muslim thought; a perfect example of why we need to be aware of the preconceptions we bring, as well as those that have been brought, to reading the Qur'an.

13

AL-BAQARA

'CHILDREN OF ISRAEL'

40. *O Children of Israel! Remember the blessings which I bestowed upon you, and fulfil your covenant with Me as I fulfil My Covenant with you, and fear none but Me.*

41. *Believe in that which I reveal, confirming what you possess, and be not the first to reject Faith therein, nor sell My Signs for a small price; and fear Me, and Me alone.*

42. *And do not confound Truth with falsehood, and do not knowingly suppress the Truth.*

43. *And be steadfast in prayer; and spend in charity; and bow down in prayer with all who thus bow down.*

44. *Do you bid others to piety and forget (to practise it) yourselves, while you recite the Scripture? Will you not then use your reason?*

45. *Seek help in patience and prayer: it is indeed hard, except to the humble in spirit,*

46. *Who know that they will have to meet their Lord, and that to Him they shall return.*

47. *Children of Israel! Remember My bounty which I bestowed upon you, and that I preferred you above all humankind.*

48. *Then guard yourselves against a day when one soul shall not avail another nor shall intercession be accepted, nor shall compensation be taken, and no helpers are at hand.*

49. *Remember when We delivered you from the people of Pharaoh: who afflicted you with cruel suffering, slaughtering your sons and debauching your women; and that was a grievous trial from your Lord.*

50. *Remember when We cleft the sea before you and thus saved you and drowned Pharaoh's people within your very sight.*

51. *Remember when We appointed for Moses forty nights of solitude, and in his absence you took to worshipping the calf, and did grievous wrong.*

52. *Then, even after that, We pardoned you in order that you might give thanks.*

53. *Remember We gave Moses the Scripture and thus a standard to discern right from wrong that you might be guided aright.*

54. *And remember Moses said to his people: 'O my people! You have sinned against yourselves by worshipping the calf: So turn (in repentance) to your Maker, and kill the guilty among yourselves; that will be best for you in the sight of your Maker.' And thereupon He accepted your repentance. For He alone is Oft-Returning, Most Merciful.*

55. *And remember you said: 'O Moses! We shall never believe in you until we see God openly', whereupon the thunderbolt struck before your very eyes.*

56. *But We raised you up again after you had been as dead that you might give thanks.*

57. *And We gave you the shade of clouds and sent down manna and quails, saying: 'Eat of the good things We have provided for you: they did Us no wrong; it was themselves they wronged.'*

58. *And remember We said: 'Enter this town, and eat of the plenty therein as you wish; but enter the gate with humility, and say: "Repentence" and We shall forgive you your sins and amply reward those who do good.'*

59. *But the sinners altered the words which had been given them; so We sent down a plague from heaven as a punishment for their iniquity.*

60. *And remember when Moses prayed for water for his people; We said: 'Strike the rock with thy staff' and twelve springs gushed forth. Every group knew its own place for water. So eat and drink of that which God has provided, and do not act corruptly, making mischief on the earth.*

61. *And remember when you said: 'O Moses! we cannot endure one kind of food (always); so pray to your Lord for us that He may bring out what plants there are on earth—green herbs, cucumbers, garlic, lentils, and onions.' He said: 'Would you exchange what is of lesser worth for what is better? Go back in shame to Egypt and then you can have what you are asking for!' And it was thus that humility and wretchedness overshadowed them and they were laden with the burden of God's anger: all this because they disbelieved God's revelations and slew the prophets wrongfully out of disobedience and persisted in transgressing the bounds of what is right.*

62. *Surely, they that believe (in this revelation), and those who are Jews and Christians and Sabaeans—all who believe in God and the Last Day, and do righteous deeds shall have their reward with their Lord; and no fear shall be on them, neither shall they grieve.*

63. *Remember when We made the covenant with you and raised Mount Sinai above you: 'Hold fast to what We have revealed to you! Remember what it contains that you might remain conscious of God.'*

64. *Then, even after that you turned away, and had it not been for the Grace of God upon you and His mercy you would surely have been lost.*

65. *And you know full well about those amongst you who transgressed the Sabbath: and We said to them: 'Be as apes, most wretched!'*

66. *So We made it an example to their own time and to their posterity, and a lesson to all who are conscious of God.*

67. *Remember when Moses said to his people: 'God commands you to sacrifice a cow.' They said: 'Are you mocking us?' He said: 'I seek refuge with God against being so ignorant!'*

68. *They said: 'Pray to your Lord for us that He make clear to us what she is to be like.' He said: 'God says: it is a cow neither too old nor too young, but of middling age. Now do what ye are commanded!'*

69. *They said: 'Pray on our behalf to your Lord that He make clear to us what her colour should be.' Moses said: 'He says it is a yellow cow, bright of hue, a joy to behold.'*

70. *They said: 'Pray on our behalf to your Lord that He point her out to us, for cows are all alike to us and we, God willing, shall be guided.'*

71. *Moses answered: He says: 'A cow neither yoked to plough the earth nor to water the fields; sound and without blemish.' They said: 'At last you have brought out the truth.' And so they offered her in sacrifice, although they had almost left it undone.*

72. *And remember when you killed a soul and disputed among yourselves about the crime: But God always reveals what you hide.*

73. *So We said: 'Strike the dead man with a piece of the cow.' This is how God resurrects the dead and reveals His wonders to you; perhaps you will understand.*

74. *Then, even after that your hearts were hardened: becoming like a rock or even harder. For among rocks there are some from which rivers gush forth; and some have cracks from which water flows; and there are some which fall down for awe of God. And God is not unmindful of what you do.*

75. *Can you really expect them to believe in the message sent to you, when a group among them would hear the word of God and then pervert it, knowingly, after having grasped its meaning?*

76. *For when they meet those who have attained to faith they say: 'We believe': But when they meet one another in private, they say: 'Do you speak to them of what God has revealed to you, so that they dispute with you before your Lord?' Have you no understanding (of their aim)?*

77. *Know they not that God knows what they conceal and what they proclaim?*

78. *And there are among them unlettered folk who have no real knowledge of Scripture, but follow only wishful fancies and mere conjectures.*

79. *Woe, then, to those who write Scripture with their own hands, and then claim 'This is from God', that they may sell it for a trifling gain! Woe to them for what their hands have written! Woe to them for the profit they made!*

80. *And they say: 'The Fire shall touch us for a few days only': Say to them: 'Have you received a promise from God—for God never breaks His promise—or do you attribute to God something you cannot know?'*

81. *Nay, those who seek gain in evil, and are encompassed by their sins, these are inhabitants of the Fire: There shall they dwell forever.*

82. *But those who have faith and do good deeds, they are inhabitants of the Garden: There shall they dwell forever.*

83. *And remember We made a covenant with the Children of Israel: 'You shall worship none but God; be kind to your parents and kindred, orphans and those in need; speak kindly to people; be steadfast in prayer; and pay the poor due. Then you turned away, except a few among you, and recanted.*

84. *And remember We accepted your covenant that: 'You shall not shed one another's blood, nor shall you drive one another out of your homes.' And this you solemnly ratified, and to this you can bear witness.*

85. *But there you are, killing one another, and driving one party among you from their homes; joining forces against them, in sin and hatred; and if they come to you as captives, you ransom them, though it was not lawful for you to banish them. Do you then believe in one portion of the Book and disbelieve another? And what is the— reward for those who do so, save ignominy in this life, and on the Day of Resurrection away to the most grievous doom. God is not unmindful of what you do.*

86. *All who buy the life of this world at the price of the life to come—their punishment shall not be lightened nor shall they be helped.*

87. *We revealed the Book to Moses and We sent after him messengers in a succession of apostles; We granted Jesus the son of Mary clear signs and strengthened him with the holy spirit. Whenever a messenger came to you with something that was not to your liking, did you not grow arrogant, calling some liars and killing others?*

88. *And they say, 'Our hearts are shrouded.' Nay, God has cursed them for their unbelief. Little is their faith.*

89. *And when there comes to them a Book from God, confirming the truth already in their possession—and [bear in mind] they had previously called for God's help against those without Faith—when there came to them that which they knew [to be the truth] they would deny it. God's curse is on those without Faith.*

90. *Miserable is the price for which they sold their souls, that they should disbelieve in what God has revealed, in envy that God would make His Grace descend on whomever He wills of his creatures! And their lot was anger piled upon anger. And a humbling punishment awaits those who reject Faith.*

91. *When it is said to them, 'Believe in what God has sent down', they say, 'We believe [only] in what was sent down to us': and they deny the truth of everything else, although it be a truth confirming what they themselves possess. Say to them: 'Why then did you kill previous prophets of God, if you are true believers?'*

92. *Moses came to you with clear signs; yet while he was away you worshipped the calf and acted wickedly.*

93. *And remember We covenanted with you and raised above you the towering Mount (Sinai): (Saying): 'Hold fast to what We have revealed to you, and listen': They*

said: 'We hear, and we disobey': And they were made to drink into their hearts love of the calf because of their faithlessness. Say: 'Vile is that which your belief commands if indeed you are believers!'

94. Say: 'If an afterlife with God is to be for you alone, to the exclusion of all other people, then you should long for death—if what you say is true!'

95. But never will they long for it, because [they are aware] of what their hands have sent ahead in this world: and God has full knowledge of evildoers;

96. And you shall find them the eagerest of men for life. And of the idolators there is one of them wishes if he might be spared a thousand years: but the grant of such life will not save him from punishment. For God sees full well all that they do.

97. Say: 'Who is an enemy to Gabriel!' For he it is who has revealed this Scripture to your heart, by God's leave, confirming that which was revealed before it, a guidance and glad tidings to the believers;

98. Whoever is an enemy of God and His angels and His messengers, of Gabriel and Michael, surely God is the enemy of all who deny the truth.

99. We have sent down to you manifest signs (ayat); only the dissolute can disbelieve them.

100. Is it ever so that when they make a covenant, a party of them cast it aside? The truth is most of them believe not.

101. And when a messenger from God came to them, confirming what they already possessed, a group among them to whom Scripture had been sent turned their backs on the Book of God, as if they did not know!

102. Instead they followed what the evils ones used to practise during the reign of Solomon. But it was not Solomon who disbelieved; rather it was the evil ones who taught humankind sorcery and such things as were revealed at Babylon to the angels Harut and Marut. But these two taught no one without first telling them: 'We are but a temptation to evil: so do not disbelieve.' Yet they learned from these two how to create discord between man and wife. But whereas they can do no harm to anyone with their sorcery, except by God's leave, they learn what harms them, and does them no good. They know full well that he who deals in sorcery has no share in the good of the life to come. And surely evil is the price for which they sold their souls, if they but knew!

103. Had they believed and been conscious of God, the reward from their Lord would have been best, if they but knew!

104. O you who have attained to faith! Do not say [to the Prophet], 'Listen to us', but rather say, 'Have patience with us', and be attentive listeners, since grievous suffering awaits those who deny the truth.

105. It is never the wish of those without Faith among the People of the Book, or among the polytheists, that any bounty should come down to you from your Lord. But God singles out for His Mercy whom He will, for God's grace is limitless.

106. *None of Our revelations do We abrogate or cause to be forgotten, but We substitute something better or similar: Do you not know that God has power over all things?*

107. *Do you not know that to God belongs the dominion of the heavens and the earth? And besides Him you have neither patron nor helper.*

108. *Or do you wish to question your Messenger as Moses was questioned of old? But whoever chooses to deny the truth rather than believing in it has strayed from the right path.*

109. *Among the People of the Book there are many who from selfish envy wish they could turn you back to unbelief after you have attained to faith—even after the truth has become clear to them. But forgive and pardon them, until God shall make manifest His will; for God has power over all things.*

110. *And be steadfast in prayer and pay the purifying dues (zakat): for whatever good deed you do, laid by for your souls in this life, you shall surely find with God, for God sees all that you do.*

111. *And they say: 'None shall enter Paradise unless he be a Jew or a Christian.' These are their own wishes. Say to them: 'Show me your proof if you are truthful.'*

112. *Yes, indeed: everyone who surrenders his whole self to God and is a doer of good shall receive his reward from his Lord; and all such need have no fear, and neither shall they grieve.*

113. *The Jews say: 'The Christians have no valid ground for their beliefs'; and the Christians say: 'The Jews have no valid ground for their beliefs.' Yet both recite the Book. The ignorant repeat their statements. But God will judge between them on the Day of Resurrection regarding that upon which they differ.*

114. *And who is more impious than he who forbids that in places for worship of God, God's name should be celebrated and devotes himself to their destruction? These shall not enter them except in fear. For them there is nothing but disgrace in this world, and in the world to come, a terrible punishment.*

115. *To God belong the East and the West: Wherever you turn, there is the face of God. For God is all-Encompassing, all-Knowing.*

116. *They say: 'God has fathered a son': Glory be to Him. To Him rather belongs all that is in the heavens and on earth: everything obeys His Will.*

117. *Marvellous Creator of the heavens and the earth! When He decrees a matter, He merely says to it: 'Be', and it is.*

118. *The ignorant say: 'If only God would speak to us! If only a sign would descend upon us!' This too was said by past generations, word for word. Their hearts are alike. Indeed, We have made all the signs manifest unto people who are endowed with inner certainty.*

119. *Verily, We have sent you with the truth as a bearer of glad tidings and a warner; and you are not accountable for the denizens of hell.*

120. *Never will the Jews or the Christians be satisfied with you unless you follow their creeds. Say: 'God's guidance is the only true guidance.' If you follow their whims*

after the knowledge which has come to you, then you would have in God neither patron nor champion.

121. *Those to whom We revealed the Book [and who] study it as it should be studied: They are the ones who believe in it. But those who repudiate it, they are truly lost.*

122. *O Children of Israel! Remember my bounty which I bestowed upon you, and that I preferred you above all others.*

123. *Then guard yourselves against a Day when no soul can atone one whit for another, when no ransom is accepted for it, when no intercession can profit it and no helpers are at hand.*

124. *And remember when his Lord tested Abraham with certain commands, which he fulfilled: God said: 'I will appoint you a leader of men.' Abraham said: 'And of my offspring as well?' God answered: 'Evildoers shall not enjoy My covenant.'*

125. *Remember when We set up the House as a place of assembly for humankind, a sanctuary: 'Take the station of Abraham as a place of worship.' And We commanded Abraham and Isma'il to sanctify My House for those who walk around it, or use it as a retreat, or bow, or prostrate themselves (in prayer).*

126. *And remember Abraham said: 'My Lord, make this land secure, and grant its people fruitful sustenance, such of them as believe in God and the Last Day.' God answered: 'And whoever disbelieves, for a while will I grant them their pleasure, then shall consign him to the torment of Fire—a wretched journey's end.'*

127. *Remember when Abraham and Isma'il were raising up the foundations of the House [they prayed]: 'Our Lord, accept this from us: for You alone are All-Hearing, All-knowing.*

128. *'Our Lord, make us surrender ourselves to You, and of our descendants a community which surrenders itself to You; and show us our ways of worship; and forgive us; for You are All-Forgiving, Most Merciful.*

129. *'Our Lord, send them a Messenger from amongst themselves, who shall recite to them Your verses and instruct them in Scripture and wisdom, and make them pure: for You are Almighty, the All-Wise.'*

130. *Who therefore abandons the religion of Abraham, except he be foolish-minded? We chose Abraham in this present world, and in the world to come he shall be among the righteous.*

131. *Remember when his Lord said to him: 'Surrender', He said: 'I have surrendered myself to the Sustainer of the Universe.'*

132. *And this was the legacy that Abraham entrusted to his children, as did Jacob; 'Oh my children, God has chosen the pure religion for you; see that you die, not save in surrender.'*

133. *Were you witness when death came to Jacob? When he said to his sons: 'Whom will you worship after I am gone?' They said: 'We shall worship your God and the God of your fathers, of Abraham, Isma'il and Isaac, the One God. To Him we surrender.'*

134. *Those are a people who have passed away. They have earned their reward, and yours is that which you earn. You will not be held responsible for what they did.*

135. *They say: 'Become Jews or Christians and you will be rightly guided.' Say: 'Nay, rather the creed of Abraham, a man of pure faith; he was no idolator.'*

136. *Say: 'We believe in God, and what was revealed to us, in what was revealed to Abraham, Isma'il, Isaac, Jacob and the Tribes, in what was revealed to Moses and Jesus, in what was revealed to the prophets by their Lord. We make no distinction between any of them: And to Him we surrender.'*

137. *If they then believe as you believe, they are rightly guided. If they turn away, it is they who are in discord. God will deal with them on your behalf; He is the All-Hearing, the All-Knowing.*

138. *The hue of God is upon us! And what better hue than God's? It is Him we worship.*

139. *Say: 'Do you argue with us about God, He is our Lord and your Lord. Our deeds belong to us and to you belong your deeds; Him we serve sincerely.*

140. *Or are you saying that Abraham, Isma'il, Isaac, Jacob and the Tribes were Jews or Christians? Say: 'Are you more knowledgeable than God? Who is more unjust than he who conceals a testimony he has received from God?' God is not unmindful of what you do.*

141. *Those are a people who have passed away. They have earned their reward, and yours is that which you earn. You will not be held responsible for what they did.*

This is a very long section, yet it seems to me that it needs to be viewed in its entirety to grasp its significance. The passage weaves backwards and forwards, interlacing its reference to the past and the present of the time of Revelation. I regard this passage as essential to understanding the Qur'anic conception of religion, and vital for coming to terms with the plurality of religion in history and the present day. Furthermore, this passage is one of the best demonstrations of how the Qur'an simultaneously addresses multiple frames of reference. There is the past time of previous prophets, the present of the time of Muhammad and the diversity of the peoples who formed the community of Medina, while it also infers and relates to all subsequent history, from Muhammad's time and our own, as well as addressing today and our future. Each of these frames of reference is necessary to appreciate the implications of these verses. If Muslims are to play their part in making multifaith, multicultural societies a lived reality, as this passage and others throughout the Qur'an insist they must, then here is where we begin to wrestle with the very human obstacles that must be overcome.

Here for the first time the Qur'an makes extended references to revelation and religious communities which precede the revelation to Muhammad, 'those that went before' who have already been mentioned. It refers to the reaction and treatment meted out to previous prophets as a context for understanding the problems in Medina at the time of the Prophet. It gives examples of how communities in history have deviated, distorted and disregarded the message brought by prophets. These examples expand on some of the themes alluded to in 'the Hypocrites', and clearly relate to the challenge faced by Muhammad and the fledgling Muslim community. The historic contexts, both preceding and including the time of Muhammad, are relevant to all subsequent time. The examples identified relate to the human interpretation of religion, what people made of God's Word in the course of history. They provide principles by which to interrogate how Muslims since the time of the Prophet fared in translating the Word of God, the Qur'an, into an organised religion, Islam, and the basis for communities and nations where Islam is the predominant religion.

The principles also speak directly to the questions of how to live in a world of diversity and difference and how to operate a multifaith society. The Qur'an insists on the ethics of mutual acceptance. This acceptance is rooted in the recurring themes of continuity and commonality. Each revelation is from God and therefore further confirms the Oft Forgiving, Oft Returning nature of God. The essence of the messages over time is always the same: a guidance on how to live a just, equitable and peaceful life; how to make the world a better place for everyone. Human perversity as well as ignorance can turn what is open and available to all into intricate, complicated means to divide people. Instead of God consciousness and guidance being the moral principles which bring people together, it becomes the embodiment of the most irreducible differences, the cause of irreconcilable dispute. This passage is emphatic that the overarching duty of religion is the same for everyone, and therefore provides a means for people of faith and good conscience to work together.

First, and most obviously, in this passage, the Qur'an is addressing Prophet Muhammad and the small community of believers who followed him on his flight from Mecca to Medina. This *sura* is the first to be revealed after the *hijra*, literally the migration, when the Prophet and his small persecuted band of followers abandoned their homes and possessions and made their way to a new city, Yathrib, which was renamed Madinat ul-Nabi, the city of the Prophet. The migration in the year 622 CE marks the beginning of the Muslim calendar.

Reviled and oppressed by the Meccans, the Prophet and his followers were invited to take refuge by residents of Yathrib who had accepted the message preached by Muhammad. But Yathrib/Medina remained a mixed community. So the Qur'an also addresses itself to this population. Apart from those citizens who had embraced Islam, there are Jews and Christians, as well as polytheists, those who still worshipped the various deities of pre-Islamic Arabia. And we don't need to be reminded of the tensions that can be caused by a sudden influx of migrants, especially ones with different religion and customs! Added to which the new arrivals were a source of potential danger for the citizens of Medina. The Meccans continued to regard the new religion as a strategic threat to the prosperity of their city. This is the context, the circumstances and the people addressed.

But there is more. For this passage concerns itself with the history and development of both the Jewish and Christian religions. It refers to the past to help explain the present in the Medina of the Prophet, and to help guide the new community of faith, the Muslims, on how to deal with their contemporary difficulties and shape their future. What is being said in very particular circumstances has meaning and relevance for people everywhere at any time, including the present day. To get to the meaning one has to think through and with all these overlapping frames of reference. No one perspective is sufficient in itself.

The understanding I take from this is that acceptance of plurality is a basic requirement. Diversity is a fact of life, a theme dealt with in many places in the Qur'an. Acceptance is based on two things: the presumptive perpetuity of diversity; and that diversity is both an intentional part of God's plan as well as a test for all people of faith and good conscience.

There is a clear presumption that Jewish and Christian communities will continue to exist. The Qur'an is establishing the basis on which Muslims should understand and come to terms with the existence of these other religious communities and not fall into the all too human traps of responding as Jews and Christians in Medina did to the arrival of Muslims and the revelation of Islam.

The principal basis for acceptance is continuity. Prophet Muhammad, we are told, is not bringing a new message: the 'new Prophet' is retelling an old narrative. Three familiar names—Moses, Jesus, Abraham—are discussed, not just to indicate the continuation of the monotheistic tradition, but also to establish the fact that Prophet Muhammad is part of a long line of previous prophets. And the Qur'an is explicit in verse 136: Muslims are to believe the guidance given to Abraham, Ishmael, Isaac and Joseph and their descendants, to Moses and Jesus, 'and all that has been vouchsafed to all [other] prophets by their Sustainer: *we make no distinction between any of them.*'

Continuity, acceptance and respect for all prophets are the foundation of the Qur'an's most basic message. As verse 62 says: '*all* who believe in God and the Last Day and do righteous deeds shall have their reward with their Sustainer; and no fear need they have, and neither shall they grieve.' How do we know this is the essence of the message? Because this same passage recurs several times throughout the Qur'an.

There is commonality in the guidance and warning God has given to all peoples. The basis of religion is the same for everyone. But, as this passage makes clear, religion is not only the guidance from God, it is also how human societies have understood and interpreted the message. We are confronted with the vexed distinction between what religion could, should and ought to be and what communities say and do in the name of religion, a distinction no less real in the time of Muhammad than it is today.

In reprising incidents familiar from the Bible, the Qur'an assumes a basic familiarity. It is not concerned with retelling the narratives in detail. Its style is to refer to particular known narratives to highlight significant lessons and point to very real differences. There are considerable differences between what the Qur'an tells Muslims and what is believed by Christians and Jews. Jesus is definitively a Prophet who preached God's Word, but like all other prophets he is human. Judaism is not an exclusive possession only for an ethnic 'chosen people'. Clearly these differences were among the reasons the Jews and Christians of Medina derided Muhammad, questioned his mission as a Prophet and sought to make him deviate from his mission. How we should deal with such religious differences is made clear in verse 109: 'None the less, forgive and forbear, until God shall make manifest His will.' In plural societies where there are competing claims to what is the truth of religion, forgiveness and forbearance are the necessary operational ethics of mutual tolerance—the full understanding of what distinguishes one belief from another rests with God and not human religious communities.

A community may receive guidance from God, but there is no guarantee they will remain faithful to that guidance. The example given is the story of the golden calf, but the point is more extensive. Throughout history humans have erred. In spite of worshipping the golden calf, a cardinal sin in monotheism, they were forgiven. The Children of Israel are said to have altered God's word (v.75), to feign belief (v.76) and to have claimed immunity from hell (v. 80), yet they are forgiven. This is a reiteration of the forgiveness we saw earlier in the case of Adam and his wife. Thus, forgiveness is for all, right from the beginning with Adam and his spouse in Paradise, to 'those who follow the Jewish faith and the Christians', right through the line of the prophets to the people in Medina, moving on to everyone doing 'righteous deeds' in our own time.

105

Forgiveness belongs to God and is open to everyone. But this passage dwells on the fact that recipients of previous revelations have made what should be open and available to all into exclusive and exclusionary claims to theirs being the entire and only truth. The problem here is arrogance; the word used here, *isakbara*, is the same as that used earlier to describe the behaviour of Iblis. Both Jews and Christians claim exclusive notions of Truth. All that God really requires from all believers are acknowledgement and gratitude, not an insistence that theirs is the only route to salvation. God pardons as well as guides whom He wills. Such arrogance can only lead diverse societies into animosity, tension, mutual distrust and worse. And the only real testimony to humanity's gratitude is to be found in doing righteous deeds, which includes caring for our fellow citizens and all people, no matter who they are or what they believe. It is only our actions, not theological rectitude, which will earn us the reward of our Sustainer—the very point on which this passage concludes.

There is a second story of the cow in this passage. God asks for the sacrifice of a cow. But the community comes back again and again to Moses demanding more and more specifics of the kind of cow to be offered. It is a case of religious nitpicking run riot, a genuine human perversity. A duty it would have been easy to fulfil if common sense had prevailed at the outset becomes almost impossible by seeking ever more technical conditions. The moral I see here is: beware of the legalistic mindset in operating religion. Human beings delight in the niceties of fine distinctions, dancing angels on the heads of pins without noticing how easily they are losing the needle of living faith in the haystack of religious ritual and custom. I find plenty of evidence of this among Muslims today, with the endless desire for a *fatwa* on this, a *fatwa* on that. They place their confidence in a legalistic mindset that is often as out of touch with common sense as it is unfamiliar with the complexities of the contemporary world.

While two incidents of the cow provide the name of this entire *sura—Al-Baqara*, The Cow—there are plenty of other examples of human perversity in the face of revelation. Prophets have had to struggle with the doubts, derision and dissatisfactions of their people. There are people who will not believe until they see God with their own eyes. There are unlettered folk with no real knowledge of Scripture who follow 'only wishful fancies and mere conjectures'. There are those who write Scripture with their own hands and claim 'This is from God'. There are those who refuse to see the continuity and confirmation of their own faith in new revelation, even though it brings the same glad tidings and enjoins the same duties. There are those who insist heaven is only for people who follow their exclusive brand of religion. 'The Jews say: "The Christians have no valid ground for their beliefs"; and the Christians say: "The Jews have no valid ground for their beliefs." Yet both recite the Book. The ignorant repeat their statements.' The litany of failings includes those who deny access to places of worship and destroy them. After all the cautionary examples of the multiple ways humanity has found to distort, pervert and corrupt God's guidance, there is a clear conclusion: 'Those are people who have passed away. They have earned their reward and yours is that which you earn. You will not be held responsible for what they did.' Potentially we can always restart with a clean slate, rather than continue the animosities and failings that deformed history. We do not have to inherit the errors of our forefathers. This is where it is so essential to keep the Qur'an's simultaneous past, present and future, its overlapping multiple frames of reference in mind.

The problem, however, is how readily human frailty manages to recreate the failings of the past again and again, to dedicate itself to the preservation of tradition by doing what previous generations did.

I find this long and complicated passage immensely hopeful. It is a timeless summons to an open, tolerant approach not just to Islam but to living with diversity and difference in a multifaith society. It summons us all to the better angels of our nature. It reminds us of the essential religious truth: 'To God belong the East and the West: Wherever you turn, there is the face of God. For God is all-Encompassing, all-Knowing.' It is not we humans who own and possess religion for our own purposes. Religion is how God consciousness and God's guidance can aid us in finding a better way of living in a world that is multifaceted, a world of wonderful diversity. I think it should be read in conjunction with the Book of Micah chapter 6, verse 8 in the Bible, which reads: 'He hath showed thee, O man, what *is* good; and what doth the Lord require of thee, but to do justly; and to love mercy; and to walk in humility with thy God.' There is a way to transcend our differences for the sake of doing what is right in the eyes of God.

14

AL-BAQARA

A 'MIDDLE COMMUNITY'

142. *Foolish people will say: 'What turned them away from the direction of prayer they once followed?' Say: God is the east and west: He guides whomsoever He wills onto a straight path.*

143. *Thus, We have appointed you a community of the middle way, so that you might bear witness to humankind, and that the Messenger might be a witness to you; and We did not appoint the direction of prayer which you once followed, except to distinguish he who follows the Messenger from he who turns on his heels. Indeed it was a grave matter, except to those whom God has guided. But God would not allow your earlier faith to have been in vain. Towards mankind, God is All-Caring, Compassionate to each.*

144. *We see you turning your face for guidance to the heavens. So, now We will turn you in a direction of prayer that will please you. Turn your face in the direction of the Sacred Mosque: Wherever you may be, turn your faces in that direction. Those who have been given the Book know well that that is the truth from their Lord. God is not unaware of what they do.*

145. *Yet were you to bring to those that have been given the Book every kind of manifest proof, they would not follow your direction; nor will you follow their direction; nor indeed do some follow each other's direction. Were you to follow their whims, after having received knowledge, you would then be truly unjust.*

146. *Those to whom We brought the Book know this as well as they know their own children; but some of them knowingly suppress the truth.*

147. *This is the Truth from your Lord: be not among those who doubt.*

148. *For every community there is a direction of their own, so hasten to do good deeds. Wherever you may be, God will ultimately gather you in. God has power over all things.*

149. *From wherever you come forth, turn your face in the direction of the sacred Mosque; that is indeed the truth from your Lord. And God is not unmindful of what you do.*

150. *From wherever you come forth, turn your face in the direction of the Sacred Mosque; and wherever you may be, turn your face towards it: so that people can have no argument against you, except those among them that are unfair; so fear them not, but fear Me; that I may complete My bounty upon you, and that you may be guided aright.*

151. *Even as We have sent among you a Messenger of your own, who recites to you Our revelations and purifies you, and instructing you in Scripture and Wisdom, and teaches you that which you knew not.*

152. *So remember Me and I will remember you; and give thanks to Me, and deny Me not.*

We move immediately from a passage with the overarching moral that the purpose of all religion is always the same, to have faith and do good deeds, to one that distinguishes and differentiates. This passage provides the definition of Muslims as a distinct community, a community defined by a particular observance: turning towards Mecca when offering prayer. While this will differentiate the Muslim community, it does not alter nor should it detract from the qualitative characteristics this community must embody in its internal operations and external relations. They are to be a community of the middle way.

Every community has its own traditions and rituals; their purpose is to summon us to 'vie...with one another in doing good works'. Our differences, far from setting us at odds, should encourage us to work together. How we live is what will be judged, and for which everyone will be individually accountable, in the Hereafter. The conjunction of setting this eternal and universal challenge in the midst of a passage which creates the very difference which will distinguish Muslims from other communities is characteristic of the style of the Qur'an, and I think highly significant. This new difference is declared following all the warnings and cautionary examples in the previous passage. Also, it refers us back to the interplay of the ideas of sundering and spreading corruption on earth being the actions of 'those who are losers' discussed previously. The difference is declared after a clear context of already established ideas is presented.

Up to the point of the revelation of this verse, Muslims faced towards Jerusalem during prayer. When in Mecca, and during the first sixteen months of his stay in Medina, the Prophet prayed facing Jerusalem. Now, he is instructed to turn towards the Kaaba, the 'inviolable place of worship', the building whose foundations were laid and purified by Abraham together with Ishmael, whose story is included in the preceding passage. This change will unite all subsequent generations of Muslims by providing them with a common focus, and gives Islam a unique distinguishing feature from other monotheistic faiths.

The 'foolish' amongst the Jews and Christians of Medina mock this change. The Prophet has to explain the change from Jerusalem to Mecca not just to the Jews and Christians but also to his own community. They are reassured that their previous devotions were not in vain, they were not praying in error or invalidly. The Qur'an reminds us that faith involves much more than simply which direction one faces during prayer. It has symbolic significance, but it is not the essence of faith: 'God is is the east and the west' (v.142); or, as we read later on, 'true piety does not consist in turning your faces towards the east or the west' (2:177). The real spirit of Islam lies elsewhere.

The true definition of Muslim society is a qualitative one: it must be 'the middle community', 'a community of the middle way'. The word used here is *wasat*, which signifies the middle part of anything. It is the point distant from either extreme, the best part of everything. While the translations 'middle community' and 'a community of the middle way' can be used interchangeably, I prefer 'a community of the middle way'. To me it infers and recalls the idea of the 'straight path', which is mentioned in the first verse of this passage. Like the 'straight path', the concept we discussed in *al-Fatiha*, 'the community of the middle way' is a qualitative conceptual tool. It is a means of orienting and evaluating how society is organised and operating. It is a means of questioning whether society is on the right course, doing what is right, not just in the form of ritual observance but across the whole spectrum of thought and action. Thus the *ummat wasat*, the community of the middle way, signifies a just, equitable, balanced, moderate people, who shun extremism of all types. It is by their moderation that the Muslim community should become an example, a 'witness', to others—just as the Prophet Muhammad himself is a model of modesty and fair dealing for Muslims.

It seems clear to me that, while those who follow the revelation given to Muhammad will turn towards Mecca in prayer, the continued existence of other religious communities is implied once again: 'For every community there is a direction of their own, so hasten to do good deeds.' Doing differently should not be made into a distraction from the true purpose of faith. Doing differently is not meant to sunder what has been joined. All communities in all their diversity ultimately are interconnected and interrelated by being creations of God and by the fact all will return to God for judgement in the Here-after. Then it will not be the distinction of their direction of prayer that counts but their good deeds.

Muslims have generally seen the notion of the 'middle community' in geo-graphical terms: Muslim societies have occupied the middle belt of the globe, stretching from Morocco to Indonesia. But that I think is incidental. Or, if you will, it is the historic product of empire building. Anyway, Muslims now live all over the planet. Some commentators, like Sayyid Qutb, have suggested that the notion of the 'middle community' is a device for judging others: 'the middle-of-the-road community', he writes, 'stands witness against other nations', 'it weighs up their values, standards, traditions, concepts and objec-tives, judging them either true or false' [8]. This idea, with its intrinsic sense of moral superiority is, I think, totally misplaced. The very terminology used shows it is falling into the pitfalls so clearly set out in the previous passage. The community of the middle way following the straight path should be making judgements on how well, or how badly, Muslims themselves fulfil their values, standards, traditions, concepts and objectives. Rather than assuming the right to judge others it should, ideally, be offering constructive engagement to all other communities to resolve the predicaments of the human condition, to make the world a better place for everyone, irrespective of what they believe. Towards other faiths, as we have seen, the Qur'an commends and authorises, avoiding argument on imponderables of absolute truth and operating mutual respect, tolerance and forbearance. And, as the Qur'an repeatedly states, indi-viduals as well as communities can only stand witness for their own actions.

It is important, in my opinion, to emphasise that the Qur'an is not suggest-ing that Muslims are *the* middle community; rather, it is pointing out that Muslims can and should always strive to become *a* community of the middle way. As such, the notion of the 'middle community' is primarily a tool of self-reflection. It implies that a balance must be sought between our physical and spiritual needs, the demands of the body and the demands of the soul. Both need equal nourishment. In the Qur'anic scheme, there is no inherent conflict between spirit and the flesh, the desire for sexual fulfilment or good food and the quest for spiritual satisfaction. We cannot neglect either; but also we can-not become obsessed with one or the other. Nor are wealth and possessions in and of themselves to be shunned, but they are to be spent. Whatever we do, whatever we seek, whatever we accumulate can be purified by moderation and 'spending', that is operating a distributive inclusive outlook in all aspects of life in an environment open, tolerant and welcoming to all. This much is widely acknowledged by Muslim scholars. But beyond that, the notion of a 'middle community' has to be translated as an all-embracing idea touching all aspects of our life and thought. It suggests moderation in our approach to religion, which should not become the sole marker of our identity, a totalitarian obsession that undermines common human values, and eventually leads to self-destruction. It points towards a balanced approach to reason and revelation, science and values, ethics and morality. It argues for a more respectful and humble approach to nature, holding ourselves responsible and accountable as trustees, people who look after and preserve the environment for future generations. It demands fair-play, equity and justice in our economic activity and moderation in our politics.

The message of the Qur'an is one thing; how Muslims actually behave in real life, and how Muslim societies shape and manage themselves, is quite another. When I look around the Muslim world, I see not 'a community of the middle way' but communities of extremes—of obnoxious, ostentatious wealth in the midst of abject poverty, of religious zealots and self-righteous chauvinists, of despots and demagogues. I see societies profoundly confused about how and in what way to be Muslim, how to express and fulfil their religious identity in the complexities of the modern world. I see communities vacillating uncertainly between a truncated and fossilised tradition and vague imaginings about how to rekindle and recapture the glories of their history. I see communities of debate and concern offering plans for modernisation, reform and revolution that turn out to be cul-de-sacs that do little or nothing to address the real problems, the dire conditions in which so many Muslims live. And I see those who peddle the panacea of violence, the quick fix of the gun and bomb, the panic politics of animosity and destruction of supposed enemies, as if that is any answer to the predicament of making a better, more peaceful and sustainable world. These are not communities displaying the quality and character they should derive from turning towards the Kaaba in prayer. And it is definitely not integrated and coherent as a community that 'races to do good deeds' (v.148).

Instead of heeding the warnings provided in the Qur'an, Muslims in their history and their present seem to be dedicated to repeating as many of the mistakes it enumerates as possible. They are sundered, divided and factional within, as much as they cherish a sense of superiority over other societies that they lack within themselves; not racing to do good deeds, but chasing all forms of human frailty and perversity with steadfast determination.

113

15

AL-BAQARA

VIRTUOUS PEOPLE

153. *O you who believe! Seek help in steadfast patience and prayer; for God is with those who are patient.*

154. *And say not of those who are slain in God's cause: 'They are dead.' Nay, they are alive, though you perceive it not.*

155. *Surely, we shall test you with something of fear and hunger, with loss of wealth, lives and crops, but give glad tidings to those who are patient,*

156. *Who say, when afflicted with calamity: 'To God we belong, and to Him we shall return.'*

157. *Upon them rest blessings from God, and Mercy, and it is they, they who are rightly guided.*

158. *Behold, al-Safa and al-Marwa are among the symbols of God. Whosoever makes the Pilgrimage to the Sacred House in the Season or at other times, it is no fault in him to circumambulate them; whoso volunteers in piety God is All-grateful, All-knowing.*

159. *Those who conceal the clear Signs and the guidance We have sent down, after We have made it clear for the people in the Book, on them shall be God's curse, and all who curse shall curse them,*

160. *Except for those who repent and reform their conduct and proclaim their faith. These I shall forgive. And I am All-Forgiving, Compassionate to each.*

161. *Those who disbelieve, and die while they are disbelievers; on them is God's curse, and the curse of angels, and of all humankind;*

162. *And under that curse they shall abide eternally. Their penalty will not be lightened, nor will they be granted respite.*

163. *Your God is One God. There is no god but He, Merciful to all, Compassionate to each.*

164. *Behold! in the creation of the heavens and the earth; in the cycle of the night and the day; in ships that plough the ocean for the profit of mankind; in the rain which God sends down from the skies, giving life to earth that is dead; and dispersing all manner of creatures; in the change of the winds, and the clouds which run their course between sky and earth: In these are signs for people who reflect.*

165. *And yet there are people who choose to believe in beings that allegedly rival God, loving them as [only] God should be loved: whereas those who have attained to faith love God more than all else. If they who are bent on evildoing could but see— as see they will when they are made to suffer—that all might belongs to God alone, and that God is terrible in punishment!*

166. *When those that were followed disown their followers, and they see the torment, and their cords are cut asunder,*

167. *The followers will say: 'If only we could have another chance, we would disown them as they have disowned us.' Thus will God show them their deeds as deepest remorse. Nor will they ever leave the Fire.*

168. *O humankind, eat of what is on earth: all is lawful and good for you. Do not follow the footsteps of Satan, for he is to your manifest enemy.*

169. *He merely commands you to commit evil and debauchery, and to speak about God that of which you have no knowledge.*

170. *When it is said to them: 'Follow what God has revealed' they answer: 'Nay, we shall follow [only] that which we found our forefathers believing in and doing.' How so, even though their ancestors understood nothing, nor were rightly guided?*

171. *The likeness of those who disbelieve is the beast which hears the shepherd's cry, and hears in it nothing but the sound of a voice and a call. Deaf are they, and dumb, and blind: for they do not use their reason.*

172. *O ye who believe! Eat of the good things We have provided for you, and give thanks to God, if it is Him you truly worship.*

173. *He has only forbidden you carrion, and blood, flesh of pig, and whatever has been consecrated to other than God. But if one is forced by necessity, without wilful disobedience, nor transgressing due limits, no sin shall be upon him. God is All-Forgiving, Compassionate to each.*

174. *Those who suppress what God has revealed of the Book, and purchase a small gain therewith, those shall eat only fire in their bellies. God shall not speak to them on the Day of Resurrection, nor shall He cleanse them. Theirs will be a painful doom.*

175. *It is they who take error in exchange for guidance, and suffering in exchange for forgiveness: yet how little do they seem to fear the fire!*

176. *That is because God has sent down the Book with the Truth, but those who differ regarding the Book are sunk deep in discord.*

177. *Virtue does not demand of you to turn your faces to the east or to the west. Virtue rather is: he who believes in God and the Last Day, the Angels, the Book, and*

the Messengers; and spends his substance, however cherished, on kin, orphans, the needy, the traveller, beggars, and for freeing human beings from bondage; who is constant in prayer, and pays the purifying dues; who fulfils the contracts they have made; and endures with fortitude misfortune, hardship and peril. These are the true believers. These are truly pious.

In what does virtue reside? How should people become and demonstrate that they are indeed 'a community of the middle way'? In what characteristics should their balance between extremes be evident? This passage juxtaposes two virtues that hold the key.

These verses ask people who have attained to faith to seek aid in patience and prayer when faced with adversity. There are many people in this world who are tested by adversity, just as the Muslims in Medina were. In our time, the world is only too familiar with refugees who have been driven from their homes, have had to flee leaving behind all their possessions, and consequently know danger, hunger and the loss of the fruits of their labour. A large proportion of such refugees today are Muslims.

To those who are patient in adversity the Qur'an gives 'glad tidings'. Is this evidence of a religious tradition that offers only fatalism? The question has always been posed and not just to Islam. But I think the question misses, or rather misconstrues, the significance of the patience to be found in prayer. In the face of adversity the first necessity is the fortitude to endure rather than succumb, and this, it seems to me, is exactly the aid to be derived from patience and prayer. The patience summoned is the inner strength and resolve to face down the adversities of one's situation. Despite their adversities the migrants to Medina were not passive and fatalistic, they were engaged in founding a new kind of society whose glad tidings were the possibility of living in a more just, equitable and righteous way. They are tested to the limit but faith is fortitude and hope.

The Qur'an provides an example of patience and perseverance by referring to the story of Hager, wife of Prophet Abraham. Hager was left abandoned with her infant son Ishmael in the desert, between two small hills, known as Safa and Marwah, located a few hundred metres from what became the site of the Kaaba in Mecca, the direction to which all Muslims were told to turn in prayer that was discussed in the previous passage. Dehydrated and distressed, fearing for the life of her child, Hagar ran to and fro between the two hills looking for water. She kept searching and praying against all the odds. Her search and reliance on God was finally rewarded when a fresh-water spring appeared in the desert. The spring is known as the well of Zamzam, it still exists

117

today, adjacent to the Kaaba. This example of patience and prayer in adversity has been incorporated into the experience of Muslims down the years. Pilgrims to Mecca relive Hagar's search by running between Safa and Marwah, when they perform the *hajj* (pilgrimage), or *umra* (lesser pilgrimage). The hills, now a long colonnaded building, are within the precincts of the Grand Mosque in Mecca. And pilgrims also collect water from the well of Zamzam, to take home as a souvenir of their experience in Mecca.

But then we come to the juxtaposition of another essential virtue necessary to 'a community of the middle way'. I would suggest that the transition from patience and prayer to the virtue of the love of knowledge in verse 164 is crucial to realising how the fortitude and endurance derived from faith becomes an active, hopeful and liberating aid—and something quite distinct from and with no connection to fatalism. It is a consistent feature of the Qur'an to use this technique to provide food for thought by making a relationship between attributes and virtues we might think about in separate contexts but which we need to understand as integral parts of following the right path.

The middle community consists of people 'who use their reason' to study the natural world and think about the physical and material laws of the universe. Indeed, they even reflect on the ingenuity we as human beings are capable of ('the ships that speed through the sea'). By linking the practice of virtue to the pursuit of knowledge, the Qur'an makes it clear that uninformed virtue has little validity. There is no real virtue in being humble and ignorant. Real virtue is humility that comes from knowledge. So, ultimately, moral excellence, the shine on basic human virtues, is acquired through knowledge and learning.

Indeed, ignorance can still lead a virtuous community to downfall. The 'men who take for worship others beside God' (v.165) are not just idol worshippers in the Prophet's Medina. They are also those, I would argue, who have idolised their political leaders, religious scholars, and the ways of their forefathers (v.170). These are the people referred to in the next two verses (166–7) as 'those who are followed' and are 'falsely adored'.

This, I think, is of crucial importance for our time. Blind imitation (technically known as *taqlid*) of religious scholars of yesteryear and today is the norm in contemporary Muslim societies. A great deal of Islamic law derives from *taqlid*; and a great deal of what religious scholars tell Muslim societies to do or not to do is based on it. Indeed, as Mohammad Asad points out in his commentary on the Qur'an, innumerable 'legal' injunctions which have little bearing on the words of the Qur'an, prohibitions in excess of what the Qur'an says, false 'attribution of religious validity to customs sanctioned by nothing but ancient usage' and absurd *fatwas* have been issued 'through subjective methods of deduction and then put forward as "God's ordinances"' [9].

There is no virtue in such blind imitation; and the Qur'an, as we read later, categorically denounces it: 'Do not follow blindly what you do not know to be true' (17:36). Instead, each believer is required to 'use reason', pursue knowledge in its widest sense, and gain the ability for discernment on moral and religious issues. As this passage makes clear, the accountability on the Day of Judgement is individual: we will be asked what we have done, not whom we followed. Thus, the followers should look not 'for one more chance in life' but towards their own critical faculties.

Critical acumen also comes into play in the discussion of 'what is lawful and good on earth'. We have already considered that the human condition is being *khalifah*, trustees, with a right to utilise the fruits of the earth. In this passage the recurrent reference to 'eat', it seems to me, needs to be considered in the wider sense of how we utilise the bounty of the earth that grows for us or is manufactured by human hands. The believers are told not to consume carrion, blood, swine, and that which has been offered as sacrifice to idols (v.173). But the prohibitions here do not only apply to food; and the prohibition itself is conditional. In the case of an emergency or necessity, what is unlawful becomes lawful. The reverse is also true: lawful can become unlawful in certain conditions, if, for example, it is acquired through unlawful means, as we learn later (5:63). The term translated as 'lawful' is *halal*, which also signifies a praiseworthy thing or action; the opposite term is *haram*, forbidden, or blameworthy. These terms have wide-ranging significance that is seldom realised.

Both have permanent and contextual aspects. There are certain things, such as murder, cheating, backbiting, which will always be forbidden. But beyond that, these concepts connect ends and means; for something to be *halal* it has to be inherently good and acquired through good means. So the fruits of theft, robbery, cheating, scam, bribery, nepotism, money laundering, monopoly, market manipulation and similar means are also *haram*. There is a perceptive line in the brilliant Pakistani film *In the Name of God* [10] where a liberal scholar (played by Nasiruddin Shah) tells a court that Muslims are 'constantly looking for *halal* meat shops with *haram* money in their wallets'.

The 'good' is defined in terms of 'sustenance': only if it sustains not just our bodies but all that which surrounds us can it be consumed. As such, lawful things themselves may not necessarily be good: a '*halal*' burger may be dripping in fat and a product of unethical farming practices. Ostensibly, the burger is lawful; but given the fact that it is bad for one's health, and injurious to the animals as well as possibly the people who work in the supply chain that deliver it to the consumer, it ought to be unlawful. The injunction to eat of the good things is not limited: it is directed against the use of things which are injurious to physical, mental, social, cultural and environmental health, even though they may not be explicitly forbidden.

Things change. What is 'good on earth' in one particular context may not be so good in another context. As such, good is not defined once and for all. It has to be constantly sought, re-established from context to context, through critical engagement. This is one of the most notable virtues of 'a community of the middle way': it adjusts to change, younger generations constantly question their fathers and forefathers, as society itself and our moral consciousness with it evolves and our understanding of what classifies as good changes.

Goodness, therefore, is not a manifestation of outward forms: it 'does not consist in turning your face towards East or West'. The Qur'an stresses the principle that mere compliance with rituals, or external forms such as beard or dress, does not fulfil the requirements of piety. Beyond belief, goodness is based on certain virtues: on patience (those 'who are steadfast in misfortune, adversity and times of danger'), on integrity ('who keep pledges whenever they make them') and on gratitude ('who keep up the prayer').

But goodness also needs to be translated into action. It manifests itself in the constant struggle for equity and social justice amongst the believers. The simplest way for an individual to seek social justice is to spend one's substance in 'God's cause'. We have in previous passages discussed how the 'straight path' as well as the 'community of the middle way' have to be understood as a distributive outlook, one that spends and uses, manages the trust it succeeds to. In this passage these concepts are given specific reference by enumerating the people one should help unconditionally: 'to their relatives, to orphans, the needy, travellers and beggars, and to liberate those in bondage'. 'Travellers', or 'wayfarers', refers to displaced people: those who due to circumstances beyond their control have been forced to move from their homes, are unable—temporarily or permanently—to return, and face hardship. It includes refugees, political exiles, asylum seekers and economic migrants. In the Prophet's Medina, those in 'bondage' were clearly slaves. The Qur'anic injunction regarding slavery is simple: 'liberate those in bondage', thus eventually leading to the abolition of slavery. Historically, Muslims did not take this injunction to its logical conclusion. Today, however, those in 'bondage' would include those trapped in poverty, people working for unsustainable wages, child labour and victims of trafficking. Clearly, 'a community of the middle way' which is constantly adapting its understanding cannot tolerate such injustices. And it seems clear in the context of this passage that 'spends its substance' does not merely refer to wealth in the form of money, the most obvious connotation. One's substance also includes the intellectual and creative abilities to devise the means to prevent injustice and want occurring.

In view of the contemporary significance attached to the idea of those 'slain in God's cause', we also need to consider this verse in its historic context, as well as the conceptual context of following the straight path as a community of the middle way. In one sense this verse is clearly contextual. The fledgling Muslim community of Medina was engaged in a life and death struggle for survival with the larger and more powerful armies of Mecca. To those who have lost loved ones, the Qur'an offers consolation and encouragement, just as it does in the case of those who are tested by fear, hunger, loss of wealth and crops. There is however another, more extensive, sense in which 'God's cause' must be understood. All who strive and do good deeds, the kind enumerated at the end of this passage, are engaged in God's cause. All who are righteous and do righteous deeds receive the promise of eternal life when they return to God on the Day of Judgement. The idea that 'God's cause' is literally a sanction for religious conflict, or acts of murder and mayhem, can have no religious warrant. It is a literalism entirely at odds with all that this passage says, indeed the entire message of the Qur'an.

When I think about this passage I cannot fail to call to mind a wonderful saying of Prophet Muhammad, which captures its essence and spirit. The saying is: pray and tie your camel. Prayer is not evidence of fatalism when it is the first step to using one's reason and finding just and practical solutions to problems. What we are asked to do is both, not either/or.

16

AL-BAQARA

LAW OF EQUITY

178. *O believers, just retribution is ordained for you in cases of murder: the free for the free, the slave for the slave, the woman for the woman. But if a brother is forgiven by another regarding what is ordained and seemly deliverance of payment made, this is an act of leniency from your Lord. Whoever aggresses after this will have a painful doom.*

179. *For the law of just retribution saves lives, O you who are possessed of understanding; so that you might remain conscious of God.*

180. *It is ordained upon you, when death approaches any of you, leaving wealth behind to make a will in favour of parents and close relatives, in accordance with what is fair. This is incumbent on the God fearing.*

181. *If anyone changes the bequest after hearing it, sin shall fall upon those who alter it. For God is All-hearing, All-knowing.*

182. *But if anyone who suspects unfairness or wrongdoing on the part of a testator, and makes peace among them, no sin shall fall upon him. God is All-forgiving, Compassionate to each.*

In practical terms, how does a community of the middle way operate? We have seen the consistent theme of the need to put religion into practice, to make it a way of life that amends the ills of society and that transcends the differences between and within communities. This passage further extends one of the essential hallmarks of the Qur'an's guidance: it sets out the norms of social life. What we learn here is that living rightly depends upon operating the law of equity, of fairness, of just and appropriate action and reaction.

Once again we need to keep in mind that the Qur'an is speaking to the problems of Arabian society at the time of the Prophet Muhammad, as well as establishing normative principles for the operation of law throughout time. The test for those who aspire to become a middle community is to distinguish between the circumstantial, that which is specific to a particular time and place, and the general principle, which will always be applicable but which needs to find appropriate form to serve the needs of another time and place.

Arabia during the days of Prophet Muhammad was a tribal society based on the notion that the sons of a clan were brothers who shared the same blood. Internecine war, pillaging and looting of caravans were widespread. Revenge and retaliation were common themes: minor tribal incidents could lead to long drawn out feuds between tribes. The 'War of Basus' began when a camel accidentally trespassed into the pastures of a neighbouring tribe and lasted for decades. In certain cases, tribes took excessive revenge: when they lost a person of noble descent, for example, they would kill many people, besides the murderer, in retaliation. Captives, both men and women, were mutilated. Famine and scarcity were annual occurrences, so certain foods were reserved for men which could not be taken by women. Women were bartered; and daughters were seen as an economic burden, leading to the practice of female infanticide.

The realities of tribal society are the particular social circumstances that form the backdrop to these verses. The Qur'an is concerned here, I think, with establishing the boundaries of fairness and equality. The Qur'an insists on absolute and total respect for human life: as emphasised in 5:45, 6:151, 17:33 and 25:68. It is not surprising, then, that the Holy Text sees murder, denying or ending someone's life, as a cardinal sin. Murder has to be punished; but there are boundaries within which justice is to be sought.

The first point I would make is that the commonalities between different religions evident in this most basic of all questions—the sanctity of human life and the just and equitable response to murder, the most cardinal of sins—are demonstration of exactly the reality and approach the Qur'an required us to be mindful of in earlier passages. Whatever distinctions the Qur'an makes in the specific principles it lays down for Muslims should never blinker us to the common principles to be found in different religious traditions. We do not stand as far apart from each other as chauvinists of any and all religions or ethical systems would sometimes have us believe.

The verse 'the free for a free' (178) can, of course, be read literally. And it leads down a familiar cul-de-sac, the same that follows from taking 'an eye for an eye', when taken to signify only what those words literally express. But uncritical literalism, the kind that does not reason with the specific and the universal, would be a gross error. Here, as in so many other places in the Qur'an, knowing the social context in which the verses were revealed and deconstructing the key words used is crucial. The term generally translated as 'retaliation' is *qisas*. It includes the idea of equality or just measure; this is why Yusuf Ali translates it as 'law of equality' and Mohammad Asad renders it as 'just retribution', which I have followed. There are two principles of equality being advocated here. First, the law is to be applied equally to all: men, women, free or not; the social status of the murderer or the victim makes no difference. Second, punishment should be proportionate to the crime.

The Qur'an refers generally to 'cases of murder'; it offers three specific outcomes: just retribution, compensation and, given its frequent exhortations and overall spirit, forgiveness. Not all murders are premeditated. There may be circumstances which alleviate the guilt: murder could be provoked, or it could be a result of temporary rage, or a result of an accident. In which case, compensation may become the just course, and it has to be made in a 'goodly manner' and fairness by taking full account of the situation of the accused.

These verses have moral import and universal implications; we can apply the general principles to our own circumstances. The term 'brother' used here to mean the victim's tribal family could be interpreted to mean society in general. Individual compensation may be financial, as suggested in these verses; but social restitution could be a just prison sentence—penal systems not being much in evidence in medieval Arabia. Indeed, it seems to me the principle of financial compensation is an element worth considerably more thought in our own time. The victim of murder is not only the individual life lost. Their entire family suffers not merely traumatic loss of a loved one but also various kinds of economic and social loss. The principle of just restitution involved in financial compensation acknowledges the needs of the other victims of the crime. The life lost can never be restored, but the victimisation of those left behind can not only be acknowledged but also addressed in practical ways.

The Qur'an seems to me to encourage one to think more broadly and profoundly than is usually the case. The function of 'just retribution' is not revenge but protection of society. Its words could not be more unequivocal: 'The law of just retribution saves lives.' Clearly, this has direct relevance to the historic context of seventh-century Arabia, but also it has universal relevance. A society that operates on the principle of just retribution, through a fair and effective system of administering justice, concerned not only with punishment but reform and restitution, nurtures its humane instincts. It is a society that reasons with crime and the causes of crime.

When it comes to punishment, society is cautioned not to transgress, not to 'exceed the limits', but to stay within the boundaries specified by the law of equity. Equity means acknowledging the obligation not just to consider degrees of culpability in the crime but also obligation to all those victimised by the crime. I would suggest that we get so bogged down in familiar arguments about crime and punishment, the hoary old chestnuts of debate, that we miss something more obvious. We are ever ready to say that the Qur'an is applicable through all time and circumstances—then fail to see how it can always refresh our understanding and way of thinking about problems. We fall into complacency, instead of continually questioning whether our thinking has gone as far and realised as much as the Qur'an suggests.

The breadth of meaning and application of the law of equity is made clear in the logical progression of this passage. Once again we have an instance of the juxtaposition and conjunction of seemingly dissimilar instances where a common principle applies. We move from 'just retribution' to 'just distribution' in the verses which deal with inheritance.

The Qur'an asks that a proper will be made in good time, so that confusion and feud may not follow after one's death. The will, we learn later, has to have two witnesses (5:106). The end product has to be respected by all concerned and cannot be altered; and the trust must be discharged with due diligence. However, if the deceased has made a mistake, and a dispute results when someone corrects it, the matter is to be settled by peaceful negotiations.

The emphasis is not just on making a will but also on its content. The concern is to achieve equity as the operation of the distributive principle we encountered in previous passages. Wealth should not accumulate in fewer and fewer hands; inheritance is a means of distributing wealth throughout society. A reasonable amount has to be left to one's parents and close relatives, particularly those in dire circumstances. The rest is dispersed to one's offspring according to a formula specified in 4:11–12, which is usually read in conjunction with 2:180–82.

Provision for parents is mentioned before all other 'close relatives', and it seems to me to highlight a way of reading all the verses dealing with inheritance; but most of all it informs our understanding of the central principle, the law of equity. It is not merely a case of honouring one's parents, but of recognising that in later life one's parents may have greater difficulty in providing for themselves. The principle of equity seeks to be proportionate and appropriate to need.

In 4:11–12, we read that a son should have the equivalent of two daughters. However, if there are only two daughters, then they should get two-thirds of the inheritance, and if there is one daughter she should get half of the inheritance. There are other proportions for other members of the family. Let us see what is happening here.

In the Arabia of the Prophet Muhammad, females were not entitled to any inheritance. On the contrary, women were used as property to be bought and sold or owned and inherited and assigned as payment for debts. Inheritance was the sole preserve of those who wielded the sword; boys below puberty, the infirm and the elderly could not inherit either. The Qur'an repeals all this and establishes new rules. It insists that women have a right not just to inheritance but also, by corollary, to property.

However, as is so often asked—and a vast deal is made of the point—why should a daughter only get half as much as a son? The answer has nothing to do with patriarchal attitudes in Arabian society at the time of the Prophet, or in any society at any time for that matter. The Qur'an is instituting a reform, but one that recognises human and social realities. Paradoxically, in terms of inherited wealth, the system works in favour of women for a rather simple reason. When a man marries, he takes financial responsibility for the whole family as patriarchy and honour demanded, and Islamic reform endorsed; his inheritance would be spent on all the family, wife and children included. When a woman marries, according to the system the Qur'an introduces, her inherited wealth remains solely her own property; her husband, or indeed her children, had no rights over it. Or looked at from the other perspective, a woman could expect to become part of a household where her immediate needs would be a claim on and be met by her partner, unlike the social obligations expected of men. Divorce or widowhood are also possibilities women might face, therefore it is equitable that they should have their own independent resources to meet their potential needs.

The proportions set out in the inheritance laws are thus designed to disperse wealth and property throughout society to guard against need. Equity does not mean that everyone gets the same; rather that distribution is based on reasonable need according to actual circumstances. Indeed, the eradication of need is a fundamental principle that recurs throughout the Qur'an, as we have already seen. Here we have an instance of the consistency with which general principles can be applied: the law of equity begins within the family, with the provision we should make from the wealth and property we own for our nearest and dearest, and then expands to embrace the whole of society, the whole of humanity. It is worth noting that devising a means to calculate the distribution of inheritance on the basis of social equity as outlined in the

Qur'an led Al-Khwarizmi (*c.*780–850), the Persian mathematician, to develop algebra [11].

The need to understand and distinguish the specific circumstances of Arabian society at the time of the Prophet Muhammad was basic to the approach of all the great scholars of Islamic history. However, times change, circumstances change and what we are required to do, surely, is to work out how the law of equity should apply in our time. The rules and regulations that Muslims regard as their tradition were formed in history and demand the application of critical reasoning, not blind following. It is not only the case that in our time gender roles are understood in different ways. The very nature of work as paid employment is vastly different, as are the needs of providing a sustainable way of life, therefore the law of equity has to be interpreted in a different way. If both men and women work, and carry equal financial burdens, the law demands that a daughter and a son get equal shares. Failure to admit such a change would be to remain oblivious to the implications of the idea of balance. A balance is something that shifts to ensure we remain within the boundaries of the law of equity.

17

AL-BAQARA

FASTING

183. *O you who believe, the fast is ordained upon you, as it was ordained on those who came before you, so that you might remain conscious of God;*

184. *(Fast) for a fixed number of days. But if any of you is ill, or on a journey, then a number of other days. For those who cannot bear it, a penance: the feeding of a poor person. And whoever does more good than he is bound to do does good unto himself thereby; for to fast is to do good unto yourselves, if you but knew it.*

185. *It was the month of Ramadan in which the Qur'an was sent down as a guidance to mankind and a self-evident proof of that guidance, and as the standard by which to discern the true from the false. Those among you who witness it shall fast throughout it; but he that is ill, or on a journey, then a number of other days. God wills that you shall have ease, and does not will you to suffer hardship; but [He desires] that you complete the number [of days required], and that you extol God for His having guided you aright, and perhaps you will be thankful.*

186. *If My servants ask concerning Me, behold, I am near: I answer the prayer of every suppliant when he prays to Me: Let them respond to Me and believe in Me, so that they might follow the right way.*

187. *It is lawful for you, on the night of the fasts, to lie down with your wives. They are as a garment to you and you are as a garment to them. God knows you used to cheat; but He has turned His face towards you and forgiven you; so now go in and lie with them, and seek what God has ordained for you, and eat and drink, until the white streak of dawn can be distinguished from the black streak; then complete your fast till the night appears. Do not lie with them in periods when you retire for devotional prayers. These are the bounds set by God, do not infringe them. Thus does God make clear His signs to mankind, so that they might remain conscious of Him.*

188. *Do not consume each other's wealth in falsehood, nor argue the matter with judges, in order to consume a portion of people's wealth unjustly, knowing well what you are doing.*

189. *They ask you concerning the new moons. Say: 'They are times appointed for humankind, and for the Pilgrimage.' It is not a virtue that you approach houses from their backs. Virtue is to be pious. So approach houses from the front, and fear God so that you may prosper.*

As a religious institution, fasting is as universal as prayer. Jews fast on Yom Kippur, the Day of Atonement, one of the holiest days in Judaism. Hindus fast during certain times of the year, such as the Durganavami festival, to purify the mind and the body. Christians observe Lent, a period of renunciation in the run-up to Easter, and have been recommended by Jesus to fast (Matthew 6:16, 17). The monks of Mount Athos, being Greek Orthodox, fast up to 200 days in a year.

In Biblical times, fasting was a sign of mourning, sorrow, affliction, or approaching danger. The Qur'an institutes fasting as a form of worship, as both an individual and collective act, that has to be carried out for 'a certain number of days'. The Sacred Text emphasises the moral and spiritual aspects of fasting and suggests that its purpose is to 'learn self-restraint' (v.183) by controlling one's natural desires. It is prescribed as one of the four main religious rituals, along with daily prayer, payment of *zakat* (the obligatory poor tax) and *hajj*, the pilgrimage to Mecca.

The fast begins 'when the white streak of dawn can be distinguished from the black streak' (generally, about an hour and half before dawn) and continues till sunset. During this time, one abstains not only from food but drink and also sex, all kinds of disorderly, abusive and aggressive behaviour, and worldly temptations and desires. The indefinite period in verse 184 becomes the definite duration of 'the month of Ramadan' in the next verse. But verse 184 provides us with an interesting hint that I think is lost in translation. Those who cannot fast, because they are too ill or too old, are asked to feed and help the poor instead. But if they can do much more than that, of their own free will, it is better for them.

Fasting involves hardship. The word used for doing 'much more' is *tatawwu*, which has the connotation of spontaneously doing good. It also means acting with effort. These two ideas are also connected with fasting itself: it is both an instinctively good act and one that requires effort. The last part of the verse, 'And whoever does more good than he is bound to do does good unto himself thereby; for to fast is to do good unto yourselves, if you but knew it' seems to acknowledge the fact that fasting requires serious effort. I think the idea of effort in all forms of Muslim worship is crucial. It suggests that as individuals and communities Muslims should inculcate the notion that serious effort is essential for genuine spiritual attainment.

Given all the physical hardship and effort required to fast, there are exceptions. People on medication or those travelling can fast an equal number of days when they have recovered or their journeys have ended. Those with prolonged afflictions, the disabled, the elderly, pregnant women and breast-feeding mothers, don't have to fast at all. They attain their spiritual benefits by putting in real effort in what they do as a substitute.

The hardship of fasting, the effort required to refrain from fulfilling the natural desires to eat and drink and suppress numerous other temptations, are undertaken for a higher thirst: the desire to be near God. The effort is reciprocated; and God replies: 'behold, I am near'. He responds, He says, to 'the prayer of every suppliant', everyone who puts in an effort to fast. It is interesting to note that 'prayer' here does not refer to prayer in general about health, wealth and material happiness. Of course, God listens to prayers for worldly and temporal benefits, not just from believers but also unbelievers, righteous people as well as the transgressors, and, as we are told elsewhere in the Qur'an, He answers 'if He pleases' (6:41; 10:22–3, 17:67). The prayer here, a spontaneous outcome of fasting, is very specific: it is about following 'the right way' towards God. And the answer comes in the form of spiritual fulfilment by attaining nearness to God.

After fasting was established as a religious injunction, many Muslims in the Prophet's Medina thought it was illegal to have sex with their spouses during the month of Ramadan, even at night. This involved additional hardship; and the verse, 'God wills that you shall have ease, and does not will you to suffer hardship', refers to the practice of early Muslims who avoided sex for a whole month. The Qur'an equates sex with hunger and thirst as natural desires, as we shall discover in chapter 45. What applies to eating and drinking after the daily fast is over also applies to sex. There is also the idea of balance here: that the spiritual quest should not be at the expense of physical self. The body and soul need to be in harmony to attain closeness to God.

The idea of mutual balance is continued in the metaphor of 'garments' used to describe the relationship between husbands and wives (v.187). Just as garments protect one's body, so spouses protect each other. Just as garments give comfort to the body, so husbands and wives are a source of comfort for each other. Just as garments decorate and adorn the body, so the married couple embellish each other, the weakness of one is made up by the strength of the other in a spirit of mutual support. What could be more beautiful in a relationship than that?

It was the practice of Prophet Muhammad on the last ten days of Ramadan to stay in his mosque, spending day and night in meditation and reflection. He advised his followers to do the same. These are the 'devotional prayers' alluded to in verse 187. This practice is not an obligation; but many Muslims voluntarily undertake the exercise.

The Qur'an prescribes fasting during Ramadan for a rather special reason: it is the month when the Qur'an itself was first revealed. The first verses of the Qur'an, 'Read in the name of your Lord...' (96:1–5), were revealed on 27 Ramadan 611. Ramadan thus, in Muslim thought, has an intimate connection with God. It is the ninth month of the Islamic calendar, which begins with the *hijra* or migration of Prophet Muhammad from Mecca to Medina during 622. The Islamic calendar is a lunar calendar: 'they ask thee concerning the New Moons. Say: They are times appointed for mankind' (v.189). As the lunar year is around eleven days shorter than the solar year, the months drift with respect to seasons. Over the cycle of 32.5 years there is a balance: fasting can be experienced in the extreme heat of the summer as well as the shivering cold of winter; and, of course, in some parts of the world for longer days or shorter days as well.

Towards the end of this section, the analogy of eating is used in relation to property (v.188). Fasting requires one to abstain from eating, which would necessarily be eating what is legal. Now we are told not to eat, in a general sense, that which is illegal, or acquired through corrupt means. The Qur'an repeatedly condemns corruption of all kinds. The fast is a physical and spiritual discipline to control one's desires. It is a device not just for coming closer to God but also for learning the importance and true meaning of God consciousness. When the fast is over, the spiritual renewal moves on to the next challenge: to control one's passion for vanities, for greed and illegal possession. Just as we saw in an earlier passage concerning deriving sustenance by eating what is good on earth, so here too we are not to think of fasting in a narrow perspective. The task of following the right path is extensive and all inclusive: it touches all aspects of human life. As so often, the Qur'an indicates the integrative and inclusive aspect of its underlying principles by such switches of subject matter. The technique presents a challenge: to reason with the shifts of subject matter to find the connection of underlying and unifying principle. Balance and equity apply across the whole range of human life. The insight and lessons of spiritual discipline apply to and operate in all the mundane aspects of our human nature and daily life.

18

AL-BAQARA

WAR AND PEACE

190. *Fight in the cause of God those who fight you, but do not commit aggression: God loves not the aggressors.*
191. *Slay them wherever you may come upon them, and expel them from where they had expelled you; for oppression (persecution) is worse than slaughter; but fight them not near the Sacred Mosque, unless they fight you therein; but if they fight you therein, slay them. Such is the reward of unbelievers.*
192. *But if they desist, then God is All-forgiving, Compassionate to each.*
193. *Fight them until persecution is no more, and religion is for God. But if they desist, then all hostility shall cease, except against those who wilfully do wrong.*
194. *A Holy Month will substitute for a Holy Month, and sacrilege calls for retaliation. Thus, if anyone commits aggression against you, retaliate against him in the same measure. But fear God, and know that God is with those who are conscious of Him.*
195. *And spend your wealth in the cause of God, and do not with your own hands hurl yourself to destruction; but do good; for God loves those who do good.*

And so we arrive not at the heart of the Qur'an but rather at the predicament of our time. These verses are some of the most controversial, bandied around by some Muslims to justify indiscriminate violence and by some non-Muslims to argue that Islam is inherently violent. Both are widely off the mark. There can be no doubt that these verses now condition relations between Muslims and non-Muslims, therefore they require careful reading and clear understanding by all. They have immense bearing on what Muslims should demand of themselves and how non-Muslims should hold us to account.

135

My question is simple: how does one get from the definitive declarative statement that opens this passage—'but do not commit aggression: God loves not the aggressors'—to a blanket warrant for violence? Answer: only by distorting one's reason and ignoring how this passage fits within the whole of the Qur'an's moral and ethical framework.

In reading this passage, it is necessary to keep the cautionary notes I have made in mind. First, no passage can be taken out of context; all must be read in conjunction and in light of their relationship to the whole of the Qur'an. Second, we have to remember the Qur'an was revealed over a period of 23 years and addresses itself both to the actual circumstances of a real community of ordinary human beings as well as to all people for all time. This means that apart from needing to know what problems confronted the Muslims at the time of Revelation, we also have another major factor to consider: the mindset, the outlook the Qur'an seeks to promote.

In this passage the Qur'an is speaking to ordinary flawed human beings in a terrible predicament. It is a predicament that humanity has been all too capable of recreating down through history, so the specifics directed to one time and place have relevance far beyond the particular circumstances. And what I find so hopeful and uplifting is that in these circumstances the Qur'an does not expect people to be perfect and follow a counsel of perfection; and yet, simultaneously, it raises their souls and minds to the path of perfectability. It limits the permission to resist, while giving guidance on how to strive to do better, how to limit the damage human beings can cause to themselves, other people and the world in which they live. It offers limits and restraints that lead towards bettering the human condition; it points to ways of learning how to make peace. The Qur'an is consistent in being a manual for reform, not a one-off leap to the ideal, but a process, an ongoing task, an effort that must continually be made by mind and soul, a course to be returned to time and time again.

Let us start by looking at the context in which these verses were revealed. The tiny Muslim community, numbering no more than a few hundred people, is under siege. There is open hostility between Muslims and various Arabian tribes, particularly the Quraysh of Mecca. Having failed to suppress Islam in Mecca, and knowing that Muslims have found refuge in Medina and are gaining strength, the Quraysh have taken up the sword to annihilate the Muslims once and for all.

The Quraysh are preparing for a major battle—the battle of Badr (c.624)—which will decide whether Muslims survive or perish. The Quraysh are committed to the complete destruction of the Muslim community, as a later verse makes clear: 'they will persist in fighting you until they turn you away from your faith, if they can' (217).

So what options do the Muslims have? In these ultimate circumstances permission is given to the Muslim community, who up to this point had refrained from fighting, to fight in self-defence. The verses were revealed *in situ* when hostilities were in progress and the very survival of the Muslims as a community was at stake.

And there are specific instructions in these verses which are just that: specific to one historic situation. For example, the personal pronoun in the word 'slay them' makes it clear that the Qur'an is referring to those who are engaged in hostilities against the Muslims, specifically the Quraysh. These persecutors had driven Muslims out of their homes in Mecca. So the followers of the Prophet are given permission to 'expel them from where they had expelled you'. They occupied the Sacred Mosque in Mecca, and the Muslims are asked not to fight within its precincts if possible.

And yet, in these circumstances Muslims are told not to 'transgress limits'—by which is meant commit atrocities, kill women, children or non-combatants, or burn down property or destroy cattle and fields, or respond disproportionately to aggression—for transgression could lead to self-destruction: 'do not with your own hands hurl yourself to destruction' (v.195). And if the enemy ceases fighting, Muslims must lay down their arms; only hostility is to be met with hostility. Thus, the fight is resistance not to exterminate the enemy but only to persuade them to cease hostilities.

There are, then, general principles here which have broader applications. The only possible justification for war according to the Qur'an, the fundamental principle if you like, is self-defence. The only legitimate enemy is those who wage war against you—a principle that is also laid down in 22:39 ('permission to fight is given to those against whom war is being wrongfully waged') and again in 60:80 and 4:91. This is why the three battles of the Prophet, Badr and Uhud, and the Battle of Trenches, were all defensive in character. The last one was in fact not a battle at all: the defence, a trench around Medina, was so good that the enemy was unable to cross it and turned back after a couple of months laying siege out of sheer boredom. The corollary is that aggression is forbidden, Muslims are not to begin hostilities: 'do not commit aggression' for 'God loves not the aggressors'.

Defensive fighting in the Qur'an is related directly to oppression. Oppression, persecution, we are told, are worse than 'slaughter'. As history shows, oppression can lead to unspeakable atrocities, the ongoing denigration and humiliation of human dignity by denying people their freedom and right to flourish and prosper. Oppression and persecution demean both the oppressor and the oppressed [12]. They fuel continual hatreds and generate new conflicts by denying the rightful liberties and opportunities to thrive that should be enjoyed by all people. They are the living death of the spirit inflicted on the innocent. It was to prevent just such an occurrence that the Qur'an permits the Muslims of Medina to stand up and fight against the oppressors of Mecca who are torturing and abusing those Muslims who did not migrate from the city with the Prophet, as they abused and preyed upon Muslims before the migration.

In a later verse the Qur'an considers the nature of oppression: 'if they do not let you be, and do not offer you peace, and do not stay their hands'; in other words, oppression is continuous suppression, that denies the right and freedom to live according to one's conscience and identity and allows no option for peace. The word often translated as 'oppression' is *fitna*. It incorporates the idea of persecution, suffering, slaughter, sedition and constant distress. It is also synonymous with hindering people from practising their faith. It is in these circumstances that war, which the Qur'an later in this *sura* describes as a 'heinous thing' (v.217), becomes legitimate. It is this fight against oppression and for survival that the Qur'an sees as just war 'in the cause of God'.

The phrase 'in the cause of God' has nothing to do with fighting for the propagation of faith, which is not mentioned once in the Qur'an. The 'cause' here is strictly liberation from persecution and oppression. Neither does the verse 'until persecution is no more and religion is for God' (v.193) have anything to do with the domination of Islam and the subjugation of non-believers. If it did, I would have severe doubts! Rather, it points to the end result of freedom from oppression: God can be worshipped without fear of persecution. Indeed, the phrase 'religion is for God' implies worship in general by all faith communities. This is made clear in 22:40 where those who fight oppression in 'the cause of God' liberate 'cloisters and churches and synagogues and mosques in which God's name is much remembered' and which otherwise 'would have been pulled down'. The words used are exactly the same: 'religion is for God'. The message of these verses is that the final outcome of fighting against oppression should be that there is no persecution on the basis of religion and everyone is at liberty to hold their chosen belief. There is no tension here with the pluralist outlook we have found in all the earlier passages.

In my opinion, the opposite interpretation, that fighting is to be continued till all people accept Islam, not only makes a mockery of the spirit of the Qur'an but makes numerous other verses—such as the one we read later in this *sura*, 'there is no compulsion in religion' (v.256)—totally meaningless. It also renders all those verses where the Qur'an exhorts the believer to make agreements with other communities superfluous.

This, however, has not stopped certain scholars from interpreting these verses in exactly this way. For example, Sayyid Qutb, the intellectual ideologue of Muslim Brotherhood, interprets v.190 as 'fighting in Islam must be undertaken only to promote the aims defined by Islam: to make God's word supreme in the world' [13]. He goes even further in his interpretation of v.192: 'But if they desist, know that God is much-Forgiving, Merciful'. Simply desisting from fighting, says Qutb, is not good enough. The enemies are 'required to renounce their denial of God and their rejection of His message' [14].

But this is by no means a common interpretation. Maulana Mawdudi, the founder of the Jamaat-e-Islami of Pakistan, who is frequently lumped with Qutb, offers a totally different interpretation of v.192. 'What is meant by "desisting"', says Mawdudi, 'is not the abandonment of unbelief and polytheism on the part of the unbelievers but rather their distance from active hostility to the religion enjoined by God. The unbelievers, the polytheist, the atheist, has each been empowered to hold on to his belief and to worship whomsoever and whatsoever he wishes' [15].

This passage, 2:190–95, is usually read in conjunction with a number of other verses where we find the injunction to fight, such as 4:76, 84, 89, 91 and 9: 5, 12, 14, 29, 36, 123. But the verses that have attracted most attention, both from the classical commentators and critics of the Qur'an, are 9:5, known as 'the sword verse', and 3:149, known nowadays as 'the terror verse'. Given their relevance to this passage, it is worth discussing these verses here.

I don't see the sword verse, 'kill the associators (*mushrikin*) wherever you find them, and take them, and confine them, and lie in wait for them at every place of ambush', as a command to all and sundry. Once again, it is a specific instruction to those in the thick of battle. The first part of the verse speaks of 'sacred months' when a truce of a sort was supposed to be in operation; but with the exception of the tribes of the Bani Damrah and the Bani Kananah, who respected the treaties they made with Muslims, all other tribes frequently violated their agreements and continued to kill and persecute Muslims. Indeed, violation of agreement was a common characteristic of the Arabian tribes in their relations with Muslims. Here again, the survival of the Muslim community was at stake. Muslims are thus urged to use the tactics of warfare to defend themselves, but as before, once the enemy 'repents', that is hostilities cease, they must be allowed to 'go their way'. On the battlefield too, the enemy did not play fair and abide by widely accepted tribal agreements. Muslims followed the injunction to desist from fighting, and would sheathe their swords when the enemy laid down their weapons. But the Quraysh often took advantage of this and practised deception, thus killing many Muslims. This verse therefore expresses total exasperation about 'those with whom you make an agreement, then they break their agreement every time' (8:56); and these are the specific people to whom this verse refers.

When taken out of its specific context, the sword verse can be used to justify all variety of violence. As I noted in chapter 3, it is the favourite verse of both fictional and real villains; followed closely by the terror verse: 'We will put terror into the hearts of the unbelievers. They serve other gods for whom no sanction has been revealed' (3: 149). Yet, the apparent meaning attributed to the terror verse could not be further from the true spirit of the Qur'an. Here, the Qur'an is addressing Prophet Muhammad himself. The verse was revealed during the Battle of Uhud (c.625), when the small and ill-equipped army of the Prophet faced a much larger and well-equipped enemy. He was concerned about the outcome of the battle. The Qur'an reassures him and promises that the enemy will be terrified by the Prophet's unprofessional army. Seen in its context, it is quite clear that it is not a general instruction to all Muslims, but a commentary on what was happening at that time.

Unfortunately, the voices that portray such specific, on-the-spot commentary and instruction as clear universal commands have a strong appeal for some disillusioned Muslim youth. However, those who do what the Qur'an demands, who 'think', 'reflect' and most of all read verses in their proper context, are brought abruptly back to two insuperable propositions: one, do not commit aggression; two, the fight against oppression does not and should never initially be by force of arms. Doing justice, working for justice, ensuring that justice and equity are made real in society is a constant task, the progressive and insistent requirement of the Qur'an; that is its path of peace. This is why the passage concludes by providing quite another sense of 'the cause of God': requiring Muslims to 'spend their wealth' to 'do good' rather than hurl themselves to destruction. These phrases relate to all that we have discussed in previous passages in regard to 'spending' in the most extensive sense of utilising the whole range of human abilities to build just, equitable, open and tolerant societies. This verse integrates the conditions where human failure and perfidy may create the conditions of conflict into the broader framework of the Qur'an's moral and ethical exhortations. It is the broader framework which creates and insists on limits. Only when under direct, physical attack does fighting in self-defence become a legitimate alternative.

But there is one other reason why young and disillusioned Muslims who feel under threat, marginalised and misunderstood are so easily caught up in the seduction of the gun. We have to acknowledge that virtually all biographies of the Prophet and so many books by Muslims on the history of Islam dwell endlessly on the battles for survival of the original Muslim community. Muslims are taught more about the details of those few battles, conducted mostly as successions of single combat and lasting in the case of both Badr and Uhud less than a day, than the details of a career of twenty-three years during which the Prophet faced down oppression by constructive peaceful means. We are too intoxicated by the historic military successes of Muslim imperialism, though there we pick and choose much more carefully. And we all seem to forget that consistently the consensus of the *ulama*, the religious scholars, of India denied the legitimacy of declaring war against British colonialism because the practice of Islam and survival of the community itself was not under threat, however much the opportunities to thrive might have been prejudiced.

Our world has been very good at generating injustice and oppression. The followers of all faiths have been less than exemplary in championing the ways of peace and just peaceful coexistence. Humanity as a whole has failed in not transgressing the limits. On the contrary it has found innumerable ways to operate oppression and persecution, to deny the rights and dignity of 'other' people. War, even war for survival, is indeed a 'heinous thing' that does injustice and usually perpetuates the cycle of oppression by creating new conditions in which it can thrive. I read the Qur'an as a way to think and learn about how to make peace, justice and equity triumphant, because that is not something war can achieve. But I am equally at ease with the proposition that war can only be a last resort. It can be undertaken only when attacked and threatened with extermination; only to make an aggressor desist. Most assuredly, I do not think this is something Muslims have to apologise for—they just have to ensure they go no further!

19

AL-BAQARA

HAJJ

196. *And perform the Pilgrimage (Hajj) and the pious visit (umra) for the sake of God. But if you are prevented, send an offering for sacrifice, such as you can easily afford, and do not shave your heads until the offering reaches its destination. And if any of you are ill, or diseased in the head, in compensation either fast, or feed the poor, or offer sacrifice. And if you are safe and secure, then whoever breaks his state of consecration in the period between the umra and the hajj shall give whatever offering he can easily afford. He who cannot afford it should fast three days during the hajj and seven days on his return, making ten full days. This is for those whose household is near the Sacred Mosque. So fear God, and know that God is severe in punishment.*

197. *The Hajj takes place in familiar months. Whoever undertakes the Pilgrimage during these months shall abstain from promiscuity, no vice and no discord is allowed during the pilgrimage. Whatever good you do is known to God. And make provision for yourself, but the best of provisions is God consciousness. So remain conscious of Me, O you possessed of understanding.*

198. *It is no sin for you to seek the bounty of your Lord (by trading during pilgrimage). When you return from Arafat, remember God at the Sacred Monument, and remember Him as He has guided you, although before that you had indeed been among those who go astray.*

199. *Then surge onward with the multitude of other people, and ask for God to forgive you your sins. For God is All-forgiving, Compassionate to each.*

200. *When you have performed your holy rites, remember God, as you remember your fathers, or yet more devoutly. There are among them such as pray: 'Lord! Give us in this world!' but they will have no portion in the Hereafter.*

201. *But there are among them such as pray: 'Our Lord! Give us good in this world and good in the Hereafter, and defend us from the torment of the Fire!'*
202. *To these shall fall a share of what they have earned; and God is swift in reckoning.*
203. *Remember God during the appointed days. He who hastens to leave in two days commits no sin, he who stays commits no sin, if he be God-fearing. Then remain conscious of God, and be assured that to Him you will ultimately be gathered.*

It is the greatest annual gathering of humanity, when almost three million people from all corners of the globe, representing a myriad of nationalities, ethnicities, languages and cultures, join in the greatest collective act of religious witness. It is the *hajj*, the pilgrimage to Mecca, the subject of this passage. But far more than providing the most amazing logistical act of witness, the *hajj* provides some of the most important insights into the essence of Islam and the worldview it seeks to inspire.

As classical commentators note, it conveys to the living some inkling of the gathering that awaits us all on the Last Day, when all the souls of all people who have ever existed will stand together before God to be judged. Participation in the *hajj* is also a real demonstration and experience of the way that Islam integrates the individual and the collective. It generates an extraordinary sense of community, of unity with the emphasis on equity. The unity of the *hajj* is based on the eradication of all distinctions of race, culture, colour, class. All pilgrims are dressed alike; ideally a king or a billionaire may walk alongside a pauper and not know the difference. If, in the eyes of God, such distinctions are of such little moment, then we have reason not to be too beholden or over-powered by them in our daily lives; it is evidence of the balance we should strive to achieve. The *hajj* is proof there are things more important than the social conventions of human invention, which can be perverse and contrary to the balance that Islam seeks to guide us towards. But then, there is the even more profound insight that in a community with unity and equity, there is no dissolution of individuality. The most often repeated statement of the pilgrims is the ultimate personal statement: '*Labeik!*' 'Here *I* am!' In this sea of humanity, before God each individual is known in their uniqueness, just as each will ultimately be judged and charged with responsibility only for their individual actions and intentions.

It seems to me that the *hajj* resolves one of the great enduring philosophical disputes: the supposed contradiction between the collective and the individual. The distinction has been made into a thorny issue, a set of irreconcilable opposites, a call to diametrically opposed systems of government. It has divided societies and peoples and has been responsible for some of the greatest atrocities of history. To experience the *hajj* is not so much to resolve this nexus of argument but rather to witness it dissolve as an illusory distinction. All people are individual and unique, but necessarily and inevitably must live within communities, in human groupings among and with other people. We are faced not with a contradiction but with realities that must be balanced. In being conscious of God, the Creator and Judge of all, we find the understanding and guidance to effect this balance. It is not just the great mass of humanity gathered together bent on a single purpose that makes the *hajj* such a moving, humbling and inspiring experience; it is the profundity of the way of thinking it teaches us about our relationship to God, to other people and ourselves.

Hajj is one of the main pillars of Islam, an obligation for all Muslims to perform once in their lives, if they are able. It was the last of the major obligations to be instituted. According to the most reliable sources, it was made obligatory only in the ninth year of the *hijra*. It was established by this passage, known as the '*hajj* verses', after the Muslims led by Prophet Muhammad had retaken Mecca, and all pagan idols and shrines had been removed from the Kaaba, the house of Worship originally built by Prophet Abraham towards which all Muslims turn when they pray. The Kaaba is the black draped cube at the centre of the Sacred Mosque in Mecca.

The word '*hajj*' means 'effort'; like fasting, the performance of *hajj* requires spiritual and physical exertion. While these verses of the Qur'an establish this institution for Muslims, they describe few of the rites of *hajj* as we have come to know them. It is through the example of the Prophet, in the reports of how he performed the pilgrimage, that we learn how these various pieces of *hajj* are put together in a set of rituals that culminate in the supreme hours of a Muslim's life.

The *hajj* takes place in the month of *Dhul-Hijjah*, the twelfth month of the Islamic calendar, and falls on the 9th, 10th, 11th and 12th of that month. It is a journey that requires the pilgrims to 'take provisions' with them to ensure they do not suffer from any financial problems both during the travel and once they get to Mecca, where they will spend some time. But it is typical that even as the Qur'an makes something obligatory, it recognises the difficulties that ordinary people may face and institutes alternatives, so that none are excluded. So, just as with fasting, there are exemptions: those who cannot travel for any reason can make compensation by 'fasting, or feed the poor, or offer sacrifice'.

The Qur'an requires the pilgrims to be at a place called 'Arafat'. The name of this valley comes from the root word *arafa* meaning 'to know': something happens at Arafat, as I know from experience, that enables the believers 'to know' they are in the presence of God. It requires a 'sacrifice'; and eventually shaving one's head as an act of humility.

During the five days of *hajj*, pilgrims from all over the Muslim world come together in Mecca, pray and worship in unison, and move constantly from place to place. Before entering the holy areas, they are required to be in a state of grace. They abandon their worldly thought and desires and put on *ihram*, two white, unsewn sheets of cloth. The actual pilgrimage starts with the performance of *tawaf*, walking seven times round the Kaaba. After *tawaf* comes *sa'y*, when the pilgrims run between the hills of Safa and Marwah. These hills are now joined by a covered walkway within the Sacred Mosque in Mecca. The ritual is in memory of Prophet Abraham's wife Hager, as discussed previously.

The night of the 8th *Dhul-Hijjah* is spent at the hill town of Mina, near Mecca. The 9th is the day of Arafat, the supreme moment of the *hajj*. The pilgrims leave early to cover some five miles, arriving at Arafat before midday. When the sun passes the meridian, the ritual of *wuquf*, or standing, begins. The entire congregation, nowadays well over two million, prays as a single entity. They are joined by Muslims everywhere who observe this day as one of the two Eids, the high points of the Muslim calendar. The sacrifice of a sheep or goat or other animal gives the name to this Eid: *al Adha*, the feast of sacrifice. The meat of the sacrificed animals is then distributed in charity. Today, with so many pilgrims, finding ways to distribute the meat is not the least of the logistical challenges. In Muslim communities around the world, *kurban*, the meat of sacrificial animals, is distributed among the entire community. It is prized as a means of participation, of feeling near to the great gathering in Mecca.

Immediately after sunset, there is a mass exodus from the enclosed plain of Arafat to the more open area of Muzdalifah, a couple of miles away, where the night is spent under the open sky. On the morning of the 10th, the pilgrims return to spend three days in Mina. During this second stay in Mina, the pilgrims sacrifice an animal and engage in 'Stoning the Devil'; three small pebbles are thrown at each of the three masonry pillars marking the different spots where the Devil tried to tempt Prophet Abraham—a gesture that symbolises the pilgrims' intention to cast out the 'evil within'. Once these rites are performed, the pilgrims conclude their *hajj* by removing their *ihram* and shaving their head or cutting their hair.

The complex rites of *hajj* are performed in 'quick pace' and in a 'peaceful condition'. The holy areas are inviolate and nothing within can be harmed:

animals, plants, not even a fly. The pilgrims shun all signs of vanity and refrain from combing their hair, wearing perfume or clipping their nails. The whole being of the pilgrim should be completely devoted to *Allah* without attention to appearance. At the most intense moments of knowing God's presence, knowing the presence of the great mass of humanity and knowing oneself, the ego should be suppressed, for in the power of these experiences we are most truly humbled. Desire, including sexual desire, should be put aside. The pilgrims come to Mecca dishevelled and covered with dust to seek God's mercy and crave His forgiveness. From the moment they don their *ihram*, the pilgrim declares, 'O Lord, here am I in response to your call'. Throughout their journey, they 'celebrate His praises' by uttering '*Allah-u-Akbar*' (*Allah* is the Greatest) and 'There is no God but *Allah*'.

These verses institute the *hajj* as the climactic point of Muslim existence. But they also make clear the theme of continuity, an important aspect of the mindset of Islam. The *hajj* was an ancient rite established in Arabia long before Islam. This is evident in the reference to its taking place 'in familiar months': these are the Islamic months of *Shawwal*, *Dhul-Qi'dah* and *Dhul-Hijjah*. The point being made is that they should not be altered. At the time of Prophet Muhammad, pilgrimage was completely assimilated into Arabian pagan practices. Idols punctuated the Kaaba and pagan customs had introduced certain undignified and discriminatory practices. The tribe of Quraysh who inhabited Mecca and guarded the Kaaba together with some of their allies were raised to the position of a religious aristocracy. They were allowed to perform certain rites fully attired, while members of other tribes had to shed their clothes, which were regarded as unclean, and either perform these rites completely naked or to obtain 'ritually clean cloth' from the Quraysh. The strict pagan code also prohibited those wishing to perform the rite from consuming any food other than Meccan food. The pilgrimage was a major source of income and prestige for Meccans, and in part explains their initial hostility to the new religion of Islam, its Prophet and his followers, who were seen as a threat to the institution that brought trade and profit to the city.

Of all the practical manifestations of Islam, the *hajj* has captured the imagination of Muslims everywhere. Many save all their lives to go on a once-in-a-lifetime journey. Some still cover long distances on foot over a period of years, thus demonstrating an unparalleled devotion. In Southeast Asia, in Malaysia and Indonesia, for example, it is customary for people to visit everyone they know and take leave of them before setting off on *hajj*. The custom dates from the time when *hajj* was not only a journey of a lifetime, but a journey from which many might never return. To become a *haji* or *hajjah*, one who has made the pilgrimage, marked a great change in one's life, and the title is an honour as much as an honorific; those who return are considered renewed and invested with an intensified sense of spirituality.

I performed the *hajj* five times during the years I lived in Saudi Arabia in the 1970s. On one particular *hajj*, I walked from Jeddah to Mecca, and everywhere in the holy areas, with a donkey. I can say without doubt that there is no experience on earth like that of *hajj*: to see the pilgrims, all dressed in white, move like a mighty river, meandering and swirling, in a great tide of devotion and reverence. The sound of their pleading voices and the patter of their hurrying feet fill the air with awe. Despite the enormous numbers and the different places from which they come, there is an overarching feeling of brotherhood and sisterhood. Under the open sky in Muzdalifah, one discovers that whatever the cultural, social, national or ethnic background of the pilgrims, they all, as Malcolm X says in his autobiography, snore in the same language [16]. And yet, the experience is intensely personal: it is me standing before God, uttering His praises, quivering with emotion, thirsty for spiritual fulfilment, asking for His forgiveness. It is an experience hard to describe, for what is felt defies language. Once you have stood at Arafat, alone in a congregation that spreads on all sides as far as the eye can see, you 'know': you feel the Grace of God. That's why, I suspect, the attraction of *hajj* is so compelling for Muslims.

There is also the lesser pilgrimage, the *umra*, which consists in performing a limited set of the rituals that make up the *hajj*. The great distinction is that while the *umra* brings one to Mecca and provides people with the enormous sense of being before God that comes from visiting the Kaaba in person, the *umra* remains an individual occasion, or something undertaken by small groupings of families and friends. *Umra* can be performed at any time outside of the *hajj* season. It is a memorable achievement for any Muslim who lives outside of Mecca, but it can never match the majesty of the crowning experience of one's life that is the *hajj*.

As ever with the Qur'an, there is consideration for practical matters in the midst of even the most supreme religious moments. Pilgrimage made Mecca a centre for trade. The Muslim pilgrims who come to Mecca are told it is 'no sin' for them 'to seek the bounty of your Lord (by trading during pilgrimage)'. Down through history this has indeed been a bounty: it enables pilgrims to finance their journey from all corners of the globe. It has made the *hajj* a major institution for the exchange not just of goods but also of ideas. Indeed, some of the greatest thinkers of Muslim civilisation made performing the *hajj* a rationale for extensive travel during which they lived, worked, learned and taught on what were extensive, circuitous travels rather than a there-and-back-again journey. A whole genre of literature records both the spiritual and mundane exploits of such pilgrims.

And again the Qur'an is concerned to point to the distinction between inward meaning and outward form. Pilgrimage is not just for material gain, for benefit in this world, even if it is no sin to trade while on pilgrimage. The bounty to be sought must always be a balance: 'Our Lord! Give us good in this world and good in the Hereafter.' The bounty we seek must be balanced by the remembrance and consciousness of God that we accumulate. And it must be a distributive and active bounty that we employ, or as we have discussed previously 'spend', in renewed commitment to making the world a better place for all.

20

AL-BAQARA

APOSTASY AND MIGRATION

204. *Now there is a kind of man whose views on the life of this world please you. He calls upon God to witness what is in his heart; yet is he the most contentious of adversaries in dispute.*

205. *When he departs, he goes about the earth spreading corruption and destroying crops and cattle. God loves not corruption.*

206. *When it is said to him, 'Fear God', his arrogance drives him into sin. Hell will settle his account, an evil resting place, indeed!*

207. *And there is a kind of man who would willingly sell his own self to please God. And God is gentle to His servants.*

208. *O you who believe! Enter the fold of peace, all of you. Do not follow in the footsteps of Satan, for he is to you a manifest enemy.*

209. *If you stumble after clear signs have been revealed to you, then know that God is Almighty, Wise.*

210. *Are they really waiting for God to come to them in cloud shadows together with angels—although by then all will have been decided, and unto God all things will have been brought back.*

211. *Ask the Children of Israel how many manifest signs We revealed to them. And one who alters God's blessing after it has come to him, God is severe in punishment.*

212. *To those who disbelieve, the life of this world has been made beauteous. They mock those who believe. But they who are conscious of God shall be above them on the Day of Resurrection. And God bestows his bounty on whomsoever He wills, beyond all reckoning.*

213. *Mankind was one single community. Then God sent forth prophets as heralds of glad tidings and as warners; and with them sent down the Book with the Truth, to*

judge among humankind in matters in which they disputed. But none other than the selfsame people who had been granted this [revelation] began, out of mutual jealousy, to disagree about its meaning after clear signs were sent to them. Then God guided the believers to the Truth, regarding which they differed. For God guides whomsoever He will to a path that is straight.

214. *Or do you think you will enter the Garden without undergoing that which befell those who passed away before you? They were afflicted with misery and hardship, and they quaked, to the point that the Messenger and the believers with him cried: 'When comes God's help?' Ah, surely, the help of God is near!*

215. *They ask you what they should spend on others. Say: 'Whatever of your wealth you spend for good goes to parents and kindred, the orphans, the poor and needy, the wayfarer.' And whatever good you do, God is aware of it.*

216. *Fighting has been prescribed for you, although it is a matter hateful to you. But it is possible that you hate a thing which is good for you, and that you love a thing which is bad for you. God knows, and you know not.*

217. *They ask you concerning fighting in the Sacred Month. Say: 'Fighting in it is a heinous thing; but to turn people from the path of God, to deny Him, to prevent access to the Sacred Mosque, and expel its people: that is more heinous in God's sight.' Persecution is worse than slaughter. They will persist in fighting you until they turn you away from your faith, if they can. But if any of you should turn away from this faith and die in unbelief, their works shall come to nothing in this world and in the Hereafter, those are the inhabitants of the Fire; therein shall they dwell forever.*

218. *Those who believed and those who emigrated and exerted themselves in the path of God, these have hope of God's Mercy. God is All-forgiving, Compassionate to each.*

Once again we come to the thorny issues of how to operate religion, how to live a religious life in this world. This passage reprises themes we have already encountered to set a context for two particular concepts: apostasy, the renouncing of faith after having embraced it, and migration. Both are placed in the context of dissension, the all too evident human talent for arguing about meaning and claiming possession of the truth. I must admit I did not find this passage easy, and the selections I made from among the translations reflect the way I came to a sense of the connections it makes.

We begin by considering two alternative models. There are plausible leaders, populists, the kind who wear their religion as a divine warrant and offer what people want to hear about success in this world. Two things distinguish such people: they are 'most contentious of adversaries in dispute' and they end up spreading corruption on the earth that causes the destruction of crops and cattle. Clearly the readiness to identify and contend with adversaries and its end product of causing real devastation are connected. The link is arrogance, the primal sin as we have already seen. The arrogance is both proclaiming they have the only answer for the ills of the world, which everyone should follow, and the readiness to argue and dispute, which inevitably leads to conflict with those who have other views about how to live. We have met their kind and the issues they raise in earlier passages.

The alternative model is provided by those 'who would willingly sell his own self to please God': people who would forego their personal interests and getting ahead in this world to do what is right, that is to make the greatest effort to follow God's guidance as best they can.

The comparison prompts the reflection that all who aspire to faith and surrender to faith should model themselves on the latter, not the former. What is commended to those who believe, v. 208 literally says, 'enter wholly into self surrender'. It may, therefore, seem perverse that I have followed the translation of this term as 'enter the fold of peace, all of you'. Apart from the fact that I find the phrasing elegant, I made this choice because it does two things. First, it conveys what I understand as the purpose and meaning of the religion, the basic message that is conveyed in the Qur'an: making a world of peace and peaceful co-existence. Second, this form of words unlocked an insight into the connections I see being made in this whole passage. Self-surrender is the most basic concept of faith, it is the condition of placing total trust in the certainty of the existence of God and recognising that one is the creation of a Merciful and Compassionate Creator. The consequence of such consciousness is giving one's self over completely to doing what God has commended, trying to live in this world to earn one's place in Paradise in the Hereafter. The 'fold of peace' is then a state of personal certainty and acceptance, a coming to terms with one's true nature. It is also recognition of the real nature and purpose of the world in which we exist. It is the state of being that one should strive to achieve, a state of being in stark contrast to the arrogant, worldly, domineering and destructive populism identified at the beginning of the passage; dedicated commitment to working peacefully being the best way to make a better world based on justice, equity and dignity for all.

Surrendering oneself to God, entering the fold of peace, is no guarantee. It does not make people perfect. Self-surrender is the starting point, the point from which one sets off in search of the straight path, seeking to make a community of the middle way a reality. However, we can all expect to stumble. We live in a far from perfect world. As we have seen, following the straight path is an extensive task requiring continual critical self-reflection as well as profound reasoning to understand and wrestle with the injustices and inequities in the world around us. In this endeavour, we can derive support and encouragement from the fact that God knows our intentions. Faith does not make us perfect, but continual striving, despite our failings and what stems from these failings, is not a worthless exercise.

What brings us to enter the fold of peace, to commit ourselves to self-surrender by achieving consciousness of God in all aspects of our life? There are people who refuse to believe without a sound and light show of demonstrable, tangible proof. In an increasingly secular world, there are many who find religion incomprehensible and beyond belief. There are also many who hover on the fringes, not discounting religion entirely but unable to commit to belief. And there are many people who find religion wanting because they find believers fallible, not good advertisements for the virtues of faith, and therefore suspend their judgement about the message and guidance from God. By the time such people get the definitive proof they seek, at a point where all will be made clear, that is in the Hereafter, it will be too late to take the option for faith.

The Qur'an returns to the example of the Children of Israel once again to remind us that following God's guidance is not easy. Despite multiple instances of definitive proof, the 'signs from God' they received, nevertheless they engaged in all the ways by which human interpretation distorts, deforms and perverts revelation to suit their own tastes; and hence they were punished—and repeatedly forgiven.

Those who disbelieve value the beauties and bounties of this world. In an age of consumerism and celebrity culture, where people judge and are judged by what they have, it is not hard to distinguish what is intended here. By contrast, people of faith should not be besotted with the material things of this world, even if they are mocked for setting different standards. We are coming to the heart of the matter here. In one sense the instances and arguments that are outlined here have contextual historic reference to the Muslims who, for the sake of faith, became refugees, leaving behind their families and possessions and migrating to Medina. The migrants had to start again. They lived frugally. What mattered to them was not worldly wealth but building a different kind of society, dedicated to different values. The example of the migrants stands the test of time; in which case the verse ends by suggesting that worldly wealth and success are neither indicators nor proof of being on the right path. The bounty of God is 'beyond all reckoning', because it is not merely material but also spiritual and extends not merely to considerations of this life but also to the life to come. Those who are conscious of God and surrender to God, who seek his bounty in the most extensive sense, will be above those who prospered in this life on the Day of Reckoning.

All humankind was once one community, states v.213. Muhammad Asad makes a long argument on this point. He invokes the idea of a state of 'primitive mentality' as the original condition of humankind, with all its overtones of a social evolutionary understanding of human history. I think this is rather at odds with the Qur'anic vision of the human condition, as well as beside the point of what is being said here. I take this to be, surely, that all humanity began endowed with the same moral and ethical faculties and capacity. The story of Adam we considered earlier defines the conceptual origins of all humanity. All humans throughout history began with the capacity for knowledge, including knowledge of God and with the same message. Adam, conceptually the first man, was also the first prophet. Islam, as scholars have agreed, can be understood as natural religion. The significance being drawn here is that all humankind was one community in the sense of having the same basis and opportunities to live a righteous life in all the differences of their ways of life: languages, cultures, races and creeds. My problem is not with the idea of evolution, as we will discuss later. It is with the idea of the primitive. The 'primitive' has been employed to deny the moral sense, and inherent moral worth, of different societies [17]. To consider any society at any time in history 'primitive' is to assert both a material and moral superiority. It is to cast judgements that can only cause dissension and conflict. We ought to be only too familiar with how in history this self-righteous moral superiority has been made the rationale for many forms of oppression and persecution that have spread more than their fair share of corruption around the globe.

The Qur'an, I would argue, is not saying that this original condition of being one community is somehow before the fact of revelation, nor, I think, that revelation is the reason we are no longer a single community. Rather, I think once again we are brought back to an obvious conclusion. It was humanity's predilection for defining differences, for disputing over identity and belief, which sundered the single community. A succession of prophets, 'heralds of glad tidings' and warners brought the means to judge, to reason and resolve the disputes that divide and separate peoples and societies from each other. Yet, once again, people who received revelation out of 'mutual jealousy' fell into disagreements about its meaning. Of course, we should remember that while in this and earlier passages the Children of Israel are cited, Christians are also included, and both stand as examples of the timeless temptation and errors that face all followers of organised religion. The verse ends with the clear statement that, despite the disputes and contention, God guided the believers to the Truth. I take this to mean that within all religions, indeed all societies, among all people there are those who hold to the straight path. And for me the clear implication is that on the straight path we can and perhaps should strive to be one community: the community of common humanity in all our diversity and differences working together to make a better world.

All human beings began with the same potential and possibilities, the same sense of values. It was human diversity which 'sundered what God had joined'. Revelation exists to enhance and clarify the scales of human judgement—to refine the ability to choose and discern between different courses of action. And still people disagree about the meaning, implications and application of these messages from God. This verse speaks to the simultaneous contexts of past, present and future. It has considerable relevance in today's world where we can, on the one hand, imagine a global community but, on the other, cannot eradicate racial prejudice and hatred or rabid nationalism and all the other ills that divide people. The moral challenge remains the same, and it is a challenge to everyone, no matter what their faith or no faith.

Making choices and striving to live according to God's guidance is no simple option, and often may mean making choices that bring hardship and misfortune in this world. Attaining to and following the path of faith is no guarantee of a blissful life in the complex muddle that humanity has made of this world. But God's succour, the strength to be derived from faith in God, is always near. So perseverance is called for.

And immediately, we are reminded of the qualities of life that constitute following the straight path. It is dedicating oneself to 'spending', to caring for the real needs of family and kindred, the poor and the needy, the wayfarer, no matter who or what they are. We need to think with a distributive and inclusive mentality, employing the resources of this world to improve the circumstances and secure the good of 'others'. I take 'others' in the most extensive sense of all people who do not belong to my nationality, religion, identity, culture or race. This inclusive care constitutes the peaceable way of making the world a better place.

Then we come to the clincher, in the sense of where this passage has been leading us, at least in my suggestion: 'Fighting is ordained for you, even though it be hateful to you.' So I see this entire passage as relating back to the earlier discussion on war and peace. It deals with the proper reticence we should have for violence and warfare, the last resort argument, and that while it might be 'ordained' in the sense of being inevitable under certain circumstances, it always comes with limits and should be against our better judgements.

We can hate something that is good for us, just as much as we might love a thing that is bad for us. The line of judgement we have to make concerns the conditions, the circumstances that make the last resort inevitable. War is heinous, but the balance is that 'persecution is worse than slaughter'. Sometimes it is necessary to defend those who are being demeaned, denied their freedom and rights, who are made second-class citizens or worse because of who they are or what they believe. I agree with Asad that this verse must be read in conjunction with 190–93, 'do not commit aggression', as it is definitely not a blanket warrant for going to war, but rather an argument about the judgement that has to be made between two evils. It is clearly addressing the historic context of the time of the Prophet while generating universal principles. There are obvious parallels, far too many of them, in our own time where communities have been left to suffer oppression, persecution even genocide, without the rest of the world springing to their aid. However, it seems to me that every universal principle we derive from the Qur'an should come with one caveat: the examples it provides are moral examples. As I have been arguing throughout, as times change so the means we use to apply these moral principles can and perhaps should change. There are more ways than going to war to fight oppression, combat persecution and defend the dignity and freedom of those afflicted. Sometimes it may be impossible to find another way, but that does not mean we should stop trying to find peaceful means; though equally it can mean, however heinous, it may be necessary literally to fight for the sake of a greater good. The trouble is that human beings have been much better at devising the means of destruction, the techniques of war and array of modern weaponry than devising strategies for making peace. I am not sure how, but I am sure that remaining within the 'limits' we discussed earlier still apply as rules of war.

Now we come to the connection that, in my mind, links the beginning of this passage with its ending. We start with the plausible populists and their self-righteous rhetoric. I think here the Qur'an is directing us towards the fire and brimstone preachers. These are the people who constantly and obsessively talk about God, loudly pronounce their faith in Him and invoke Him on every occasion, but who in reality do nothing but 'spread corruption'. They are led, more than anything else, by the arrogance of their own convictions. I find such people wherever I look in the Muslim world: listen to the speeches of some of our religious scholars, the declarations of the Taliban, and the rhetoric of many followers of the 'Islamic movements'. The real devotees of God spend their lives quietly and earnestly, 'to please God'.

A favourite device of the 'contentious' ones is attacking the faith and belief of others. But it is not just the faith of others, the non-Muslims, that they attack; their most vehement assaults are focused on those Muslims who in their opinion are deviating from their prescribed path, or worse: who have left Islam altogether. In their eyes, apostasy is a cardinal crime, punishable only by death.

The technical term for apostasy in Islam is *riddah* or *irtidad*; an apostate is called *murtadd*. The Qur'an does not, contrary to popular belief, prescribe any punishment for apostasy. On the contrary, it advocates total freedom of conscience, conviction and belief.

In this passage, those who leave Islam are mentioned twice. The first time, those who 'backslide' in verse 209 are told that they should know 'God is Almighty, Wise'. The second mention, in verse 217, is specific to the Muslims in Mecca and Medina who were being persecuted relentlessly; and the persecutors were not going to stop 'until they turn you away from your faith'. The Qur'an tells these Muslims that if they renounce their faith they will be losers both in this world and in the Hereafter. In neither of these cases does the Qur'an suggest that apostasy is a capital crime, or indeed that it is a crime at all! Frankly, if that was the case I would lose my faith.

Instead, the Qur'an leaves matters of faith to individual conscience. Faith is strictly between an individual and God: 'For God guides whomsoever He will to a path that is straight' (v.213). Later in this *sura*, as we shall see, we have the most categorical of all statements on freedom of belief: 'There is no compulsion in religion' (v.256). Thus, everyone is free to believe or not to believe. To emphasise this point, the Qur'an tells us elsewhere that if God wanted everyone to hold the same belief, He would have created a world—a rather boring one in my opinion—solely of believers: 'If it had been God's will, they would have believed, all who are on earth!' (10:99). Not only is one free to believe or not, one is also entitled to act according to whatever one believes and does not believe: 'Say: everyone acts according to his own disposition: But your Lord knows best who it is that is best guided on the way.' (17:84).

But more than that, the Qur'an acknowledges that belief is not a static phenomenon. There are those, we learn elsewhere, 'who believe then disbelieve, then believe again, then disbelieve' (4:137). So there is constant two-way traffic and shifting of lanes: believers of one religion may turn to another religion; and believers of today may turn out to be atheists of tomorrow, and vice versa. But for everyone who turns away from faith, there is someone who turns towards faith: 'should one of you turn back from his religion, then God will bring a people, whom He loves and who love Him' (5:54). There is a balance, of a sort, that is always maintained.

Towards the end of this passage, those who are persecuted for their belief and are forced into exile are given hope. There is an obvious historic context: the people 'who believed and those who emigrated and exerted themselves in the path of God' are the early Muslims in Mecca. They had no option but to migrate to Medina along with the Prophet Muhammad. But I think there is also a general point here. The Qur'an sees migration as an option for all those who suffer religious intolerance, or other forms of oppression and persecution. This is not just the way of the Prophet Muhammad, but most prophets. Prophet Abraham, who was threatened by his own people, had to go into exile: 'I will emigrate for the sake of my Lord' (29:26; also 37:99). Moses and the Israelites had to flee the oppression of the Pharaoh: 'So he escaped from there, vigilant and fearing for his life, and said "My Lord, deliver me from these oppressors"' (28:21).

The Qur'an sees migration as a beneficial exercise. It is encouraged not just to escape oppression but also in the pursuit of learning. We have already encountered the other side of the equation: migrants and refugees are to be helped and supported. They add intellectual and economic capital to a community, fill gaps in the labour markets and contribute to the economy of both countries: the one they have left behind and the one they have made their new home.

The moral imperative to oppose oppression and persecution as well as to aid those who flee its clutches should remind us that we still can be one community, a community of common humanity. Such a community must exert itself in practical, humane ways to protect the weak, the needy, all those who suffer, whatever their origin, belief or identity, because they are, just like us, God's creatures: part of the sacred trust it is our duty to sustain and nurture.

21

AL-BAQARA

MARRIAGE AND DIVORCE

219. *They ask you about wine and gambling. Say: 'In them both lies great sin, as well as some benefit for humankind; but the evil that they cause is greater than the benefit which they bring.' They ask you what they should spend; say: 'What is surplus to your needs.' Thus does God make clear to you His signs: in order that you may reflect.*

220. *on this life and the Hereafter. They ask you about orphans. Say: 'To improve their condition is best; if you mix their affairs with yours, they are your brothers; God knows the dishonest from the honest. Had God willed, He could have caused you hardship: God is Almighty, All-Wise.'*

221. *Do not marry idolatresses, until they believe: A slave woman who believes is better than an idolatress, even though she pleases you. Do not give in marriage to idolators until they believe: A male slave who believes is better than an idolator, even though he pleases you. These people will lead you to the Fire. But God beckons you to the Garden and forgiveness by His leave. He makes clear His signs to humankind; perhaps they will remember and reflect.*

222. *They ask you about menstruation. Say: 'It is a vulnerable condition: So keep away from women in menstruation, and do not approach them until they become clean. When they have cleansed themselves, then come unto them as God has commanded. Truly God loves those who turn to Him in repentance and He loves those who keep themselves pure and clean.*

223. *Your wives are your tilth; so approach your tilth as you desire, and send [good deeds] before you for your souls; and fear God, and know that you shall surely meet Him, and give glad tidings to those who believe.*

224. *Do not make God, because of your oaths, an excuse for you not to do good, or act rightly, or make peace between people; God is All-hearing, All-knowing.*

161

225. *God will not call you to account for thoughtlessness in your oaths, but will hold you to account for what your hearts have earned; and God is All-forgiving, All-forbearing.*

226. *For those who forsake their wives, a waiting for four months is ordained; if they then change their minds, God is All-forgiving, Compassionate to each.*

227. *But if they are determined on divorce, God is All-hearing and All-knowing.*

228. *Divorced women shall refrain from remarriage for three menstrual cycles. Nor is it lawful for them to hide what God has created in their wombs, if they truly believe in God and the Last Day. And their husbands have the better right to take them back in that period, if they desire reconciliation. And women have the selfsame rights in conformity with fairness, but men are a grade more responsible than them. God is Almighty, Wise.*

229. *Divorce can be uttered twice: and then she must be retained in honour or released in kindness. It is not lawful for you to take back anything you have given them, except when both parties have cause to fear that they would be unable to keep within the bounds set by God. If you fear that they would be unable to keep to the bounds of God, there is no blame on either of them if the woman gives back something in order to free herself. These are the bounds set by God, so do not transgress them. Whoso transgresses the bounds of God, these indeed are sinners.*

230. *If he divorces her, she shall not thereafter be lawful to him until she has married another husband. If the other husband divorces her, no blame attaches to either of them if they re-unite, provided they feel that they can conform to the bounds of God. Such are the bounds of God, which He makes plain to those who understand.*

231. *If you divorce women, and they reach their appointed term, either take them back in kindness or release them in kindness. Do not hold them back against their will, or to be vindictive. He who does so wrongs his own soul. Do not make the revelations of God a laughing stock, and remember God's blessing upon you, and the Book and Wisdom he has sent down wherewith He edifies and instructs you. Fear God, and know that God is Omniscient.*

232. *And when you divorce women, and they reach their appointed term, do not deter them from marrying their husbands, if they mutually agree on equitable terms. This is an admonition to everyone who believes in God and the Last Day. This would be better for you and more pure in heart. God knows, and you know not.*

233. *The mothers shall suckle their children for two whole years, for those who desire to complete the term. Upon the father rests the duty of maintenance and clothing, affably granted. No soul is burdened except with what it can bear. No mother shall be made to suffer because of her child, nor father on account of his child. The same duty rests upon the heir. If they both decide on weaning, by mutual consent, and after due consultation, there is no blame on them. If you decide to deliver your children to a wet-nurse, no blame attaches to you, provided you pay what you have agreed upon, fairly and affably. Fear God and know that God sees all that you do.*

234. *And if you die and leave widows behind, they shall hold themselves apart for a period of four months and ten days: When they reach their appointed term, no blame shall attach to you regarding what they might honourably do with themselves. God is well acquainted with what you do.*

235. *Nor shall any blame attach to you if you allude to a marriage proposal with these widows or else keep it to yourself. God knows that you shall propose to them. But do not make promises to them in secret, unless it be in fair and honourable speech. Do not tie the knot of marriage until the recorded period has reached its term. And know God knows what is in your hearts. So take heed of Him; and know that God is All-forgiving, All-forbearing.*

236. *No blame attaches to you if you divorce women, not having touched them yet or settled any marriage settlement on them. But provide for them, a rich man what he can bear, and a poor man what he can bear. Let this be provided fairly and affably and let this be an obligation upon all who would do good.*

237. *And if you divorce them, not having touched them yet though having settled upon them a marriage settlement, then (pay) the half of what you have settled, unless they forgo this right or else he who holds the knot of marriage in his hand forgoes it. Yet if you forgo this right, it would be nearer to piety. Do not forget to be generous to one another: For God sees all that you do.*

238. *Perform your prayers regularly, especially the Middle Prayer; and stand in God's presence in humility and devotion.*

239. *But if you are in a state of fear, then pray while walking or riding. When you again feel secure, remember God and how He taught you that which you knew not.*

240. *Those among you who die and leave widows behind should bequeath their widows a year Qur'an maintenance and no eviction. But if they leave, then no blame attaches to you regarding what they do with themselves, if they do so honourably. God is Almighty, All-wise.*

241. *For divorced women maintenance is decreed, fair and affable. This is an obligation on the righteous.*

242. *Thus does God make plain His revelations to you: so that you may understand.*

Here we have what, at first sight, appear to be a number of disconnected topics of different moment. Once again, I suggest, we need to think through the conjunction, the bringing together of these seemingly disparate points, to find the link. Submitting ourselves to the effort of thinking and questioning is, as I have argued consistently, the essence of reading, the basic requirement for understanding. In this passage we are faced with a subject that has become a vexed issue in Muslim society. And not only in Muslim society; for here we come to the perennial topic where critics find both Islam and Muslims wanting in their attitude to and treatment of women. In our time, liberating Muslim women has even been made into a justification of war! Therefore, in light of all the fury and drivel as well as the depressing evidence of what Muslims justify in the name of their religion, might I suggest we all take a deep breath. We all come to reading with our own ideas and experience, along with all the assumptions, prejudices and predilections that includes. Too often we read through and with these assumptions to hear, confirm and understand the ideas with which we began. My emphasis in approaching the Qur'an is precisely the opposite.

Submitting ourselves to the Qur'an should mean testing and interrogating all our ideas and experiences afresh. Specifically, we need to approach these verses not through the perspective of what we know of *Shari'a*, Islamic law, and how it has been interpreted and practised by Muslims in history as well as today in different parts of the Muslim world. The questions we should be asking are whether what we now know of the *Shari'a* constitutes the only way these verses can be read. We should be asking whether the patriarchal and often misogynist attitudes of most Muslims actually match up to what the Qur'an says. Has Muslim society, and especially its learned scholars, interpreted the Qur'an to suit attitudes already prevalent in society? Have the customs and ideas of other times and places been inveigled into or overlaid upon what the Qur'an itself says? Are we in fact dealing with a certifiable example of Muslims falling into the pitfalls of interpretation and distortion that the Qur'an so clearly warns against?

There are those who read these verses with a degree of feminist indignation. I would not suggest there is no cause for indignation. However, it is necessary to look at the words used and not invest them with innate offensiveness and knee-jerk reaction. The semantic implications and the resonance of words seamlessly stir our own social conditioning on subjects such as pure and impure, normal and abnormal, what is respectful and what is demeaning. Reading the Qur'an is about getting beyond these blinkers as far as our intelligence and diligence will permit.

These verses move from drinking and gaming to treatment of orphans, suitable marriage partners, questions of divorce, to making oaths and matters of inheritance—quite a range. But I would argue that the first topic, drinking and gaming, gives a powerful clue to the consistent theme. The key, I suggest is intoxication, things which stir the passions and yet also by their very nature cloud the judgement. Questions of marriage and divorce, like all the other topics here, bring human passions into play. An oath, for example, can be uttered in the heat of the moment. So consistently, in each instance, we are guided to the need to make clear-headed, sober judgements, the kind that lead to justice and equity for all concerned.

The Qur'an repeatedly moves from soaring expressions of spiritual verities to details of mundane human behaviour. A full appreciation of our relationship to God is, as the Qur'an has been saying from the very beginning, found in how we act upon and live out God consciousness in all the aspects of our daily life. Worship is expressed not just in prayer but also in how we deal with mundane activity. It requires finding the right balance in all our activities, not being intoxicated with our self-interests or passions, but being ever mindful of the need for clear and sober judgement so that we apply the moral and ethical guidance of the Qur'an as far as we are able in even the smallest aspect of our lives.

Pre-Islamic society in Arabia was into binge drinking. Wines were made in most households, drinking was seen as a sign of high culture, and drunkenness was valued as a sign of wealth and eminence. Gambling was a close second to drinking. A popular method used for gambling involved throwing a jumble of arrows which were used to draw lots. Each arrow defined a share, from zero to three or four. The person who drew nought had to buy a camel, which was slaughtered, and the meat distributed according to the shares drawn by each participant. Like drinking, gambling too was seen as a source of pride and honour. Given that tribal Arabs valued pride and honour above all, it is not surprising that gambling and drinking led to excess. Both habits contributed to perpetual tribal feuds and constant wars.

The Qur'an sought to transform Arab society; and the whole of this passage is devoted to aspects of social transformation. Verse 219 is the first time the Qur'an mentions drinking and gambling; and it is worth noting that it acknowledges there is 'some profit' in both. But the social costs are greater: for a society to prosper and progress, drinking and gambling had to be abandoned. The injunction forbidding these comes later, in 5:90, which asks Muslims to shun them in order to be 'successful'. But from the specific example we should draw a more general principle. It is not just wine that is to be avoided on these grounds: all variety of intoxicants are included, from liquor to drugs, hard or soft, that affect the mind and hence the ability to make balanced judgements. Similarly, gambling would include all games of chance—including the national lottery. Both, we learn in 5:91, cause 'enmity and hatred to spring in your mind'; and, as such, thwart the development of genuine prosperity and well-being. The total transformation of Arab society after the emergence of Islam, I think, was in significant part due to this prohibition. It allowed the noble aspect of the Arab character, their industrious and intrepid nature, their courage and frankness, to come to the fore.

A particular consequence of unending fighting and warfare in Arab society was that many children were left orphans. So the Qur'an moves immediately to the care of orphans, who must be looked after in a manner that is 'for their good'. Orphans should not be treated as a separate class, as they usually had been, but as equals: 'your brethren'. They should not be left to live on the charity of others, but should be an integral part of a family. Guardianship of orphans, taking them into one's family and care, which involves taking responsibility for their rights to property and inheritance, must be dealt with honestly. When we think of how much of literature down the ages, and in so many societies, deals with stories of orphans deprived of their birthright, the principle is obviously of universal relevance. The intoxicating prospect of access to someone else's wealth is to be resisted.

We then move on to marriage and divorce, another important area for social transformation. The pre-Islamic Arabs had a number of rather strange marriage customs. Men married frequently, taking as many wives as they liked, and would dispose of their children if they could not provide for them. Divorce was easy and frequent, and having set aside a wife a man might then remarry her. The Qur'an tells them not to make a habit of this; marrying a woman twice is enough. There was another prevailing practice: men would swear oaths to abstain from sex with their wives, thus leaving them in limbo: they would neither be divorced and free to remarry nor be treated as proper wives. Some women could pass their entire life in such bondage. The Qur'an tells these men that after four months of abstention they should consider themselves divorced—or re-establish conjugal relationships (224–7). There was also a tradition of provisional divorce: a woman could be divorced for a short period and then taken back. The Qur'an tells these men to make up their mind, 'either keep or release them in a fair manner'.

As we have noted so often before, the Qur'an deals with the real and actual conditions of the time when it was first revealed and of the society to which it was revealed. In our reading we have to take account of the practices and attitudes it was seeking to change. And from the nature and means of transformation it sets out we need to look for the moral and ethical principles, the consistent values which can be applied to any society at any time in history, which is another way of saying we need to identify the values with which to interrogate our own experience, ideas and prejudices.

The principles the Qur'an introduces as a catalyst for social transformation all work to establish balance and bring about greater justice and equity in human behaviour. We can summarise these as:

1. Husbands and wives have the same rights: 'And women have the selfsame rights in conformity with fairness'. (228)
2. Divorce is not necessarily a bad thing, but it should be an amicable affair, and women have an absolute right to divorce, without giving any reasons: 'there is no blame on either of them if the woman gives back something in order to free herself'. (229)
3. To ascertain a possible pregnancy, and hence the parentage of the child, divorced women should wait before taking a new partner: 'Divorced women shall refrain from remarriage for three menstrual cycles.' (228)
4. Divorced women are entitled to alimony: 'For divorced women maintenance is decreed, fair and affable.' (241)
5. Widowed women should have arrangements made for their welfare by their husbands: 'bequeath their widows a year's maintenance and no eviction'. (240)
6. Mothers should breastfeed their children for two years: 'Upon the father rests the duty of maintenance and clothing, affably granted.' (233)

All these reforms were introduced into a society where the majority of women had no free will. Verse 221 clearly suggests that in the task of transforming society, those who believe in the new course of action are better suited and able to support each other. Clearly both have equal responsibilities in making the practical, conceptual and moral change that must occur. Those who have invested commitment in faith and the new ways of living that it demands are more natural companions and helpmates, more likely to abide by the limits it sets and the outlook on life it requires. The sharing of the obligations and responsibilities of society by men and women is a recurrent feature of the Qur'an. Many verses are addressed to the 'believing men and the believing women' or the 'believing women and the believing men', not as separate categories but bracketed together in a mutual task, because no society can function properly unless it uses the talents and potential of all its citizens; clearly, a lesson too many Muslim societies, now and in history, have chosen to ignore! The classical commentators regard the reference to 'slave' or 'bond' person, depending on the translation, as being in the sense of the name Abdullah, which literally means 'slave of Allah'. Just like the marriage practices mentioned above, the institution of slavery existed in Arabia, and the Qur'an had a clear, balanced, transformative position on the subject, like every other injustice.

All of the regulations arising from marriage and divorce work to ensure equity and fair dealing in what is the most basic of human relationships. It is perfectly clear that the Qur'an regards marriage as a basic institution of society, the foundation of its prime building block, the family. In marriage, as everything else, the emphasis is on equitable fair dealing and the need for kindness and affability by both parties. Marriage is an intense relationship, and the Qur'an does not expect it will always work. The dissolution of a relationship, with divorce, is where passions get most heated, and most particularly where there should be fair dealing which is equitable to the interests of both parties. However, there seems to be an underlying point of great significance working throughout this passage: the right of the individual not only to fair provision but to their individual identity and their freedom to make choices about their own lives. This links the regulations for the treatment of orphans, of women in marriage and divorce, as well as the children of divorced couples. Decisions made on behalf of orphans should respect the integrity of their birthright, not dissolve their identity and property in that of their new guardians. Women have a right to a marriage portion, their dowry, as well as to maintenance in the event of divorce. The paternity of a child should also be clear. Children have a right to know who their parents are, not least since they will have a claim on both their mother and biological father. Hence the need for women not to remarry until it is evident whether they are pregnant or not, which applies both to divorce and widowhood. It seems to me the specific mention of maintenance for women who are breastfeeding relates to divorced women. The claim is on the biological father to accept responsibility for the needs not just of his child but also its mother on whom the child is totally dependent. However, it would seem that a mother can decide not to complete the two years of breastfeeding. The clear principle is that 'no mother shall be made to suffer because of her child, nor father on account of his child'. And this applies through all the varied permutations of actual human relationships that might arise, in marriage, divorce or widowhood. It is the principle that matters, and we have to find a way to apply it through all the changing circumstances of time and social conditions.

Verse 228 in many translations is given as men being 'a degree' above women. A great deal rests on the interpretation and emphasis given to this statement. It cannot be wished away, it must be discussed. The subject of verse 228 concerns a woman waiting three months after a divorce, during which time she may or may not be found to be pregnant, and at which point the divorce becomes final. The Qur'an suggests that 'their husbands would do better to take them back during this period', if they wish to do the right thing. Both husband and wife have the right to annul the marriage, but, as Asad notes, 'since it is the husband who is responsible for the maintenance of the family, the first option to rescind a provisional divorce rests with him' [18]. The verse is simply making a statement of fact about the social conditions of the time. However, it can be read another way: the husband has a degree of edge because during those three months he can remarry. Either way, this is not an ontological statement about the status of men and women. It is a very specific reference to the role of men in divorce in Arabia during the Prophet's times. And it carries two implications: first, that while divorce is permissible it is not commended; and second, that children are best reared with and by their natural parents.

There is all the difference in the world between reading passages or extracts within the context of the entire Book and taking one reference out of its specific context and universalising its implications. I would be the first to acknowledge that the latter is exactly what far too many Muslims have done, to the detriment of women and Muslim society as a whole. The only antidote to such misogynistic nonsense is to read the Qur'an as a whole. As we shall have cause to discuss in more detail later, the idea of men being a degree above women is consistently contradicted by the totality of the Book. The issue evaporates in the sense I have made from reading various translations and commentaries that clearly refer the words to the context of the burden of ongoing financial responsibility in circumstances where both parties retain individual choice and freedom to decide. 'And women have the selfsame rights in conformity with fairness, but men are a grade more responsible than them.'

A slightly different aspect of the same kind of controversy relates to the simile in verse 223. Here in some translations wives are likened to 'fields' or, as Yusuf Ali translates it, 'tilth', the form I follow. I take the simile to mean that women, like 'mother earth', are good at nurturing humanity: they not only endure hardship during childbirth but also breastfeed and nourish their children, keep the family together, and are the repository of some of the most humane (or feminine, if you like) values of society. Just like the earth, they bear fruit, cultivate civilisation, and need to be approached with love, attention and respect. In an agrarian economy, society holds as self-evident the importance and value of nurturing, taking great care with, husbanding in another sense one's fields or tilth. In a desert environment the fields and date groves of towns and oases are even more precious, hard won and hence deserving of care and attention. To me this seems to heighten the significance and meaning attached to the kindness and affability, as well as the justice and equity, due to women. In the context of time and place, women are likened to the most precious resource that society has at its disposal, rather than being referred to in a denigrating and demeaning way. And we should not forget that, whether translated as 'go into your fields whichever way you like' or, as the sense I have made of it, 'so approach your tilth as you desire', it is bracketed with the reminder to 'send good deeds before you for your souls'. The intoxication of passion and human desire never obviates the need for remembering the spiritual balance that must be appreciated in all things.

Apparently 'go into your fields whichever way you like' has another connotation altogether. Haleem provides a rather bizarre footnote to this verse: 'when the Muslims emigrated to Medina, they heard from the Jews that a child born from a woman approached from behind would have a squint' [19]. So, the suggestion is that the Qur'an provides the Muslims with assurance that this is not so!

The classical commentators have discussed the issue of 'approaching from behind' in some detail. Al-Tabari, for example, furnishes us with many opinions, concluding with his own that anal sex is forbidden as vaginal sex is the only way to conceive. The classical commentators also provide us with a reason why this verse was revealed. A rather feisty and liberated woman of Meccan origin asked the Prophet, through one of his wives: was 'sex from behind acceptable?' The question arose, apparently, because this practice was quite common among the Quraysh in Mecca but unknown to (the original) inhabitants of Medina. She seems to have got a positive answer!

However, I don't think it is as clear cut as this. When it comes to marriage, the Qur'an emphasises the equality of both partners. And that equality continues when it comes to sex: the desires of both partners have to be taken into consideration. I certainly don't find any problem with this passage. If we are prepared to think beyond the historical and cultural blinkers and not impose our own hang-ups on the words of the Qur'an, a healthy, mutual and balanced sexual life becomes part and parcel of the good life, and why would one want to argue with that?

The subject of menstruation (v.222), about which the Qur'an is a great deal more up-front and open than has been the norm in Western society, is another subject of controversy. Here we are faced with another problem of translation, in particular Yusuf Ali's translation which describes menstruation as 'pollution'. Indeed, Ali's translation of most verses in this passage is problematic; and his footnotes are particularly misogynist. Pickthall suggests it is an 'illness', which does not take us very far either. Asad describes menstruation as a 'vulnerable condition'. Haleem gives it as: 'Say, menstruation is a painful condition.' Haleem's version suggests the verse is trying to point out that sex during menstruation can be painful for some women and it is thus best avoided. This reading might seem to be borne out by other references elsewhere in the Qur'an; for example menstruating women for the duration of their period, along with pregnant women and breastfeeding mothers, are not required to fast during Ramadan. It is because of the wider connotations of menstruation being bracketed with pregnancy and breastfeeding that in the end I determined to go with 'vulnerable condition' since there are a host of various health and well-being issues associated with menstruation.

I think the verse does two things: first, it openly acknowledges the biological nature of women; and second, it brings forward the themes of consideration and kindness, of dealing fairly with women's concerns, which run through all the verses dealing with marriage and divorce in this passage. What can never be tolerated is using the God-created biological nature of women as a rationale for making them somehow less worthy, indeed less 'religious' than men, which unfortunately is the kind of nonsense one too often hears from traditional scholars and repeated by far too many Muslim men, to their vast demerit. Misogyny is inveterate as well as inventive in working its pernicious hold on society. A sensible reading of the books of *Hadith* collections of the sayings of the Prophet is a worthwhile antidote; they are a secondary source for understanding the Qur'an, and all contain sections devoted to menstruation. They show conclusively that women, far from regarding menstruation as something which prejudiced them in terms of religion, took an active interest in how their religion recognised the totality of their biological nature. Equally, these question and answer sessions with the Prophet show how women were concerned to establish how they could carry out their duties and obligations in the fullness of their biological identity.

There is one other point that has to be dealt with. How are the words 'clean' and 'cleansed' to be interpreted? For many readers this is a further example of the pollution/purity problem. I would suggest that this predicament comes from thinking through cultural assumptions rather than rather obvious fact. Other religions, including Judaism and Catholicism, have elaborate doctrine and ritual with particular reference to menstruation. A great deal of this doctrine can be traced to the interpretative superstructure built on the story of Eve as the temptress who caused Adam to fall from grace. As we have already seen, the Qur'an's rendering of the story has no such implication. Mrs Adam, like her husband, sinned, was forgiven and is born into the world sinless and pure, which includes her female biology. And this is the conceptual status of all human beings as far as the Qur'an, and Muslim opinion, is concerned. But the history of interpretation in other religions creates an instant sensitivity which can cause impassioned reactions to particular words. In keeping with the principles being commended in this passage, therefore, I would suggest a calm and clear use of reason. Consider a society without the modern aids of sanitary provision, especially for women's particular needs; only very few studies even by female anthropologists venture to consider such matters, but when they do their findings make a world of difference [20]. The logical outcome of such a thought, however much I blush, is that 'clean' and 'cleansed' have a perfectly ordinary, sensible and innocent literal meaning.

It is undoubtedly the case that male readings of the Qur'an have predominated in history. But, thankfully, in recent times women's readings have re-emerged, and what characterises them is their confidence and security. You will find no suggestion that they feel charged with 'pollution', let alone second-class personhood. Indeed, it is not only women scholars but Muslim women in general who defy and disown all the fabrications of misogyny that have been foisted on them by male Muslim 'scholars'. The trouble is that women's sense of self-worth, the strength they take from the Qur'an, is no guarantee that in the real world of Muslim custom and practice they get the fair and equitable treatment that is their right according to the provisions laid down in the Qur'an. Muslim women are forever being told by the *ulama*, the scholars, that in Islam they have an exalted status, a supremely important role and numerous rights, such as to personal property, withheld from women in other religious and social systems; and yet despite all that, they are on the receiving end of far worse than is their due. It is on the basis of full recognition of the nature and needs of women that the Qur'an seeks to build companionship, mutuality and fair dealing in consideration, kindness and affability as the basis for marriage, divorce, indeed all aspects of relations between men and women. Those are the principles on which we need to operate today.

22

AL-BAQARA

QUALITIES OF LEADERSHIP

243. *Have you not reflected upon those who left their houses, in their thousands, for fear of death? And how God said to them 'Die', then brought them back to life? God is bountiful to humankind, but most of humankind will not render thanks.*

244. *Then fight in the cause of God, and remember that God is All-hearing, All-knowing.*

245. *Who shall be the one who offers up to God a handsome loan, which God shall multiply for him many times? It is God who holds back or gives in abundance, and to Him you shall return.*

246. *Have you not reflected upon the notables of the Children of Israel when, after the days of Moses, they said to a prophet among them: 'Appoint for us a king that we may fight in the cause of God'? He said: 'Do you promise, if fighting is enjoined upon you, that you will fight?' They said: 'What prevents us from fighting when we have been driven out of our homes along with our children?' Yet when fighting was enjoined on them, they turned away, all but a few of them. God has full knowledge of those who do wrong.*

247. *Then their Prophet said to them: 'God has appointed for you Saul as king.' They said: 'Why should he reign over us when we have a better claim to kingship than he does, nor has he been granted abundance of wealth?' He said: 'God has chosen over you, and increased him abundantly in knowledge and bodily prowess. God grants rule to whomsoever He wills. God is All-encompassing, All-knowing.'*

248. *Their Prophet said to them: 'The sign of his kingship is that the Ark will come to you in which there is tranquillity from your Lord, and a relic from the family of Moses and the family of Aaron, borne by angels. In this is a sign for you if you are true believers.'*

249. *When Saul set out with his soldiers, he said: 'God is about to test you at a river. Whoever drinks from it is not my follower, whoever drinks not is my follower, save one who scoops a scoop with his hand.' They drank from it, all but a few of them. When he passed across the river, he and those who believed with him, they said: 'We have no might today against Goliath and his troops.' Those who believed they would meet God said: 'How often a small force has overcome a numerous force, by God's leave, and God is with those who stand fast.'*

250. *When they came out to do battle against Goliath and his troops, they said: 'Our Lord! Pour down steadfastness upon us and make our feet firm and grant us victory over the host of unbelievers.'*

251. *So they defeated them by God's leave, and David killed Goliath; and God granted him kingship and wisdom and taught him what He willed. Had God not restrained humankind, some by means of others, corruption would surely overwhelm the earth. But God is limitless in His bounty to all the worlds.*

252. *These are the revelations of God, which We recite to you in truth. And you are indeed one of the messengers.*

253. *Some of these apostles We have endowed more highly than others; of their number there are some to whom God spoke and He raised in some degree. And we bestowed clear wonders upon Jesus the son of Mary, and strengthened him with the Holy Spirit. And if God had so willed, succeeding generations would not have fought each other once revelations had come to them. But they fell into dissension, and some of them believed and some disbelieved. And if God had so willed, they would not have fought each other; but God does what He wills.*

254. *O you who believe! Spend out of what We have provided for you, before a Day comes when there will be no bargaining, nor friendship nor intercession. The unbelievers are the evildoers indeed.*

As we have already discussed, the Qur'an provides a message of continuity expressed in its many references to narratives, personalities and prophets that are familiar from the Bible. In each instance these references are used to demonstrate that possessing Divine guidance is one thing; preserving it, implementing it and living by it are other matters. Human beings are flawed, prone to error and can find innumerable ways of circumventing or diverting God's good news to serve their own short-sighted ends. These references to the past are not mere history; they stand as cautionary warnings of the challenges that will face the Muslim community in seeking to build, as well as successive generations of Muslims up to our own day and into the future.

This passage tells the story of Moses' flight from Egypt, thus reintroducing once again the themes of oppression, migration and fighting for survival, which have already been discussed. The 'thousands' mentioned in verse 243 are the

Children of Israel who were forced to leave their homes because of persecution and fear of death. The Qur'an tells this story, and the stories of Talut/Saul and David and Goliath that follow, as short parables, assuming familiarity with the details and using the known narrative to highlight a particular moral.

Moses and his followers were in a double bind. The state of bondage in which they were kept in Egypt was a metaphorical death, a slow intellectual and spiritual strangulation. This is the underlying meaning the Qur'an consistently gives to oppression and persecution. They also faced real death: orders had been given for their male offspring to be put to death. Moses tries to persuade them to enter the Holy Land but they refuse. The Israelites end up wandering the wilderness, looking for an alternative home. On God's command, Moses orders them to fight and drive the Canaanites out of Palestine. But they refused to fight; and as a result, a whole generation perishes in the desert. But the next generation overcomes the Canaanites, finds the Promised Land and, in this sense, the Israelites are 'brought back to life again'.

This passage also continues the theme of social transformation. The story of Moses is related to show that sometimes it becomes necessary to stand up to oppression, when people are 'torn from our homes and our children'. There are circumstances when the refusal to challenge oppression is not a viable option. The story is meant as a warning to Muslims who had been driven out of Mecca and had been living in exile in Medina for about a year. The Qur'an repeatedly acknowledges the reluctance of some Muslims to resort to fighting, as we saw in an earlier discussion. Fighting, war is a 'heinous thing'; but 'persecution is worse than slaughter', it is the conceptual and metaphorical death of a people. So, here the Qur'an uses this parable: follow in the footsteps of the Israelites and you will have the same fate. To safeguard your future, indeed to survive, there is no alternative but to give a 'good loan' to God (v.245): that is, sacrifice your wealth, and 'fight in the cause of God' (v.244).

The brief mention of Moses is followed by the story of Talut, mentioned in verse 247, who is thought to be Saul of the Bible. The story in the Qur'an is not much different from the Bible narrative in 1 Samuel 8:19–20. The Israelites beseech a 'prophet among them' to 'appoint for us a king, that we may fight in the cause of God'. Their wish is granted. Saul is appointed by God as their ruler. Then two things happen. First, despite having been driven out of their homes along with their children, the Israelites refuse to fight their oppressors. Second, they quibble about Saul's qualifications to reign over them. Both matters raise the question of leadership.

In the first instance, we have to consider how the request for leadership comes about. We are told that the Israelites demand the appointment of a leader from a prophet who is among them. Prophets, as we are told throughout the Qur'an, are messengers and warners sent by God to remind humanity of their duties to God. The Israelites are clearly facing a dire situation. They are subject to oppression and persecution. We are told they are specifically asked whether, if a leader is appointed for them, they will promise: 'if fighting is enjoined upon you, that you will fight?' So in one sense the community is looking for a leader to take responsibility for difficult decisions which they could, and perhaps should, have the means to make for themselves. The purpose of revelation, as we have seen so often, is to make clear the duty of believers to confront and eradicate injustice, even if in the final analysis that means fighting. We have discussed that 'fighting in the cause of God' is legitimate only in defence, when subject to aggression. It is a concept that has a more extensive meaning than armed conflict, but there are times when this becomes unavoidable. So the question 'Who shall be the one who offers up to God a handsome loan...?' is not something to be delegated to a leader, but an option that, when circumstances demand, can and should be answered by all members of the community. While it is far easier to be led, to be told what to do, in fact the message of God and the judgement of what is necessary in particular circumstances should be evident to all.

The second point about leadership is that even after pleading for a leader to be appointed and being told that 'God has appointed for you Saul as king' the Israelites were not satisfied with the choice. They question Saul's appointment: how can he be our leader, they say, when he is not even wealthy, nor has the social status to rule over us? The moral here is explicit: it is not wealth or power or social status but intellectual and physical capabilities that should be used to judge who is and who is not fit to rule.

Talut/Saul's appointment does not mean that rulers are appointed by God. Of course, 'God grants rule to whomsoever He wills' (v.247): but to do that He does not have to tell us specifically who our political leaders should be. Rather, we are told the criteria by which we should select our leaders. Elsewhere in the Qur'an, we read that we should put our trust in those who are worthy of such trust (4:58); we should choose our political leaders carefully and ensure they are capable of delivering the goods in terms of justice and equity. One of the key concepts of the Qur'an, *shura*, I think has a direct link with democracy. The believers, we read in 42:38, respond to their God not just by keeping up their prayers, but they also 'conduct their affairs by mutual consultation'. *Shura*, or mutual consultation, is how political authority is acquired in 'a community of the middle way', and how God grants authority to whomsoever He pleases. There is a collective responsibility on each individual within the community to share the duties and obligations of decision-making; just as, having selected a leader, there is an obligation on the community to follow that leader in doing what is right and may be necessary in difficult circumstances.

I will have much more to say about Islam and democracy later. But it should suffice here to state that the Qur'an does not look at the powerful and the unjust with much favour. This is also evident from all that we have learned so far about virtue, oppression, equity and the middle community. Thus, the suggestion that the powerful can lay claim to political legitimacy simply by virtue of their power is, in my opinion, a totally untenable position.

That the powerful have little legitimacy is also clear from the next story: that of David and Goliath. The powerful tend to end up spreading tyranny and strife and driving people from their homes; and, as the parable emphasises yet again, it becomes necessary for the weak to stand up to them to restore order and justice. Saul warns them that they are to be tested and not to drink from a river, which represents the allures of ease. The weak among them drink and then declare: 'We have no might today against Goliath and his troops.' Whereas we see that those who believe recognise that it is not the size of their army but the strength of their convictions, the rightness and justice of their cause, that are crucial. In difficult circumstances believers have to rely on patience, steadfastness and wisdom as their instruments for subduing the powerful.

It is worth noting that when Saul became king he went through a transformation himself. A sign of his authority was the gift of tranquillity, or 'security' as Yusuf Ali translates it, which he received from God (v.248). The Bible suggests this was a transformation of the heart: 'As Saul turned to leave Samuel, God changed Saul's heart' (1 Samuel 10:10). Significantly, the Qur'an locates tranquillity not in the mind but in the heart: 'It is He Who sent down tranquillity into the hearts of the believers that they may add faith to their faith' (48:4). When the mind has had its say and all is said and done, faith finds its location in the heart. It is a tranquil heart that engenders sincerity, humility, respect, courage and all the other virtues necessary for the exercise of power. The Qur'an seems to be saying that the ultimate function of power, political and otherwise, is to free the world from oppression and strife, and bring it 'back to life again' by restoring peace and tranquillity.

The passage ends with a crucial reference to dissension and division of opinion, which follows previous revelations to other prophets and suggests that such division is a human characteristic; one that Muslims in history have not been spared. What is suggested in verse 253 is that divergence of opinion among human communities is part and parcel of the process; it does not preclude people attaining to faith, in history or now, but it is a test that people can fail. We are free to disagree, but we bear responsibility for the consequences of dissension, as much as for the choices we make through free and open debate. It is not the difference of opinion we should be concerned with, but how we make choices among and between such differences of opinion, how we select the best path among the divergent views. There is all the difference in the world between differences of opinion, without which and through which a consensus is formed, and dissension, which by definition denies the need or possibility of achieving consensus.

In conclusion, all believers are called on to 'spend out of what We have provided for you'. We have met this concept before. On the Day of Reckoning there will be 'no bargaining, nor friendship nor intercession'; each will have to answer for the choices and decisions they made. In the context of a discussion of the appointment of leaders and then of the endowment of apostles, it is quite clear that shifting responsibility to them will not do anyone any good. It is human beings who have interpreted, responded to or distorted and deformed the messages brought by apostles of God. It is human beings who have to be steadfast and determined in following the straight path of righteous deeds, whether well-led or not. It is, in the final analysis, not a question of leadership. What will be judged is the quality of individual commitment by each and every citizen to work to create a community of the middle way. Working together in consultation is not about being led, but about understanding and holding to values and principles, doing good deeds, spending our efforts and accepting individual accountability for our responsibility to make the world a better place.

23

AL-BAQARA

MAJESTY OF GOD AND FREEDOM OF RELIGION

255. *God. There is no God but He, the Living, the Everlasting. Neither slumber seizes Him nor sleep. To Him belongs all that is in the heavens and on earth. Who is there shall intercede with Him, save by His leave? He knows all that lies before them and what is after them. Nor can they grasp aught of His knowledge, except as He wills. His Throne extends over the heavens and the earth, and upholding them wearies Him not. He is the Most High, the Sublime.*

256. *There is no compulsion in religion: Truth stands out clear from Error: whoever rejects evil and believes in God has grasped the most trustworthy handhold, that never breaks, for God is All-hearing, All-knowing.*

257. *God is the Protector of the believers: He leads them from the depths of darkness into light. As for those who disbelieve, their patrons are idols that bring them out of light into the depths of darkness. These are the rightful owners of the Fire, they will abide therein forever.*

Here we come to the passage that for me is the heart and soul of the Qur'an. It begins with the verse that is second only to *al-Fatiha* in familiarity to Muslims. Known as *Ayat al Kursi*, the Throne verse, it was considered by classical commentators to be the most excellent verse in the Qur'an. It is a popular subject for calligraphy, and in a great diversity of calligraphic forms finds a place on display in millions of Muslim homes around the world. And yet it is the juxtaposition of *al Kursi* and the following verse that for me encapsulates the essence of the Islamic worldview.

Ayat al Kursi is the most beautiful statement of the power and majesty of the Almighty. It reveals God as the creative and sustaining force behind all existence, the Divine who is all-knowing and always aware, a ceaseless, unwearying presence conscious of each individual in all their activities: what we show as well as what we conceal, what has happened to us and what awaits us. Such power and majesty can only be made evident to human beings by God alone. It is only by God's will that we can come to know the Divine that is far beyond human consciousness or capability.

Knowledge is a crucial aspect of the Divine. And the emphasis throughout the Qur'an on God's knowledge is reflected again and again in the impetus this gives to the exercise of human intellect to understand and appreciate better both God's creation and the meaning and operation of God's guidance to humankind. The use of reason is essential to making the right decisions, making the right qualitative judgements on how to act in this world and how to distinguish right from wrong. The word *Kursi* means throne, but in Muslim thought and parlance it has become inseparable from the concept of knowledge. Knowledgeable and learned people are referred to as 'People of the Chair', and this is the origin of the professorial 'chair'. Many of the terms we associate with universities derive from Arabic, a legacy of the institution's origin in Muslim civilisation, from which it was borrowed wholesale by European society during the Middle Ages.

But what truly takes my breath away is what immediately follows this most ringing evocation of the Divine: 'let there be no compulsion in religion'. It is the most profound declarative statement in the Qur'an. It is not the business of any human being to coerce another in matters of faith or religion. The all-powerful gives us complete freedom to believe or not believe, to follow whatever religion we choose. The ability to attain to faith is innate in human nature, and the means to attain faith is provided by revelation. Only our willing, informed convincement is the true measure of God consciousness. By implication, for individuals or society to coerce people is to interfere with and arrogate to themselves authority over a relationship which can exist only between God and each individual soul.

What is being made clear, it seems to me, is that God is beyond any need or requirement. God does not need worshippers; it is human beings who need consciousness of God. Faith and religion, we are told, are based on recognising the distinction between truth and error; they are an exercise of reason and intellect, a work of knowledge as well as of spirit. Willing, informed and reasoned belief is laying hold of 'the most secure handhold that never breaks', a phrase I find the most liberating, empowering and comforting in the Qur'an.

Religion that is free from all coercion refers to belief in God as embodied in the verse of the Throne. The word for religion, and Islam's own self-description, is *deen*. As these verses make clear, *deen* is a way of knowing, being and doing, a way of life. What is more, this way of living, based on God consciousness, brings God near to us, it illuminates our lives.

Muslims frequently say that religion, their *deen*, is a total way of life. What this means is that just as belief in God is a free, informed choice, so the consequence of belief is about making choices about seeking what is best for oneself, one's family, for society, for the whole of humanity and the world, in all aspects and actions of daily life. And part of living one's *deen*, since we cannot live in splendid isolation, is seeking out and working for the free, willing collaboration of other people in the project of making the world the best possible place we can. A reflection of this is that the Arabic word for city, the concentration of human cohabitation, is *medina*, from the root *deen*. It was the new name given to Yathrib after Prophet Muhammad migrated there from Mecca and began to organise the new religion.

Community organised by consent of the governed, it seems to me, follows from the proposition of religion as a way of life embraced by the consent of free will. The distinctions that illuminate how to live are the values and principles revealed by God for human betterment, which we accept as a consequence of faith. In opting for the light we willingly commit ourselves to working for justice and equity, and put ourselves on the right path.

The word used in this passage for evil is quite interesting: *at-taghut*. The evil ones are those who exceed their legitimate limits, and arrogate powers, wealth and lordship that do not belong to them—leading to arrogance and worship of other things beside God. Evil is interfering with, distorting and turning to the wrong ends, the free choices of free individuals. There is little point in saying we have free will if we are not free to exercise the option to abide by the constraints of moral and ethical behaviour of our own volition. And of our own volition it is necessary to turn away from the excesses of intoxication with worldly wealth and power, from arrogance and indulgence, from naked consumerism, especially that which squanders, wastes and despoils the human spirit and the world in which we live. That is the light that leads us away from the darkness of ignorance and unconsidered, short-sighted judgements.

I also think it is significant in conjunction with the preceding passage and its discussion of leadership. God and God's Word, which we are free to follow or not, are the real source of leadership and authority. It is the task of freely consenting individuals to opt to follow this guidance. The task of remaining loyal to, debating, implementing, adapting and applying this guidance cannot be delegated to leaders, for that would be to denigrate the freedom we have been given. The task is to find the right balance, the appropriate form of social organisation where free individuals can, by their willing consent, cooperate with one another, whatever they believe or don't believe, to make the world a better place for all. This is the objective laid out in God's guidance and the most profound expression of worship and praise of the Almighty.

24

AL-BAQARA

ARGUING WITH GOD

258. *Are you not aware of him who argued with Abraham regarding his Lord, because God had granted him kingship? Abraham said: 'My Lord is He who gives life and causes death.' He answered: 'I grant life and deal death.' Said Abraham: 'God causes the sun to rise from the East; cause it then to rise from the West.' Then the unbeliever was dumbfounded. God guides not the tyrants.*

259. *Or else like the man who passed by a town, in ruins with its roofs caved in. He said: 'How will God bring this back to life, after its death?' God caused him to die for a hundred years, then resurrected him. God said: 'How long did you remain thus?' The man replied: 'A day or part of a day.' God said: 'No, you remained thus a hundred years; but look at your food and drink; they show no signs of age; and look at your donkey: Thus We shall make you a symbol to humankind. And look at the bones, how We bring them together and clothe them with flesh.' So when this was made clear to him, the man said: 'I know that God has the power to will anything.'*

260. *Remember when Abraham said: 'My Lord! Show me how You give life to the dead.' God said: 'Do you not then believe?' Abraham said: 'Yes, but so that my heart can be at peace.' God said: 'Take four birds, and teach them to obey you; then place a part of them on each hill, then call them. They will come flying to you. Then know that God is Almighty, Wise.'*

At first glance these stories seem unclear. And yet these verses deal with the most central issues of religion and the most enduring subject of human fascination. Belief in a Creator is to accept not only that life and death exist, but that there is a power beyond the natural processes of which we are aware. It not only created life and death as we know them, but can also bring about life after death. The trouble is the existence of life after death is beyond human perception and direct knowledge. Nevertheless, being human, we have inordinate curiosity, an infinite capacity to speculate, theorise and look for proof. There is even the temptation to think that the knowledge we can accumulate has, or will eventually enable us to have, power comparable to that of the Creator. There is no greater mystery in our existence than having faith in the Hereafter. So, perhaps, to expect the explanation to be simple would seem over optimistic.

I think the Qur'an is making us aware of distinctions, as so often, of different categories and orders of things we need to differentiate if we are to make sense of faith as a way of living. There are a couple of points to note here. First, the words used for life and death, *hayat* and *maut*, are as applicable to individuals as to societies, nations and civilisations, and to flora and fauna. Second, the parables are not literal; they have a visionary import. The Qur'an lets its readers engage their minds and imagination to decipher whether the incident being described is literal or a vision: the context, the nature of the incident and references to history guide us towards developing an understanding of their meaning.

The debate between Abraham and the king sets out the distinction between earthly and divine power, and introduces the concept of *zulm*, which means wrong, but is particularly associated with wrong in the sense of tyranny and corruption. This argument with the king refers us back to the subject of leadership, the theme running through the preceding passages. Abraham makes a statement of belief: 'My Sustainer is He who grants life and deals death.' In response the king makes a statement of fact: 'I too grant life and deal death.' What is the distinction here? Certainly, kings, emperors and governments command the power of life and death over people. They can empower society to flourish, or they can cause devastation through war. They can act according to law, even according to God's guidance, or they can bend the law, moral or human, to serve their will and ends. They can ensure that people get the resources they need to sustain life, or they can misappropriate or withhold these resources. But however much power an earthly ruler has, it is not the creative power of the Almighty, the power to call the universe into existence, to cause the laws of nature to operate and to sustain them endlessly without effort, as explained in the verse of the Throne.

Ultimately, all earthly powers are subservient to and derivative from the creative power of the Almighty. And the point of understanding this distinction is that kings, emperors and governments are just as much in need of God consciousness, of abiding by the limits and balance of God's guidance, as any individual. Recognising the limits of their power, recognising humility before the creative, sustaining power of God and God's ultimate judgement over all human beings is as necessary to kings as to paupers. No accumulation of and command over earthly power, power over nations and their people, exonerates or relieves rulers from responsibility if they do wrong and are guilty of *zulm*.

It is not only rulers who have to use their judgement. Citizens too have the right to judge how rulers use their power, for as we have seen in so many previous passages everyone has a duty to oppose and seek to eradicate the misuse of power, the tyranny of oppression and persecution which is a demonstration of earthly power over life and death.

The commentators have suggested that the king arguing with Abraham is Nimrod, an ancient king, son of Kanan, the arrogant and presumptuous ruler who built the Tower of Babel. His people would come to him to get food; and he would ask: 'Who is your Lord?' To get food, they had to reply: 'You are.' Nimrod was a sun-worshipper. Hence Abraham's argument: if he had control over life and death then he could also control his deity, the sun, and make it rise from the West. Nimrod then becomes 'dumbfounded' because he realises that his assertion is opposed to his own belief. Yet, as with many other characters referred to in the Qur'an, the identity of the king is not specified. Essentially it is not who he is but the attitudes he typifies that are important. It is the misguided sense of power and mastery that is significant. In a world suffused with God consciousness, such vainglory has no place, indeed has to be opposed. Abraham is in fact speaking truth to power, a duty incumbent on all who believe.

The next section of this passage concerns what might be described as the rise and fall of empires. This is an idea that occurs frequently throughout the Qur'an. References to the succession of earthly powers, which flourish, hold sway and then come to naught, are used as important insights. In this instance, a man passes by the ruins of a town. He puts me in mind of the tourists who visit the ruins of Pompeii, or some other ancient site. The man asks that most human of questions: if all that was so solid, so impressive an expression of power and mastery, can so visibly crumble and pass into ruin: 'How could God bring all this back to life after its death?' Commentators point out that this is similar to the story of Prophet Ezekiel as related in Ezekiel 37:1–11, where it is presented as a vision.

The parable given in answer is not merely that God, the Creator of all things, including all the laws of nature, can will whatever He chooses. It is also a warning about the delusion of time. We perceive time as well as the power of kings and empires, cities and civilisations in earthly terms, the terms of our own mortality, which gives us an illusion of permanence. Our perception is constrained by the limitations of human experience. God deals in eternals, in dimensions beyond our human perception. The promise of the Hereafter, of returning to life after death, is not about life as we know it here and now. The God who created the laws of nature could suspend them. But learning how to live with and within the normal workings of the laws of nature, rather than asking for them to be suspended, is the real test of faith; just as it is our preparation for life in another dimension, the life after death.

And so we return to Abraham, who at the beginning of the passage made the statement of belief: 'My Sustainer is He who grants life and deals death.' Clearly, as a Prophet of God, Abraham was a believer. Yet even he wants incontrovertible proof. So he argues with God: 'My Lord,' he says, 'show me how You give life to the dead.' God retorts: 'Do you not believe?' 'Yes,' he replies, 'but just to put my heart at rest.' So even though he believes, Abraham still has a nagging doubt in his heart: he wants knowledge that can be proved. I find the distinction here fascinating: between knowing as belief and knowing as provable knowledge.

The classical commentators found this verse to be the most puzzling in all of the Qur'an. Most suggest that the birds have to be cut up, and their pieces placed separately on hilltops, if they are to rise from the dead. I think it has nothing to do with cutting up the birds. I see it in a less perplexing way: on one level it simply confirms the possibility of doubt, which as we have seen is an important theme running through *sura Al-Baqara*. If even a prophet can doubt and question God, it is little wonder that ordinary human beings do so too. The answer to Abraham's question comes as a parable. I take the parable in its simplest meaning: birds can be trained—like homing pigeons—to return to their master. What is the Qur'an but a training manual for human nature, a way to ensure we return to our Master and Maker? As human beings, we learn how the laws of nature operate and use this knowledge to our benefit and advantage. But we too are part of the laws of nature; faith is a capacity of our created human nature, but it is also a capacity that must be trained and exercised to grow strong and fulfil its potential. The word used for birds in this passage, *tair*, has other meanings: the cause of good and evil, the source of misery and happiness, the origin of rise and fall. So the birds, like the birds in Hitchcock's famous film of that name, are complex creatures signifying a number of different ideas.

Coming as it does after the most exalted expression of the power and majesty of the Almighty, and the declaration of complete human freedom to believe or not to believe, there is another significance to be drawn from this passage. The freedom to believe is also the freedom to enquire, ask questions, to doubt and to think our way through the most difficult and enduring of earthly problems.

25

AL-BAQARA

CHARITY AND USURY

261. *The likeness of those who spend their wealth in the cause of God is like a grain of corn which brought forth seven ears, in each ear a hundred grains. God multiplies his bounty to whom He pleases: and God is Infinite, All-knowing.*

262. *Those who spend their wealth in the cause of God, and do not follow up what they spent with reminders of their generosity or causing offence, shall have their reward with their Lord. No fear shall fall upon them, neither shall they grieve.*

263. *Kind words and forgiveness are better than charity followed by hurt. God is All-sufficient, All-forbearing.*

264. *O you who believe! Render not vain your alms-giving by stressing your own benevolence and causing offence, like one who spends his wealth in order to flaunt it before people, but believes neither in God nor the Last Day. His likeness is to a boulder with a little earth upon it: a downpour strikes it leaving it hard and bare. Such people can do nothing with what they have earned. God guides not those who are impious.*

265. *But the likeness of those who spend their wealth, desiring the pleasure of God and to strengthen their souls, is as a garden on high fertile ground. A downpour strikes it and it produces double its yield; if not a downpour, then soft rain. God sees full well all that you do.*

266. *Would any of you wish to have a garden with date-palms and vines beneath which rivers flow, and in which are all kinds of fruit, and then be overtaken by old age, and with only weak children—that it should be caught in a fiery whirlwind, and burnt up? Thus does God make clear His signs to you; that you may reflect.*

267. *O you who believe, spend of the good things which you have earned, and from what We brought forth from the earth for your benefit. Do not give in alms the inferior*

portion thereof, which you yourselves would not accept except with closed eyes. And know that God is All-sufficient, All-praiseworthy.

268. *Satan promises you poverty and commands you to commit sin. God promises you His forgiveness and bounties. And God is Infinite, All-knowing.*

269. *He grants wisdom to whomsoever He wills; and whoever is granted wisdom has indeed been granted wealth abundant; but none remember except those with understanding.*

270. *And whatever you spend on others, whatever vow you take, God knows it. But the unjust have no helpers.*

271. *If you make public your free gifts, it is well. But if you conceal them and deliver them to the poor, that would be best for you, and will atone for some of your ill deeds. And God is well acquainted with all that you do.*

272. *It is not required of you (O Messenger) to make people follow the right path. It is God, rather, who guides whomsoever He wills. And whatever of good you may spend on others is for your own good, when it is spent seeking the Countenance of God. Whatever good you spend shall be rendered back to you, and you shall not be wronged.*

273. *It should go to the poor, those who are constrained in God's cause and cannot move about in the land; an ignorant person would think them rich because of their self-restraint. You shall know them by their mark: they do not beg from people with importunity. And whatever good you spend, God knows it well.*

274. *Those who spend their wealth by night and by day, in secret and in public, shall have their reward with their Lord. No fear shall fall upon them, neither shall they grieve.*

275. *Those who gorge themselves on usury behave as one whom Satan has confounded with his touch. They say: 'Buying and selling is but a kind of usury.' But God has permitted trade and forbidden usury. Hence, whoever becomes aware of God's admonition and thereupon desists shall keep his past profits; and his affair is up to God. But those who relapse, they are destined for the Fire, therein to abide forever.*

276. *God has blighted usury and blessed free giving with manifold increase. God loves not the impious lawbreaker.*

277. *Those who believe, do good works, perform their prayers and pay the poor due shall have their reward with their Lord. No fear shall fall upon them, neither shall they grieve.*

278. *O you who believe, fear God and abandon what remains of usury, if you are true believers.*

279. *If you do not, be forewarned of conflict with God and His Messenger. If you repent, you shall keep the capital of your wealth, neither wronging nor wronged.*

280. *If a debtor is in difficulties, let there be respite until a time of ease. But if you remit [the debt] by way of charity, it would be better for you, if only you knew.*

281. *Fear a Day in which you shall return to God, when each soul shall be paid back that which it has earned, and they shall not be wronged.*

Once again the Qur'an turns from the sublime and rarefied questions of faith to the utterly practical and mundane. This passage expands on the necessary requirements to effect communal transformation. It focuses on two agents of social change, one positive and one negative: charity and usury. And in the aftermath of a global economic boom and spectacular bust, it has strong contemporary relevance.

The Qur'an is concerned that we understand the nature and purpose of charity: there are right and wrong ways in which it can be dispensed. For believers, it is an 'affirmation of their own faith'. Charity is accepting an obligation towards and responsibility for the living conditions of our fellow citizens, our fellow human beings. The most fundamental basis of the Qur'anic vision is that we cannot be good in isolation. As demonstrated in so many contexts in *sura Al-Baqara*, the real affirmation of faith is to appreciate the common humanity of all people and work to improve life for everyone. This improvement must be achieved by respecting, preserving and uplifting their human dignity. The objective of charity is to create a world of justice and equity, of opportunity for all. Poverty is a pernicious condition which erodes human dignity and blights human potential. It is the duty of believers to intervene and work to eradicate this blight.

The entire thrust of the etiquette of charity set out in this passage is that it must operate to undermine, rather than emphasise, the divisions in society. Charity should not highlight the distinctions between haves and have nots; it should be conducted not just to eradicate those differences but by submerging and ignoring those distinctions. This is achieved as much through how charity is delivered as in the effects that giving has on the lives of its recipients. The Qur'an suggests something very profound: charity should consist of the best we have to give, not the kind of things we would ourselves disdain to possess. Charity is not about giving away our cast-offs; it is not about a paternalistic attitude that looks down on those in need and suggests that second best is good enough for the poor; charity is not about hand me downs: it is offering a helping hand up.

Giving in charity is distinct from *zakat*, the obligatory poor due, a tax payable by all Muslims on an annual basis. *Zakat* is one of the pillars of Islam and it creates a central communal fund designed to be used for specific social welfare purposes. These verses make clear that paying *zakat* is not the end of our obligation and responsibility to others. Wherever need endures, so too does the obligation to do whatever is in our power by distributing and sharing, 'spending' the good things we have been given.

While giving in charity is necessary to achieve the objective of the Qur'an— the betterment of the poor, of society and humanity as a whole—it has some major pitfalls. Charity must not become a vanity project. It must not merely serve to illustrate how much more some people have than others. A harsh word can undermine all the good that charity may bring: 'kind words and forgiveness are better than charity followed by hurt' (v.263), the kind of hurtful words that humiliate those in need by making them feel inadequate because they are poor. Likewise, charity distributed to emphasise one's benevolence defeats its purpose, which is improving the understanding and fellow-feeling between those who give and those who receive.

Charity is not given to gain favours of others, to acquire status in society, or to draw attention to oneself, 'to be seen by men': all of which are rather common in contemporary society. I cannot argue with the objective of Band Aid, Comic Relief and Pudsey Bear in his annual events, but shouldn't we question whether they have become a convention that depends on drawing attention to our giving, on suggesting that only if we get fun and entertainment and a pat on the back for our efforts are we prepared to give to those in need? Are we really doing the right thing in encouraging children to go from door to door rustling up sponsorship so that they can give money to charity? Is that how we should teach the real etiquette of charity to the next generation? Such strategies to raise charitable donations are part of a world that fears compassion fatigue. While there is nothing wrong in giving 'charity openly', provided it is done in the right way, the most important lesson is that there never should or can be a case for compassion fatigue. Charity is solely to earn God's pleasure, whose Compassion is Infinite; our duty is to try and mirror this unending compassion, on which we depend, in all activities including charity. It is an act of worship that connects us directly to God. It remains a duty, a constant obligation until such time as we eradicate poverty and the causes of poverty, and need and the causes of need. It is a double imperative: on the one hand, to appreciate its true meaning; and on the other hand, to operate it in an appropriate manner to serve the real interests of its recipients, not our assessment of what is good enough for them.

I love the similes used in this passage. We have 'grains of corn', 'garden on a hill', arable land that benefits from rainfall, and rocky land that cannot grow anything. The similes introduce a new kind of logic: where things increase by subtraction. So spending one's wealth to support humanity and humane causes is like 'grains of corn that produce seven ears, each bearing a hundred grains' (v.261). Thus, one adds to one's wealth by actually subtracting from it. If you are true to the technique of giving, you 'double' your yield, your reward is in Heaven and here in this world, like a garden on a hill that benefits from a rainfall. But if you do not follow the basic rules for giving, then you are 'like a rock with earth on it: heavy rain falls and leaves it completely bare' (v.264): it is in fact not charity at all but a pretentious act designed to gain fame and fortune, perhaps increase your sales or commodity value, and fill column inches in newspapers and slots on television. The idea being conveyed here is that genuine charity, given generously, constantly and continuously, 'by night and by day, in private and in public' (274), will not make you poor but rich. This is why in this passage we are told no less than three times that 'those who spend their wealth in God's causes' should have confidence in their actions: there is 'no fear for them, nor will they grieve' (v.274). It will make the whole of humanity richer by enabling a more equitable and balanced world. The richness implied is social as well as personal and spiritual.

But what are 'God's causes'? The 'needy' are described as 'wholly occupied in God's way and cannot travel in the land (for trade)' (v.273). 'God's way' here does not mean engagement solely in what are conventionally seen as religious activities. Rather, it means serving, and providing services for, humanity at large: working for the betterment of society, seeking socially beneficial knowledge, researching diseases to fight illness, building schools and hospitals, helping refugees and displaced people, providing support to victims of natural disasters or man's inhumanity to man, and fighting injustice, inequity and social ills. Such 'needy' individuals and social institutions, too preoccupied with serving humanity, cannot engage in economic activities, but need constant and continuous support from the believers to survive and flourish. When the Qur'an talks about giving 'charity openly', it seems to me it is referring to subscriptions for works of public utility, for the advancement of social and public welfare.

And I would suggest that genuine charity, as described here, means disowning the idea that the rich somehow know more and know better than those in need. I am thinking particularly about the kind of attitudes associated with foreign aid, which often creates dependence rather than self-reliance, which gives technology and services that enable donor nations to make a net profit on the deal, or which fail to empower the indigenous knowledge and skills of the recipients [21].

The call to give to charity, emphasised again and again in this passage, can be seen as the Qur'an's way of urging Muslims to establish pragmatic and perpetual institutions for the social transformation of society. Across the Muslim world, such institutions were known as *waqfs*, 'pious foundations'. Muslims seeking spiritual advancement would leave a legacy in the form of property or a plot of land as a trust in perpetuity to be used for the benefit of humanity. The individual establishing the *waqf* would specify its purpose clearly, and appoint a legally responsible person or group to carry out its function with knowledge and experience. Such trusts supported universities and hospitals, scholarship and learning, and funded research and travel. As George Makdisi shows in his detailed study, *The Rise of Colleges* [22], *waqfs* played a vital part in enabling the flourishing of science and civilisation in the classical era of Muslim civilisation.

Contemporary Muslims, I believe, have forgotten the intellectual, educational, scientific and cultural dimensions of charity. Charity amongst Muslims is now associated almost solely with building mosques and responding to natural disasters. We need to recover the scope, imagination and creativity these verses imply in ways relevant to the extent of need in contemporary society at home and abroad.

The passage moves from discussing charity to usury, from an institution that builds community and society to one that blights and destroys social cohesion; from the broad basis of human sympathy to the annihilation of all sympathetic human affections. Islam is by no means unique in seeing usury in a negative light. It is regarded as evil in most religions and religious philosophies. In *The Divine Comedy*, Dante, who has a particular aversion to Islam and its Prophet, places usurers in the inner ring of the seventh circle of hell, below even suicides [23]. Indeed, it is heartening in the aftermath of the global economic crisis to see the religious leaders from among Jews, Christians and Muslims campaigning together, on the basis of their common opposition to usury, for amendment to the problems of the culture of debt.

The Qur'an distinguishes between trade and usury. The essential difference has to do with sharing mutual risk. Historically, this meant developing distinctive forms of contractual relationships and instruments for funding trade, most of which ended up being borrowed from Europe. In trade, it meant that those with capital—the bankers and investors or capitalists, for short—shared the risk of making a loss along with the hope of making a profit. Lending money on usury insulates the capitalist from risk. In event of a loss, the entire burden is borne by the borrower, the one who uses his or her physical and intellectual labour to begin a new undertaking. The lender merely sits back and counts the profit; the debt must be repaid irrespective of whether the enterprise suffers an actual loss. Hence trading and usury are distinct. Trade has the potential to increase the wealth of a society, brings peoples and cultures together; usury makes the rich richer. And, which is worse, it can trap people and states in perpetual debt. It divides society and increases the hardship of those most in need: it undermines the moderation and strong sense of social justice of 'the middle community' and is diametrically opposed to the law of equity. As such, usury is a tool of oppression.

The emphasis on charity suggests that the Qur'an is unambiguously on the side of the poor. It does not want the rich to grow richer at the expense of the poor by sinking them in greater misery, a direct product of usury. This, however, is not just an issue of social and economic justice but also of morality. Usury's worse effects are on our moral well-being: it generates a love of wealth, makes us selfish, and leads us to think, like Gordan Gekko in the film *Wall Street*, that 'Greed is Good'. Not surprisingly, the Qur'an takes an unequivocal stand against usury, and compares those who devour usury to those touched by the devil, which in this case stands for Mammon: 'those who take usury will rise up on the Day of Resurrection like someone tormented by Satan's touch' (v.275). There are echoes here of the story of Adam and his wife being led by the arrogant Iblis to transgress limits and boundaries of ethical behaviour.

The Qur'anic term for usury is *riba*. The Hans Wehr *A Dictionary of Modern Written Arabic*, widely regarded as a standard work, translates *riba* as 'interest' or 'usurious interest' [24]. But the term, which originates from the verb *r-b-a*, also means 'to grow, to exceed', to add, to swell, to add an excess over and above the necessary. *Riba*, as Asad notes, contains the idea of 'the exploitation of the economically weak by the strong and resourceful' [25]. Given that the Qur'an sees oppression as a prime sin, I would suggest that *riba* is not just about interest, but also about all forms of economic exploitation of the poor: such as disproportion in the amount of tax paid by the poor, as well as the disproportionate allocation of taxpayers' money. Real equity is not spending the same on everyone, but sufficient according to need. Those who are poor should command sufficient allocation to tackle the problem of poor schools, and hence the lack of access to educational opportunities. The same goes for health provisions, cultural marginalisation and all those things that end up victimising the poor, simply because they are poor.

The 'usury verses' (275–82) were amongst the last verses of the Qur'an to be revealed. The Prophet died soon afterwards, and his companions could not question him about the extensive meaning of *riba*. Classical commentators, such as ibn Kathir (1301–73), who relied extensively on the sayings of the Prophet and his companions' interpretations of the Qur'an, thus had serious problems both in understanding and explaining these verses. This, I think, is a blessing in disguise. Economic exploitation is like plasma: it is difficult to contain, morphs into any shape and size, and devours anything in its path. It takes different forms in different societies, depending on their principal modes of production and technological status.

So the nature of *riba*, in its fullest sense of economic exploitation, cannot be delineated once and for all. As Asad rightly notes, 'our answers must necessarily vary in accordance with the changes to which man's social and technological development—and, thus, economic development—is subject' [26]. Hence, while the Qur'anic condemnation of the concept and practice of *riba* is unequivocal and final, every successive Muslim generation is faced with the challenge of giving new dimensions and fresh economic meaning to this term which, for want of a better word, may be rendered as 'usury'.

We live in a time beset by the consequences of economic disasters. As we contemplate the results of subprime mortgages; the escalation in house prices which keeps increasing numbers of even moderately affluent people off the housing ladder; our economy fuelled by an increasing debt burden on everyone; derivative trading that seeks to make money out of mis-selling to the poorest; increasing disparities between the pay of private employers and even the top management of public bodies as against the rest of the workforce; the billions paid in bonuses to those who manipulate the stock market to make money from money: there is pertinent pause for thought in this passage. Untrammelled consumerism has brought us a world of stark contrasts as well as an increasing gap between rich and poor. I see this passage as speaking directly to contemporary concerns.

Therefore, we need to tease out the general principles established in this passage which can steer us *away* from the path of *riba*. We return to the similes of 'grains of corn', arable land and the garden. Making money from money is an arid exercise: in the long run it brings little benefit to a society as a whole, and is like a rocky land where 'rain falls and leaves it completely bare'. Just as seed cast on the ground unaccompanied by labour or rain would not grow, so expenditure and investment of money has to be accompanied by physical or intellectual labour to produce wealth that benefits all. Credit and debt are a scourge: they are like 'a garden of palms and vines' that is 'struck by a fiery whirlwind and struck down' (v.266), leaving you in your old age feeble and your offspring destitute. Those who are suffering from a debt-burden, individuals and states, are to be helped; and where possible their debts have to be written off as an act of charity (280). And, just as a tree should not continue growing beyond a certain point, lest it ends up devouring and destroying the rest of the garden, so individuals and societies cannot continue to grow economically without destroying the very society and environment that sustain them. The moderation that is the characteristic of the 'middle community' must also be reflected in its economic activities. The Qur'an urges Muslims to be neither miserly nor extravagant: 'Do not be tight-fisted, nor so open-ended that you end up blamed and overwhelmed with regret' (17:29).

Ultimately, the Qur'an argues, we are all dependent upon God's bounty. How we 'use' or 'spend' is crucial to making society and all its citizens 'prosper' and flourish, which are the criteria on which we will all be judged. None of us can totally insure ourselves against risk, which comes in multiple forms, because none of us can foresee the future. What cannot be avoided should therefore be shared; that is the law of equity. Usury is about making those that have proof against loss insulated from the risks and perils they unfairly push onto others. Sharing risk is a way of recognising the contribution of both labour and capital in making a better society. Every soul has to be paid in full for the toil and trouble of its physical or intellectual labour, as much in the here and now as it will be in the Hereafter. This is the basis of the distributive outlook we have discussed previously.

I know of no society that has, as yet, got the balance right. However, I do think that in this passage we are given the means to devise objective tests that should be employed to interrogate the ways of the world. What the Qur'an presents by overlaying and interlacing the spiritual with the mundane is a guidebook, an operator's manual for social transformation, the qualitative reform that has to be sought as much today as at the time of revelation.

26

AL-BAQARA

WITNESS

282. *O you who believe, When you give or take credit among yourselves for a stated term, write it down. Let a scribe write down in your presence, in all fairness. Let no scribe refuse to write as God has taught him. So, let him write and let the debtor dictate. Let him fear God, and let him not diminish a jot from it. If the debtor is feeble-minded, weak, or is unable to dictate, let his guardian dictate in all fairness. Summon two witnesses from among your men. If two men are not at hand, then a man and two women, of such as you approve as witnesses, so that if one forgets, the other can remind her. Nor should witnesses be reluctant if summoned. And do not be reluctant to write it down, whether small or large, up to its set term, for this is fairer in God's sight, more reliable as evidence, and more likely to prevent doubts. However, if it concerns an immediate commercial deal that you transact among yourselves, no blame attaches to you if you do not write it down. And have witnesses whenever you trade with one another, but neither scribe nor witness must suffer harm. If you do them harm, this would be an offence on your part. And remain conscious of God who teaches you; and God has full knowledge of everything.*

283. *If you are on a journey, and do not find a scribe, let there be a surety handed over. If you trust one another, let the trustee fulfil his trust, and let him fear God, his Lord. And do not conceal evidence; whoever conceals it, his heart is tainted with sin. God knows full well all that you do.*

At first sight this passage would seem to be a logical part of the previous discussion on charity and usury. Certainly, it is the Qur'an at its most practical. I take it as a separate passage, mainly because of the interpretation it has received and the general misconstruction and controversy attributed to it.

How, after all we have just found out about applying rules of equity and fairness, of building inclusiveness and fellow feeling in pragmatic ways, could the Qur'an turn around and make the veracity of women half that of men? It is clear to me, and any reasoned reading, that that is precisely not what is being said. Such a conclusion would defy what the Qur'an consistently argues elsewhere, and is testimony to the ease with which misogyny and patriarchal prejudice has been read into the text to turn meaning on its head.

During the time of the Prophet Muhammad, Arabia was an illiterate society; reading and writing were not the norm. In this passage, the Qur'an continues the theme of social transformation with the emphasis now on a cultural shift from an oral society to a literate one. The theme of usury, concerned with the ethics of lending and borrowing money, naturally leads us, in the longest verse in the Qur'an (282), to the subject of contracts. Once again, the objective is to enshrine the principles of justice and equity through mechanisms for transparency and openness that promote fair dealing, honesty and harmony while addressing questions of the imbalance of power between participants in business deals. We have to notice not merely the detail, but the consistency of the underlying principles that order the diverse aspects of human activity mentioned in the Qur'an.

The believers are advised to write down any business arrangements they contract, rather than simply rely on memory as was normally the case in seventh-century Arabia. Those who could not read or write are urged to use the services of a professional scribe. On the whole, writing is emphasised as a more exact and clear way of keeping records: it is 'more equitable in God's eyes, more reliable as testimony, and more likely to prevent doubts arising between you'.

It is interesting to note that it is not the lender but the borrower who is asked to dictate the contract: 'let the debtor dictate'. I think this is to balance the power equation between the lender and the borrower. The lender cannot make a unilateral contract, writing down whatever he wishes. It must be the borrower who makes the reliable written statement of what has been agreed in the contract. The borrower is urged to be honest and 'fear God'.

It is possible that a borrower may not be in a position to dictate the contract or to be able to negotiate the contract justly. The word translated by Haleem as 'feeble-minded' is rendered by Yusuf Ali as 'mentally deficient'; but it has no such meaning: political correctness notwithstanding, it is a sign of our changing attitudes, and our awareness of the connection between language and equality, that no one would nowadays use such a term [27]. The allusion here is to someone who is too young or too old, and hence may find the transaction or terms of contract difficult to understand. These people need the help of a guardian, who must also be honest and fair in writing up the contract. In the period when these verses were revealed, such people would most likely be orphans who had to rely on their guardians to ensure their property and other inheritance rights were justly and contractually protected.

However, just writing down the contract is not good enough. The contract has to be witnessed. And here we come to one of the most controversial passages in the Qur'an.

The Qur'an suggests that witnesses should be 'two men', or failing that 'one man and two women'. But these are not just any witnesses; they come from 'those you approve as witnesses'. So those who act as witnesses have to satisfy the parties engaged in transaction, and these parties themselves reflect the norms and values of the society from which they come.

Much has been made of this section of verse 282; it has been interpreted to mean 'two women equal one man'. On the basis of this interpretation, classical as well as modern commentators have argued that women lack common sense, they are less reliable, and indeed somewhat inferior to men. Those who take such a position often justify their claim by citing dubious, and often fabricated *Hadith*, or sayings of the Prophet Muhammad: sayings which are in stark contrast to the overwhelming body of evidence in *Hadith* and the biographies of the Prophet, which show the recipient of God's revelation as a man who treated his wives and other women with the utmost respect, and operated and encouraged the social equivalence of men and women explicit and implicit in the Qur'an. It is common for what are supposedly more pious and puritan segments of Muslim societies, including traditional scholars and thinkers, to have no compunction in asserting openly that women are feeble-minded, irrational and timid [28]. Some other Muslim groups even invoke science to justify their claims about the inferiority of women. It is safe to say that misogyny rules. This is an inversion of the meaning in the Qur'an, and thus a serious perversion of Islam.

However, it is by no means a failing exclusive to Muslim society. The nonsense talked by so-called Muslim scholars is exactly the language and terms that were used for centuries in Western society. Derived initially from the Bible, this mindset led to women being viewed as chattels, first of their fathers and then their husbands. Exactly such rhetoric was used in the long campaign to secure voting rights for women in Western nations. There are many Muslim countries today where women have the vote, indeed Muslim countries led rather than followed in producing women prime ministers. There are however notable exceptions. It is sadly the case that the antiquated rhetoric endures regardless of the strides that Muslim women have made in education, the professions, even politics. It endures from the blinkered addiction to traditional interpretation. Traditional interpretation on the subject of women is not only wholly offensive in its preservation of failings and errors, it is also schizophrenic. Those selfsame religious scholars who fulminate about the irrational and feeble-minded character of women are just as likely, with a straight face and no hint of reflection, to turn around and extol the excellence and superiority of the status, role and rights that Islam has granted to women.

The obvious point to note is that this verse categorically does not say that women lack common sense, or are feeble-minded or inferior in any way. The issue of two women witnesses relates specifically to commercial transactions. And we have to consider the context in which such transactions would occur in the patriarchal society of seventh-century Arabia. Furthermore, it must be clear from the context of the principle the Qur'an is putting forth that this is not a statement on the status of women. The emphasis in this verse is on justice, where the debtors, guardians, the scribes as well as the witnesses are all urged to act justly, to play their part in securing the social transformation that is required to bring society to a higher moral condition.

In this verse the context is not just important—it is all there is! We have already seen that women in Arabian society did not have a great deal of free will, and did not play an important part in public life. Of course, there were exceptions: the most notable being Khadijah, the first wife of the Prophet, who persuaded him to go on a business trip on her behalf—a prelude to their romance and eventual marriage. But on the whole they were not involved in financial transactions, and lacked experience in this regard. Moreover, women tended to stay in their own domains and did not go out to bazaars and markets, mosques and courts, as often and commonly as men. So, the very least we can say is that this advice relates to a specific society in a particular period. The second woman is there to support the first, and help her out if needed: 'remind her'. The two encourage each other to come forward to do their public duty, that is to be active participants in creating a more just and equitable society. And if one of the female witnesses is coerced, manipulated or otherwise forced to change her testimony by some unscrupulous male, not an unlikely event in the kind of society we are dealing with, the two could support each other and stand firm.

The requirement of two female witnesses is not something to be projected forward. It is a backward glance to the circumstances of the society the Qur'an seeks to change, a means by which it can transform itself. Its continued relevance occurs because many Muslim societies today still need to make just the same transformation. Under such conditions, the Qur'an says that if you cannot find two satisfactory male witnesses, then have one satisfactory male and two satisfactory female witnesses. But an explicit reason is given for this provision: 'if one of the two women should forget the other can remind her'. Now, the point about a specific reason is that it can change with changing times and circumstances. That's why we cannot take a provision such as this as a general rule or command. General rules in the Qur'an are simply stated as fact, as for example: 'there is no compulsion in religion' (256). But context-specific verses tend to have conditions or reasons attached.

We also need to see this verse in relation to what the Qur'an says elsewhere. As a whole, the Qur'an does not locate spirituality, agency, morality, or individuality in gender. On the contrary, it insists on the equality of humanity, men and women, races and nationalities, colour and cultures; as such, it often mentions men and women in parallel to emphasise explicitly their ontological equality: 'For men and women who are devoted to God—believing men and believing women, obedient men and obedient women, truthful men and truthful women, patient men and patient women, humble men and humble women, charitable men and charitable women, men who fast and women who fast, men who protect their chastity and women who protect their chastity, and men who remember God frequently and women who remember God frequently—God has prepared forgiveness and a rich reward' (33:35).

There is another, equally important, reason why it is absurd even to think, let alone claim, that this verse is suggesting that 'two women equal one man'. When it comes to witnesses, the Qur'an suggests that different situations require different kinds of witnesses. When making a bequest, for example, any two men will do (5:106). For witnessing a divorce, two witnesses, male or female, are acceptable (65:2). If a husband accuses his wife of cheating, then her testimony rules over his (if this was turned into a general ruling, then women would be superior to men!) (24:6). And if a husband wants to take things further, then he has to produce four eye witnesses to justify his claim (24:4).

A main purpose of the emphasis on different kinds of witnesses is to encourage the believers to reflect on the nature of evidence. What constitutes reliable evidence? Whom can you trust? The Qur'an suggests one should examine the context of each particular situation and then decide who would make a viable witness: what kind of experience is needed, and how many witnesses one would need to confirm the validity of a particular event. The witnesses themselves have a serious burden to bear: they cannot conceal their testimony; they are required to come forward unhesitatingly when needed and be just and truthful in their testimony. They have to bear witness for the sake of God, even though it may be against themselves, their parents or relatives (4:135).

What the Qur'an seeks, I think, is to lay the foundations of a literate, reflexive society. If you have to write things down then you have to learn to read and write—the availability of scribes notwithstanding. If you have to examine the context of each situation, then you have to think seriously not just about what constitutes evidence but also about your society as a whole. The 'middle community' cannot function on rumours and heresy; it seeks to be reasonable, to use reason and work with thorough and viable evidence in its daily economic, social and political transactions.

The 'problem of women', so evident in Muslim societies, has nothing to do with the Qur'an: it is a problem created by Muslims in history which draws on a tradition of interpretation. Classical commentators, as products of their age, were often misogynists. They came from cultures which had a long tradition of seclusion of women, as well as the veiling and subordination of women, all of which they managed to integrate into their reading and interpretation of the Qur'an. Traditional modernists have uncritically followed in their footsteps, both out of respect and as an excuse for confirming their own prejudices. Modern history has also created conditions in Muslim societies that have made them more conservative than earlier eras. In the face of the challenges of radical change, sections of Muslim society have sought to turn back the clock rather than think forward according to the principles of the Qur'an. The prevailing traditionalism, based on narrow, literal and out-of-context reading of the Qur'an, is responsible for the plight of women in Muslim societies—and it is the main hurdle to the progressive change that the Qur'an itself seeks.

This traditionalism has been devised and elaborated without the voice of Muslim women scholars. It is to the growing ranks of learned sisters in Islam that we must look to balance our understanding. Without women's voices and women's readings, we can have no truly inclusive contemporary interpretation of the Qur'an's meaning. Without listening to 'the believing women' we cannot transcend the hypocrisy and unreasonable nonsense put out by so many traditionalists to the detriment of Muslim society and civilisation as a whole.

27

AL-BAQARA

PRAYER

284. *To God belongs all that is in the heavens and all that is on earth. Whether you reveal what lies in your souls or whether you conceal it, God will call you to account for it, forgiving whom He wills, and punishing whomever He wills, for God has the power to will anything.*

285. *The Messenger believes in that which has been revealed to him from his Lord, as do the believers. All believe in God, His angels, His books, and His apostles making no distinction between any of His messengers. They say: 'We hear, and we obey. We await Your forgiveness, O Lord, unto You is the journey's end.'*

286. *God does not burden a soul with more than it can bear. To its credit, that which it has earned; and against it, that which it has deserved. 'Our Lord, Condemn us not if we forget or fall into error. Our Lord, Lay not on us such a burden as You did lay on those before us. Our Lord, Lay not on us a burden greater than we have strength to bear. Pardon us, forgive us and have mercy on us. You are our Protector; so grant us Your support against those who stand against faith.'*

Our reading began with the first *sura*, *al-Fatiha*, which is the basis of all the cycles of Muslims' five daily prayers. We conclude our reading of *sura Al-Baqara* with a passage devoted to the subject of prayer that ends with a prayer. The close of *Al-Baqara* indeed reprises the references to belief in God, His angels, His books and His apostles with which it began. The Qur'an overlays, returns to and interweaves its themes so that we emerge from reading returning to first principles, but with a deeper sense of the meaning of its words.

Al-Fathia provides a summation of what Islam is and teaches; *Al-Baqara*, the longest chapter, provides an overview of what the Qur'an means as spiritual and practical guidance to humankind. Throughout the rest of the Qur'an the themes included in these two chapters are expanded and explored, reprised and restated with the addition of more detail. The circularity and interweaving of the style are invitations to search for interconnection, to read each verse, each passage in relation to each other and in the context of the whole, to remember at each instant, with each word, that there is nothing in isolation and that everything that is being said is constantly referring to past, present and future. It is a lot to take in; there is, I find, always more to learn and struggle to understand. So it is fitting that *Al-Baqara* ends with the most human and humane of prayers.

This closing passage opens where the Qur'an itself began, emphasising the absolute sovereignty of God. Here is a restatement of the 'Lord of the Day of Judgement' to remind us that from God nothing is concealed. All people, believers and non-believers alike, are ultimately accountable in exactly the same way for their own thoughts and actions. No one, including believers, has an automatic right to forgiveness. Forgiveness is earned by effort. God forgives or punishes 'whom He wills'. In this common end we find the commonality and unity of all humanity through all time. The task, the challenge faced by each individual is always the same: to make the effort, to do deeds in this life which earn God's pleasure.

The first principle for believers is to uphold God as absolute sovereign of the heavens and the earth, for everything belongs to Him. He has absolute authority: 'He has power over all things.' We fully understand ourselves, our human relationships and our relations to the whole of creation only when we appreciate the supremacy of the creative power that brought everything into being, sustains it in being and invests it with meaning and purpose. To be conscious of God is to look at the world in a distinctive way: humbly, with awe and wonder, with a duty of care, with responsibility for making the most of all that has been created for our use and benefit. We are not lords of this world, not masters and owners, but trustees accountable to a higher authority in all our thoughts and actions.

Belief in God is followed by conviction in his guidance; and his angels, his revealed texts, and his prophets. The Qur'an emphasises that believers do not make distinctions between any of God's prophets but respect them all equally. From this should come respect for those who follow the revelations to earlier prophets. At heart, the messages each brought contain the same glad tidings. It is human perversity, through dissension, mutual jealousy, through failure to understand God's purpose in the diversity of our identities and ways, that distorts and divides the common effort required of all people of faith.

The *sura* ends with a prayer which the Muslim Community, encountering severe hardship in Medina, is urged to recite. I find the emphasis in this prayer on human frailties fascinating and significant. Believers can, of course, commit a sin knowingly. But the mistakes stressed here arise from unintentional error, faulty judgement or forgetfulness. These are truly human attributes. The point is not just that we need forgiveness, for sins committed knowingly and unknowingly. We also need to be aware that these very weaknesses are what make us human. Belief does not make us exempt from human weakness. Belief is the context in which we work to deal with and through our weaknesses in all our humanity.

The prayer comes in two parts. The first expresses certain desires on our part as God's creation: take us not to task if we forget or do wrong unintentionally; do not place on us the heavy burden that was placed on people before us, and do not overburden us with more than we can bear. It all ends up as a plea for the preservation of our humanity. The second, corresponding part acknowledges God as our Creator and asks for absolution: 'pardon us', 'forgive us' and 'show us Mercy'. Together, the two parts not only define our relationship with God but also the nature of our humanity: our ability to be broken by afflictions, suffering and atrocities.

Verse 286 says: 'God does not burden a soul with more than it can bear'. This 'burden' is not an earthly burden. Clearly the suffering, hardship and injustices we see around us can and do compromise human dignity and drive many mad with pain. This is precisely why we pray for freedom from such afflictions. And, as believers, we are duty-bound to stand up to and try to do something about them, to struggle constantly for the preservation of our common humanity and the increase of the practical delivery of justice and equity to all human beings, as well as the natural world.

The burden mentioned here relates to our individual responsibility and accountability to God. It is our final judgement which is limited by our individual capacity—and that includes our ability to do something about the untold suffering we see all around us. This is precisely why the verse goes on to say that each soul 'gains whatever good that it has done, and suffers its bad'. We shall not be judged, the Qur'an tells us, if we do not have the ability to achieve the perfect results in all that needs to be done, or are forced to abstain because of our lack of capacity. What matters is doing as much as we are able, and using our intelligence to appreciate what should be done. The religious temper is to open our hearts, minds and spirit to the understanding that things can be better; that as things are, they do not ever and always need to be.

The promise that the Qur'an makes, like the promise of other monotheistic faiths, is the promise of hope: there is always hope of guidance and forgiveness. And the greatest hope of all is the enduring, infinite compassion and mercy of the All-powerful. It is a call to effort, in full acknowledgement of all our frailties and failings in this life. It will be the individual and personal dispensation on which we rely on the Day of Reckoning, because we are known according to our capacities and the opportunities presented to us in life. Each is judged only according to how they faced up to the problems and made the most of the potential of their times. God is Absolute; we are indeed creatures of our times. All we can do is the best we are able, to make things better by raising our aspirations to the ideals and values for transforming society set out in the Qur'an. When we do this, we have 'grasped the most trustworthy handhold, that never breaks' (v.256).

Part Three

THEMES AND CONCEPTS

28

INTRODUCTION

We have completed a reading of only two chapters of the Qur'an: *al-Fatiha and Al-Baqara*. Yet as summation and overview they communicate the essential message, illustrate the extraordinary nature of the text and the special character of its style. Indeed, *Al-Baqara* has introduced and covered the gamut of the themes, injunctions and principles to which we will turn in this part of the book.

The Qur'an can be read on various levels. It can simply be an act of worship and devotion: as *al-Fatiha* is read during daily prayers, or the verse of the Throne is used in devotional recitations. It can be read for religious guidance: to discover the articles of faith and importance of performing certain obligatory acts of Islam such as *zakat*, *hajj* and fasting. Moreover, the Qur'an can be read, as we have been trying to read it, to tease out contextual and deeper meaning, to gain guidance for contemporary problems, and to think with. It can also be read at a mystical level, as the Sufis do, to gain esoteric and metaphysical insights. And, of course, as with all religious texts—the Torah, Bible, Bhagavad Gita, or the teachings of Buddha—it can also be studied as a scholarly endeavour, which requires some training, expertise and considerable study. What one takes from the text depends on how one reads, the purpose and effort invested in engaging with the Qur'an.

At this point it is worth reflecting on the principal technique we found essential: context. Appreciating the text and engaging with its meaning, I have argued, depends on becoming aware of the multiple distinct contexts the Qur'an addresses and distinguishing between them. As a commentary on the life of Prophet Muhammad, and the people, customs and culture of Arabia during his times, understanding the Qur'an requires knowing something about the life and personality of Prophet Muhammad and the circumstances and background of the Arab community in which he lived. The general cultural milieu and the specific circumstances within which each verse is revealed have a direct bearing on the ability to understand the kernel of universal truth embedded in the text, to distinguish the time-bound from the enduring principle which is timeless, in the sense that it has to be applied within the specific circumstances of the succession of times and places that comprise human history.

The other essential in clarifying the significance of context is to consider how individual verses are connected with other verses elsewhere in the Qur'an, and how the parts are integrated within the whole. We need to read the Qur'an, as the text itself demands, with some intellectual rigour. What we cannot do is to take a given verse, divorced from its context, and say this is precisely what it means. This is not a way of reading the Qur'an; rather it is a means of justifying one's own bias and prejudices.

Interpretation, of course, is a human endeavour. Any reader will bring his or her own experiences, cultural background, understanding of contemporary circumstances and intellectual ability to his or her reading. And that reading, like my own, will have its natural limitations. So no reading of the Qur'an can be a definitive, final word on the Sacred Book. We cannot, therefore, consider any interpretation of the Qur'an to be universal and eternal; and we must look at any such claims with scepticism, whether they come from classical commentators or their modern counterparts, Muslim scholars or Western experts on the Qur'an. Our approach to, and understanding of, the Qur'an has to develop and evolve continuously with the passage of time and changes in our circumstances. So interpreting the Qur'an is a dynamic, living process, involving adaptation, additions, abandonment, refinement and improvement.

However, this is not to say that all readings of the Qur'an are necessarily time-bound or simply a reflection of a reader's background and circumstances. A socially rational interpretation of certain general verses is possible: we can all agree that a verse such as 'there is no compulsion in religion' (2: 256) or 'God does not love the transgressors' (2: 190) can be read objectively and has common meaning. Appreciating the universal import of certain general verses is, I think, particularly important if our concern is interrogating the text rather than justifying our preconceived ideas or pre-existing social beliefs. There is an objective core of meaning in the Qur'an that is accessible to all fair-minded readers.

From the outset I sought to temper the traditional approach of reading the two initial chapters verse by verse. I focused my reading on what are to me distinct passages, each of which dealt with particular themes. It was considering the text in these discrete passages that gave me the clearest insight into structure and style, while awareness of a central theme and its implications illuminated connections between what might at first sight appear disconnected or extraneous verses. Recognition of a central theme or concept focused attention on interconnection as the way in which juxtaposition, simile, metaphor and parable worked to expand the potential meaning and implications to be drawn from the passages under consideration.

Interconnection is not merely a feature of particular passages within specific chapters; it is for me the defining character of the Qur'an as a whole. The traditional exercise of exploring the text verse by verse, by its very nature cannot yield insights into the broader themes, essential concepts and universal meaning of the Qur'an, nor can concentrating our attention on just two chapters. We need to examine the themes and concepts we have encountered, such as the Qur'anic notion of prophecy, or the idea of community, or nature, as they are reflect in the Sacred Text as a whole.

This is what we have to do next.

29

PROPHETS AND REVELATION

Prophecy is one of the major themes of the Qur'an. God guides humanity, away from error and sin and towards goodness and justice, through prophecy. Prophecy brings 'good news' about humanity's potential for advancement and elevation, and warning that we can sink, as individuals and communities, into the depths of ignorance and barbarity. The function of prophecy is to put humanity on the track of physical and moral advancement, to inspire nobler and higher sentiments and inspire and instil in men and women virtues that take them closer to the Divine. Prophecy is thus not only the method through which God communicates His Message to humanity; it is also a sign of His mercy and favour.

The Qur'an presents prophecy as a universal phenomenon: 'we have despatched a messenger to every nation' (16:36). All prophets are equal, 'we make no distinction between any of them' (3:84), but 'We have made some Messengers more excellent than others' (2:253). Muslims are required to believe in the revelation of every single one. The prophets are not just the bearers of the Divine message, but they also, through their lives, demonstrate how the message is to be interpreted in practical life. This is why they are 'only human beings' (14:11) who come from within the community. They understand the suffering of the community, are anxious about its turmoil, and are trusted by all (9:128–9). They are chosen because of their pure character and special personalities, and endowed with knowledge and wisdom to 'recite His signs' (3:164) to their communities. They become guides and leaders, and communicate the revelation from God to their people without fear and with resoluteness and patience.

But what is revelation? The Qur'an's answer to the question is given in 42:51–2: 'it is not granted to any mortal that God should speak to him except through revelation or from behind a veil, or by sending a messenger to reveal by His command what He will: He is exalted and wise. So We have revealed a Spirit to you [Prophet] by Our command: you did not know before what the Book is nor what faith is, but We have made it a light whereby We guide whomsoever of our servants.' What we are being told is that God does not speak directly to a prophet, but the communication, or revelation, comes from behind a veil in the form of a light that is infused in the prophet's mind or heart. The prophets thus know and can perceive things in the way other humans cannot. It is interesting to note that the agency of revelation is not made clear: the 'messenger' who brings revelation is left undefined, and the message itself comes in the form of a 'Spirit'. We can conjecture that the messenger is an angel. In the opening verses of chapter 53, the Star, which is generally accepted as referring to Prophet Muhammad's vision in the Cave of Hira where the revelations actually began, the revelation is taught to the Prophet by someone with 'mighty powers and great strength, who stood on the highest horizon'. Some translators and commentators suggest it is an angel, or more specifically, Angel Gabriel (or Jibreel). But it could also be the Spirit mentioned in 42:51. Elsewhere in the Qur'an, angels and the Spirit are mentioned together as two different entities. In 'The Night of Glory', for example, 'angels and Sprit descend again and again with their Lord's permission on every task' (97:4); and 'on the Day whose length is fifty thousand years', 'angels and Spirit ascend to Him'. (70:4). Whatever the agency of revelation, the revelation itself is both seen and felt: '[The Prophet's] own heart did not distort what he saw' (53:11), which suggests that it is both an intuitive and a visionary experience. But ultimately, revelation remains a Divine mystery, as it must. It is a spiritual phenomenon and, as such, not amenable to any form of purely rational analysis. It can only be judged by its end product, the quality of the text it produces: what does it actually say, what eternal truth does it communicate, and does it stand the test of time and last for eternity? The truth of the revelation that infused Prophet Muhammad with a 'Spirit of Our command' is embodied in the Qur'an itself.

The Qur'an distinguishes between two types of prophets: *rasul* and *nabi*. Although both are divinely inspired, only *rasuls*, or messengers, receive revelation in the form of a Book: 'these were the men to whom we gave the Book, and authority, and prophethood' (40:78). Thus, while every *rasul* is a *nabi*, not all *nabis* are *rasuls*. As communicators of revelation, both *rasuls* and *nabis* serve as 'witnesses' to the Divine Message. On the Day of Judgement, these 'witnesses' will be called and truth will be clear from falsehood: 'We shall call a witness from every community, and say, "produce your evidence", and then they will know that truth belongs to God alone; the gods they invented will forsake them' (28:75).

Adam was the first *nabi* and Muhammad is the last *rasul*. In between, the Qur'an mentions 23 other prophets, many being familiar names from the Bible: Idris (Enoch) (19:56–7, 21:85–6); Nuh (Noah) (6:84); Hud (11:50–60); Saleh (11:61–6); Ibrahim (Abraham) (6:83, 11:69–76); Isma'il (Ishmael) (6:84, 19:54–55); Ishaq (Isaac) (11:70–74); Lut (Lot) (7:80–84); Ya'qub (Jacob) (11:71); Yousef (Joseph) (6:84 and the whole of *sura* 12); Shu'aib (7:85, 11: 84); Ayyub (Job) (6:84); Musa (Moses) (6:84, 20:9–99); Harun (Aaron) (6:84, 20:90); Dhu'l-kifl (Ezekiel) (21:85–6, 38:48); Dawud (David) (6:84); Sulaiman (Solomon) (6:84); Ilias (Elias) (6:85); Al-Yasa (Elisha) (6:86); Yunus (Jonah) (6:86); Zakariyya (Zachariah) (6:85); Yahya (John) (6:85) and Isa (Jesus) (3: 45–8; 43:57–9; 19:88–98; 5:116–17; 19:16–36; 5:46–7; 5:72–5; 43: 63–5). All these prophets are one community; they communicated the same message of the unity of God and the importance of upholding justice and equity (42:13).

Two prophets receive particular attention. The first is Jesus, who is mentioned in no less than 93 verses. The Qur'anic name for Jesus is Isa; but he is also referred to as the 'Messiah', 'Servant', 'Messenger', 'Word', 'Sign' and a 'Prophet' to whom a Book was revealed. He was born of virgin birth, performed various miracles, and preached the Gospels. The Qur'an's take on Jesus is illustrated in 3:45–50:

The angel said: 'Mary! God gives you news of a Word from Him, whose name will be Messiah, Jesus, son of Mary, who will be held in honour in this world and the next, who will be one of those drawn nearer to God. And he shall speak to people in his infancy, and in his adulthood. He will be one of the righteous.' She said: 'My Sustainer! How can I have a son when no man has ever touched me?' The angel answered: 'Thus it is: God creates what He wills: when He wills a thing to be, He but says unto it, "Be", and it is. He will teach him the Scripture and wisdom, the Torah and the Gospel. He will send him as a messenger to the Children of Israel: "I have come to you with a sign from your Lord: I will make the shape of bird for you out of clay, then breathe into it and, by God's permission, it will become a real bird; I will heal the blind and the leper, and bring the dead back to life with God's permission."'

While Jesus is said to be born of divine decree, the Qur'an emphatically says he is not the son of God, and emphasises the point by frequently referring to him as the 'Son of Mary'. Indeed, to accept Jesus as the son of God would be tantamount to denying the fundamental and all-pervading Qur'anic message of the unity and transcendence of God: 'They say, "God has children!" May He be exalted! He is the Self-Sufficient One; everything in the heavens and the earth belongs to Him' (10:68). Similarly, it would be a negation of the Qur'an's basic teachings if the trinitarian notion of 'God the Son' is accepted: 'Those who say, "God is the Messiah, son of Mary", are defying the truth' (5:17). Jesus himself, according to the Qur'an, made no claims to divinity. Indeed, God will question him on the Day of Judgement about such claims: 'When God says, "Jesus, son of Mary, did you say to people, 'worship me and my mother as two gods alongside God?'", he will say, "May You be exalted! I would never say what I had no right to say; if I said such a thing You would indeed have known it"' (5:116). The Qur'an also denies that Jesus was crucified to death, but acknowledges his ascension into heaven, which is both a sign and affirmation of his prophethood: '(They said): "We have killed the Messiah, Jesus, son of Mary, the Messenger of God." They did not kill him, nor did they crucify him, though it was made to appear like that to them...' The overall conclusion: 'The Messiah, the son of Mary, was only a Messenger; other messengers had come and gone before him' (5:75). [1]

The second prophet is Muhammad, who is naturally given considerable space as the Qur'an is addressed to and through him. Surprisingly, his proper name only occurs in the Qur'an four times. Like Jesus, who is given a universal significance in the Qur'an—he is 'a sign to all beings' (21:91)—Muhammad too is a witness, guide and mercy to those who devoted themselves to God (16:89). The two prophets are going to play a prominent role in the eschatological drama of the last days [2]. But unlike Jesus, Muhammad does not perform miracles. His only miracle is the Qur'an itself.

Muhammad is 'the unlettered prophet' (7:157) who is endowed with an 'exalted character' (68:4). His responsibility is simply to communicate the message of God: 'So [Prophet] warn them: your only task is to give warning, you are not there to control them' (88:21–2). This he does in a loving, kind and gentle way: 'had you been severe and harsh-hearted, they would have broken away from about you' (3:159). He is accused of being a fortune-teller, a mad man, and a poet by a society where poets were thought to be invaded by spirits when they delivered their poetry. He is none of these things, says the Qur'an, but the last prophet: 'Muhammad is not the father of any of your men, but he is the Messenger of God and the Seal of the prophets' (33:40).

So, one of the special features of Muhammad is that the Divine message comes to an end with him. But why, one may ask, does prophecy stop with

Muhammad? The conventional Muslim argument is that religion has evolved through history, the message of God becomes more developed and refined from one prophet to another, and reaches its final form in Islam. As proof, Muslims present Islam, with some sense of moral superiority, it has to be said, as the most perfect and complete religion. There is also a simple observation that can be used as evidence. No other prophet has actually emerged after the Prophet Muhammad. This does not mean that no claims to prophethood have been made; the twentieth century has been witness to all sorts of strange religious movements, from New Age syncretism to Scientology. But no successful prophet has appeared, no Divine text has come to light, and no global religion with billions of adherents has arisen.

I would argue that in theory Islam is indeed a perfect religion: 'this day have I perfected your religion and completed My favour on you and chosen for you Islam as a religion' (5:3). But its practice, being a human endeavour, can never be perfect. Indeed, in some cases, as we have already seen, the practice of what goes under the rubric of Islam can be quite destructive. Muhammad is 'the Seal of the prophets' because the message of God has reached its natural conclusion: all that is left is to understand the message and its actualisation in individual, social and communal life, which is an eternal struggle. However, the fact that Muhammad is designated as the last prophet does mean that his followers have a special responsibility: they have to prove, by their behaviour, that his message is indeed the final and perfect form of religion. Here the evidence is seriously flawed!

Muslim modernists present a second argument to defend the finality of prophecy. By the time Islam appears in the world, and the Qur'an is revealed, humankind has become rationally and morally mature. Reading, writing and systematic thinking are beginning to emerge and gain some ground. The benefits of ethical and moral behaviour are recognised and appreciated. So the need for further revelations becomes superfluous. But, 'the fact that man is still plagued by moral confusion', Fazul Rahman notes, 'and that his moral sense has not kept pace with his advance in knowledge, in order to be consistent and meaningful, this argument must add that man's moral maturity is conditional upon his constantly seeking guidance from the Divine Books, especially the Qur'an, and that man has not become mature in the sense that he can dispense with the divine guidance' [3]. Given that advances in knowledge, by their very nature, generate a host of moral and ethical problems and dilemmas, there will always be need for Divine guidance. But should our 'moral maturity' be defined solely in terms of Divine guidance? I would suggest that the argument also works the other way round: we come to realise the true significance of Divine help, and the fact that we cannot resolve our dilemmas without it, only after becoming morally mature. So this argument has a few shortcomings.

I think our understanding of why the Qur'an describes Muhammad as the last prophet has to be based on something else. And it is this: after Muhammad, we do not need another 'chosen' man to guide us through the moral morass of human existence. We may be 'mature' in relation to some issues; and not so mature in relation to other new, emerging and more complex issues. Either way the responsibility for resolving our moral and ethical dilemmas rests squarely on our own individual and collective shoulders. Moreover, it is our responsibility, I would argue a duty, to create a fair and equitable society. There will not be a new Moses to lead us to the Promised Land; or a new Jesus to save our souls; or, indeed, a new Muhammad to establish a just social order. The end of prophecy is a sanction against our intrinsic inclination to look perpetually for a Messiah so we can place all our burdens and responsibilities on his shoulders. It suggests, in particular, that it is our own responsibility to stand up to tyranny and oppression. The prophets serve as our models, they motivate us to do good and behave morally, and they are our ideal spiritual guides. But following prophetic example also means speaking truth to power and waging a struggle against cruelty and domination. After all, this is exactly what every prophet in history did and had to do. In particular, we learn from the Qur'an, the prophets waged struggles against three types of people, personified in the story of Moses by Pharaoh, Haman and Korah (40:23–9). The three are respectively the symbols for the ruling elite, the corrupt administrators and the phenomenally rich, who work together to accumulate power, thwart distribution of wealth and subjugate and marginalise most of society. What the prophets achieved, or tried to achieve, in the past, we have to do in our own time.

The Qur'an describes a special event in the life of the Prophet Muhammad known as the 'night journey'. It is a journey that takes the Prophet Muhammad from Mecca to the mosque in Jerusalem: 'Glory be to Him who made His servant travel by night from the sacred place of worship to the furthest place of worship, whose surroundings we have blessed, to show him some of Our signs' (17:1). This part of the night journey, known as *isra'*, is the first stage of *mi'raj*, the Prophet's Ascension to Heaven. Here, Muhammad 'soared up and stood, poised on the highest point of the horizon; then he approached and came on down, and stood two bow-lengths off or even closer'; and 'he saw some of his Lord's greatest signs' (53:1–18).

Muslim scholars differ in their opinion about whether the Ascension was a bodily journey or a spiritual experience. Tradition even has the Prophet riding a white mystical beast, Buraq, taller than a donkey but smaller than a mule. Its step is said to cover a distance equal to the range of its vision. The prophet tied it up in Jerusalem and then went up through the seven heavens, meeting other prophets as he went, culminating with Ibrahim. Myths even have Muhammad bargaining with God about the number of times Muslims are supposed to pray during the day.

But the Qur'an makes it clear that *isra'* and *mi'raj* are spiritual journeys, a vision. Later on in 'the Star', the *sura* which contains the description of *mi'raj*, the event is clearly described as a vision: 'the vision we showed you was only a test for people' (17:60). Muhammad saw the 'Lord's greatest signs' with a spiritual eye. The experience gave him hope at a time when his situation in Mecca was of utter helplessness.

Given his character, his spiritual enlightenment and the fact that he is the recipient of revelation, the Prophet is the ideal model of behaviour for Muslims. Indeed, the Qur'an tells us that 'in God's messenger you have a fine model for someone who looks forward to (meeting) God and the Last Day, and mentions God frequently' (33:21). Someone who is held in such high esteem commands both admiration and respect; and Muslims go out of their way to show due respect to the Prophet. At the Qur'an's suggestion (33:56), we send blessings on the Prophet every time we mention his name: 'peace be upon him'. Out of respect, Muslims prefer that the Prophet is not depicted in images. We try to emulate the Prophet and model our behaviour on his. And, not surprisingly, we are upset when he is disrespected or depicted in an insulting manner [4].

While the Prophet is the ideal model to emulate and respect, can we also say that he is perfect in all ways?

I think the assumption that the Prophet was perfect in all regards, common amongst both classical and contemporary jurists and religious scholars, is logically inconsistent with the fact that he was a human being. To be human, by nature, is not to be perfect. To assume that the Prophet was a perfect human being is to conflate his personality with the original source of revelation: God. The Prophet himself never made this claim; the doctrine of *isma*, or infallibility of the Prophet, emerged later when his sayings and actions, the *Sunna*, was formulated.

The Qur'an points to the Prophet's humanity on a number of occasions, when he is corrected or indeed admonished. On one occasion, he was addressing a group of Quraysh leaders in Mecca. A poor blind man, ibn Umm Maktoom, interrupted him. Unaware that the Prophet was busy, ibn Umm Maktoom asked him repeatedly to teach him some verses of the Qur'an. The

Prophet was not pleased at his repeated interruptions, grimaced and turned away from him. The following verses were then revealed criticising his behaviour:

He frowned and turned away,
Because a blind man came to (interrupt) him.
What do you know? He [the blind man] might be purified [by the guidance of the Qur'an]?
Or he might receive admonition, and the teaching might profit him?
As to the one who regards himself as self-sufficient,
You gave him your full attention,
Though it is not you to be blamed if he rejects the guidance.
And the one who came to you striving earnestly,
With fear in his heart,
You were inattentive to him.
By no means should it be so! For it is indeed a message of instruction to all people [not only the rich].
Therefore let who so will, keep it in remembrance. (80:1–12)

Not only was the Prophet a human being, he was also a person of a particular time and a particular place. As such, he could not transcend the limitations of his society and his times. He dressed according to the customs of his society, he performed his daily functions within the limitations of this society, and the environment he created around himself depended on the tools and instruments available to him. We therefore need to separate what is particular to his time and circumstances from what is eternal in how he lived out the message of the Qur'an. And what are eternal in the life of Muhammad, I would argue, are his humanity, the norms and values he exemplifies and personifies in his character and everyday behaviour. I think it is important for Muslims to stress constantly the Prophet's humanity, rather than focus on the minutiae of how he looked, how he brushed his teeth or the medicine he used.

In *sura Al-Baqara*, we came across a verse that I deliberately passed over. It addressed the Prophet directly: 'It is not for you [Prophet] to guide them; it is God, who guides whomsoever He wills' (2:272). It is not the Prophet, however, who needs this reminder. It is us. We need to be reminded that ultimate guidance comes only from the Qur'an; the Prophet exemplifies aspects of how we can translate this guidance into our lives, use it to build communities and establish just and equitable societies: how we can interpret and live the message of the Qur'an. This makes him an extraordinary human being.

However, the Prophet is always a conceptual model caught in the exigencies of his own time. This caveat applies not only to details of personal habits and dress, but must surely extend to the circumstances by which the nascent Muslim community he led secured its existence [5]. For example, the revelations on warfare, the fight to survive as a community of faithful, addressed to Muhammad are entirely contextual. The fact that warfare, internecine as well as between peoples and nations, has remained a dominant feature of Muslim history is testament to a failure of moral maturity to assert itself. Legitimising recourse to warfare by references to the experience and actions of the Prophet is to elevate one aspect of his life and the message he brought over and above the extensive evidence for the demands for peaceful co-existence, for resolution of dispute by peaceful means. The Qur'an is explicit that peace with justice and equity for all is the objective to which human beings must strive. Islam is by no means the only religion which has found the entirely human seduction of imperialism and conflict an easier call to answer than the Qur'anic message of peace-making. It is no less a blot on the comprehension of Muslims than it is of any other people of any other faith or no faith. Finding another better way to be human is the enduring demand inherent in divine guidance.

For me, the greatest implication of all we learn about prophethood in the Qur'an is that of universalism. The attention given to the plurality of prophets, named and unnamed, as well as the fact that all people have received guidance from God, creates the most important context that challenges our understanding. We have not only to reason our way through the specifics of the message given to Muhammad and the rootedness of this revelation in his time and place; we have also to seek the intersection of this specific revelation with the transcendent moral vision of which all peoples and communities in history have had their share. The Prophethood of Muhammad exists to make clear the recurrence of God's message and help us to transcend the limitation and narrowness of our perspectives shaped by tribalisms, factionalisms, sectarianisms or nationalisms. The search is not merely to follow the Prophet as best as we can, but also to seek God's pleasure as a way to realise and respond to the search for the divine in all people, whoever they are.

30

ABROGATION AND CHANGE

Wherever possible, I have tried to link passages in the Qur'an with events in the life of the Prophet Muhammad. These events can be found as a continuous narrative in classical biographies of the Prophet, known as *Seerah*, such as ibn Ishaq's *Life of Muhammad*, written in the eighth century [6]. The *Seerah* is essential for us to discover when a particular *sura*, or a section within the *sura*, was revealed; and give each *sura* a place in a definite chronology. The establishment of such a chronology brought the concept of abrogation to the fore. Abrogation is the principle by which verses revealed later in time took precedence over apparently contradictory passages revealed earlier.

The principle of abrogation, or *naskh*, is allegedly taken from the Qur'an itself. In 2:106, we read: 'any of our messages that we abrogate or consign to oblivion, We replace with a better of a similar one'. But abrogation is a rather tricky, not to say sticky, theory. Muslim scholars differ on what it is and how to apply it. Various classifications have been developed about what is abrogated with what. On the whole, confusion reigns.

The most common example of abrogation we find in the literature relates to wine and intoxicants. First, in 16:67, we are asked to reflect on where alcohol comes from: 'From the fruits of date palms and grapes you take sweet Juice and wholesome provisions. There truly is a sign in this for people who use their reason.' Then we are told, in 2:219, that alcohol can be both good and bad, but the bad outweighs the good: 'They ask you (Prophet) about intoxicants and gambling: say, "There is great sin in both, and some benefit for people: the sin is greater than the benefit."' We now move to the instruction to avoid alcohol while praying: 'You who believe, do not come anywhere near the prayer if you

225

are intoxicated (*sukara*), not until you know what you are saying' (4:43). Finally, the believers are asked to avoid alcohol altogther: 'You who believe! Intoxicants and gambling, idolatrous practices, and (divining with) arrows are repugnant acts—Satan's doing; shun them so that you may prosper' (5:90–91).

What is happening here is fairly clear. The rules are tightening over time as the community adapts to its new faith. We can explain the differences in verses by the fact that the less prohibitive verses were revealed earlier during the Meccan period. Which is my first problem with the theory of abrogation: the Meccan *suras*, which deal with spiritual aspects, human behaviour and issues of morality and ethics, become systematically less important.

But this type of abrogation relies solely on agreement on the dates of the verses in question. What if this is not patently clear? Also, we are not always sure which verse is connected to which event in the life of the Prophet Muhammad. So how are we to decide in such cases which verses abrogate others?

Such complications have led scholars to disagree on exactly how many verses in the Qur'an have been abrogated. In the eighth century, Az-Zuhri, one of the earliest authorities on *Hadith*, claimed that 42 verses had been abrogated. In the eleventh century, the number increased to 238, and then 248. Then it went down drastically: the Egyptian theologian al-Suyuti, who flourished in the fifteenth century, reduced it drastically to 20; and the eighteenth-century Indian Sufi scholar Shah Wali Allah brought the number down to 5.

Moreover, what abrogates what has not been limited to the Qur'an. Some Muslim scholars have even argued that examples and sayings of the Prophet, the *Sunna*, can abrogate the Qur'an. This argument has been used, for example, to justify stoning to death for adultery, a punishment that does not exist in the Qur'an. As far as I am concerned, the Qur'an is the primary source of Islam; it cannot be abrogated by the secondary source, the *Sunna* of the Prophet.

There are other problems with the whole notion of abrogation. One of the verses most commonly used to justify abrogation, 'when We substitute one revelation for another' (16:101), is Meccan and came before most of the Medinan verses that are said to be later abrogated. It seems rather strange to me that this verse is used to justify something that didn't exist at the time it was revealed. A Meccan verse cannot logically talk about abrogating something that will happen in the future in Medina. Moreover, when we look at the few verses used to justify abrogation, we can see that they can be interpreted in other ways. They do not, in my opinion, refer to the passages of the Qur'an, but earlier revelations such as the Torah and the Bible. The context of 2:106, quoted above, shows this is the case: the verse is addressing the Jews.

I think the theory of abrogation is a red herring. It has been used to tie Muslim religious thought in knots, and justify the unjustifiable.

So, how do we interpret various earlier verses in the Qur'an that seem to contradict what was revealed later in the Qur'an?

Contradictions in the Qur'an play an important creative role. They point out that even good things can have a downside: that the pursuit of good can sometimes lead to production of evil. They force us to consider opposite viewpoints, clashing perspectives, and thus prevent us from making oversimplified analyses. And contradictions emphasise the simultaneous and contextual logic of the Qur'an. Staying with the theme of intoxicants, consider the two descriptions of alcohol: in 16:67 alcohol is praised; but in 5:90 it is connected to gambling and denounced. As statements, both are simultaneously true: alcohol obviously has good qualities; but in excess it affects the mind, 'stops you remembering God and prayer', and leads to socially disruptive behaviour. The contextual logic here points in a number of directions. The excess of one thing, which may have a good content, alcohol, can lead you towards another, totally destructive thing, gambling. This is in fact exactly what was happening in Mecca during the time of the Prophet. The Meccans engaged in binge drinking which often led them to indulge in a second vice, gambling, and together the two led them to fights, scandals and blood feuds. Similarly, the fanatical zeal to do good, even though based on good intention, can also cloud one's judgement and lead to destructive results. The point is that good is contextual; what may be seen as good in one particular situation may become bad in another. It is worth noting that in describing wine in glowing terms, the Qur'an suggests that it 'truly is a sign for people who use their reason'. The point is that one needs to keep a balanced, rational perspective on things. Good is not always a priori given; it needs to be constantly interrogated, thought about and discovered through sustained reasoning. And it has to be seen in a changing, dynamic context: what is 'wholesome' in one context may not be so in another.

So, contradictions in the Qur'an cannot be dismissed simply as inconsistency. Rather, they suggest that the world is not amenable to one-dimensional solutions, and no particular partial view can encompass the whole. Verses that appear contradictory often expand on what was said earlier, or explore the same issue from a different perspective or in a different context. To prove a particular point, the Qur'an uses one argument and sometimes another. It explores the same idea in different contexts, so that verses about the same topics can have different aspects. The underlying themes that emerge relate to change, changing contexts, multiple perspectives and constant struggle to discover what constitutes goodness in particular circumstances.

227

The whole notion of change and changing contexts is quite evident from the wine verses we have been looking at. There are three ideas of change in these verses: first, the commands relating to alcohol are changing; second, the society that the Qur'an is talking about is evolving and changing; and finally, the context that the Qur'an is dealing with is itself changing. The obvious thing to note is that this change is not instantaneous; it does not involve a major upheaval or a revolution. It is a gradual, evolutionary change. While emphasising that change is essential, the Qur'an insists that it should be measured and lead to social and cultural transformation without turmoil or violence. It is not change that should lead society; rather, society should lead change.

Equally important is the point that change necessitates shifts in perspective. As Muslim society develops and changes, moves from Mecca to Medina, the theme of alcohol gets a different expression at each stage. Different perspectives on alcohol are revealed at different stages, enabling the Muslim community to adjust to change; and it is forbidden only when Muslim society has reached a level of maturity in Medina. What this suggests is not that one verse is abrogated by another, but that a society has to be able to fulfil certain criteria before it can implement particular injunctions of the Qur'an; and that it is necessary for a society to adjust to change as it evolves and changes itself.

The apparent contradictions and changes in expression according to context are the Qur'an's way of teaching how to separate the permanent from the temporary, the transient from the abiding: how to change while remaining, in terms of worldview, values and norms, the same. When the teachings of the Qur'an are understood to exclude all possibility of change—which is what the theory of abrogation is all about—the end result is to make static what is essentially dynamic in nature. A society that claims to be based on God-given eternal values cannot function without wrestling with and striving to reconcile the categories of permanence and change. Muslims have singularly failed in this regard over the last few centuries. That is why they seem to be stuck in historic times.

31

TIME AND HISTORY

The themes of time, the dynamics of change, and processes and patterns of history are interwoven throughout the Qur'an. The titles of some chapters, particularly the *suras* revealed in Mecca and found towards the end of the Sacred Text, focus our attention on the nature of time. These headings describe the phases of the day: 'Dawn' (103), 'The Morning Brightness' (93), 'The Declining Day' (103), 'The Night' (92). There is a sense of movement in the titles themselves; and we can extrapolate that just as the day changes into night, time and history also continue to move. Other titles draw our attention to future time: 'That which is coming' (56) and 'The Inevitable Hour' (69), suggesting that time and history are heading towards a final conclusion, a singularity, if you like.

My favourite *sura*, chapter 103, which is frequently recited at the end of a meeting or a gathering, directly invites us to 'consider time'. Its Arabic title is *Al-'Asr*, a word that has a number of connotations all relating to time. In everyday parlance, it is translated as afternoon, as in 'the 'Asr prayer'. But the term embodies the notion of movement. Hence, some translators, such as Pickthall and Haleem, render it as 'The Declining Day'. But it can also simply mean 'time', or as Asad translates it, 'The Flight of Time', or as Yusuf Ali has it, 'Time Through the Ages'. The emphasis is on movement of time, a time that cannot be recaptured. The *sura* suggests that time is valuable, it should be seen as an opportunity to pursue truth and do good, otherwise it would be lost and we would be lost along with it. The whole chapter reads: 'Consider the flight of time! Man is bound to lose himself, except those who believe, do good deeds, urge one another to truth, and urge one another to steadfastness' (103:1–3).

229

Man is therefore trapped in time, which is constantly changing. Indeed, the Qur'an suggests that change is the inevitable corollary of life: everything changes; except, of course, God who is Timeless and above time: 'Say, "He is God the one, God the eternal"' (112:1–2). All creation is thus not only subject to change but has to accommodate and adjust to change, or 'lose' itself. Indeed, even the Word of God (not to be confused with God Himself) is subject to change, as we read in 16:101: 'We substitute one revelation for another.' So God Himself changes His Word according to the needs of time and the inevitable changes of circumstance. The Prophet too had to accommodate to change: first he prayed facing Jerusalem, then, after the instruction from the Qur'an, he changed his direction towards Mecca (2:142, 144). So change is the only constant in the universe.

Time changes and moves on, but it has certain characteristics: it is relative; it may flow at different rates in different settings. There will be a 'Day whose length is fifty thousand years' (70:4); and there is a night, 'The Night of Glory', which can extend to 'a thousand months' (97:4). It is perceived differently by different people with different perspectives. We see this in the parable of the 'Companions of the Cave'. The young men were seeking refuge; they asked, 'Our Lord, grant us Your mercy, and find us a way out of our ordeal.' They hid in a cave and slept: 'We sealed their ears in the cave for years.' But when they woke up, they could not figure out how long they had slept, and thought they had only slept 'a day or part of a day' (18:10–11, 19). So a very long period of time can be perceived as short; and vice versa.

There was time before we appeared on this earth. The opening verse of chapter 76, which has the dual title of 'Man' (or rather human being) and 'Time', asks: 'Was there not a period of time before man, when he was not yet a thing to be thought of?' There is a dual suggestion here: that there was time before man appeared on the planet, and there was time before an individual is born 'out of a drop of sperm' (76:1–2). Moreover, time does not end with one's life. It is still there in that the world continues. But it is also still there for the person who is no longer alive, in the sense that his or her deeds, good or bad, continue to affect the environment and history—right up to the 'Inevitable Hour'.

What about the time in-between, after birth and before death, the time of our lives, the time we spend on this earth? It is, of course, quite trivial in cosmic terms. But we perceive it rather differently. Preoccupied with our busy lives, we seldom contemplate the fact that our time on earth is very limited. Unless some calamity forces us to reflect on our mortality, we seem to think and behave as though we will live forever. Some even chase immortality, through medicine and magical portions, through fame and fortune, through technological defiance of the inevitable. But we ought to contemplate just how truly short our lives actually are. Even shorter than we perceive, as the dialogue with God on the Day of Judgement hints:

He will say: 'How long did you remain on earth, in number of years?'
They will respond: 'We remained for a day or part thereof. Ask those who count.'
He will say: 'You remained only a short while, if only you knew.' (23:112–14)

The suggestion is that our time on earth is precious. It should not be devoted to seeking pleasures, or, as the title of chapter 102 states, 'Striving for More', for which there is 'No need'. Those 'who amass riches, counting them over, thinking they will make them live forever' (104:1–3) ought to think again. The person 'who pushes aside the orphan and does not urge others to feed the needy', those 'who pray but are heedless of their prayers', and 'those who are all show and forbid common kindness' ought to consider future time (107:1–7) in two respects: the costs of their actions for future generations and the home they leave behind (the theme of nature and environment explored in chapter 38); and the consequences of their behaviour for the life after death and the home they may inhabit in eternal time, which begins on the 'Day when people will be like scattered moths and the mountains like tufts of wool, the one whose good deeds are heavy on the scales will have a pleasant life, but the one whose good deeds are light will have the Bottomless Pit for his home' (101:49). Again and again, the Qur'an urges its readers not to 'love the fleeting life' (76:27), but to provide for the time and life to come. This life is life in precious time: we 'will have stayed [in this world] no longer than a single hour' (10:43). We are urged to make the best use of this time and pay heed to our life in the Hereafter, where time has a different measure.

The time before us also needs special attention. The Qur'an gives particular consideration to history and is full of historical passages. But it is not history as we know it: chronological, detailed analysis of events and personalities, a comprehensive narrative of good and bad old days. Rather the Qur'an uses history as a guide to the pitfalls of the future. The emphasis is always on the lessons that can be drawn from the historical narrative. The short picturesque passage at the beginning of 'Daybreak' is a good example:

Have you [Prophet] considered how your Lord dealt with [the people] of Ad, or Iram, [the city] of lofty pillars, whose like has never been made in any land, and the Thamud, who hewed into the rocks in the valley, and the mighty and powerful Pharoah? All of them committed excess in their lands, and spread corruption there: your Lord let a scrounge of punishment loose on them. Your Lord is always watchful. (89:6–10)

The *sura* goes on to contrast history with human nature. The main theme is how oppression, greed and love of wealth destroy people and places, cultures and civilisations, converting their glory and greatness to decay and destruction.

The narratives of ancient people in the Qur'an are used for four specific purposes. First, to encourage the study of history: 'many ways of life have passed away before your time. Travel about the earth and see what has happened to those who gave lie to truth' (3:137). Second, to promote the development of historiography: what use is the study of history if one cannot develop theories and ideas on ideologies, cultures and social foundations which bring power and prosperity to nations and civilisations or lead them into decay? The analysis of time past 'should be a clear lesson for all men, and guidance' (3:138). Third, the believers are challenged to redeem the history of the future; to put these lessons into practice. Like Moses, history can be used 'to bring your people out of the depth of darkness into the light'; and serve as a reminder for 'all who are patient and grateful in adversity' (14:5). And finally, as an accumulation of these goals, to infuse a consciousness of history.

History in the Qur'an is thus presented as the motor of change [7]. While change is constant, leading either to progress or to decay, there are certain historical reasons behind every change. The Qur'an does not want believers to accept change passively, inevitable though this is, but to change things actively. It seeks, I would argue, to release the moral energy of people and societies to shape history and hence make genuine progress.

Not surprisingly, progress in Qur'anic terms is not based on wealth, technology or splendour. Civilisations rise and fall; cultures flourish and decay; ebb and flow in power are transitory fluctuations. All superpowers and technological civilisations have allotted periods: 'there is an appointed term for each community, and when it is reached they can neither delay nor hasten it, even for a moment' (74:49). What matters in the final analysis is not might, power, the affluence of material means or even the accumulation of knowledge, but righteous conduct.

I think the Qur'an is suggesting that righteous behaviour and good deeds should be the greatest legacy of time and history, which is a sad reflection on all humanity. Our time on earth is connected to the time that went before us and the time that will come after us: all woven into a tapestry in which time and eternity exist together. Even though we are embedded in our own time, we ought to be aware of other dimensions and perspectives on time, and take them into account as we live our lives. We should remember that all history has contemporary relevance. Each generation sees episodes of history from its own perspective. Each generation must draw its own lessons from history, and move forward by adjusting to change. For when all is said and done, 'God does not change the condition of a people unless they first change their conditions themselves' (13:11).

Time and history are perhaps the best examples of themes by which the Qur'an seeks to challenge the limitations and complacency of our understanding. Revelation demands that we constantly think outside the box of our earthly concerns by keeping in mind the intersection of time and timelessness. The point of intersection is ever-present; but what it demands, counsels and guides us to may need to be different in every instance. If we stand firm on time, the model and example limited to just one narrow vision of time and one instance of the intersection with history, we can, and probably inevitably will, end by bringing evil or the unconscionable from good, by neglecting the good we should be engaged on putting into action. Tradition is a human construct fashioned in time; it is the legacy of history which the Qur'an suggests is neither substitute nor a sure approximation of righteousness. The only tradition worthy of the Qur'anic vision is one that continually redefines itself by the pertinence and appropriateness of its moral and ethical precepts to deal with the issues of today.

32

TRUTH AND PLURALITY

The plurality of religion is a constant and reccurring theme in the Qur'an. Far from adopting a hostile attitude to other religions, the Qur'an promotes acceptance of religious plurality and treats other religions with equality. It recognises that different faiths have different laws and ways of knowing and understanding God, but emphasises the common ground of 'doing good': values and morals that promote goodness, virtue and peace are integral to all faiths and more basic than differences in outward form and rituals. The challenge for humanity is to come together in peace and harmony, despite religious and theological differences.

We have already seen that the Qur'an uses stories from the Old and the New Testaments to illustrate some of its arguments. Both the Torah and the Bible are regarded by the Qur'an as revealed texts. 'It was God', we are told, 'who revealed the Torah (to Moses): therein was guidance and light' (5:44). And to Moses, God said: 'I have chosen you for Myself. Go, you and your brother, with My signs, and make sure that you remember me' (20:41–2). Regarding the New Testament and Jesus, we read: 'We sent Jesus, son of Mary: We gave him the Gospel and put compassion and mercy in the heart of his followers' (57:27). The 'name of God is commemorated in abundant measure', not just in mosques but also 'in monasteries, churches, synagogue' (22:46). The term used in the Qur'an to describe both Jewish and Christian communities is 'People of the Book', who are said to be constantly 'humbling themselves before God' and who 'will have their rewards with their Lord' (3:199).

Despite this, controversy has arisen relating to certain verses which are used to argue that the Qur'an does not look at Jews with favour. Verse 5:82 is a good example: 'You Prophet', we read, 'are sure to find that the most hostile to the believers are the Jews and those who associate other deities with God; you are sure to find that the closest in affection are those who say "We are Christians" for there are people devoted to learning and ascetics.' The context of this verse has a familiar contemporary ring. It was revealed in Medina where the Jews exercised considerable political power. Moreover, the Meccans who migrated to that city with the Prophet were canny businessmen, and the Jewish clans who predominated in certain crafts feared that the migrants would capture their trade; hence the animosity. The verse describes the particular situation in Medina at a particular point in time. And at that time it represents a very human situation, one which posed a challenge to the nascent Muslim community. In no instance is it more important to remind ourselves that the Qur'an is not and cannot be reduced to a record of the doings of the Prophet and the first Muslim community in all their fallibility. The record of their dealings with the Jewish community in and around Medina is problematic, and part and parcel of the conflict of the time. It is not a general ruling. The Qur'an is the compendium of God's guidance for all people for all time, which looks beyond the exigencies of even an era of Prophethood. We can be sure the particular relations of the first Muslims and the Jews of Medina are not general propositions: it could hardly be so since it would violate what the Qur'an is saying repeatedly elsewhere.

Jews and Muslims, I think, are closer to each other than Muslims and Christians. Both have similar codes of conduct, laws and jurisprudence (the *Shari'a* in Islam and the *Halacha* in Judaism). The dietary arrangements of both religions are almost the same (*halal* and *kosher*); and charity is an important feature of both (*sadaka* and *tsedaka*). This is why, I think, Jews and Muslims have had excellent relations in history: when persecuted in Christendom, Jews always found a welcoming refuge in Muslim lands; in Moorish Spain, Jews and Muslims produced a dynamic, learned society with a strong accent on multiculturalism [8].

But regardless of 5:82, Muslims and Christians have not enjoyed a close relationship in history. I think this is largely because of the Christian doctrine that salvation can be obtained only through Christ. In history, Christianity made orthodox belief and rigorous policing of heresy the foundation of citizenship. Beyond the ambit of orthodox Christianity existed only those who were deemed inherently inimical and hostile. It was an exclusivist concept, not a recipe for ecumenical courtesy. It produced a history which continues to cast a long shadow over contemporary events and attitudes [9].

But it is not only Judaism and Christianity that are based on revealed Truth. The Qur'an also mentions another community: the Sabians (2:62). In the Prophet's Medina, the Sabians were those who believed in divine mystery and followed the Gnostic path. In contemporary times, I would argue, the Sabians represent all those with mystical tendencies, who promote self-awareness of God and 'do good'. For these people too, we are told, 'there is no fear': 'they shall have their reward from their Lord'. We can expand this circle of faith communities even wider. If prophets have been sent to every nation, then every religious community has some aspects of the Divine Truth. Sufi scholars in India, for example, have argued that Ram and Krishna, highly revered in Hinduism, could be prophets. And Hindus are a people of the Book as they have the Vedas, which contain an abstract idea of God and describe *Ishwar* (God) as without shape and human attributes (*nirankar* and *nirgun*), a notion not too far removed from the monotheistic conception of God. And Sikhs, with their emphasis on the Unity of God and reliance on the teachings of Sufi saints, are clearly a faith community with aspects of Divine Truth. Such considerations led Shah Waliullah, the eighteenth Indian reformist Sufi, to postulate the idea of *wahdat al-deen* or 'unity of religions' [10]: an idea that has common currency amongst Sufis.

I think that the Qur'an supports this position. Every community, we are told, has 'appointed acts of devotion' (22:34), symbolic ways of worshipping and adoring God. And we read in 2:148, 'each community has its own direction to which it turns'. Every faith community has its own individual path that it takes towards God and finds its own way 'to do good' and be virtuous.

Thus, the Qur'an envisages a religiously plural world, where different communities share different aspects of the Divine Truth. Each religion is unique in its beliefs, rituals and forms of worship. But underneath the external differences there is an internal unity; and the Qur'an places a strong accent on this unity. The emphasis should lead us to appreciate religious pluralism as well as promote religious harmony.

Of course, this is not always the case. Some may even argue it is seldom the case. I would certainly agree that while Muslims always take pride in the record of tolerance and multiculturalism in their history, in today's world we do not live up to our heritage. And even our view of history may have too rosy a glow. Muslims are often too complacent, too ready to overstate their case, rather than investigate their failings. Communal tensions, political expediency and the dictates of power have been features of Muslim polities as of other societies. And when we are stiff-necked and indulge in holier than thou attitudes towards other faiths, we are explicitly out of line with the spirit and the letter of the Qur'an.

To promote religious harmony in a world of religious plurality, the Qur'an provides a number of guidelines. First, the faith communities are urged not to take an extremist position: 'People of the Book do not go to excess in your religion, and do not say anything about God except the truth' (4:171). Second, they are urged to deal with each other in the best of all possible ways: when arguing about God they should argue in the 'most courteous way' (16:125) and 'say what is best' (17:53). Third, they are advised not to revile the beliefs of each other, indeed even the beliefs of the polytheists (6:108); and, when accosted by others for their own beliefs, they are urged to 'walk humbly on earth' and reply: 'Peace' (25:63).

Of course, treating each other with respect, and speaking in a gentle and kind manner, is sometimes just not enough, particularly when it concerns fundamental religious differences. Here, the Qur'an offers an ultimate fallback position: declare a truce and move on:

> Say: 'O unbelievers! I do not worship what you worship,
> Nor do you worship what I worship;
> Nor will I ever worship what you worship,
> Nor will you ever worship what I worship,
> You have your religion,
> And I have mine.' (109:1–6).

The most important guidance given by the Qur'an, however, is a riposte to all people of all faiths: that God Alone knows all! It is a reminder that ultimately faiths define their differences in terms of practise, worship and rituals, ordered by theological, that is human, interpretation. But flawed human beings can have only a tenuous hold on weighty theological distinctions about the nature of God, the Hereafter, the nature and circumstances of forgiveness and redemption and other such issues. Yet it is a consistent feature of human nature to contend and argue, to go to war to kill and to die for the sake of what we can never know nor of which in this life can we possess the whole truth; only God Alone knows the answer to these questions and will make them clear to us, not in this world but only in the next. All the etiquette the Qur'an offers about religious debate underscores this point; just as all it has to say about human communities over complicating and over interpreting and turning revelation to their own ends makes the same point.

It may be human to be fascinated by imponderable questions relating to faith, what we regard as the big questions of existence. But what the Qur'an is also telling us clearly and repeatedly is that giving in to this impulse—the desire to appropriate and domesticate God to our level of understanding and pronounce definitively on matters that belong to God alone—is the most basic distraction from the true path of faith, which is doing good, bringing forth justice and equity in ourselves, the life of our society and relations with other peoples.

Instead of focusing attention on what we can never know in this existence, the Qur'an again and again insists that the true testament of faith is harnessing all our intelligence, energy and commitment for those things we can affect. It is within our power, indeed it is the true meaning of a life of faith, to work to change ourselves and the societies in which we live to ensure the dignity of every human being, and that we nurture and husband every part of God's creation. Anything that diverts us from the enormity of making the right and appropriate moral and ethical choices that lead us toward the betterment of the human condition is, in the Qur'anic view, a waste of time and energy. God consciousness, the motive force of faith, is about doing, making and being, not contorting our understanding by trying to ponder the mind of God. Instead of arguing over theological issues, we should ensure that there is freedom, equity, fairness and accountability in human societies, that there is full participation for everyone, no matter what they believe or who they are. We have to ensure the eradication of poverty and give everyone the dignity of fair wages and gainful employment according to their abilities, economic justice for all and education for all. These are only some of the explicit areas of human life to which the Qur'an devotes particular attention and which thus become the substance of living faith. These problems are hard enough to tackle, as history and our own day prove again and again. But they are essential tests of our faith. At the core of all religion is this selfsame message, so collaborating on the moral challenge of daily life is the clearest proof of God consciousness, however we conceive of or worship God.

The Qur'an's pragmatic approach to religious pluralism is really quite amazing. There is no notion of supremacy here. Believers of all faiths, and none, are urged to recognise that religious differences exist and will continue to exist. They are asked to put their differences aside and collaborate with each other: 'Say, "People of the Book, let us arrive at a statement that is common to us all' (3:64).

I find the idea that Islam will somehow reign supreme and dominate the world, believed by some Muslims, to be errant nonsense from the perspective of the Qur'an. The Qur'an does not expect, or indeed suggest, that everyone will accept Islam or that the world will become a monolithic religious entity under the tutelage of some imagined global 'Islamic Caliphate', as some Muslims would have us believe. But it does expect that everyone should have the freedom to believe what they wish—let there be no compulsion in religion—and that believers of different religions can and should co-exist in harmony and mutual respect. Humanity is one; but it is a humanity that thrives on diversity and difference—as we shall see in the topic of the next chapter.

33

HUMANITY AND DIVERSITY

Equality is a recurrent theme of the Qur'an. All human beings are 'the children of Adam' and have been 'honoured' and made to 'excel' (17:70). Furthermore, as God's creation we become truly human when the breath or spirit of God is breathed into each and every one of us. Therefore, we all deserve to be treated with equality and dignity.

But the Qur'an goes on to make some more explicit points. All human beings, whatever their creed, race, class and culture, are equal, we are told. And it is not just the individuals who deserve respect. The 'diversity of your tongues and colours', we read in 30:20, are 'His signs'. So discrimination is forbidden not just on the basis of colour, but also on the basis of language and culture. The Qur'an insists that all languages and cultures are equal, equally important for maintaining diversity, and have to be valued equally. Thus Arabic is as important as, say, Swahili, Urdu or English; one language cannot claim superiority over the other. And the culture of, for example, Australian Aborigines is as important and deserving of respect as European cultures. One cannot assimilate the other; or relegate the other to the margins.

In the 'diversity of your tongues', the Qur'an tells us, 'there are messages' for those 'who posses knowledge' (30:22). What could these messages be? One obvious message is that diversity and difference are the very essence of God's creation. Everything exists in multiples and in diverse forms. Only the uncreated God is one. Another message, I think, is that diversity is a prerequisite for survival itself. When diversity is diminished—a language disappears, one culture is assimilated into another, flora and fauna are eradicated—we and our world are diminished. Diversity makes it possible for us to exist and live in our terrestrial abode and thrive. Equally, it enables us to engage with one another, to recognise each other, and hence to know each other. This is the subject of one of my favourite verses in the Qur'an: 'O humankind! We have created you male and female, and made you nations and tribes, that you may know one another' (49:13). Recognition through difference does seem somewhat paradoxical. But the paradox here is more apparent than real. The verse, I think, provides another advance on our understanding of diversity, adding the political and social entities within which we live to the list of purposeful and meaningful diversity of human existence [11].

What is it we can know of each other if we live in different nations, with different religions, different languages, being people of different races and cultures? It seems to me these are the elements that define identity. And to me the Qur'an is saying that identity is central to our capacity as human beings first to know ourselves and then through knowing ourselves as God's creation know other people equally as God's creation. Only when we are grounded in our own identity can we learn how to extend to others the obligations and responsibilities, the rights and the duties we claim for ourselves.

The challenge the Qur'an poses is one that has endured through human history and that in most instances people have flunked: to be able to see ourselves in and through the differences between our own way of life and that of other people. But it has to be said that Muslims were more tolerant in history than they are nowadays. It is easy to care for and respect people who look, talk, think, act and believe as we do. This is as true of Muslims as of other civilisations, peoples and nations, now and in history. The test for us all is to see common humanity and the possibility of working for the common good in people who have different beliefs and are radically different from us.

There is another element we should not forget in the intentional nature the Qur'an gives to the diversity of human identity. We learn about the world by coming to know the place where we are born, the people among whom we live—our family and community—and through the wider associations of our tribe or nationality. We domesticate our knowledge, and this is necessary. Differences of place, environment, of culture and all the elements of diverse identity are therefore necessary parts of the knowledge we need to care for the entirety of God's creation. No one people can or will know everything about the diversity of the world; we need each other and the differences in our identities, experience and knowledge to survive and thrive.

The Qur'an clearly guides us to appreciate, to cherish and learn from the diversity of human identity and the positive contributions it makes to human existence. But as history demonstrates, there is a catch. Human frailty leads people time and again to fall so in love with their own identity that, instead of valuing it, diversity becomes a source of fear. Other people become a threat. Preserving our own identity becomes a reason for war, for seeking to dominate and even eradicate other people. The Qur'an concludes the verse that explains the purpose of identity with the antidote to vainglorious nationalism: 'the noblest of you in the sight of God is the one who is most deeply conscious of Him' (49:13). The competition between peoples of different identities is the common challenge to be conscious of God and live according to God's guidance, as we each know and understand it. And if we abide in God consciousness we cannot disrespect, let alone harm, anything of God's creation, no matter how strange or bizarre it may appear.

The verses dealing with human diversity move in tandem with the verses we looked at in the previous chapter on religious plurality. Both lead to the same conclusion. Diversity and difference are necessary, they form the basis on which we must find ways to focus on the things we can control as we work to bring forth justice and equity on the basis of fair dealing, dignity and respect for all people, no matter who they are, nor how different they are. National, cultural and even religious identity, the traditions in which we are brought up, are not ends in and of themselves. They are the means at our disposal to appreciate the true meaning of what is universal. Our identity is the means through which we come to know God, and it is God the Creator of all in all its diversity who is truly universal. God consciousness is not one size and one way fits all. Being conscious of God is how we can come to do right by each other, respecting all the different ways there are to achieve the same ends of justice and equity for all by doing, thinking and being different.

It is a great step, but through knowing the humanity of other people in all their differences we can also come closer to knowing God. By being conscious of the oneness and supremacy of God, we should gain the compassion and insight to know other people and respect them as they deserve.

When we reflect on all the human misery and bloodshed caused by racial hatred and nationalism; when we reflect that these horrors are not dead letters, things of the past but active deformities today in so many places around the globe; we can measure how far we fall short of true God consciousness, whoever we are, wherever we live and however we worship. This much we do know. Clearly, what remains for us to learn is how to do differently by one another.

I think the Qur'an's outlook on pluralism is particularly relevant in an age when the foundations of identity seem to be weakening [12]. We talk of multiple identities and 'ethnic minorities', but we seem to be unsure of how we are supposed to 'live together' while maintaining distinctive and different identities; or indeed how it is possible to have complex and multifaceted identities. And we also have, throughout the world, the weakening of family structures and neighbourliness. Modernity undermines the small-scale units that should be the building blocks even of mass society. The small scale of family and neighbourhood, of face-to-face relationships, are where we learn, or should learn, the basics of moral and ethical action and compassion, tolerance and live and let live. It is far harder to appreciate the meaning of these concepts in the abstract, about society en masse, without the practical lessons of give and take necessary to live in strong families and vibrant neighbourhoods. It seems to me we need a great deal of courage and inspired thinking to have the confidence to value the differences of our identity and go forward together to build a society where all these differences do not separate us but enable us to come together more fully as a community or a nation. This is what the Qur'an is telling us. And this, it seems to me, is the real objective we all should be working towards.

34

INDIVIDUAL AND COMMUNITY

The central aim of the Qur'an is to establish a just and equitable social order. Each individual and society as a whole, working through its institutions and agencies, has a role to play in this endeavour. We can only realise our full potential to be good people individually if we all work together to create the conditions that support, encourage and promote well-being and betterment for all people. Therefore there should be no tension between the individual and society, since both should share a common goal.

The basic proposition in the Qur'an is that none of us is or can be an island. We might be able to imagine living on a desert island, but that is no realistic model for how we actually live. We exist only in connection to other people: our family, our neighbourhood, our community and country. All our memories are about our school, our workplace, our place of worship, the clubs, associations we join, the friends we hang around with: places full of other people as well as ourselves. Since we're stuck with other people, the only important question is: how do we make the best possible world for ourselves in relation to other people? And that requires doing right by others, so that they will be fair with us. Quite clearly, the Qur'anic vision is at odds with the proposition coined most famously by Jean-Paul Sartre that 'hell is other people' [13]. As we have already seen in considering the themes of plurality and diversity, other people are not only unavoidable, but learning how to deal with them justly and equitably, with dignity and respect is essential to righteousness, perhaps a major aspect of genuine worship of God.

The term the Qur'an uses for 'community' is *umma*. It is a concept much abused nowadays. For extremists, the *umma* is some sort of monolithic entity that must be ruled by a global Caliphate. For some non-Muslims, *umma* suggests that Muslims living in the West cannot be trusted, indeed represent a fifth column or potential enemy within, because they can never be fully loyal to the country they have adopted as their home. To me, both ideas are utter nonsense.

Both views fail to realise that *umma* is a moral concept. As we see from 58:7, 'there is no secret conversation between three people where He is not the fourth, nor between five where He is not the sixth, nor between less or more than that without Him being with them, whoever they may be'. In Christianity, the idea that Christ is present in community, that a church is the body of Christ, is central. In Islam, the moral glue that holds a community together is God. But both Islam and Christianity agree that the experience of God is to be found in relationships, in the connections between people, in how a group of people become a community.

The single most important implication of *umma* is not that Muslims are a global community, but that Muslims should be defined by how they become a community in relation to each other, other communities, and the natural world. The *umma* exists in the efforts we make in thought and action to live up to and live out the moral precepts of the Qur'an. Moreover, the *umma* is not a single cultural entity, as we discussed in the last chapter; it is composed of nations and tribes, colours and tongues, the purposeful units into which we are born. What unites this *umma* is common moral purpose. So this community does not follow the lead of any one group, such as the Arabs, but seeks to achieve the same moral ends through and within the diversity of all its constituent groups. As both concept and practice, it is meant to be a demonstration of diversity within unity. In other words, there may be many ways to achieve the same purpose; so long as the means and ends are consistent with the moral guidance and precepts of the Qur'an, no one way is inherently better than another.

As practice, the *umma* exists as far as Muslims follow the injunctions of the Qur'an [14]. Muslims, we have already seen, are described as a 'middle community' (2:143): a balanced *umma*. By following the law of equity and establishing justice with dignity and compassion for all, they become 'the best *umma* singled out for people' (3:110). Being a community means that 'the believers are brothers' (49:10); 'the believing men and the believing women are friends and allies one to another' (9:71); and collectively they are as impregnable 'as a building reinforced with lead' (61:4). The individual members of the community have responsibilities, some of which are mentioned in 49:11:

'Believers, no one group of men should jeer at another, who may after all be better than them; no one group of women should jeer at another, who may after all be better than them; do not speak ill of one another; do not use offensive names for one another.' The best individuals in this *umma*, the Qur'an tells us, are those who are the most pious and God-fearing or have *taqwa* (49:13).

It is the concept of *taqwa*, I think, that relates individuals to society. Most Muslims think that *taqwa* is acquired through prayer and devotion, reading the Qur'an and engaging in extra worship (*dhikr*, remembering God) in the middle of the night. Now, of course, *taqwa* has this personal dimension, which is about strengthening our relationship to God. But I think *taqwa* must also manifest itself through our human relationships, our relations with all of God's creations. As we strive individually to appreciate the attributes and nature of God, so we must try in our own imperfect way to reflect these qualities towards all that is also part of what God has created. For me, *taqwa* is a sign of how you treat those who are less fortunate than you, how loving and caring you are, how you display humility and respect, how you interact with your environment, how you participate in building a viable and dynamic community. And it is not something that you acquire or advertise; it is something that is recognised in you by others, the community and society.

The social activity that binds Muslim society together, what makes the *umma* the best community, is that it 'enjoins good and forbids evil' (3:104, 110; 9:71). Now I must admit that this is one of the most misused injunctions of the Qur'an. It is used as a charter by all self-appointed moral supervisors who think they know what is best for everyone else. In its worse forms, we have the state-sponsored moral police harassing citizens for alleged moral shortcomings in Saudi Arabia and Iran. But the injunction has nothing to do with moral policing.

The principle of doing good and preventing bad is that both individual and society work in harmony to promote virtue; both 'cling firmly together by means of God's rope' (3:103). I consider this to mean we have to concentrate not only on individual acts of goodness, but also work to ensure that the institutions and organisations of our society are fit for the purpose of giving everyone the best opportunity to fulfil their potential and flourish. It is about making the right choices about the provision of services—everything from energy and sewage to schools and hospitals—so that the needs of all people are catered for. It is about building peace, ensuring mutual tolerance, working for and insisting on good government: all actions necessary to build *taqwa* in a society. It is about making reasoned and informed choices about science and technology and all the ethical questions they raise. It is about inclusion and participation for all people in the life of society; no individual or group can attribute absolute power to themselves to determine the affairs of the community or to arbitrate on the issues of morality and ethics. Rather, the affairs of the community should be determined by mutual consultation (42:38). This was the way of Prophet Muhammad himself (3:159); and this must be the way of Muslim community and society.

Unifying all these efforts is the recognition that both the individual and the community are accountable before God. God will judge what individuals do within a community and how the community itself behaves as a collective.

The most basic social unit on which the Qur'an focuses most attention is the family. But the family it envisions is not a nuclear family consisting only of your spouse and children; it is both your parents and grandparents and all your relatives [15]. This extended family includes even your friends and neighbours. 'Be good to your parents, to relatives, to orphans, to the needy, to neighbours near and far' (4:36). Again and again, the Qur'an asks the believers to be kind to their parents (31:14; 46:15–16; 17:23–5) and look after them in their old age. Mothers in particular are singled out for attention: 'his mother bears him with one fainting spell after another fainting spell', 'she gives birth to him painfully' and 'weans him for two years'. Never, we are told, say to either parent: 'Ugh, nor scold either of them', the Arabic term used in the Qur'an, 'uf', being a sound indicative of contempt, dislike and disdain.

Living with other people requires that we respect their individuality and freedom to be themselves, so we are required to respect each other's privacy. This injunction is given a specific form in 24:27–8 where the believers are asked 'not to enter other people's houses until you have asked permission to do so'. But 'entering a house' I think should be taken as an example of the general principle of not violating the privacy of others in any way. Moreover, Muslims are instructed not to annoy, slander or defame each other. 'Those who undeservedly insult believing men and women', we are told, have committed a 'flagrant sin' (33:58). And when the believers hear a lie, 'they should think well of their own people and declare "this is obviously a lie"' (24:12).

The Qur'an emphasises mutual trust, family life, individual responsibility, *taqwa* and community building to avoid what it calls *fitna*. The believers support one another, we read in 8:73, because if they don't, 'there will be persecution in the land and great corruption'. *Fitna* has a number of meanings, including temptation, sedition, persecution, treachery, dissension and corruption. We are all responsible for working to ensure these scourges do not take root in our society, or if they exist for bringing them to an end. Where *fitna* exists it will inevitably undermine the moral basis of society and lead it towards self-destruction, which includes destroying the physical environment in which we live.

How we live together is the measure of not only our humanity but our faith and consciousness of God. Finding the right balance between individualism and common endeavour is the key to self-preservation and the preservation of the standards and guidance of the Qur'an. The Qur'an argues that an egalitarian society, based on mutual trust, where the individual and community work for the same common goals, is the best way for all to prosper and thrive.

In a time of rampant individualism we are weaned, it seems, to follow Sartre in finding other people an impediment to our self-actualisation, the self-realisation of our own personal desires. As the distinction between the rich and famous, the gap between the wealthiest and the rest becomes ever more extreme, a pervasive culture of envy spurs an individualist creed concerned with getting the best one can for oneself. I would not say this equates exactly to 'and devil take the hindmost'. But at the centre of social and political life, there is the ongoing argument about individual and collective provision for the basic services that sustain and nurture well-being. The Qur'an argues this is not a case of either/or, but of both; a responsibility on all to contribute to basic services for all, as well as the obligation to make individual contribution by those who have the means to provide for those in need. The centre of the argument should, it seems to me, be shifted to how we strike the proper balance and move towards eradicating need, rather than debating individual rights that would release those with abundant means from a sense of obligation to their fellow citizens.

35

REASON AND KNOWLEDGE

The Qur'an is generously sprinkled with references to learning, education, observation and the use of reason. Indeed, reason, after revelation, is the second most important source for discovering and delineating the 'signs of God'. The cosmos is presented as a 'text' that can be read, explored and understood with the use of reason: 'in the alternation of night and day, in the rain God provides, sending it down from the sky and reviving the dead earth with it, and in His shifting of winds there are signs for those who use their reason' (45:5). Thus, reason is a path to salvation; it is not something you set aside to have faith, it is the means to attaining faith, a tool of discovery and an instrument for getting close to God.

The Qur'anic notion of reason, however, is much more than simply logical deduction [16]. Reasoning per se can become instrumental and lead to oppression. By simply focusing on the most rational and efficient way of doing things, instrumental reasoning, as critical theorists and social philosophers such as Jurgen Habermas [17] have pointed out, can lead to all sorts of social, economic and political problems. By concentrating on 'how' a goal is to be achieved, we often overlook 'why' the goal is sought in the first place, and whether it 'ought' to be pursued at all.

It is to avoid the problems of instrumental rationality that the Qur'an connects reason to salvation: 'They will say, "if only we had listened, or reasoned, we would not be with the inhabitants of the blazing fire"' (67:10). If reasoned actions lead to salvation, then it follows that they have to be undertaken within a value system: when both the ends and means are just and equitable, when the 'how' is connected to 'why' and 'ought'. These questions are best

251

answered, according to the Qur'an, not just by using the mind, but also the heart.

It is interesting to note that the Qur'an often uses 'reason' in juxtaposition with 'listening', as in 67:10. Every reasoned argument has a counter-argument. While understanding comes from reasoning, it does not come with reasoning alone. We are also required to listen to the counter-argument and take it into consideration in our reasoning process. When the Qur'an says that those who throw scorn at the believers are doing this 'because they are people who do not reason' (5:58), it is emphasising that the counter-arguments are falling on deaf ears.

We reason, according to the Qur'an, not just with our minds but also through listening and seeing; true comprehension is reached when all the faculties, including the heart, come into play. Those 'with hearts they do not use for comprehension, eyes they do not use for sight, ears they do not use for hearing' are like 'cattle', 'entirely heedless' (7:179). Blind followers are not necessarily irrational, they simply stick to the paradigm they know and trust: the ways of their forefathers (43:22–3), the traditions of Great Men long dead (43:22), the ideas that 'they do not know to be true' (17:36) which have passed their 'use by' date. True knowledge, the Qur'an tells us, is produced through arguing and listening to the arguments of others, through criticism, self-criticism and counter-criticism.

So the elitist idea that faith can only be explained and taught by scholars cannot be justified using the Qur'an. I see it as a ploy by religious scholars to control religious thought. Knowledge, the Qur'an makes clear, is not the domain of a chosen few. Rather, every individual should seek knowledge as a religious duty.

It is with this holistic notion of reason, which employs all our faculties and eschews blind devotion to a single paradigm, that the Qur'an invites us to reflect, ponder and pursue knowledge. The emphasis on knowledge in the Qur'an is eye opening: again and again, we are urged to study nature, explore the cosmos, measure and calculate, discover the situation and histories of other nations, travel the earth in search of knowledge, learning and wisdom: 'It is He who has made the sun a shining radiance and the moon a light, determining phases for it so you might know the number of years and how to calculate them. God did not create all this without a true purpose' (10:5); 'It is He who spread out the earth, placed firm mountains and rivers on it, and made two of every kind of fruit; He draws the veil of night over the day. There truly are signs in this for people who reflect' (13:3); and 'Say, "Travel throughout the earth and see how He brings life into being"' (29:20).

The word used for knowledge in the Qur'an is *'ilm* [18]. It signifies that knowledge is a form of remembering God. Those who study God's 'signs in the creation of the heavens and earth' are remembering God, 'standing, sitting and lying down' (3:191). Thus, the pursuit of knowledge becomes a form of worship which is accorded special status in the Qur'an. Conventional types of worship does not necessarily make the worshipper intelligent, clever or wise. (And, I have to say, I know many devout worshippers who are anything but.) But knowledge can increase understanding, comprehension and lead to wisdom. That is why the Qur'an asks: 'what about someone who worships devoutly during the night, bowing down, standing in prayer, ever mindful of the life to come, hoping for his Lord's mercy?' And answers: 'how can those who know be equal to those who do not know?' (39:9).

The Qur'an seeks to establish a society of 'those who know', a knowledge society, a society where reason and reflection, thought and learning, are not only valued but grounded in everyday reality. The situation in the Muslim world today, where science and learning are conspicuous by their almost total absence, where irrationality and fanaticism are the norm, indicates just how far many Muslims have deviated from the teachings of the Qur'an [19].

The world of faith that the Qur'an implies is one of reasoned argument among multiple points of view between Muslims as well as people of other faiths and no faith. As we have seen, knowledge derives from seeking to transcend the limitations of our narrow perspectives. But knowledge like everything else has to be sought and exists within moral and ethical parameters. The search for knowledge can neither liberate nor exonerate us from careful consideration of consequences and risks, of the means and purpose by and for which it is sought. The pursuit of knowledge is a basic requirement. However, that does not necessarily mean all enquiries, all techniques, all objectives for seeking knowledge are good or blameless in and of themselves. It is not merely that the search for knowledge needs to be conducted with humility, but we also have to recognise that ignorance is a constant companion of knowledge: our ignorance of the questions we do not ask. We need to appreciate the fact that as human knowledge has accumulated, so has our ignorance. The quest for knowledge is a challenge to seek to comprehend that which serves the purpose of achieving greater justice and equity for all, while accepting that however much we know, we remain limited, finite and fallible beings who do not know all. In a Qur'anic perspective, knowledge does not confer mastery and it always carries responsibilities and obligations to distinguish between what we can do and whether it ought to be done.

36

CRIME AND PUNISHMENT

Crime and punishment are not a major theme of the Qur'an. Out of the 6,200 verses in the Qur'an, Abdel Haleem tells us, '70 verses discuss personal law, 70 verses civil law, and 20 judiciary matters and testimony'. Moreover, these tend to deal with general principles such as justice, kindness and charity, rather than detailed laws: even legal matters are explained in language that appeals to the emotions, conscience and belief in God. In verses dealing with retaliation (2:178–9), once the principles are established, the text goes on to soften the hearts of both parties: offender and victims [20]. Despite the fact that only a handful of verses deal with punitive injunctions, the issue of crime and punishment has become controversial, not because of what the Qur'an says, but how the matter is treated in Islamic law, or *Shari'a*. It is thus assumed, by Muslims and non-Muslims alike, that the Qur'an must devote considerable space to offences and sentence: this is why it is worth examining this theme here.

The main concept associated with the Qura'nic view of criminal justice is *hadd* (plural *hudud*); it literally means 'limit' or 'boundary', and signifies the limit of what is tolerable and permissible and what is not. In Islamic legal parlance, *hudud* has come to signify 'fixed punishments', which cannot be changed because they are designed to prevent crime. However, when we examine the term in the Qur'an and compare it with how it has come to be used in Islamic law, we immediately come across a discrepancy.

The word *hadd* is mentioned fourteen times in the Qur'an. Indeed, we have already encountered the term in 2:229–30, where it is mentioned no less than six times, in our discussion about divorce. After instructing the believers that divorce can only happen twice, and laying down guidance about how wives should be treated, the verse tells us that 'these are (*hudud*) the bounds set by God: do not overstep them', and concludes: 'these are *hudud Allah* which He makes clear for a people who know'. The obvious point to note here is that there is no reference to punishment of any kind! When we examine the occurrence of the term elsewhere in the Qur'an (as in 2:187, 9:97, 65:1, 4:12–13, 58:3–5), it becomes clear that it is intended as a moral guideline: it describes the boundary within which good and virtuous human conduct is located, where decency resides. This becomes quite clear in the chapter entitled 'Repentance', 9:112: 'The believers are those who turn to God in repentance; who worship and praise Him; who bow down and prostrate themselves; who order what is good and forbid what is wrong and who observe (*hudud Allah*) God's limits'.

Thus, from the perspective of the Qur'an, *hadd* has nothing to do with punishment and everything to do with establishing the moral tone of the Muslim community. Nevertheless, this did not prevent classical jurists from establishing *hadd* punishments, particularly for adultery, theft and murder. The Hudud Ordinance of Pakistan, for example, is all about such punishments [21].

The Qur'anic term for sexual crimes is *zina*. It is problematic in that it can mean adultery, fornication or rape. But *zina* is perceived, and indeed translated, simply as 'adultery'. The Qur'an prescribes two kinds of punishment for adultery. In 4:15, we read: 'if any of your women commit a lewd act, call four witnesses among you, then, if they testify to their guilt, keep the women at home until death come to them or until God shows them another way'.

There are three points to note in this short verse. First, the evidence required to prove adultery is exceptionally high: so high, in fact, that it is almost impossible to prove. Adulterous liaisons are not usually conducted in plain sight of four witnesses, and only eye witnesses rather than gossip, rumour or suspicion will suffice. Second, even with evidence, guilt is proven only with a confession. Third, the punishment that follows is confinement until such time as the guilty party is shown 'another way'. That is, they repent. So the overall emphasis here, I think, is on the guilty party to seek forgiveness and find an alternative way of fulfilling their sexual desires.

Later, the Qur'an complicates matters—as it always does—to keep the believers on their toes! So, we have 24:2: 'strike the adulteress and adulterer one hundred times'. Let us put some context here. The Qur'an was revealed in a society without state institutions, such as prisons. It had to provide answers that were immediately applicable to the society it was addressing. Justice had to be dispensed, and it had to be seen to be done. Hence, the advice: 'ensure that a group of believers witness the punishment'. The punishment, in my opinion, is totally contextual. It does not have universal import. Moreover, before it can be carried out it still requires the stringent burden of proof and evidence mentioned in 4:15. And there is a warning that we need to pay attention to: 'those who accuse honourable but unwary believing women are rejected by God, in this life and the next' (24:23).

The Qur'anic term most often used in connection with theft and murder is *qisas*. It is normally translated as 'retribution', as in 2:178: 'you who believe, fair retribution is prescribed for you in cases of murder'. In a footnote to his translation, Abdel Haleem explains that *qisas* etymologically means 'to track down' [22]. For classical commentators, *qisas* was synonymous with 'making a thing equal with another thing'. But the term has a much wider meaning in classic Arabic lexicons, ranging from 'to pursue someone' to 'investigate by following one's footsteps'. I think what the term implies is that the criminal should be pursued, tracked down, the crime investigated, and the culprit should be punished fairly with due process of the law—all these meanings are implicit in the term. I find the conventional reductive rendering of *qisas* as 'blood for blood' both appalling and a reflection of a medieval, tribal mindset.

We can say much the same about punishment for theft as for striking the adulterers. 'Cut off the hands of thieves, whether they are men or women, as punishment for what they have done' (5:38) has to be viewed in the context of a tribal society whose norms it reflects. It is not meant to be a universal injunction for all times. The universal principle is that justice should be done and seen to be done; and fair punishment should be handed out according to the norms of a society.

This leads to the conventional Muslim wisdom that the Qur'an advocates mandatory capital punishments. Hence, we see the prevalence of capital punishment in Saudi Arabia, Iran, Pakistan, the Sudan and other Muslim countries. I beg to differ.

There are three reasons for this. First, there is the notion of compensation. The guilty party can be forgiven by its victims. The main verse used to justify capital punishment, 2:178, goes on to say: 'if the culprit is pardoned by his aggrieved brother, this shall be adhered to fairly, and the culprit shall pay what is due in a good way'. So compensation is presented as a part of the whole package of 'fair retribution'; it should not simply be seen as an eye for eye.

Second, there is the overwhelming emphasis on repentance: whatever the crime, whatever the punishment, it does not apply merely to those 'who repent later and make amends' (24:5). In all four instances where the Qur'an specifies a punishment for an offence, it stresses that the door to atonement and reformation is always open. So 5:38, 'cut off...', is immediately followed by 'but if anyone repents after his wrong-doing and makes amends, God will accept his repentance' (5:39). This is also consistent with the overall spirit of the Qur'an.

Third, the Qur'an sees human life as sacrosanct: 'take not life, which God has made sacred' (6:151). 'If anyone kills a person', we read in 5:32, 'unless in retribution for murder or spreading corruption in the land—it is as if he kills all humanity, while if any saves a life, it is as if he saved the life of all people'. Would this apply to an innocent person executed by some miscarriage of justice? I think so. Therefore, capital punishment is not presented in the Qur'an as a norm, but as the last resort in exceptional cases.

What would these exceptional circumstances be? I think they apply to those who, to use a common Qur'anic phrase, 'spread corruption in the land'. These would include hardened, violent or depraved criminals who have no understanding of repentance and changing their ways—and here I would include terrorists. These are people who defy the norms of any decent society; they operate over the outer limits, beyond the boundaries of *hudud*, the parameters prescribed by God for human behaviour.

The point is that *hudud* represent the outer limits of human actions and not the norm. They do not apply as a general rule, but are the exceptions applicable in extreme circumstances. The other essential point is that a limit defines not only the extreme consequence that can be resorted to in unusual circumstances: most importantly it also implies and entails the existence of a system within the limits. We cannot understand the limit, or know when it has been reached, without giving even more attention to what should exist within the limit. No proper appreciation of the Qur'anic view of crime and punishment can or should exist without first giving priority to establishing a social system that is just and equitable. It is the responsibility of the entire society to ensure that operational means of delivering genuine justice and equity, fair opportunity for all are provided. Inequality and injustice—scourges such as poverty, oppressive hierarchies that exclude and demean groups or individuals—any of the perversions that human society has managed to invent and tolerates must have a bearing on how we think and understand the validity of applying the limit. We cannot make people good, but we can and should strive to create conditions where there is every incentive and encouragement for people to respect each other and treat each other with dignity, in which case the limits could retreat almost to vanishing point.

The other consideration we should take account of in thinking about a bounded system, a society that recognises limits, is that it is free to adopt any measures, any form of legal arrangements, any ordinances and bylaws that fall within the limits to promote, encourage or indeed punish behaviour. It can and should devise appropriate means to ensure that circumstances never reach the limits. Muslims seem to have lost sight of this fact. If we have responsibility for making a good society, we have responsibility to enact the procedures to bring it into being and sustain it in operation. The *hudud* are not the only legislation there is or can be; rather they define, or should define, exactly the point we do not want to arrive at.

The Muslim tragedy is that living on the edge, making appeal to and seeing virtue only in the limits, has become the norm. It is a flaw not merely in Islamic law; it exists most resolutely in popular understanding of what constitutes Islamic law and what living as an operative Islamic society should mean [23]. In the process, Muslim societies have, not surprisingly, become extremist. Our problem is not merely making a transition from the contextually rooted specific to general laws; we also need to concentrate on the norms of the human society we are guided to create, and frame our laws on the basis of dignity and mercy. The limit is harsh; the norm we lose sight of is the way of compassion, mercy and good governance that delivers human dignity for all.

The urge to punish offenders is by no means exclusive to Muslim society. The fear of crime and belief in the efficacy of punishment represent a general, pervasive climate of popular opinion. The sense I take from the Qur'an is that rather than devise ever more laws and punishments, what a good society needs is more reflection, investment of creative thought and planning on the subject of reformation. Finding the means to bring an offender to appreciate the consequences of their actions is not easy. Rehabilitation is only a soft option where people have lost faith and confidence in the concept of repentance. Genuine moral reform can be the safest long-term guarantee for society. However, it is unlikely to occur without addressing the predicaments and circumstances that lead people to commit crimes in the first place. It is not a case of making society responsible for the existence of crime, but an appreciation that distributive justice and equitable opportunity are part of the means to secure the reform and rehabilitation that are the true proof of repentance. Simply locking people up and throwing away the key is the soft option. Learning the practicalities of administering mercy and compassion, forgiveness and repentance in the real world is fraught with difficulty; but as far as I am concerned, it is a goal for which we ought to strive.

37

RIGHTS AND DUTIES

In the Qur'an there is no 'middle management': every individual has a direct relationship to God and is ultimately responsible for his or her actions. It is a basic principle of the Qur'an that 'each soul is responsible for its own action; no soul will bear the burden of another' (6:164). However, given God's Infinite Mercy and Benevolence, we can always pray for others to be forgiven. As for ourselves, as individuals and as communities, we have certain rights as well as responsibilities.

The idea of human rights in the Qur'an is firmly based on the notion of human dignity. The Qur'an provides a direct and uncompromising affirmation of the dignity of human beings: 'We have confirmed dignity on the children of Adam' and 'favoured them specially above many of those We have created' (17:70). This dignity is neither something that is earned, nor is it based on righteous conduct; it is innate, the natural endowment and God-given right of everyone, whoever they are, pious or sinners, whatever their race, colour, creed or nationality. And it can never be compromised.

The idea of human dignity is combined with the Qur'an's equally categorical stand on justice and equity: 'Be ever steadfast in your devotion to God, bearing witness to the truth in all equity; and never let hatred of anyone lead into the sin of deviating from justice' (5:8). This, the prime human right in the Qur'an, is echoed in the first article of the 1948 Universal Declaration of Human Rights: 'all human beings are born free and equal in dignity and rights. They are endowed with reason and conscience and should act towards one another in a spirit of brotherhood' [24].

Many other principles of the human rights convention can also be seen in the Qur'an [25]. For example, 17:33 states 'do not take life, which God has made sacred', which can be read to mean 'everyone has the right to life, liberty and security of person' (article 3). 'Whenever you judge between people, you should judge with justice' (4:58) implies that 'everyone has the right to recognition everywhere as a person before the law' and 'all are equal before the law and are entitled without any discrimination to equal protection of the law' (articles 6 and 7). And 'do not devour one another's wealth to no good purpose' (2:188) can be interpreted, and has been interpreted, to mean 'everyone has the right to own property' and 'no one shall be arbitrarily deprived of his property' (article 17). The injunctions 'do not let one make fun of another, do not defame one another, do not insult by using nicknames, do not backbite or speak ill of one another' (49:11–12), 'do not spy on one another (49:12) and do not enter any houses unless you are sure of the occupant's consent' (24:27) can all be read to mean 'no one shall be subjected to arbitrary interference with his privacy, family, home or correspondence, nor to attack upon his honour and reputation; everyone has the right to the protection of the law against such interference or attacks' (article 12). We have already seen that the Qur'an forbids displacing communities, sending people to exile, and recommends that asylum seekers and refugees should be protected (article 17). It is quite evident that the Qur'an establishes many of the human rights that we find in the UN Declaration of Human Rights.

But the Qur'an goes further. A dignified life is only possible, the Qur'an argues, if one has the basic necessities of life, such as food, clothing and shelter. So the hungry have the right to food, the naked the right to be clothed, the homeless the right to be housed: 'the needy and the destitute have a right to their wealth' (51:19), that is both the wealth of individuals and the collective wealth of society. In the Qur'anic framework, a crucial aspect of human dignity is the absolute right of individuals and communities to the essential necessities without which life cannot be sustained. The bounty of God cannot be restricted (17:20); and everyone has the right to be free from want, from abject poverty that undermines human dignity. So the Qur'an already balances the outlook over which the United Nations became politically and ideologically divided by incorporating the substance of what became the alternative charter of human rights, the International Covenant on Economic, Social and Cultural Rights [26]. In its balanced approach, the Qur'an takes us beyond the framework of the vexed negotiations behind the UN conventions.

The difference between the Qur'anic view of rights and the various UN conventions is that in the Qur'anic framework rights are equated with duties, and both are interdependent. Humankind has the 'right' to survive, for example, only insofar as it performs the duty of maintaining the world—that is, that it acts as a proper trustee (*khalifa*) of God and fulfils properly and appropriately the responsibilities and trust that God has placed on humanity. In the Western scheme, the emphasis is on the individual; the Qur'an, in contrast, gives equal importance to the community and the notion of group rights. In the Western liberal tradition, the focus is on personal freedom that signifies the ability to act. In the Qur'an the emphasis is on the ability to be, to exist. It is necessary for the community not just to survive but to provide a social, cultural and spiritual environment where an individual can realise his or her full potential to be. The overall concern of the Qur'an is not just the rights of the human but the rights of humanity, including the humanity of the individual.

All this, however, does not mean that Muslims should be against the conventional notion of human rights—even though, perversely, some are. The idea that people deliberating in international bodies to establish conventions on human rights is an illicit activity which somehow undermines the authority of the Qur'an is, in my opinion, the height of folly. Getting as many people as possible to recognise basic principles, which as I have argued are entirely consistent with the Qur'an, is undoubtedly a good thing. Enunciating principles is not the issue, but actually making them real and available equitably to all. Muslim societies have been notably lacking in that regard, as have many others, whether they subscribe to the UN conventions or the Qur'anic route. But also, it means that some Muslims are concerned about the limitations of conventional thought, the thinking and implementation behind the UN conventions, and would like to take the human rights discourse a few steps further—a point I argued at great length in my book *Postmodernism and the Other* [27].

As we considered in a previous chapter, the entire substance of the divide between the Universal Declaration of Human Rights and the International Covenant on Economic, Social and Cultural Rights turns on the enduring argument in Western thought between individual and collective rights. The Qur'an's answer is a unified framework where the same moral and ethical rights and responsibilities apply to the individual as to the society incorporated as a political and social entity. The state is not empowered at the expense of the individual, nor is the individual seen as rightful in battling against the proper work of the state in ensuring equity for all.

The problem is not with principles. The problem is the interpretation and implementation that bedevil activity on behalf of the UN conventions as much as on behalf of the Qur'anic viewpoint. Instead of redundant argument about which declaration is more perfect, a genuine effort to see whose activity is more humane and life-enhancing for those denied their rights by whatever code would do a great deal to carry us beyond nitpicking on the head of a pin.

38

NATURE AND ENVIRONMENT

The Qur'an contains a 'theology of ecology'. The themes of the unity of nature and our responsibilities towards the environment run throughout the Sacred Text. Nature is invoked in numerous verses; these verses relate nature first to God, then to humans. Nature is also frequently used both to illustrate the power and majesty of God and to suggest that far from being chaotic, natural phenomena have stability and regularity and hence utility for humans. The Qur'an unifies the natural order of the cosmos under the single sovereignty of God; and constantly urges us, as we have already seen, to study, understand and appreciate the order of things. Moreover, the most central concepts of the Qur'an have a direct bearing on ecological thinking and environmental action.

The most important concept in the Qur'an, from which everything else is derived, is *tawheed*, or the unity of God. God, according to the Qur'an, is One and the absolute possessor of the universe. He is its merciful Sustainer and unquestioned Master. He has created all that is in it, and brings new things into existence, by His command: 'It is He who gives life and death, and when he ordains a thing, He says only "Be" and it is' (40:68). His creation obeys His rules, or 'laws of nature', which enables them to fit into the order of things: 'He gave everything its form, then gave it guidance' (20:50). The emphasis on 'life and death' in relation to creation, which occurs regularly in the Qur'an, is important. It suggests that while God is Infinite, His creation is not. Everything except God is 'measured out' and created for a fixed period: 'we have created all things in due measure' (54:49).

The idea of measuring here should not be confused with predestination. It implies that creation has a 'finite' or 'limited' dimension. And it suggests that there are patterns, predictability, dispositions and trends in nature. The universe operates according to rules (even though some of these rules may follow chaotic patterns), regulations (even though some of these may be based on random probability) and laws (even though some of these may be contextual). When the Qur'an refers to natural phenomena, the emphasis is always on ordered, well-knit, regular and predictable nature: 'the sun, too, runs its determined course laid down for it by the Almighty, the All Knowing. We have determined phases for the moon until finally it becomes like an old date-stalk. The sun cannot overtake the moon, nor can the night outrun the day: each floats in its own orbit' (36:38–40). The point being that only when natural events are seen as phenomena within an ordered and predictable universe can they be studied rationally and eventually be comprehended and used for the benefit of humanity. Apart from demonstrating the power and majesty of God, nature is also there to serve the needs of humans. The earth gives way to the plough of the farmer, and winds bend the sails of the seamen (43:10–12).

Tawheed becomes an all-embracing value when this unity is asserted in the unity of humanity, unity of man and nature, and the unity of knowledge and values. As such, nature is not there simply to be exploited and abused. Indeed, given the intimate connection between nature and man, its abuse is nothing but self-abuse. Just as human life is sacred, nature in the Qur'an is a religious, hence sacred, institution. The earth, 'with its fruits, with its palm trees with sheathed clusters, its husk grains, its fragrant plants' (55:10–13) is there for our benefit. But it has to be treated with respect, justice and balance: 'He has set the balance so you may not exceed the balance: weigh with justice and do not exceed the balance' (55:7–9). The earth and its environment have rights. And its first right is the acknowledgment that we do not own it. We have not created it and hence we cannot own it. Rather, we have it on trust from its rightful owner. The concept of *tawheed* emphasises that nature has no meaning without reference to God; without Divine purpose it simply does not exist. This is why the Qur'anic term for nature is 'created order'.

The second most important concept in the Qur'an is the concept of *khalifa*. It is usually translated as 'vicegerent' but I prefer 'trustee'. That human beings are *khalifa* or trustees of God on earth is made clear in 2:30 where God tells the angels: 'I am putting a *khalifa* on earth'. The *khalifa* comes as a representative of a higher authority. He or she has no exclusive right to anything. The function of trustees is to carry out their responsibility diligently and ensure that the trust survives and thrives. As trustees of God on earth, it is our individual and collective responsibility to maintain the balance or harmony of nature, preserve and conserve the environment with all its flora and fauna, and treat all God's creation with due respect and reverence. Thus, we are not independent of God but are responsible and accountable to God for our activities on the planet: scientific and technological, industrial and business, individual and collective. The trust, maintaining the integrity of the earth and its environment, is a test from God; and we will be judged on how our responsibilities as trustees are carried out: 'It is He who has made you trustees on earth and raises some of you above others in ranks, to test you through what He gives you' (6:165). The ranking here is not the hierarchy of rich and poor—this would go against what the Qur'an says elsewhere and the utmost importance it gives to the notion of equality and human dignity. Rather, the rank in question is the rank of virtue: it is about righteousness and knowledge. I would argue that virtue here includes environmental virtue: some of us excel in our environmental good deeds over others. The Qur'an repeatedly asks us to compete with each other in doing good, including that which is good for the environment. Also, this would imply rank in the sense of possession of knowledge and capabilities to utilise and affect the environment: the more one possesses and uses, the greater the responsibility to do so with prudence, to guard against degradation and damage as an integral routine of how nature is exploited [28].

Nature, therefore, is a trust or *amana*, and a theatre for our moral and ethical struggle. While we enjoy temporary control over nature, we have no sovereign authority. The Qur'an views nature essentially in a teleological perspective, and therefore the claims of our 'dominion' over her has no place in the Qur'anic perspective. Here, the teachings of the Qur'an are diametrically different from those of Christianity. In Christianity, nature is 'fallen' and is viewed as opposed to grace. Hence, St. Augustine declared that nature is 'unredeemed' [29]; it cannot teach us anything about God and thus has no theological or spiritual value. Salvation comes by humbling nature. Nature devoid of God's presence and grace can, then, as Francis Bacon said, be 'tortured' to yield its secrets [30]. But in the Qur'an, nature is a 'sign' of God: 'there truly are signs in the creation of heavens and earth, and in the alternation of night and day, for those with understanding, who remember God standing, sitting, and lying down, who reflect on the creation of heavens and the earth' (3:190–91). As such, nature is necessary for both our survival and salvation as well as for 'understanding'. All creation is sacred; there is no such thing as a profane planet. Looking after the environment, and maintaining harmony and balance between people and nature, are thus part of our function as human beings. When we fail in our custodianship of nature, we also fail as human beings and become strangers in our terrestrial abode. When we cease to appreciate the beauty of our planet, we also forget our true origins and final destination. To be mindful of God, the Qur'an tells us, is to be truly close to nature.

But being close to nature does not stop us from experiencing its wrath. If nature behaves according to the will of God, one may ask, how can we account for natural disasters? This is one of the enduring questions of the human condition. Our relationship with nature includes the trauma of natural disasters which, as we so often witness in today's world, overwhelm communities with death and devastation. It seems to me that the power of nature, the awesome might and even intimidating power, are indeed part of the majesty of God. But I do not take that to be either a fatalistic acceptance that disasters happen or the idea of natural disaster as a punishment from God per se.

First, we have to be clear what we are talking about. Often what we call natural disasters are in large degree man-made tragedies. Human activity exacerbates and compounds the effects of the forces of nature working away by their own rules and regulations. So here we have to ask how sensitive and prudent human activity has been in appreciating the laws of nature and creating social, economic and environmental practices which work in harmony with the possibilities and potential of natural events. Human failure to be aware of or respect the laws of nature, or the effects of human greed, environmental degradation and irresponsible activity can hardly be blamed on God when they devastate lives [31]. Building communities on flood plains and concreting over green fields that would allow excess water to run off are not acts of God but human activity that disregards the likelihood of flooding. The same is true of droughts. If land is overexploited, trees cut down and no prudential systems maintained to store up resources in good years against the likely occurrence of lean years, who is to be blamed? And as we know, or should know by now, drought and famine are functions of poverty, human injustice and inequity. Famine is never the product of a total lack of food either in one country or in the world as a whole; it results from the inability, the lack of means to purchase food by the poorest and most vulnerable, and it is they who pay the price in suffering.

Second, the awesome power of nature is a reality, but a reality, as I have emphasised, that we are commended to study and seek to understand. If nature is a 'sign' for those who 'understand', then that understanding must include the knowledge to prevent natural disasters, or at least to limit their destructive consequences. Earthquakes happen. Yet many cultures, traditional indigenous ones as well as those at the cutting edge of modern science and technology, have mastered techniques to construct buildings that do not collapse in even the strongest earthquakes. Think of the walls of Inca towns, built with what we would call rudimentary tools, yet still standing long after the destruction of the culture that made them and with it the knowledge, understanding and respect for nature it included. We have acquired the knowledge and capacity, for example, to create tsunami warning systems—but not the social and economic justice to ensure all those who are vulnerable are warned and protected.

Third, I take the idea of respect for the powers of nature, the need to study and attempt to understand them and then to organise our social and economic systems prudentially to account for those awesome powers to be the essence of the concept of *khalifa*. The whole point about the Qur'an is that it requires us to use joined up and interconnected thinking. So the power of nature cannot be considered separately from how we interact with nature. The emphasis the Qur'an places on justice and equity requires us to give equal care to the environment and the welfare and well-being of each and every human being. These are our non-negotiable responsibilities and duties which permit us to live harmoniously with nature and each other.

However, I have to add one other point, a theme we have already encountered in the Qur'an: the concept of risk. Human beings are not omnipotent but limited, we are intelligent and perfectable as moral beings but never omniscient—God alone knows all. So for me, there never will be a time when we fully understand all the powers of nature, nor will we ever be able to control those powers completely. There will always be risk, the risk of being taken unaware by the action of natural forces, subject to disaster. The Qur'an emphasises that in the face of risk the right action is to ensure it is shared as equitably as possible. We must accept responsibility, a duty of care for those overtaken by disaster and the troubles it brings. This is not a counsel of 'just sit back and take it', nor the uncaring vengeance of a wilful, cruel God. It is the endowment, not always easy to accept, of being created with free will and given the liberty to exist and make our own way and choices in an ordered universe of awesome power. It would be so much easier, I accept, to live in a cotton wool world where everything is benign. We don't; and looking for someone or something to blame, as far as I'm concerned, is a complete distraction from the essential business of doing everything we can to make the best possible world out of the one we do inhabit.

Muslim societies of the classical period were not free from natural disasters. Nevertheless, love and conservation of nature were a major concern for traditional Muslim communities.

Amana and *khalifa* are not just theoretical concepts. They were actualised, translated into specific policies right from the time of the Prophet Muhammad. The Prophet established two types of inviolate zones bordering around towns and watercourses: *haram* and *hima*. The *haram* zones, within which certain activities were forbidden, were maintained around wells, watersources, towns and cities. Around wells a space was left to protect them from impairment, to provide room for their operation and maintenance, safeguard their water from pollution, and provide resting areas for livestock, and room for irrigation facilities. Around rivers and natural watercourses, people could not carry out any activity that would pollute their water. Around towns and cities, people could not cut trees or forage or burn, to ensure that wildlife and their habitat were protected and the carrying capacity of the town or city was not exceeded. The *hima* zones were set aside outside cities specifically for the conservation of forests and wildlife. The Prophet declared the area surrounding Medina as *hima*; and, within the city, he established a number of *haram* zones. Following the Prophet, the rightly guided Caliphs extended and created many other inviolate zones. Caliph Umar, for example, established the *hima* of ash-Sharaf and the extensive *hima* of ar-Rabdah near Dariyah. A number of *himas* created during the classical period still exist in Saudi Arabia today.

The instruments of *haram* and *hima* were an integral part of Islamic law, *Shari'a*, during the classical period of Muslim civilisation; as were animal rights, which were extensively debated, as can be seen in such classics as 'Disputes Between Animals and Man', part of *The Epistles of the Brethren of Purity*, written in the tenth century [32]. The Qur'anic verse 'all the creatures that crawl on the earth and those that fly with their wings are communities like yourselves' (6:38) led to the first full-fledged charter of 'the rights of livestock and animals', first formulated by Ibn abd as-Salam, who flourished during the thirteenth century. Environmental aspects of the *Shari'a* also played an important role in town planning. Traditional Muslim cities, such as Fez [33], were not only surrounded by inviolate zones, but their use of water within and around the city was also exemplary. Cities were built around rivers: fresh water was extracted upriver, while used water was deposited downstream. Any activity that would pollute or contaminate the river was forbidden by the *Shari'a*. A city had clearly delineated limits; and its population or its boundary were not allowed to exceed the carrying capacity of the river. Popular culture too reflected the love of nature and the urge for conservation. The titles of such classical Sufi works as *Gulistan* (The Rose Garden) and *Bustan* (The Fruit Garden) by Sadi Shahrazi [34] and Farid al Din Attar's *The Conference of the Birds* [35] provide ample evidence of this.

Contemporary Muslim societies have lost much of their traditional consciousness and concern for the environment. The reasons are varied: not least, the decline of Muslim civilisation itself, along with the ravages of colonialism and then the mad rush for modernisation. But in the age of climate change, I would argue, Muslims are duty-bound to return to the ecological insights of the Qur'an and to implement them in their individual lives, as well as their use and treatment of the environment. The preservation and conservation of our flora and fauna, the diversity of which is truly amazing to behold, is a religious duty and a moral responsibility for all Muslims. If Muslims fail to play an active part in looking after the gardens and rivers of the globe, to reflect on the needs of the 'spread out earth', to use our reason to develop appropriate policy and strategies for safeguarding the future of the planet, we will be ruined both here and in the Hereafter: 'It is He who spread out the earth, placed firm mountains and rivers on it, and made two of every kind of fruit; He draws the veil of night over the day. There truly are signs in this for people who reflect. There are, in the land, neighbouring plots, gardens of vineyards, cornfields, palm trees in clusters or otherwise, all watered with the same water, yet we make some of them taste better than others; there truly are signs in this for people who reason' (13:3–4).

39

ETHICS AND MORALITY

A book of guidance is ultimately a book about ethics and morality. So it should not surprise us to discover that the Qur'an contains numerous verses and passages about moral and ethical concerns. Scripture's moral guidance has meaning only for those who believe; or are perceptive enough to understand the 'signs' of the Grace of God and appreciate that the universe has a moral purpose. It is of little consequence to those who see without insight, who do not follow 'the ways of peace' and 'what pleases Him' (5:16). Hence, the Qur'an's moral exhortations are couched, in the words of Bishop Kenneth Cragg, in 'the perpetual perhaps' [36]. Perhaps those who believe will be able to connect the dots and see this wisdom in its true perspective. Perhaps, those who do not believe may also gain something from these teachings. Perhaps, a reader of the Qur'an has enough intellectual acumen to appreciate the pragmatism of its moral insights. Perhaps. What is necessary, I think, is a sense of awe and gratefulness.

Gratitude is the prime moral value of the Qur'an and the foundation of its ethics and morality [37]. Again and again, we are asked to be thankful to God. The 'signs' of God are there to see 'for every steadfast and thankful person' (14:5); God provides 'you with good things so that you might be grateful' (8:26); and 'God always rewards gratitude' (4:147). Gratitude comes both from the heart and the mind. It is a reflection of the feeling of awe at the wonders of God's creation, it is dismayed neither by terror nor by despair, and, like true love, it cannot be forced or controlled. Yet, unlike love, it generates perspective and discernment that lead to critical capacity and critical awareness. This is why gratitude in the Qur'an is always connected to God's favours, and the believers are asked to say, 'Lord, help me to be truly grateful for Your favours to me' (46:15).

In contrast, the Qur'an sometimes deplores the behaviour of ungrateful, graceless people: 'most of them do not give thanks' (10:60). Even though God is 'bountiful to people, most of them are ungrateful' (27:73).

Both gratitude and ingratitude manifest themselves through service or lack of service to humanity. Gratitude has external as well as internal, personal, dimensions. Externally, it expresses itself by working to improve the lives of others and enhancing the environment we inhabit. We have already seen that the Qur'an gives great importance to charity, to helping the orphans, the needy and the old, and spending one's wealth on good causes. Helping those less fortunate than oneself is not an incidental, a part-time concern for the believers: gratitude demands that in one way or another one's entire life is devoted to promoting equity and human dignity, peace and harmony, and conserving and preserving the environment. The most profound way of thanking God is to enhance our humanity and beautify the garden of His creation. The challenge is collective, as well as individual. The same moral and ethical principles are an exhortation and imperative for the community. The greatest gratitude is to organise and operate an entire society that delivers human dignity, peace and harmony, justice and equity for all—Muslim and non-Muslim alike. Indeed, the whole point of the Qur'an's moral and ethical principles is that they are not branded products, not a special preserve of Muslims alone. In a complex heterodox, multicultural society, they cannot be achieved by Muslims in isolation. They are principles that dictate the need for common aims and objectives, for collaboration with people of other faiths and no faith, a fact for which we should be truly thankful, since it offers a realistic way to achieve peace, if we learn to implement the guidance properly.

Internally, gratitude is about two specific values that the Qur'an mentions repeatedly: patience and moderation. 'Be patient' (46:35), we read, for it is the patient who ultimately have faith and hope in God: 'those who believe seek help through patience and prayer' (2:153). The Qur'an divides patience into three components. First, patience requires endurance: 'endure patiently whatever may afflict you' (31:17). But endurance in the face of affliction is not fatalism. It is about steadfastness, the second element of patience. Affliction is endured patiently because there is always hope if, with determination, we steadfastly follow the path of virtue. This is why the believers pray: 'Our Lord, fill us full of patience and make our feet firm' (2:250).

Third, patience is about self-control and seeking righteousness without being distracted by the glamour of the world or materialistic and physical desire: 'content yourself with those who pray to their Lord morning and evening, seeking His approval, and do not let your eyes turn away from them out of desire for the attraction of this worldly life' (18:28). The Qur'anic idea of patience is not passive but proactive. In expressing our gratitude to God by seeking equity and justice, we can err by straying into self-righteousness, feebleness or violence. This is why patience is associated in the Qur'an with strength, discipline and persistence. It is not about succumbing to misfortunes and hurdles, but control of the self in the face of opposition, resolve in the task of striving for social transformation. The function of patience is to persevere, against all odds, as one seeks to change what is, into what ought to be.

Moderation has two elements. First, moderation requires restraint in all we do [38]. Whether the good we seek is service to others or charity, we need to follow the middle path: 'do not be tight-fisted, nor so open-handed that you end up blamed and overwhelmed with regret' (17:29). Temperance is necessary, the Qur'an tells us, even in worship: 'do not be loud in your prayer, or too quiet, but seek a middle way' (17:110). And we should certainly be moderate in what we say and what we do: 'go at a moderate pace and lower your voice, for the ugliest of all voices is the braying of asses' (31:19).

Second, moderation based on gratitude requires humility. Humility is acceptance that perhaps we don't have the full story, the whole truth, the absolute definitive answer. The Qur'an declares: 'God does not love the arrogant' (16:23). The advice not to 'strut arrogantly about the earth' (17:37) refers not just to hubris towards others but also towards the flora and the fauna of the planet, the kind of built environment we create and how we study and seek to understand nature. The Qur'an promises paradise to those who 'do not seek superiority on earth' (28:83) and 'call on your Lord humbly and privately' (7:55). Humility, particularly personal humility, can sometimes be confused with weakness. Thus, just like patience, the Qur'an links humility with strength: 'Seek help with steadfastness and prayer—though this is hard indeed for anyone but the humble, who know that they will meet their Lord and that it is to Him they will return' (2:45).

Now the purpose of all this moderation and patience is not just individual salvation. Clearly, individuals will benefit, in this world and the next, by following the moral guidance of the Qur'an. But these moral precepts also have a social dimension. Societies also need to be moderate and patient, and shun the pursuit of superiority in favour of modesty and gratitude. The personal and the social moral imperatives lead in the same direction: the well-being of and harmony in society. The Qur'an challenges the individual and society to transcend their will to power for working together to address the moral and ethical concerns of humanity as a whole. By answering God's call 'to that which gives you life' (8:24) we can, perhaps, enhance our humanity and enrich life in all its exuberance and fullness.

But that still leaves a burning question: why do bad things happen to good people, best efforts go awry and the worst of human potential regularly make its appearance, and even win the day. No one of faith can be so lacking in imagination as to be unaware of the problem; I have certainly spent a great deal of time pondering this question. As I see it, faith is no gold chip guarantee, nor is that what the Qur'an necessarily promises. The first, inescapable reality of faith is that this life is not all there is. The essence of belief in the Hereafter, our continuation beyond this life, is exactly the reason to persevere in doing as much good as one is able, despite the bad things that happen. Only if one loses sight of the life in the Hereafter is there a reason to give up when best efforts turn to dust in your hands and society seems to be going to hell in a hand basket before your eyes.

Second, if bad things are a negation of the promise of faith, and the outcome of gratitude to God is good results, then faith itself becomes an entirely materialist proposition. It is very easy to reduce this equation to the personal and individual counsel of self-satisfied complacency, the sanctimonious self-righteousness that says so much 'good' done, so many reward points accumulated—'I'm all right, Mate; pity about you!' In my opinion this is exactly where the Qur'an's insistence on the social dimension is so essential and so great a saving grace. When is the state of the world such that anyone can simply rest assured?

Faith is not a guarantee. We have free will, freedom of choice and responsibility for our actions as limited human beings—people with a lot to learn. Faith is a guide, a source of resolve, a reservoir of strength in striving to make things better, not a certainty that all will be well. It is we fallible humans who have put in the effort to make it work and keep it up and running. Faith is about the work we have to do, not something that will be done for us because we have faith. If simply believing and being grateful were enough, we would neither have free will and personal responsibility nor live in a world with other people equally as free as ourselves. But having faith, seeing ourselves and our problems in a larger perspective, are the reason to persevere despite our personal failings and those of people around us. And that is something to be grateful for—given how bad things can get.

40

READING AND WRITING

'Read' was the first word to be revealed to the Prophet Muhammad. The revelation that is the Qur'an began on the night of 27 Ramadan 611, when Muhammad was meditating in the cave of Hira near Mecca. We know that he was unlettered. Tradition tells us that 5 he replied, 'I am not of those who read.' But the revelation insisted that he reads. 'What shall I read?' the Prophet asked eventually. 'Read', came the reply, 'in the name of your Lord who created: He created man from a clinging form. Read! Your Lord is the Most Bountiful One who taught by means of the pen, who taught man what he did not know' (96:1–5).

These first verses make it clear that reading has a special place in the Qur'an. But reading requires something to read. So it is closely followed by writing, the use of the pen, the instrument through which we come to know what we 'did not know'. Reading and writing are thus exercises in discovery, a path that leads humanity to glory and perfection. Reading and writing are essential not just for the reflective society the Qur'an seeks to build, but also for generating culture, producing new knowledge and hence building a dynamic, thriving civilisation. They are the basic tools that God has taught us to facilitate communication (55:4) and instil critical thought in human beings.

The Prophet Muhammad himself placed a great deal of emphasis on writing things down. In this, he was simply following the advice given in 2:282 to put things down in writing: 'have a scribe write it down justly between you'. One of his first acts after arriving in Medina was to write a constitution for the city that guaranteed security and religious freedom, established a system of taxes and mechanisms for resolving conflicts [39]. When the Prophet returned to his birthplace, after the conquest of Mecca, he forgave all those who had persecuted and driven him out of the city, but gave some of them an important responsibility: to teach ten Muslims how to read and write. Reading and writing are thus at the very core of Islam.

But the pen can be used for promulgating good as well as promoting evil. The opening verses of chapter 68, which is called 'The Pen', illustrate the point. 'By the pen! By all they write!' it begins, 'Your Lord's grace does not make you [Prophet] a madman' (68:1–3). One of the first allegations of the people of Mecca against the Prophet was that he was mad. Such assertions do not become true simply because they have been written down. But 'by what they write' has a double meaning. It is, of course, a general reference to what people write. But it also refers to the Qur'an itself which was being written down by a coterie of scribes as it was being revealed [40]. The allegation of madness was directed as much at the Prophet as what was being revealed to him—the Qur'an. While refuting the allegations against the Prophet, the Qur'an asks of the accusers: 'do they have [access to] the unseen? Could they write it down?' (52:41). In other words, could you justify your allegations by writing something enduring and eternal like the Qur'an, the 'Noble Reading'?

The written word can thus serve a number of purposes. In its literal sense, the Qur'an tells us, the word—spoken or written—is always an expression of one's ethical and moral intent. Hence, the Qur'an divides the word into two categories. 'A good word is like a good tree whose root is firm and whose branches are high in the sky, yielding constant fruit by its Lord's leave.' In contrast, 'an evil word is like a rotten tree, uprooted from the surface of the earth, with no power to endure' (14:24–6). The good word, good writing, is not only a form of solace, a mode of communicating thought, experience, insight and knowledge from individual to individual, generation to generation, from one culture to another; it is also something that will endure and survive the test of time. And good words also have the blessings of the One who creates them in the first place: 'God will give firmness to those who believe in the firmly rooted word, both in this world and the Hereafter' (14:27).

The good words, however, cannot be read in any which way. We need to read and evaluate what we read; without critical awareness we cannot attain the best possible meaning: 'listen to what is said and follow what is best' (39:18). There are numerous and different ways of reading. Something written with good intention can be read in a bad way. Reading, the Qur'an tell us, is always an exercise in interpretation. And the choices we make in reading a sacred text like the Qur'an itself are always ethical choices.

This brings us to the great conundrum of Muslim society today: the appalling literacy rates in so many Muslim countries, and worst of all when one considers the literacy rates for women. How on earth did we, the believers, get ourselves into such a dreadful mess? There can be no excuses, particularly when we have the example of Muslim history where free education, public institutions such as libraries and centres for scientific enquiry with free public access existed alongside the systematic efforts to translate and make available in written form as much of the learning of the world as could be accumulated [41].

There are however reasons. The home-grown reasons include the veneration Muslims have for the oral form of the Qur'an: we get excited when we hear that a young man has become a *hafidh* and can recite the Qur'an cover to cover by memory, but we should not think that this is an education by itself. That we love to hear the Qur'an recited is not and should never be a reason for assuming that nothing more is required for an individual to learn to genuinely read and write. It is no substitute for ensuring that everyone is literate. When so many Muslims around the world are not native Arabic speakers, being able to recite the Qur'an is no qualification for fulfilling the Qur'an's emphasis on reading and writing in one's own language. Then there is the veneration for rote learning and memorisation which began with the Qur'an and has remained the basis of formal religious education up to and including today. These techniques may have been valid once upon a time. Today they are an impediment to the development of critical consciousness, which the Qur'an itself insists is what reading is for. Then there are a host of reasons that have to do with the consequences of history, the legacy of colonialism, the tension between tradition and modernity that made preserving Islamic tradition with its oral Qur'an, memorisation and rote learning the last redoubt of cultural survival and independence. The results, nevertheless, are diametrically opposite to what the Qur'an itself teaches. There are also the consequences of underdevelopment and lack of resources to invest in education.

All these reasons notwithstanding, I am at a loss to understand how Muslims can not only tolerate but also endorse this state of affairs. The duties and responsibilities of believing women being the same as those of believing men, denying women an education only increases the harm. A society steeped in illiteracy, I believe, cannot really claim to be guided by the Qur'an—even though it may label itself as an 'Islamic republic'! Tackling illiteracy is thus the most urgent task facing Muslim societies today.

Literate culture, a culture of books, is barely tolerated in many Muslim societies. Those who produce books have the unfortunate habit of having ideas.

These book-borne ideas often serve as a challenge to both religious and state authorities. Reading and writing invite oppression almost everywhere in the Muslim world. Debate, tolerance and a diversity of viewpoints, concern to advance knowledge and enhance understanding—these are troublesome and potentially dangerous threats to the powers that be. Conformity, a passive population that does not ask questions but merely mouths familiar certainties, is much more tractable, fit to be told what to think and what to do. But it is not my vision of what a People of the Book should be!

Part Four

CONTEMPORARY TOPICS

41

INTRODUCTION

Reading the Qur'an thematically has enabled us to connect various verses in different parts of the Qur'an and see the text in much more holistic terms as interconnected, bound together by the interrelationships of what it is saying. I would not suggest the connections to each theme were exhaustive, but most certainly they allowed us to draw more general conclusions when compared to verse-by-verse analysis. Moreover, a thematic reading also allowed us to use tools of critical analysis ranging from semantics, hermeneutics and cultural theory to contextual analysis and old-fashioned intellectual (Socratic) questioning. In the process, I hope we have seen that the whole can sometimes produce a bigger, more nuanced and hence more moral picture than the parts.

Anyway, there are two conclusions that I would like to draw, both of which go against the grain.

The ultimate goal of the Sacred Text is to provide moral and ethical guidance. But morality does not end with the Qur'an—a common assumption amongst most Muslims. Morality begins with the Qur'an. The Qur'an paints the boundaries of the moral universe in broad brush strokes, points to the outer limits, and illuminates universal precepts. After that, it asks believers to explore, enhance, expand and develop their own understanding of morality and ethics according to their own context and times. This is what being a trustee of God is all about.

We can say the same about knowledge. The Qur'an is undoubtedly a book of knowledge. But all knowledge does not converge into the Qur'an—it is not the sum of all knowledge, a common Muslim fallacy. On the contrary, knowledge diverges from the Qur'an: its emphasis on reasoning, criticism, reading, writing, observation, accuracy and travel are impetuses for the general pursuit of knowledge; the Qur'an presents knowledge as cumulative, something that builds up over time.

And so to a frequently asked question: why are Muslims so far removed from the enlightened teachings of the Qur'an?

My answer is that this is largely due to three category mistakes. Most Muslims think that the only valid interpretation of the Qur'an is the one made in history, particularly by the first generation of Muslims. This, in my opinion, is a theory of decline: no progress is possible if all progress has already been made in history, over 1,400 years ago. In addition, moral evolution comes to a grinding halt if you think that all morality ends with the Qur'an, and we, our conscience and modern knowledge have nothing to do with expanding or discovering contemporary moral insights based on the principles of the Qur'an. Finally, your fate is really sealed if you believe that the Qur'an is a repository of all knowledge and there is nothing for you to discover. These three category mistakes undermine the ethos of the Qur'an, and are the main causes of the degeneration, discord and current impasse in Muslim societies.

This is a failure of Muslim reasoning. As a result many Muslims are quite incapable of articulating moral positions on contemporary issues. Or perhaps one should say that their approach to answering the moral dilemmas of contemporary times does not take the present, its knowledge and complexity seriously, preferring comparisons with the world as it was centuries ago. Such dedication to historical interpretations far too often ends up justifying the unjustifiable with outmoded quotes and slogans.

The discrepancy between theory and practice, I fear, becomes even more evident when we look at some of the burning issues of our time, such as the veil and treatment of women, sexuality, politics and freedom of expression. The Qur'an's position on such issues cannot be stated simply by lifting individual verses out of context and interpreting them on their own as 'the final word' of God. Rather, as in the thematic section, we need to make connections with other verses of the Qur'an, elsewhere in the text, examine the context, and tease out what the Qur'an is saying to us in our time. The purpose of the exercise is not to discover some sort of 'absolute truth', which is known only to God, but to get a more holistic and nuanced picture.

42

THE *SHARI'A*

Given that *Shari'a* is often described as 'God's Law' and has become central to Muslim existence, one would expect the term to appear frequently in the Qur'an. However, strictly speaking, *Shari'a* is not a Qur'anic concept—unlike such concepts as *'adl* (justice), *khalifa* (trusteeship) or *jihad* (sustained struggle), which are repeatedly mentioned, discussed and elaborated in the Qur'an.

The word *Shari'a* occurs, in variations, twice in the Qur'an. In 45:18 we read: 'We have sent you O Muhammad on a clear religious path.' The path referred to here is clearly the path of the Qur'an and the guidance that it provides. In 5:48 we are told: 'We have assigned a law and a path to each of you.' The reference here is to guidance that God has provided to all nations and communities through His prophets, according to the time and condition of each community. In neither case can we infer that the term *Shari'a* represents a codified canon of unchanging law designed to exist for all time.

Literally, the word *Shari'a* means 'the way to a watering hole', a place where one can drink, refresh and revive oneself. The term came into vogue in the eighth century, during the Abbasid period when Islamic law was beginning to be institutionalised. The *Shari'a* was socially constructed in history [1] not just as law but also as morality. It is now used to mean simultaneously both law and morality.

The *Shari'a*, we are told, is divine and cannot be changed [2], so one would expect it to have a direct relationship with the Qur'an. Yet, few aspects of the *Shari'a* are directly based on or derived from the Qur'an itself. If, for example, we look at the *Muwatta'* [3], the seminal legal text by eighth-century jurist Imam Malik (*c.*711–95), whose example was followed and is claimed as the

285

founder of one school of thought on Islamic law, we see that the Qur'an is there only as an embellishment. Malik relies extensively on *Hadith*, the traditions of the Prophet Muhammad. The point is significant for a fundamental reason. Those concerned to implement a system of administration and justice turned to *Hadith* precisely because the Qur'an itself provided such sparse legislative injunctions. How it was to be made the basis of governance for a rapidly expanding domain required additional debate and thought. The most obvious source of practical information was how Muhammad, the messenger and principal teacher of its meaning, had acted as the leader of an actual community. Something else also came into play when the *Shari'a* was being formulated: Arab custom. Here too Malik was influential. He was the only putative founder of a school of thought never to leave Arabia, spending his life in Medina. How the Prophet determined matters in the context of Arab custom then played a central role in shaping Islamic law, its growth and development.

Classical jurists divided the sources of Islamic law into two main categories: principal sources and supplementary sources. Principal sources included the Qur'an, the *Sunna* (the actions and authentic Traditions of the Prophet), *ijma'* (the consensus of the opinion of the religious scholars) and *qiyas* (judgements based on juristic analogy). Supplementary sources, developed over a period of time, included *istihsan*, *istisla* and *'urf*. *Al-Istihsan*, literarily 'seeking the good', was a principle developed by Imam Abu Hanifah (699–765), founder of the Hanafi School of Islamic Law. It means that laws should be based on equity and justice as defined by God in the Qur'an and expressed in the *Sunna*. *Istisla*, or seeking what is correct and wholesome, was the principle developed by Imam Malik. It emphasises public interest and establishes public and individual good as the basic criteria for the development of Islamic Law. Finally, *'urf* is the custom of a particular society. Custom, the theory goes, becomes part of Islamic law where it does not violate the clear injunctions of the Qur'an and *Sunna*. The various supplementary sources of Islamic law—including analogy and opinion of the jurist, which I regard as secondary rather than primary sources—are in fact methods for utilising, drawing inference from and thus understanding the basic sources: the Qur'an and the *Sunna*. These methods, as well as the outcome of their use, are human products. What these methods, and the diversity of opinions based on them, actually demonstrate is that the Qur'an and *Sunna*, and hence Islamic law, are highly flexible and open to a number of interpretations. Unfortunately, as Islamic law evolved, juristic opinion came to be viewed in dogmatic terms, as expressing the final or finished interpretation. The real basis of Islamic law thus became not the Qur'an and

Sunna per se but the methods developed to utilise the fundamental sources and the opinions that emerged from using these methods. It is worth noting that none of the classical jurists who developed these methods ever claimed a monopoly on interpretation or regarded their opinions as the last word. It was later generations that attributed finality to their findings, as various schools of Islamic law gradually evolved, developed and were canonised.

What is regarded as Islamic law nowadays is essentially a body of juristic opinions that began to be socially constructed during the early Abbasid period of the eighth and ninth centuries. Today, what is understood as the *Shari'a* incorporates layer upon layer of classical legal rulings, known as *fiqh*, or jurisprudence, which has acquired an immutable status [4]. When people look to the *Shari'a* for guidance on a particular issue, what they are actually looking at is *fiqh*, the rulings of medieval jurists, rather than looking directly at how the Qur'an treats that issue. And these rulings define not just law but also morality. So the legal injunctions developed to solve the problems of a bygone era based on the social and cultural circumstances and understanding of a medieval society have come to be seen as the law and morality of Muslim societies for all times! It is hardly surprising then that not much of the *Shari'a* has any contemporary relevance and bears little relationship to what the Qur'an actually says. This is why wherever the *Shari'a* is imposed (and it is always imposed!), as for example in Saudi Arabia or Afghanistan under the Taliban, it reproduces the conditions of medieval times.

The discrepancy between theory as presented in the Qur'an and the *Shari'a*, which is supposed to put Qur'anic principles and injunctions into practice, arises in three forms: (1) the *Shari'a* frequently acts against the strict injunctions of the Qur'an; (2) what the Qur'an relegates to the periphery as extreme or boundary conditions, the *Shari'a* brings to the centre and makes them the norm; and (3) while the Qur'an repeatedly insists on justice, the *Shari'a* often ends up propagating injustice.

To give a few examples:

1. The Qur'an declares that 'there is no compulsion in religion' (2:256), but the *Shari'a* prescribes capital punishment for apostasy.
2. The *Shari'a* prescribes stoning to death for adultery. Nowhere in the Qur'an do we find anything remotely related to stoning. Moreover, the Qur'anic legislation on adultery, as we shall see in Chapter 46, 'Sex and Society', makes it virtually impossible to prove adultery.
3. The Qur'an asks for four witnesses to prove 'lewd' behaviour to ensure that injustice is not committed on those who are accused of such behaviour,

particularly women. The *Shari'a* treats rape and 'lewd' behaviour as equal. In the absence of four witnesses, the rape victims are treated as adulterers and punished as such; thus, under the *Shari'a*, they are doubly victimised.

4. The Qur'an, as we shall see, prescribes no specific punishment for homosexuality. The *Shari'a*, on the other hand, insists on capital punishment.

5. Virtually all of the *Shari'a* legislation regarding women—divorce, alimony, custody of children—is in fact misogynist and anti-women, whereas the Qur'an demands that men and women should be treated equally before the law.

6. The *Shari'a* makes *hudud* punishments the norm. As we have already seen, *hadd* means outer limits or boundary and is concerned with establishing the moral tone of the Muslim community. Yet, by turning it into a norm the *Shari'a* makes capital punishment a standard feature of Islamic law. Under the *Shari'a*, there seems to be only one rule: kill everybody who disagrees with you, or is seen by you as deviant, or breaks your rules. It is the total antithesis of the spirit of the Qur'an.

These few examples illustrate how far the *Shari'a* has deviated from the teachings of the Qur'an, and how little relevance it has to the Sacred Text. Its development is intertwined with the social and cultural dynamics of the development of Muslim rule, which go a long way to explaining how irrelevant, absurd and ridiculous the *Shari'a* appears in the contemporary world [5].

Why has the *Shari'a* deviated so far from the spirit of the Qur'an? The *Shari'a* developed in the midst of the historic realities of Muslim society. The vital aspects of this society need to be considered. During its early centuries Muslim history was in its expansionist phase, and *Shari'a* incorporated the logic of Muslim imperialism. The *Shari'a* rulings on apostasy, for example, derive from this logic. The same can be said of the division of the world into *Dar al Islam* and *Dar al Harb*. The *Shari'a* preserved a simplistic expansionist view which could foster hostility to non-Muslims by demarcating 'the abode of peace' (lands under the dominance of Islam) and 'the domain of war' (regions where it confronted 'the infidel'). Within its area of dominance, a complex process of adaptation and cultural change was underway. Muslim society and hence the *Shari'a* was not just a product of Arabia. It was the outcome of the interplay between a Sacred Text contextually rooted in Arabian society transported to rule over lands with their own long history of complex organisation: the Hellenised Middle East and the Persian Empire. The more those out of Arabia became intertwined with the peoples and lands over which they ruled, the more adaptation and accommodation became a two-way process. Converts to Islam brought their own cultural histories, understandings of custom as well as their social and cultural formation in different religious traditions to their interpretation and application of the Qur'an. The formation and content of the *Shariʿa* was expansive not just in terms of the dynamics of imperialism but also in human, social and cultural terms. Moreover, those who framed the *Shariʿa* were not the managers of society. They were concerned largely with individual and specific legal matters rather than with theorising the implications of their judgements for society as a whole. The dynamics and requirements of power were often at odds with the religious and intellectual elite who served as judges, framing and developing ideas of law and morality. The *Shariʿa* developed with an inner tension and division between those who governed and set themselves above society and those who framed the law.

We need to appreciate the fact that, far from being Divine, the *Shariʿa* is almost totally a human product. By insisting that an outmoded body of man-made law is Divine, we do an injustice both to the Qur'an and to ourselves. Criticism of the *Shariʿa* is often shunned and outlawed by appealing to its divine nature. The elevation of the *Shariʿa* to the divine level also means the believers themselves have no agency: since 'The Law' is a priori given, people themselves have nothing to do except to follow it. Even if the law is patently unjust, violates the basic principles of ethics and morality, it has to be followed. There is just no provision for the believers, as individuals, to engage critically with the law. Yet, the *Shariʿa*, as a way to a watering hole, should be the source from which the believers quench their thirst for knowledge and contemporary relevance. It should be a problem-solving methodology [6] that requires the believers to exert themselves and constantly reinterpret the Qur'an and look at the life of the Prophet Muhammad with fresh eyes. Just as the Qur'an has to be reinterpreted from epoch to epoch, so the *Shariʿa* has to be reformulated to accommodate and make sense of changing contexts.

Frankly, the historic methods used to develop Islamic law, such as analogy, consensus and custom, are rudimentary. They cannot meet the challenge of contemporary times. We need to rethink not just what would constitutes Islamic law in contemporary times, but also how we study and derive legal principles from the Qur'an which are relevant to our epoch. The Qur'an itself sees law as dynamic and provides ample space for change and accommodation. It provides the template of enduring values which have to be delivered to further the objectives of its moral and ethical framework according to the circumstances in which people live. Indeed, even what the Qur'an prohibits may become permissible when the situation demands: 'if someone is forced by hunger, rather than by desire or excess, then God is most forgiving, most merciful' (6:145). Moreover, the door is wide open to adopt anything new that is good, wholesome and of utility, whatever its origins: 'the unlettered Prophet' 'commands them to do right and forbids them to do wrong, who makes good things lawful to them and bad things unlawful, and relieves them of their burdens and the iron collars that were on them' (7:17). It defies both the Qur'an and logic to suggest that law and morality have not evolved or that nothing good has come out of the centuries since the *Shari'a* was first formulated.

Classical Muslim scholars, like Malik, did recognise the principle but argued that even though the law is occasioned by a specific situation, its application is universal. That, I believe, was a fundamental error. The 'iron collar' in 7:17 refers to difficult obligations imposed on the Children to Israel. It seems to me that by making universal a law that was produced in a specific situation during a specific period, the *Shari'a* has been turned into an 'iron collar' around the neck of Muslim societies, and keeps them from moving forward into the twenty-first century. Law changes as society and its needs change. Islamic law cannot be 'law' if it is frozen in history. To be considered as law, the *Shari'a* must be dynamic, constantly changing and adjusting to change, while remaining faithful to the principles of the Qur'an. Moreover, we need to distinguish between legal enactments, which are subject to change, and universal moral injunctions. Only by making this distinction can we truly understand the spirit of the Qur'an—and develop a *Shari'a* that promotes justice and equity and guides the believers to 'a clear religious path'.

We also need to recognise that the *Shari'a* has become truncated by history. As Muslim lands became subject to colonial European rule, more and more of the business of society was handed over to administration under European codes of law. It was hardly the concern of colonial administrations to inject dynamism into Islamic law, indeed it served their purpose to encourage and promote the view that *Shari'a* was an established, fixed and unchanging canon in those areas where they feared to interfere with its operation. As a distinct legal system, *Shari'a* became even more fossilised as purely a code of personal and family law. Where once studying the basis of Islamic law was the means of progressing to education in a variety of disciplines, increasingly Islamic education became downgraded to mastering an ever more fixed and limited section of purely religious disciplines. Those who knew Islamic law knew less and less of a rapidly modernising world around them. To move forward it is not the inherited, fossilised body of law conventionally termed the *Shari'a* that is necessary. What is needed, on the one hand, is a robust study of the history of ideas to unravel the immovable object the *Shari'a* has become; and, on the other hand, there is a desperate need for robust reasoning about how to recover the means of making laws consonant with Qur'anic principle and values that operate its moral and ethical framework to serve the actual needs of society. The *Shari'a* has to become a vigorous, dynamic work of human reason.

43

POWER AND POLITICS

The Qur'an describes itself as 'a guidance', a manual outlining how to live a good life. As such it is intensely concerned with all aspects of governance. It deals with governance of the self that is both spiritual and mundane, extending to all aspects of thought and daily living. The good person is the prime focus of the principles and values of its moral and ethical framework. However, self-governance, living a good life by doing good deeds, is only one aspect of the message. The Qur'an is also concerned with governance in the sense of the organisation of society. The consistent emphasis in the Qur'an is that the good person is impossible without accepting responsibility for the creation and advancement of a good society. The moral and ethical framework it outlines embraces and includes both the individual and the collective. The responsibility for undertaking transformative action is placed upon the individual working with and within the community as a whole. The Qur'an does not present a prescriptive view of a specific kind of political system or system of governance, but fulfilling its objectives, demands a style of engaging with society that could be termed participatory democracy. This vision is both distinctive and extensive.

The issues of politics and power are discussed in the Qur'an through historical and allegorical verses. These verses talk in general terms about transgression, spreading corruption on earth and limits to power with references to the history of Arabia, Egypt, Palestine as well as the Eastern Roman Empire and Iraq. The overt message is that God will deal with the tyrants of the present and the future just as He dealt with the tyrants of the past: with punishment, ruin and dishonour. The underlying meaning is that absolute power corrupts absolutely, leads to tyranny, which inevitably leads to the decline and downfall of empires and societies.

The results of abuse of power are illustrated in a number of narratives of historic people. In several places, the Qur'an asks the reader to remember 'the stories about their predecessors, the people of Noah, Ad, Thamud, Abraham, Midian, and the ruined cities' (9:70). The people of Ad, who lived in South Arabia, were endowed with great power and stature (7:69). But they became 'vain' and began to 'act like tyrants' (26:128–30). The people of Tahmud, who succeeded the people of Ad, behaved in a similar manner. Moses and his brother Aaron were sent to the Pharaoh of Egypt because he had 'exceeded all bounds' (20:43), and 'made himself high and mighty in the land and divided people into different groups: one group he oppressed, slaughtering their sons' (28:4), while favouring the other group. All three tyrannies met a similar fate: 'Have you not considered how your Lord dealt with [the people] of Ad, of Iram, [the city] of lofty pillars, whose like has never been in any land, and the Thamud, who hewed into the rocks in the valley, and the mighty and powerful Pharaoh? All of them committed excess in the land, and spread corruption there: your Lord let a scourge of punishment loose on them. Your Lord is always watchful' (89:6–14).

The import of these verses is clear: God hates tyrants. Power has to be exercised on the basis of mercy and compassion and be used to uphold justice and equity in all its manifestations.

But a further point is being made in these and similar other verses. Tyranny is perpetuated when rulers assume they have absolute power. In the Qur'an, the word for possessing power or to have power and dominion (*mulk*) is used exclusively for God. There are two exceptions: *mulk* (kingdom) and the associated word *malik* (king) are used with reference to David, Solomon and Saul, where they are said to have a kingdom and are described as prophet-rulers. But in all other places in the Qur'an, *mulk* and *malik* refer only to God, as for instance in 5:17: 'God's is the kingdom of the heavens and the earth and all that is in between' or 'Say God, Lord of the Kingdom!' (3:26). The exclusive use suggests that only God can be described as king, and absolute power belongs only to God, 'the all knowing and wise' (9:15), who has 'power over all things' (35:1). To assume absolute power is to assume you 'can withhold the blessings God opens up for people' or 'release whatever He withholds' (35:2). It is, in fact, to assume you have power over life and death; power to do as you wish; power to rule without accountability; power to sit in judgement over others and power to make law and put yourself above the law. In short, you have the power of God; or, at least, to think and act as if sharing the power of God. 'How can you be so deluded?' (35:3), the Qur'an asks. 'He does not allow anyone to share His rule' (18:26).

It is precisely to avoid absolute power, along with the oppression and tyranny that accompanies it, that the Qur'an provides guidance on who should rule, how the rulers should be chosen, why we should obey the rulers and when the rulers should not be obeyed.

To begin with, political leadership is not something that is inherited, or is automatically conferred on the basis of class or wealth. After Abraham made Mecca his home, and had purified the House of God 'for those who walk around it, those who stay there, and those who bow and prostrate in worship' (2:125), he prayed for the city to become 'a heaven of peace and prosperity for ever' (14:35). Naturally, he was concerned how the city would function and be led after his time. So: 'When Abraham's Lord tested him with certain commandments, which he fulfilled, He said, "I will make you a leader of the people." Abraham asked, "And will you make leaders from my descendents too?" God answered, "My pledge does not hold for those who do evil"' (2:124). Thus, even the descendants of a prophet have no legitimate claim to leadership. That is why when Solomon prayed for power he did not wish it to become some sort of inheritance: 'Lord forgive me!' Solomon prayed, 'grant me such power as no one after me will have' (38:35). In relating the story of Talut/Saul, the Qur'an rejects class and wealth as irrelevant for political authority: 'Their Prophets said to them, "God has appointed Talut/Saul to be your king", but they said, "How can he be king over us when we have a greater right to rule than he? He does not even have great wealth." He said, "God has chosen him over you, and he has given him great knowledge and stature"' (2:247).

Apart from prophet-kings, who are a special case, the Qur'an does not look on monarchs with favour. As the Queen of Sheba notes, 'whenever kings go into a city, they ruin it and humiliate its leaders—that is what they do' (27:34). Instead, the Qur'an suggests that power should be acquired through a social process. It should be generated, organised and distributed as a collective endeavour, involving everyone. 'Those who believe and trust in their Lord', declares the Sacred Text, 'conduct their affairs by mutual consultation' (42:38). While the Qur'an contains no reference to the notion of 'the state', the only term with any specific political connotation that appears in the Sacred Text is 'shura' or consultation. Indeed, consultation in running the affairs of the community is so important that even the Prophet is required to consult—not just those who follow him but also those who disagree and disobey him. One group disobeyed the Prophet's military orders, causing heavy loss to the Muslim army. They were not 'court marshalled', but were treated with kindness. The Qur'an refers to the incident in 3:159: 'By an act of mercy from God, you were gentle in your dealings with them—had you been harsh, or hard-headed, they would have dispersed and left you—so pardon them and ask forgiveness for them. Consult with them about matters, then, when you have decided on a course of action' (3:159). Consultation is thus a paramount principle in all affairs of the state.

It is the process of consultation that gives legitimacy to political authority. And it is because of this legitimacy that 'the people' (*al nas*, the people, is a concept that occurs repeatedly in the Qur'an indeed, it is one of the principal categories to which the Qur'an is specifically addressed) are required to obey the leaders: 'You who believe, obey God and the Messenger, and those in authority among you' (4:59). However, this compliance is not unconditional.

It is not enough that power is acquired through lawful means. The ends of power too have to be legitimate for compliance to have any meaning. Power has to be directed towards just goals if it is to be and remain legitimate. The function of a political leader is to do justice, uphold the law and work to fulfil the needs and requirements of the community. This is clear from God's advice to David: 'David, we have made you viceroy over the earth. Judge fairly between people. Do not follow your desires, lest they divert you from God's path' (38:26). Political leaders are required to uphold the law in all circumstances. Even those people who may despise them or not support them must be treated within the bounds of the law: 'do not let your hatred for the people who barred you from the Sacred Mosque induce you to break the law: help one another to do what is right and good; do not help one another towards sin and hostility' (5:2). And, like the believers in general, leaders are required to be humble and grateful to God: 'you need not grieve for what you miss or gloat over what you gain. God does not love the conceited, the boastful, those who are miserly, and who tell other people to be miserly' (57:24).

If the leaders do not fulfil their obligation to promote justice, in social, economic and political terms as we discussed in chapter 16, and uphold the law, the people are duty-bound not to obey them. The believers are told explicitly, 'do not obey those who are given to excess and who spread corruption in the land instead of doing what is right' (26:150–52); and 'do not yield to those whose hearts we have made heedless of our Qur'an, those who follow their own desires, those whose ways are unbridled' (18:28). Political leaders, even those who came to power legitimately through consultation, lose their legitimacy if they follow 'their own desires'. They are thus required to hand power back; or have power taken from them.

Power within the framework of the Qur'an is a trust, an *amana*. It is both a trust from God as 'God grants His authority to whoever He pleases' (2:247) and from the people who have been consulted and agreed to entrust the role of leadership to a particular individual. The leader is thus responsible for this trust to both: to God in the Hereafter; and to the people in this world. If this trust is not handled properly, it should be handed back diligently and without violence: 'God commands you [people] to return things entrusted to you to their rightful owners, and, if you judge between people, do so with justice' (4:58). Trust here refers especially to the affairs of government; the implication is that power should be handed back to the people, who should choose another person who can fulfil the trust of political leadership.

It is worth noting that the term Caliphate, in the specific sense of political institution, does not occur in the Qur'an. The word Calipahate is derived from *khalifa*, which as we saw in chapter 38 is best translated as 'trustee of God'. It has no connotations of a delegated political authority, or political representation, or political organisation. The verse 'He made you successor on this earth' (repeated in a number of places, such as 24:55; 35:39; 6:165), sometimes used to justify the Caliphate, has no political implication. Indeed, the notion that one group of people succeed over another, or one generation succeeds over another, contains the idea of human development or evolution rather than political structures. The conceptual introduction of the term *khalifa* in the story of Adam and his wife, as discussed earlier, deals with the creation and endowment of all humanity rather than a class of political leaders. If the political institution of the Caliphate had any importance for Islam, it would not only have been mentioned but also be repeated and discussed in many places. As God says in the Sacred Text, 'we have neglected nothing in the Book' (6:38). The Prophet does not use the term either or suggest that such a system of governance should be established. So where does the whole idea come from?

The early leaders of the Muslim community were known as *Amir al-Muminin*, leader or commander of the faithful. The title suggested that they had political and military authority. Later, the term *khalifa* began to be used in official, government circles. In the early use of the term *khalifa*, or Caliph, the political leader of the Muslim community was described as *khalifat rasul Allah*, or the deputy of the Prophet of God. This was reduced to a shorter, but more powerful, title: *khalifat Allah*, deputy of God. We can detect a slow but sure movement towards self-aggrandisement. It was a shift in terminology that came after military victory brought Muslim rule over what had been powerful and highly centralised empires.

The first four leaders to emerge after the death of the Prophet Muhammad—Abu Bakr (d.634), Umar (d.644), Othman (d.656) and Ali (d.661)—did not see or describe themselves as Caliphs or 'rightly guided'. They saw themselves as ordinary men and were simply referred to as *Amir al-Muminin*. They were sanctified much later as 'The Rightly Guided Caliphs', both to avoid disputes between Muslims and to draw a sharp line in Islamic history between legitimately elected leaders and hereditary monarchs. The Rightly Guided Caliphs were non-hereditary leaders who were chosen through various processes—election, selection, consensus amongst the majority—which can be described as democratic. They were totally accountable to the community and were questioned, challenged and held to account by ordinary citizens. They believed in consultation as an integral part of their system of governance. But the reign of three of the four Caliphs ended in murder; the last two amidst a bloody civil war.

After the period of The Rightly Guided Caliphs, the Caliphate degenerates into a hereditary system. The style and system of government of the two successive dynasties, the Umayyads and the Abbasids, were autocratic and harsh. Succession amongst the Abbasids, for example, was brutal and bloody and frequently ended with one son killing all his rival siblings [7]. The idea that the ruler is 'vicegerent of God' was also introduced by the Abbasids: their claim to absolute power could only be justified by Divine dispensation. In historic terms this process reflects acculturation to the forms and aggrandisement characteristic of the Persian emperors whom Muslim rulers displaced, rather than Qur'anic principles. The notions of accountability and consultation were drained of all their content: the Caliph's words were law while he was totally above the law. The duty of the citizens to obey the Caliph was reinforced as passive and full submission.

The injunction for 'mutual consultation', *shura*, emphasised so strongly in the Qur'an, was drained of all meaning through a process of systematic reduction. First, the religious scholars argued, consultation excludes those areas where Divine guidance in the Qur'an, and the examples and sayings of the Prophet Muhammad, are clear-cut. Then the scope of *shura* was further limited to the practice of early Companions of the Prophet, *ahl al-shura*, or a group of consultants. Their examples were to be followed in community affairs whether they were relevant or not, even though the context might have changed totally. Then the examples of the Companions of the Companions had to be copied. Then the decisions of the early jurists, who had codified the *Shari'a*, or Islamic law, had to be followed unquestionably. So society is always looking back to previous generations, rather than thinking for itself or looking forward. At the end of the process, the citizens had nothing left to do but to obey and follow. It made public opinion and public interest irrelevant, outlawed dissent, banned innovation, and promoted monocracy and absolute power. Not surprisingly, it spelled the decay and degeneration of Muslim culture and civilisation.

As a political theory, I would argue, the Caliphate has no redeeming features, nothing to recommend it. Those who demand 'the return of Caliphate', or hark back to some perfect political order, are dupes of somnambulant desires. Just as the *Shari'a* turned the believer into an empty vessel, so the political theory of the Caliphate transformed the citizens of a Muslim state into passive, obedient servants.

In more recent times, the notion of sovereignty of God has been used to similar ends. God, says the Qur'an, is 'Holder of Sovereignty' (3:26). Authority and Judgement 'belongs to God alone' (12:40; 6:57) who is All Powerful and All Knowing. If God is the Sovereign of the Universe, the argument goes, He is also Sovereign in terms of politics. Since sovereignty belongs to God, it follows that it cannot belong to the state or the people. All elements constituting a Muslim government are subject to the commandment of God, the Lawmaker. So law-making authority cannot be given, say, to a parliament, let alone the people; neither can supreme control of government affairs be vested in political parties or the people as a whole. This simplistic argument is turned into a neat, totalitarian formula.

The formula works like this. The Muslim community cannot exist as a community of believers in the Qur'an without upholding God's law, or the *Shari'a*. An 'Islamic state' [8] becomes 'Islamic' by the virtue of the fact that it *imposes* the *Shari'a* on its citizens. As the true guardians of the *Shari'a*, the religious scholars have the right and the duty to *enforce* the *Shari'a*. As such, political authority belongs in the hands of the religious scholars, or at least, the rulers must be subject to their guidance and supervision. The citizens only have the obligation of obeying the religious scholars, which amounts to obeying God, and the leaders they support. They have no right to resistance against the political rulers, as they are only exercising the authority of God, through His Law. Nowhere in this formula is there any place for free will or accountability or peoples' participation in governance or indeed independent, free-thinking citizens. Religion, politics, law and morality are all rolled into a single bundle that is directly or indirectly controlled by a single elite. Thus, tyranny, despotism and autocracy are justified in Muslim societies.

The ruler becomes beyond reproach. If he is the 'Supreme Leader', or *Welayat Faqih* (the 'Guardian Jurist'), who rules in the name of God, the Prophet and the Imams, who is both spiritual and political leader, legislator and executor, then he is in fact an absolute sovereign [9]. He cannot be questioned and all his decisions have to be accepted. He is the measure of good and evil: what he does is good, what he forbids is evil. If the king is an hereditary monarch, whose rule is supported by the religious scholars, who cannot be held accountable for their decisions or opinions, who imposes God's law on his people, then His Majesty has limitless powers to do whatever he wills. Such totalitarian systems not only perpetuate tyranny and oppression, but kill the critical faculties of their citizens, paralyse reason and thwart thought and creativity. That is why Muslim societies are intellectually dead and creatively asleep.

Of course, Sovereignty of the Universe belongs to God. As the Supreme Ruler of the universe, the affairs of the cosmos, including the physical and spiritual condition of human beings, are absolutely directed by the Will and Wisdom of God. But this will is equivalent (but not equal) to the immutable laws of nature which do not change for anyone. It is in this sense that 'authority belongs to God alone' (12:40). To argue that God's sovereignty operates in the political affairs of society in the same way as in the working of nature is absurd [10]. If His sovereignty operates through His Law, or *Shari'a*, as some would argue, then it does not amount to very much. Unlike the laws of nature which cannot be denied, acceptance of the Laws of God is optional. As God Himself says, 'there is no compulsion in religion' (2:256) so you are free to accept or reject Divine Laws. Moreover, these laws, unlike laws of nature, do not have permanency: they are open to interpretations, they can change according to context—what is *halal* (allowed) may become *haram* (forbidden) under particular circumstances, and vice versa—and they can be enforced by one political leader and removed by another. So even if the *Shari'a* is enforced by state power, it does not mean that sovereignty in it belongs to God; as we have seen, the *Shari'a* itself is a man-made historic construct, hence human beings are constantly playing with, changing and reinterpreting this sovereignty.

Sovereignty belongs to God in cosmic terms, but when it comes down to earth sovereignty it belongs to those who can make earthly decisions. The trust of responsibility and accountability for earthly decision belongs to all humanity. All decisions of state are in the hands of human beings, therefore actual sovereignty in the conduct of human affairs belongs to the people. Otherwise the Qur'an would not insist that believers conduct their political affairs through mutual consultation. It is the process of consultation itself, right across the board involving every single citizen, that confers legitimacy on political leaders, who are required to be accepted by all, and validates political decisions which are binding on all. In the Qur'anic framework, the head of state is not a deputy of God; he cannot be, as he does not have the attributes of God. Rather, he is a representative of the people who have chosen him; and, like everyone else, he is responsible to God for his actions, including the exercise of authority. All, the ruler and the ruled, have the same rights and responsibilities and are subject to the same law. The Prophet himself did not claim any rights beyond those which other Muslims had. In the actual working of the state organisation, of which he was founder and head, there was nothing to distinguish him from others. He lived in the simplest way possible, participated fully in community work, digging ditches with his soldiers and working on building sites with other labourers, and never claimed any superiority on account of being a ruler. Moreover, while some aspects of a country's law may be based on, or draw from, Divine injunctions, not all law is Divine. God does not legislate about urban planning, or what portion of the national wealth should be spent on education and research and development, or the use of communication technologies, or how we should drive. The Prophet did not declare that the Qur'an was his constitution, but framed the Constitution of Medina through a process of consultation, involving negotiations, contested arguments and the inclusion of both Muslims and non-Muslims. Laws are dynamic, they change according to context, circumstances and changing realities; and since they regulate society, society itself has the right to participate and have its say in framing laws. The supremacy of the law and public consultation in making new laws and deciding important public affairs were the cornerstones of the Prophet's political leadership in Medina. The city state of Medina recognised no superiority based on heredity, class, social status, political position or rank, or indeed any distinction between master and slave: it was a democracy beyond that envisaged in ancient Athens.

In the framework of the Qur'an, the ruler and the ruled are bound by a social contract: the ruler must uphold justice, consult the people on policy, follow not his personal desires but the interests of the citizens and the dictates of the law; and the ruled must obey and follow the leadership of the ruler. But when the rulers cease to be servants of the people, they cease to deserve to remain in authority, and must relinquish power when asked to do so by the people. The Prophet's immediate successor, Abu Bakr, made this clear in his inauguration speech: 'You have elected me as your leader, but I claim no superiority over you. The strongest among you shall be weakest with me until I get the rights of others from him, and the weakest amongst you shall be the strongest with me until I get all his rights...Obey me as long as I obey God and His Messenger. In case I disobey God and His Messenger, I have no right to obedience from you' [11].

The obligation to 'obey God and His Messenger' applies equally to 'the people'. The Qur'an warns that the majority view may not always be correct; and crowds, led by emotion, fear or moral panic, do not posses much wisdom. The Qur'an, therefore, deprecates the majority for following their whims and conjectures (6:116), lacking knowledge and understanding (7:187; 49:4; 5:103), being ungrateful (7:17; 12:38), and sometimes transgressing the rights of one another (38:24). This is why God asks the Prophet to judge between people 'according to what God has sent down. Do not follow their whims, and take good care that they do not tempt you away from any of what God has sent down to you' (5:49). The guiding principles for 'the people' have to be the moral injunctions of the Qur'an; and the demands of the public themselves have to be just, ethical and rational. In the battle for ideas, policies and conduct of public affairs, history has shown, 'many a small party has triumphed over a large party' (2:249). So minority opinion cannot be simply swept away. The voices of the minorities—ethnic communities, religious communities, intellectual groups, dissenting concerns—have to be given due respect, due consultation and due space in public affairs.

All this places a huge responsibility on Muslim people. Muslims as individuals and collectives have to ensure that they behave according to the principles of morality, justice and equity laid down in the Qur'an. They have to conduct their affairs on the basis of mutual consultation. They have to select their leaders through a transparent and open process of debate and discussion, in which all participate equally and minority voices are not drowned. They have to ensure that their leaders pursue just policies, uphold the law, treat everyone, including themselves, equally before the law and frame policies by full consultation with the people. There must also be a mechanism for peacefully taking power away from leaders who behave otherwise. Finally, it is the responsibility of the people as well as their leaders to promote social justice, equity, distribution of wealth, eradication of poverty, rule of the law, and work both within and across communities for peace and prosperity.

This makes Muslims, by definition, political creatures of the most assertive type. Politics according to the Qur'an, I would suggest, is about controlling and managing power to produce participatory governance and deliver policy through consultation, without harming society and without disobeying the commands of God. This, I would argue, cannot be accomplished by harking back to some perverted notion of Caliphate, which was in truth nothing but an imperialist monarchy, or recreating a romanticised, utopian 'Islamic state' ruled by the Mullahs. The goals of Muslim politics are best achieved by building a thriving civic society where participation and accountability are taken for granted, freedoms and rights are ensured, and bridges are constantly built between majority and minority communities, people and their leaders to promote trust and unity [12]. In the end, the final 'Judgement is for God alone: He tells the truth, and He is the best of judges' (6:57).

44

POLYGAMY AND DOMESTIC VIOLENCE

One of the longer chapters of the Qur'an, *sura* 4, carries the title 'The Women'. It makes a number of references, as the title suggests, to women and issues of gender relations. It also contains what is seen by many commentators as one of the most problematic verses in the Qur'an, 4:34, about disciplining a disobedient wife. There are also verses in this chapter that have widely been used to justify polygamy. Given the undeniable existence of domestic violence in Muslim communities, and the prevalence of polygamy in many places like Saudi Arabia and Nigeria, it is necessary, I think, to look at these verses closely for new and alternative interpretations. The Qur'an treats both polygamy and domestic abuse in what appears to be a conflicting way; but the contradictory logic of the Qur'an, as I argued earlier, has a specific creative or transformative purpose.

Polygamy is referred to right at the beginning of the *Sura al Nisa*, The Women. It starts by reminding us that men and women were created from a single soul, emphasises the importance of 'the ties of kinship', and urges the believers not to exploit orphans and consume their property. Then, we read in 4:3: 'If you fear that you cannot do justice to orphans, then marry from among [orphaned] women such as you like, two, three, four. But if you fear you will not be fair [to your wives], then [marry] only one; that is the safest course.' Conventionally, this verse has been seen as giving permission for polygamy.

The first thing to note is that the verse has a strong context. It is talking specifically about orphans. The Prophet had been involved in two battles with his enemies, the Quraysh; many Muslims had been killed, and as a consequence there were many orphans in Medina. These orphans were not being treated well. The Prophet was repeatedly being approached regarding young orphan women, as is made clear later in the *sura*: 'They ask you [oh Muhammad] concerning women. Say: God gives you His decision concerning them, and what is being recited to you in the Book concerning orphan women to whom you do not give their due, but you would rather marry them, and [also concerning younger] and weaker children' (4:127). So, it seems that Muslims in Medina were quite determined to marry young orphan women. We should also remember that this was already a highly polygamous society, where men not only had but were expected to have scores of wives. The 'permission' to marry these women is both a product of the general conditions in Medina as well as the insistence of some to be allowed to marry orphan women.

But there is a contradiction. The 'permission' has a condition. The Muslims of Medina are allowed to marry up to four orphan women with the requirement that they do justice amongst the co-wives. First, the Qur'an puts the responsibility for this justice on the individual believer: 'if you fear' that you cannot be just to all four of your wives, then stick to monogamy which is 'the safest course'. Then, further on in the *sura*, it states categorically: 'You shall never be able to do justice among women, no matter how much you desire to do so' (4:129). The contradiction here is meant to be creative: the believers are asked to reflect on their desire for multiple wives and the demands of justice and to resolve the contradiction by reflection. The goal of the exercise is a transformation: to move a polygamous society to a monogamous one. This is the Qur'an's way of banning polygamy. Instead of an outright ban, the Qur'an seeks a gradual change, based on thought and reflection.

The traditional interpretation of these verses, as one would expect, has been somewhat different. Classical jurists saw the 'permission' as legally binding and left the all-important issue of justice to the conscience of the individual. That, I would argue, was a fundamental error. It would be more reasonable to assume that if something is humanly impossible then it is bound to be violated. As such, the only logical conclusion would be that polygamy is not permitted. The function of the contradiction in these verses is to invoke thought amongst the believers on an issue of justice between genders, and to focus on the moral ideal towards which the society as a whole should move.

The moral ideal is also the focal point of the famous 'beating' verse in chapter 3. And, here too, we have a contradiction. The verse in question, 3:34, has been the subject of great controversy and has been debated endlessly. It has caused a lot of problems, even for the best scholars. As translated by Haleem, it reads: 'Husbands should take good care of their wives with [the bounties]

God has given to some more than others and with what they spend out of their own money. Righteous wives are devout and guard what God would have them guard in their husband's absence. If you fear high-handedness from your wives, remind them of [the teachings of God], then ignore them when you go to bed, then hit them.' In a couple of footnotes, Haleem explains that the verb he has translated as 'high-handedness' (*nashaza*) means a sense of superiority; and that the context of the verse suggests that a husband is allowed to hit his wife once!

Even once is too much. For if the Qur'an allows the believing men to hit the believing women, then it is sanctioning domestic violence. Most commentators, past and present, have expressed a moral unease about this verse and have resisted interpreting it as a general sanction. On the whole, traditional jurists went out of their way to emphasise that the term used here for hitting (*dharaba*) has only a symbolic significance and does not refer to physical beating. If it had to be carried out, it should be done with a 'folded handkerchief', as Razi suggests, or, as al-Tabari recommends, with 'a toothbrush or some such thing'.

But even as a symbolic act it is morally reprehensible; a point the Prophet was keen to demonstrate. There is nothing he disliked more, he stressed, than 'seeing a quick-tempered man beat his wife in a fit of anger'. What did he do when he had difficulties with his wives? Did he engage in a bit of symbolic battering? Nothing could be further from the truth.

So, what exactly is going on here? To begin with, 3:34 contradicts numerous other verses in the Qur'an where gender equality is emphasised. For example, 35:33 gives parity to men and women in every way: 'For men and women who are devoted to God—believing men and women, obedient men and women, truthful men and women, steadfast men and women, humble men and women, charitable men and women, fasting men and women, chaste men and women, men and women who remember God often—God has prepared forgiveness and a rich reward.' The logic of this verse suggests that righteous men are also devout and 'guard what God would have them guard'; and, if they fail to do so, or if they displease their wives by behaving or acting as though they were superior, women have the equal right to 'hit them'. Why would a Sacred Text that insists on equality allow one gender but not the other to act in specific ways?

The 'beating' verse also contradicts a number of verses about divorce, where the believers are asked to release their wives in a 'good way' (2:229), not to 'drive them out of their homes' (65:1), but to provide them with 'maintenance' or alimony (2:241). Throughout, as we argued in chapter 21, kindness and affability along with mutual support are the ethos. It seems strange that when a woman chooses to stay in a marriage she can be 'hit', but if she chooses to separate she is showered with love and affection. A marriage in which God sanctioned violence, common sense would dictate, is a prescription for divorce. Contradiction also emerges when we examine what the Qur'an actually says about marriage: it should be based on harmony (4:128), love and mercy (30:21), and husbands and wives should protect each other (2:187). So in marriage, as in divorce, the accent is on gentle and responsible behaviour.

I would suggest that the contradiction here deliberately directs our attention towards a specific act; and its function is to generate moral apprehension of that act. For a male-dominated society, where the superiority of men was taken for granted, the verse can be seen to express the 'natural' order of things. For such a society, moral unease is generated when this verse is compared and contrasted with what the Qur'an is saying elsewhere, its all-embracing emphasis on gender equality. As in the case of polygamy, the contradiction here forces the believers to transcend their behaviour by thinking about it. The resolution of the contradictions involves a moral choice and abandonment of certain outlooks and behaviour. Like polygamy, misogyny was the dominant norm in pre-Islamic Arabia, and extreme domestic violence was not uncommon. The Qur'an bans both: one by introducing an impossible condition, the other by reducing it to a mere symbol and presenting it as contradictory behaviour. The moral goal is to move towards a society totally free from both polygamy and misogyny and their expression through domestic violence.

But the contradiction itself may be more apparent than real. The term *dharaba* is a common Arabic root-word with a large number of possible meanings. It can be translated as beat, hit, strike, scourge, chastise, flog, make an example of, spank, pet, tap, to go away, strike out on a journey or even seduce. It is used in a number of different ways in the Qur'an itself. So why should *dharaba* be seen simply as hitting or beating? Given the general tenor of *sura* 4, where women's rights are repeatedly emphasised, injustice and oppression of women are denounced, and believers are urged to be kind to each other, would it not make logical sense to interpret, and translate, 4:34 in favour of women? It is interesting to note that despite their moral unease, the conventional commentators, classical and modern, saw 4:34 only in terms of beating [13]. Maybe this was because all of them, up until recently, were exclusively male. So it has taken a female translator to come up with a viable alternative reading. Laleh Bakhtier translates 4:34 as follows:

Men *are* supporters of wives
because God has given some of them
an advantage over others and because they spent
of their wealth.
So the ones in accord with morality
are the ones who are morally obligated
and the ones who guard the unseen
of what God has kept safe.
And those whose resistance you fear,
then admonish them and abandon them in
their sleeping places
and go away *from* them. [14]

The Bakhtier translation has two other features worth noting. She empha-sises the present tense of the verse, suggesting that the verse is describing the ground reality of the Prophet's Medina. The word she translates as 'supporters', *qawwam*, has caused as much controversy as *dharaba*. Pickthall, for example, says 'men are in charge of women'; according to Yusuf Ali, 'men are protectors and maintainers of women'; Asad says 'men shall take full care of women'; and still other translators have men as managers of women. This particular under-standing of the verse has led to the justification of numerous patriarchal traits. Men, many classical scholars argued, were the mediators of the word of God. It was their job to discipline and educate women in the ways of God. As long as Islamic law was not being violated, it was the duty of a wife to be obedient to her husband. Indeed, this obedience was given a sacred dimension by clas-sical scholars like al-Tabari and is emphasised by modern commentators like Mawdudi. By obeying their men, the inheritors of the mantle of the Prophet, women were in fact obeying God. This twisted logic was not limited to obedi-ence within the household. It was extended to the society at large: women needed a man (*mahram*) as their guardian when they went out, women could not attend funerals or grave sites, women could not represent themselves in public, women could not be leaders of the community, and a woman could not even worship God by fasting without the permission of her husband because her husband might want to have sex with her during the day! Without doubt, I think, these absurd and obnoxious rules inculcate a cultural arena conducive to rampant domestic violence and violence against women in con-servative Muslim societies. And both, the interpretation of the verse and the anti-women rules and legislation based on it, I would suggest, defy the basic logic and spirit of the Qur'an.

Men were indeed 'the protectors and maintainers of women' in the tribal and patriarchal society addressed and described by the Qur'an. It is meant as a statement of fact, not a moral goal to be pursued by the society as a whole. A proper interpretation of the verse is provided by the life of Prophet Muhammad himself. The situation in his household was quite the opposite: as long as she was alive, Khadijah, his first wife, was the manager of the Prophet's household. He worked for her in the business that she ran. She managed the finances, gave him advice and looked after him when he was distressed—she was the *qawwam*; just as the Queen of Sheeba, according to the Qur'an, was the *qawwam* of Yemen (27:29–35). In the Prophet's Medina, women played a very active part in the social and political life of the community. And after his death, the Prophet's wives became jurists and teachers.

The interpretation of *qawwam* has led many classical and modern commentators into highly dubious and dangerous territory. Arguments have been presented about various inabilities and incapabilities of women. Men are supposed to be more mature, are natural leaders and endowed with superior mental capabilities. Reading some of these comments and commentaries, I must admit, fills me with shame. To posit that women should be obedient servants of their men is to perform immense violence to the spirit of the Qur'an. I find the very idea morally repugnant.

The truth is that *qawwam* simply means 'breadwinner' or 'those who provide a means of support or livelihood'. It's a gender neutral term. But centuries of classical and modern exegesis has failed to point this out. It is left to contemporary feminist commentators, such as Asma Barlas [15], Amina Wadud [16] and Leila Ahmed [17], to demonstrate this. However the word is translated, it does not imply subordination of women or superiority of men. That would violate the more general and categorical principle of the Qur'an: 'believers, men and women, support each other' (9:71). The dominant framework within which any problematic verse of the Qur'an has to be read is that of eternal equality: equality before God and equality in responsibility on earthly matters. Which brings us to yet another meaning of *qawwam*. Elsewhere in the Qur'an *qawwam* is used to describe human behaviour towards God. Both the wife of Pharaoh and Mary sought the protection of God and accepted His truth. They were amongst the *qanitin*: those who showed obedience to God and were 'truly devout' (66:12).

Women's readings are obviously necessary to balance our interpretations of the meaning of the Qur'an. There is no genuine debate when half the population is silenced. Though there is a conundrum here: there is a saying of the

Prophet which argues that religion lies beneath one's mother's feet. In Muslim society this is undoubtedly true. I am not alone in having my first encounters with the Qur'an thanks to the efforts of my mother. Over the centuries women, as well as men, have accepted the customs and tradition derived from male readings of the Qur'an. Women have internalised these traditions willingly, not as passive acceptance of second-class status but as positive assignment to domesticity. And without women treating sons differently from their daughters, misogyny cannot persist in any land. This is not to blame women for their own victimisation. It is, however, to argue that for women, just as for men, mere reading is not enough. It is only critical engagement with words and their meanings that can take a society forward in a balanced and inclusive way.

The final point must be to acknowledge that domestic violence and subordination of women are not especially Muslim or Islamic issues, however much attempts are made to present it as such. Domestic violence exists in every society, sadly. It is not confined to any specific group or class. It has been evidenced among the highest and the lowest, the well educated as well as the disadvantaged. Neither are patriarchy and misogyny particularly Muslim traits. Indeed, in Judaism and Christianity, where women were viewed as chattels of their father and then their husband, these attitudes were fostered and far more overtly derived from religion. 'To love, honour and obey' was the basis of the marriage contract solemnised before God as a sacrament of the Church for Christian women, nor has the wording entirely disappeared. Social attitudes, however, have moved on. There has been a moral rebalancing—though it has by no means eradicated domestic violence. Muslims have every reason to learn from this and return with fresh thoughts to their own basic text where gender equality, kindness, mutuality and affability are to be found as guiding principles. However, if immense moral progress in attitudes accompanied by profound social change in practice do not eliminate domestic violence, there is reason to think more critically about its origins. In chapter 21 the discussion of marriage and divorce began with the seemingly anomalous verses relating to intoxication. The connecting principle, I argued, was control of one's passions as the means to maintain both emotional balance and sustain God consciousness. Passion, the capacity to become intoxicated with excess, is an aspect of human nature. Moral progress is not merely a matter of ideas, of critical enlightenment but also of disciplining our passions, taming the excesses to which human nature is prone, to a higher purpose. The training is to awaken and be guided by God consciousness. Both men and women need to be obedient—but only to God.

311

45

SEX AND SOCIETY

The Qur'an portrays sex as natural and wholesome. It is not something shameful, mysterious or perplexing but only another, amongst many, signs of God. Far from feeling guilty about our sexual desires, we should share our sexual passion in a deep and satisfying way and see it as a pleasure given to us by God to be enjoyed. 'Another of His signs', we read in 30:21, 'is that He created spouses from among yourselves for you to live with in tranquillity: He ordained love and kindness between you.' Thus, a life of peace and serenity requires a deep and abiding relationship based on intimacy and mutual affection.

But sex is not just an outer sign of God. It is also an inner sign that emanates from within us. It is a sign 'in your own nature' (45:3) that the Qur'an alludes to a number of times: 'On earth there are signs for those of sure faith—and in yourselves too, do you not see?' (51:20–21). Sex is thus an integral part of our *fitra*, 'the natural disposition God instilled in mankind' (30:30), our innate awareness of our origin as the purposeful creation of God.

This is precisely why sex is nothing to be ashamed of or feel guilty about. During the Prophet's time, Muslims in Medina believed that sex was forbidden during the month of Ramadan, even at night when eating and drinking is allowed. However, not everyone could resist the temptation. They felt guilty and admitted to the Prophet that they had spoiled their fast by having sexual relations during Ramadan. The incident is mentioned in 2:187: 'You [believers] are permitted to lie with your wives during the night of the fast: they are your garments and you are their garments. God was aware that you were betraying yourselves, so He turned to you in mercy and pardoned you: now you can lie with them—seek what God has ordained for you.' So sex is a gift

313

of God to be enjoyed, even in the austere month of Ramadan, which suggests that it adds to the spiritual benefit of worship.

A few verses later in the same *sura* we read: 'your wives are your tilth, so approach your tilth as you desire, and send [good deeds] before you for your souls' (2:223). We have discussed this verse and the significance of the metaphor of 'field' or 'tilth' in chapter 21. However we look at this verse, it is clear that the idea of gardening is being conveyed. Hence, the feminist scholar Laleh Bakhtiar translates the verse as 'your wives are a place of cultivation for you'. Cultivation requires preparing the ground—digging up soil, spreading the seeds, watering the seedlings, nursing the plants, tackling weeds and pests—so the 'field' can bear fruit. The advice to 'send' something good beforehand, or as Tarif Khalidi puts it, 'lay up good works for yourselves', suggests that the metaphor is pointing towards foreplay. Indeed, this is how the last part of the verse has been interpreted by most classical scholars. The Prophet too recommended foreplay and counselled men not to fall on their wives like animals, but be gentle and send 'a messenger', kisses and caresses, prior to the sexual act. The verse, I think, is also acknowledging the fact that female sexuality requires some attention and that the sexual satisfaction of wives is just as important as that of the husbands. If sex is an innate part of human nature, *fitra*, then it is equally important for both men and women. It is worth pointing out that in history women actually sued their husbands in *Shari'a* courts for the failure to provide sexual satisfaction, and had their claims upheld!

Sexual morality in the Qur'an is ultimately related to the happiness and spiritual welfare of people, both as individuals and communities. Hence, sexuality is not presented in opposition to spirituality, but as a part of God's grace that leads to spirituality. The Qur'an urges believers to take a spouse as soon as they are able to: 'marry those amongst you who are single' (24:32). But there are some single women who are out of bounds: 'Do not marry women that your fathers married ... that is indeed a shameful thing to do, loathsome and leading to evil. You are forbidden to take as wives your mothers, daughters, sisters, paternal and maternal aunts, the daughters of brothers and sisters, your milk-mothers and your milk-sisters, your wives' mothers, the stepdaughters in your care—those born of women with whom you have consummated marriage ... wives of your begotten sons, two sisters simultaneously ... Other women are lawful to you so long as you seek them in marriage, with gifts of your property, looking for wedlock rather than fornication' (4:22–4). It is worth noting that 'other women' need not necessarily be virgins; the Qur'an does not valorise female virginity. We see from the example of the Prophet's own marriages that divorced and widowed women are just as desirable marriage partners as virgins. The Prophet's first marriage was to Khadijah, who was much older than him, which suggests that younger men can—or should it be should, given that it is *Sunna*, the example of the Prophet?—marry older women and older women can marry younger men, with no sexual hang-ups.

Sex is good; but not all sex leads to human happiness and welfare. So those who are 'unable to marry' are advised to 'keep chaste until God gives them enough out of His bounty' (24:33). The Qur'an's insistence on chastity is aimed at preventing complications, unhappiness and spiritual despair. Chastity is maintained by avoiding certain kinds of sex, 'by not taking lovers or secret mistresses' (5:5), not going 'anywhere near adultery' (17:32), and by staying 'well away from committing obscenities' (6:151).

Chastity in the Qur'an is not a passive but an active concept. It is the counterpart of modesty as an interior condition produced by a commitment to values. Both modesty and chastity apply equally to men and women, to individuals as well as society. Chastity is a function of conduct, the sexual choices we make, and not of sexual identity, class, faith or human nature. One consciously and actively seeks to avoid certain actions as an individual, and society, as a whole, provides a platform which enables individuals to remain chaste. So while the Qur'an suggests that believers 'who guard their chastity except with their spouses' (23:5–6) will be happy and prosperous, it also bans prostitution, pornography and sexual provocation. 'Do not force girls into prostitution so that you may seek the display of worldly life', we read in 24:33. In 24:19, the Sacred Text asks the believer not to 'spread *fahisha*', a term with different shades of meaning, including lewdness, indecency and pornography (and, in some Muslim circles, homosexuality, which we will discuss in the next chapter).

It is to prevent *fahisha* that the Qur'an has a special take on the human body. The body per se is not something indecent. Just as sex is an innate part of our natural disposition, so is the body a natural part of our physical make-up. Just as sex is good and wholesome within certain boundaries, so the *sexed* body can only be displayed to certain individuals. Neither sex nor the sexed body can be used for public consumption. The body, as a site of desire and eroticism, should be private: 'righteous wives are devout and guard what God would have them guard in their husband's absence' (4:34). In 24:31 we find an indication of who is to be considered as part of one's private domain: 'And let them not display their charms except to their husbands, their husband's fathers, their sons, their husband's sons, their brothers, their brother's son, their sister's son, their womenfolk, their slaves, such men as attend them who have no sexual desire, or children who are not yet aware of women's nakedness, they should not stamp their feet so as to draw attention to any hidden charms' (24:31). All others are located in the public domain where chastity is preserved by lowering one's gaze (24:30).

But it is not just the women who need to lower their gaze and guard their bodies. Men too have to keep their privates private. In the Prophet's Arabia, where temperatures could easily reach 40 degrees centigrade, it was not unusual for men to sleep naked or relax in their birthday suits. Referring to them, the Qur'an suggests that people should not barge into the rooms of those who are sleeping or resting, but ask their 'permission to come in at three times of day: before the dawn prayer; when you lay your garments aside in midday heat; and after the evening prayer. These are your three times of undress' (24:58).

Thus, the emphasis is not just on the public display of the female body. But the body per se, male and female, has to be kept away from public gaze. However, preserving chastity in public does not mean that men and women should be strictly segregated, or that women should be covered in shrouds to protect them from the eyes of lustful men. The gaze itself is the real veil: and both men and women must veil themselves by averting their gaze. However, classical commentators, as is so often the case, concentrated on only one side of the equation and took the verse to mean that 'the gaze was the "messenger of fornication"'. As Asma Barlas argues in 'Believing Women' in Islam, they

sought to mitigate it not as the Qur'an does, by counselling modesty for both men and women, but by segregating and veiling women in order to protect men's sexual virtue. The Qur'an, however, rules out both male and female scopic activity. Moreover, its injunction to cast down one's eyes establishes that people must, in fact, be free to look upon one another publicly. If men and women were segregated, or if women's faces were veiled, it would not be necessary to cast down one's eyes, and thus this ruling of the Qur'an would be unnecessary. If anything, therefore, the Qur'an's ruling establishes that women can freely enter public arenas, undermining the claim of Muslim conservatives that Islam mandates secluding and segregating women [18].

It should be noted that seclusion of women and their veiling were prevalent cultural practices of the Greek and Persian worlds long before the spread of Islam to these regions. These customs and cultural norms were read into the Qur'an to become the standard interpretation of Qur'anic exegesis in history.

In contemporary times, the gaze plays a much broader role than simply ogling at the opposite sex. In a world where sex has been turned into a global commodity, and the natural desires of human beings have been commercialised, lowering one's gaze becomes a constant and monumental exercise. The sexed body is everywhere: in advertisements, on television and films, specialised magazines, the catwalk and a hundred other places. Obsession with sex is the norm. Body form, and the means to heighten the sexual display of the body, is a worldwide multi-billion industry which now sells the concept to children as much as adults. Yet this manufactured desire, this 'love of desirable things made alluring for men' (3:14), and, one might say, for women, is not about satisfying normal sensual needs. It cannot be, since the desire is insatiable, constant and perpetual. Rather, it is a desperate attempt to escape the pain of spiritual void. The gaze thus acquires a particular spiritual significance in our time. Its function is to keep the believers spiritually chaste, away from the paraphernalia and perversion, the pain and perturbations of a sex-obsessed society.

Chastity is also linked to another major obsession of our time: malicious gossip, 'tittle tattle', paranoid fixation with the sex lives of 'celebrities', and who is 'dumping' or 'dating' whom. In most cases, these are unsubstantiated rumours designed to sell newspapers, gossip magazines and increase the ratings of television shows. They also serve to occupy pitifully vacuous lives.

During the period when the Qur'an was being revealed, a rumour emerged in Medina. It was the Muslims themselves who started the gossip: 'It was a group from among you that concocted the lie' (24:11). Given the nature of gossip it spread quickly and the Muslims as a whole began to take it seriously. The Qur'an admonishes those who started the rumour: 'when you took it up with your tongues, and spoke with your mouth things you did not know [to be true], you thought it was trivial but to God it was very serious' (24:15). Those who paid attention to the chitchat are also rebuked in strong terms: 'When you heard the lie, why did you not say, "We should not repeat this— God forbid!—it is a monstrous slander"?' (24:16).

There are a number of restrictions being laid here. First, rumours about the sex lives of others should not be spread; those who engage in such 'tittle tattle' will be charged with the sin they have earned, and the one 'who took the greatest part in it will have painful punishment' (24:11). (We can surmise that gossip columnists are doomed!) The sex lives of others are just that: sex lives of others. They concern neither you nor me. They are private affairs that are best kept private and not subjected to slanderous gossip. Second, on hearing such rumours, the believers have a particular duty: 'When you heard the lie, why did believing men and women not think well of their own people and declare, "This is obviously a lie"?' (24:12). One's duty is to think good of the people who are being maligned and protect their honour and privacy. Third, gossip should not be believed without concrete evidence—when, in fact, it ceases to be mere gossip: 'And why did the accusers not bring four witnesses to it? If they cannot produce such witnesses they are liars in God's eyes' (24:12–13). Finding four witnesses for sexual misdemeanours is by no means easy: the criteria for evidence are deliberately weighted on the side of the victim. Ultimately, what should be private remains private, and the chaste are not maliciously maligned.

The 'concocted lie' in question was about Aisha, the youngest wife of the Prophet. While travelling with a caravan on a journey, she dropped a necklace. When she went back to retrieve the jewellery, she was left behind and became separated from the caravan. Eventually, she was found by a young man who escorted her back to Medina. The rumour suggested that something unlawful happened between them. A long passage in the first part of *sura* 24, 'Light', is devoted to this incident, as well as issues of privacy, gossip, slander and sexual behaviour.

When it comes to accusations of sexual misconduct, the Qur'an takes the side of the accused. 'Those who accuse honourable but unwary believing women', we read in 24:23, 'are rejected by God.' In matters of chastity, the woman's word is law; when she swears by God, the matter ends: 'As for those who accuse their own wives of adultery, but have no other witness, let each one four times call God to witness that he is telling the truth, and, the fifth time, call God to reject him if he is lying; punishment shall be averted from his wife if she in turn four times calls God to witness that her husband is lying and, the fifth time, calls God to reject her if he is telling the truth' (24:6–9). In other words, believe the wife and not the husband.

The Qur'an's treatment of adultery, fornication and 'lewd acts' in public (which conservatives would argue include what are referred to in some circles as 'PDAs': public displays of affection) follows the contradictory logic we discussed in the case of polygamy. In all cases, four eyewitnesses are required to establish guilt: 'if any of your women commit a lewd act, call four witnesses from among you' (4:15). The punishment appears quite severe: 'strike the adulteress and adulterer one hundred times. Do not let compassion for them keep you from carrying out God's law … and ensure that a group of believers witnesses the punishment' (24:2). Women accused of 'lewd acts' are to be kept 'at home until death comes to them or until God shows them another way' (4:15); in case of men, 'punish them both; and if they repent and mend their ways, leave them alone' (4:16).

Given that the evidence required to substantiate a charge of adultery, fornication or 'lewd act'—collectively known as *zina*—is no small matter, the logic of these verses seems to be that the charges could never be proven. Only a total imbecile would perform any of these acts in the full and glaring view of four witnesses. Given that the punishment for bearing false witness is almost as high as the actual crime, it would require a brave witness to come forward: 'As for those who accuse chaste women of fornication, and then fail to provide four witnesses, strike them eighty times, and reject their testimony ever after: they are lawbreakers, except those who repent later and make amends' (24:2–5). So the punishment is symbolic rather than an actual, physical penalty: it is meant to serve simply as a deterrent. Indeed, classical jurists and judges accepted the punishment in principle but, in reality, left cases of illicit sex unpunished, leaving the matter in the hands of God.

There is another reason to assume that the punishment is purely symbolic. The word used for 'strike', *jalada*, as Abdel Haleem explains in a footnote, 'means "hit the skin" with hand or anything else. There are reports that people used shoes, clothes, etc.' [19]. In Arab culture, throwing shoes is the ultimate demonstration of public disgrace, as President George W. Bush was to learn. Thus, this punishment has nothing to do with Taliban-style lashing with whips, which to my mind is an indication of the pathological, sadistic psychology of those who preside over such affairs. And it has absolutely nothing to do with the barbaric practice of stoning. In fact, the function of the punishment is to 'name and shame' the individual concerned: this is why it is a public exercise. It is in the process of 'naming and shaming' that the believers are asked to 'not let compassion for them keep you from carrying out God's law'. The final goal is actually not to punish at all, but to produce transformative behaviour that leads to repentance.

Now repentance is a very personal and private affair between God and the individual concerned. We have no real way of judging repentance; all we can do is take the words of the accused at face value. Neither do we have any means of knowing when 'God shows them another way' or what that way could be- although we can guess. The truth can only be judged by God, who is 'always ready to accept repentance' (4:16). So, the advice to leave the transgressors alone 'if they repent and mend their ways' is really the driving factor in dealing with issues of illicit sex.

The overall message for the believers is to keep within the boundaries of decency and morality. 'Those who pray humbly, who shun idle talk, who pay the proscribed alms, who guard their chastity' are 'not to blame, but anyone who seeks more than this is exceeding the limits' (23:2–7). Keep your desires under wraps, the advice goes; and do not let your 'desires exceed this limit'

(70:31). But, of course, given human nature and the conditions of the modern world, not everyone will follow the desired course. Temptation is always present. Both men and women can have illicit desires. The public space will often be corrupted. The believers are thus asked to keep away from those who corrupt the moral fibre of society: 'Corrupt women are for corrupt men, and corrupt men are for corrupt women; good women are for good men and good men are for good women' (24:26).

If sexual ethics in the Qur'an aim to promote contentment and spiritual welfare, as I have argued, why is sex in Muslim societies, one may legitimately ask, the source of so much injustice and unhappiness? Why is the female body seen as a site of female shame and male honour? How has the barbaric practice of female circumcision, an inheritance from pre-Islamic cultures, survived? The simple answer to these questions is that such notions and practices have nothing to do with the Qur'an but everything to do with cultural traditions, customs and practices. They are not exclusively Arab or non-Arab; they are derived from and are part of many cultures. As time-honoured practices and ways of thinking and operating in the world, they were inveigled into the Qur'anic framework, retained and newly re-justified with the rubric of Islam; some even became part of the *Sharia* as it evolved through the centuries and exists today [20].

Women in Muslim societies face the greatest injustice in relation to rape. Under certain *Shari'a* legislation, such as the Hudud Ordinance of Pakistan [21] or the Hudud Bill of the Malaysian State of Kelantan [22], *zina*, i.e. illicit sex, and rape are seen as the same thing and fall under the same rules. Of course, the two are quite distinct. *Zina* is consensual sex, and even though it is out of wedlock, it may involve love and mutual affection. Rape is non-consensual sex under force and duress: it is an aberration of power, violence and humiliation. Only a perverted mind would see both as the same. Yet, under *Shari'a* legislation, the rules of *zina* are applied to rape; and the rape victim has to bring four male witnesses of just character to prove the charge against her attacker. The most frequent outcome is that the rape victim is doubly victimised: not only has she been raped, but she is also accused of adultery or fornication and imprisoned! So the rules that were supposed to protect women from slander are used to sanction state violence against them. Those who frame such laws and apply them in the name of Islam are, I would argue, the real transgressors, who 'overstep His limits' and 'will be consigned by God to the Fire, and there they will stay—a humiliating torment awaits them' (4:14).

A community that strives to become a 'community of the middle way' treats issues of sexual ethics as it treats other aspects of life: with modesty and moderation, tolerance and generosity, understanding and forgiveness. Abu Bakr, father of Aisha, was the closest companion of the Prophet, and provided support to a relative named Mistah. When he heard that Mistah, an immigrant from Mecca, had participated in spreading the 'concocted lie' against Aisha, he swore he would never help this poor relative again. But the Qur'an advised him otherwise: 'those who have been graced with bounty and plenty should not swear that they will [no longer] give to kinsmen, the poor, those who emigrated in God's way: let them pardon and forgive. Do you not wish that God should forgive you?' (24:22). We should wish for others, this verse suggests, what we desire for ourselves. Ultimately, the best we can do for those who stray outside the limits of sexual ethics is to forgive. And we should pray that they, like us, enjoy God's grace to the full and have a happy and wonderful sex life.

46

HOMOSEXUALITY

The term homosexuality does not occur in the Qur'an. But the Qur'an does mention 'men who have no need of women'. We are not explicitly told who these men are, but we can guess: either they have no sexual desire at all or they desire other men. And if such men are 'mindful of God' they could, in the Hereafter, be in 'Gardens and in bliss, rejoicing in their Lord's gifts' which include, amongst other things, 'devoted youths like hidden pearls' (52:17–24). Elsewhere we are told: 'Everlasting youth will attend them—if you could see them, you would think they are scattered pearls' (76:19). There are two points to note here. The positive way male beauty is portrayed; and the fact that no negativity is attached to men who do not desire women.

It is in 24:31, which we considered in the previous chapter, that we come across 'men who have no sexual desire' who can witness the 'charms' of women. Clearly, men who have no sexual desires for women, and are thus treated like close family members, can be elderly, impotent (although whether anyone would actually advertise his impotence is open to question) or homosexuals.

Oblique references to homosexuality occur in a couple of other places in the Qur'an. In 42:49–50, we read: 'God has control of the heavens and the earth; He creates whatsoever He will—He grants female offspring to whoever He will, male to whoever He will, or both male and female, and He makes whoever He will barren: He is knowing and all powerful.' So a single offspring can be 'both male and female', which suggest that a male could have a female sexual orientation and a female could have a male sexual orientation; or, at least, their sexuality is ambiguous. Gender ambiguous people, such as hermaphrodites, were not unknown in the Arab society when the Qur'an was being revealed.

The other reference occurs in 24:60, which has been translated in rather different ways. According to Abdel Haleem: 'No blame will be attached to elderly women who are not hoping for sex, if they take off their outer garments without flaunting their charms, but it is preferable for them not to do this: God is all hearing, all seeing.' Yusuf Ali has 'such elderly women as are past the prospect of marriage'; and Muhammad Asad suggests it is 'women advanced in years, who no longer feel any sexual desires'. However the verse is translated, the essential message being conveyed here is that these women are not going to bear children and are not interested in sexual intercourse with men. The women could have passed the natural child-bearing age, or they are so old that they have no sexual desires, or they are mystic celibates—but the description can apply equally to lesbian women.

What can we learn from these indirect references to homosexuality? We note that the existence of non-heterosexuals is recognised and they are described in a matter of fact way as though they are a natural creation of God. But given that the references are so oblique, it is obvious that homosexuals are not the main concern of the Qur'an: the Sacred Text focuses on heterosexuals because they propagate and replicate the social order. Homosexuals exist, the Qur'an seems to be saying, but they are a small minority, so don't make too much fuss about them. Concentrate on the sexual mores of the majority who determine the future of society.

There is another point to consider. Given the Qur'an's emphasis on diversity, it seems strange to me that the Sacred Text would not recognise sexual diversity. When we are asked, in 17:84, to 'Say, "Everyone does things in their own way, but your Lord is fully aware of who follows the best-guided path"', should we not include homosexuals in 'everyone'? It seems that the Prophet Muhammad did. One reason the Qur'an mentions 'men who are not attracted to women' is that such men existed in Medina during the time of the Prophet. They lived outside the dominant patriarchal economy, moved freely amongst the women, witnessing their 'charm'. The Prophet accepted these men as citizens of the diverse society that was Medina with the usual stipulation that they should not break the ethical and moral codes of society.

Moreover, I think it is important for us as a religious community—indeed, all religious communities, Muslim, Christian, Jewish—to ask whether homosexuality is a natural disposition or a matter of choice. If one chooses to be gay or lesbian, then it makes sense to argue that homosexuals can, or should, change their sexual behaviour. But if homosexuality is a natural God-given dispensation, part of the *fitra* or innate human nature of an individual, which

I think the Qur'an implies, then the question of change in sexual orientation does not arise. One cannot change one's *fitra*. I tend to agree with Scott Siraj al-Haqq Kugle, the author of the luminous study *Homosexuality in Islam*, who argues that 'some human beings simply are homosexuals by disposition rather than by choice'. Science seems to confirm this assertion. Kugle writes:

There has always been a small minority of homosexual women and men in every human community, though societies define them in different ways, languages have different terms to describe them, and belief systems have different reactions to their presence. Some societies accept them and some condemn them, but none has ever prevented them from being present—whether openly or under suppression. What causes them to be present is open to question. As a Muslim, I assert that they—like all natural phenomena—are caused by Divine will, though biological process or early childhood experiences are important means by which they come into being. Whether the "cause" is God's creation, biological variation, or early childhood experience, homosexuals have no rational choice in their internal disposition to be attracted to same-sex mates [23].

It would be an unjust God who, after having given no choice to the individuals concerned, condemns them for being homosexuals. Indeed, such a condemnation would go against all the overwhelming emphasis on justice and equity that we find in the Qur'an.

But such arguments were not considered by classical and traditionalist scholars, who insist that the Qur'an condemns homosexuality. The sole basis of outlawing homosexuality is 4:16: 'if two men commit a lewd act, punish them both' (4:16). But I find it difficult to see how this verse condemns homosexuality. In the previous verse, 4:15, we read: 'if any of your women commit a lewd act, call four witnesses from among you, then, if they testify to their guilt, keep the women at home till death comes to them or until God shows them another way'. What could this 'lewd act' be? It could be any kind of sexual indiscretion from adultery, fornication, prostitution to female or male homosexuality. The fact that four witnesses are required suggests it is the act being performed in public, or at least in the full view of four adults, that really makes it indecent. The same word, *fahisha*, is used to describe the lewd nature of the acts, which suggests that it is also something that happens in public, in full view of adult witnesses. I would argue that it is the public gaze that is the issue here and not necessarily the nature of the act itself. What is condemned is lewd public behaviour—whatever the sexual orientation of the parties involved.

Nevertheless, the term *fahisha* has come to designate homosexuality in Muslim circles. So a great deal depends on how we understand this term, which can mean anything from gross indecency and transgression to gruesome deeds and even atrocities. It is in the story of Prophet Lot, mentioned in a number of places in the Qur'an, that the term is used most frequently. In 7:80–81, for example, we read: 'We sent Lot and he said to his people, "how can you practise this outrage? No one in the world has outdone you in this. You lust after men rather than women. You transgress all bounds."' The word for transgression here is *fahisha*, which in classical commentaries is said to mean 'sexually entering males'. But there is a problem with this simplistic reading.

When we consider how the word *fahisha* is used elsewhere in the Qur'an, a somewhat different picture emerges. Reading Kugle again:

In the verse that communicates Lot's prohibition, *al-fahishah* comes in the definite nominal form, "the transgression", whereas the verse about adultery mentions *fahishah* in the indefinite nominal form "transgression". This suggests that transgression is a general category including many different specific kinds of acts; one could speak of a particular transgression in specifying an act or one could speak of transgression in general to imply a whole range of acts that transgress the boundary of decency, righteousness, or legality. Not every term mentioned as "transgression" would be equivalent, morally or legally or punitively. In fact, the Qur'an often uses the term "transgression" in the plural in the narrative sections about Lot and his conflict with his community [24].

If we read Lot's story, scattered as it is throughout the Qur'an, thematically, we discover that it is not so much about homosexuality but a string of gross sexual transgressions, including widespread promiscuity, paedophilia, bestiality, the use of rape as a weapon of intimidation and power, and the sexual denigration and abuse of guests. Lot's lot were exceptionally stingy, greedy, covetous, and wallowed in filth; they robbed travellers, humiliated strangers, and exploited the needy. In 7:81, it is not only men that Lot's people lust after. They lust after male guests in order to humiliate and intimidate them, to use rape as an instrument of power. The sexual acts in Lot's story are acts of violence, above and over anything else. This is why God 'showered upon them a rain of destruction' (7:84).

We should not confuse the story of Lot as it appears in the Qur'an with that which appears in the Bible. Muslims have accepted and adopted the Biblical view of homosexuality, both in history and contemporary times, instead of engaging with the text of the Qur'an and thinking things out for themselves.

Lot also figures in 'sayings' of the Prophet that are used to justify condemnation of homosexuality, criminalise it, and prescribe punishment for the homosexual act: death by stoning. In fact, there is absolutely no evidence that the

Prophet punished anyone for homosexuality. Most of the so-called *Hadith* regarding homosexuality are at best not authentic, or worse, totally fabricated. Sayings like 'whosever you find doing the act of the people of Lot, kill the active and passive participants' or 'the one practising the act of the people of Lot, stone the one on the top and the one of the bottom, stone them both together' are not authentic: they have nothing to do with the Prophet and everything to do with the prejudices of society. The evidence actually suggests that the Prophet took homosexuals, cross-dressers and transgenders as part of a natural landscape and paid little attention to them. There are no *Hadith* or sayings of the Prophet in authentic collections, such as *Sahih Bukhari* [25], denouncing homosexuals. *Sahih Bukhari* contains a couple of stories about 'effeminate men' who frequently visited the household of the Prophet and talked and joked with his wives. These stories are mentioned largely because a particular *mukhannath*, as they are known, upset the Prophet. During a conversation with Umm Salama, one of the Prophet's wives, a *mukhannath* described a woman of another tribe in a lurid manner. When the Prophet heard the description, he banned this *mukhannath* from entering his house. It is clear from the story that the Prophet was disturbed by the unethical description, the backbiting tittle-tattle, and not by the sexual orientation of the person concerned. In the Prophet's Medina, *mukhannath*, who are anatomically male but display the gendered character of a female, had privileged access to and mixed freely with women. They had a particular social role: bringing couples together and singing and dancing during weddings. In India and Pakistan, where they are known as *hijras*, they perform the same roles today.

It is quite clear to me that the widespread and rampant homophobia of Muslim societies cannot be justified either on the basis of Qur'anic teachings or the example of the Prophet Muhammad. On the contrary, the Qur'an portrays homosexuality as a natural disposition and the *Sunna* is exemplary in its toleration of sexual orientation. The demonisation of homosexuality in Muslim history is based largely on fabricated traditions and the unreconstituted prejudices harboured by most Muslim societies. In this case, as in so many others, religion is used to support deep historic prejudices rather than reform and enlighten them.

The story of Lot, however, is not altogether irrelevant to contemporary gay culture. It is, after all, about extreme excess. While we are sexual beings, male and female, the Qur'an tells us, we are not exclusively and solely sexual but also moral agents in all spheres of human activity. Modesty is the counterbalance to our sexual appetites, which should be fulfilled away from the public sphere.

327

This applies equally to homosexuals, who like other believers are required to be modest, 'lower their gaze', and keep private things private. Contemporary gay and lesbian behaviour in Western societies, it seems to me, is anything but modest.

The obsession of gay culture with lavishing attention on looks, clothes, certain kinds of pop music and promiscuity is far from innocent; it echoes the excesses of Lot's people; and it is being aped blindly in Muslim societies as fashion. The commodification of homosexual lifestyle has more than individual excess to answer for: it is a global economy, politics and ecology that produce injustice and inequity within and between nations. The obsession of gay culture with lavishing attention on looks, clothes, certain kinds of pop music and promiscuity is far from innocent; it echoes the excesses of Lot's people; and it is being aped blindly in Muslim societies as fashion. So, it seems to me, modesty and privacy have roles to play in countering the excesses of global gay culture steeped in consumerism.

Privacy, of course, is not a licence for 'anything goes', since all our activities are known to God to whom we will be answerable. But modesty and privacy do stand guardians to the private fulfilment of our sexual nature—whatever our orientation.

47

THE VEIL

Most discussions about women in Islam begin with the veil, which is often considered an instrument of control. It is defended passionately; and attacked with ferocity—both by Muslims and non-Muslims. For centuries, the veil has been used to represent Muslim women in stereotypical terms [26]. Nowadays, it has acquired symbolic as well as political significance. But what does the Qur'an say about the veil? Is it really a Muslim institution sanctioned by the Sacred Text?

The term associated with the veil in the Qur'an is *hijab*. The word occurs eight times in the Sacred Text (19:17; 38:32; 17:45; 41:5; 42:51; 7:46; 33:53; 83:15). Literally *hijab* means a curtain, partition or screen. In none of the verses is *hijab* used in the sense conventionally understood by Muslim societies as a piece of clothing covering the head and entire body; nor indeed the items such as *burqa*, the head to toe shroud worn by Muslim women in the Indian subcontinent, nor *niqab*, the face mask worn in the Middle East, nor the all-enfolding black *chador* used in Iran nor the *abaya* of Arabia. *Hijab* is something different all together.

In some verses of the Qur'an, *hijab* is used metaphorically to refer to a separation, as in 7:46–7 where it signifies the separation between the inmates of Paradise and the denizens of Hell: 'a barrier divides the two groups with men on its heights recognising each other by their marks: they will call out to the people of the Garden, "Peace be with you!"—they will not have entered, but they will be hoping, and when their glance falls upon the people of the Fire, they will say, "Our Lord, do not let us join the evildoers". In 83:15, *hijab* is something that separates the unjust on the Day of Judgement from God: 'No indeed! On that day they will be screened off from their Lord.' And in 42:51 it is used to intimate how God communicates with humankind: 'it is not granted to any mortal that God should speak to him except through revelation or from behind a veil'.

But the verse particularly associated with the veil, the *hijab* verse, is 33:53. It reads:

Believers, do not enter the Prophet's apartment for a meal unless you are given permission to do so; do not linger until [a meal] is ready. When you are invited, go in; then, when you have taken your meal, leave. Do not stay on and talk, for that would offend the Prophet, though he would shrink from asking you to leave. God does not shrink from the truth. When you ask his wives for something, do so from behind a screen: this is purer both for your hearts and for theirs. It is not right for you to offend God's Messenger, just as you should never marry his wives after him: that would be grievous in God's eye.

When classical commentators refer to this verse, they speak of 'the descent of the *hijab*'. This means two things: the descent of a revelation from God, and the descent of a piece of material between the wives of the Prophet and the men who were visiting. There are a number of obvious points we can make about this 'descent' of the veil. The verse is teaching basic rules of behaviour to the people of Medina, living in extraordinary times. It is addressed specifically to those believers who are invited to the household of the Prophet for a meal. It specifically asks this same group of believers to treat the Prophet's wives with respect and talk to them 'from behind a screen'. And it states that no one should marry the wives of the Prophet after his death. So the verse is not only specific but emphasises its specificity. A little background context will explain why the verse is couched in such specific terms.

First, the general context of Medina during the time when 33:53 was revealed. The city was small; it provided its inhabitants with a very intimate and confined living space. The Prophet and his companions formed a tightly knit unit. The centre of attraction and activity was the Prophet's mosque, and the most coveted space was next to the mosque, where the Prophet himself lived with his wives. Even Fatima, the daughter of the Prophet, found it difficult to find a space for herself in the area. A door from the mosque led straight to the apartment of his wife Aisha. So the Prophet himself had little private space; indeed, the distinction between his private and public life had all but disappeared. But during this period Medina was also a conflict-ridden society. The Muslims had just lost a battle—the Battle of Uhud—and were in a state of crisis. Various tribes jostled for power, tensions existed between Jewish and non-Jewish tribes, as well as inter-clan conflict and conflicts within the prominent families of Medina [27].

The small Muslim community was focused not just on the Prophet but also his wives. They were of great interest to the community as a source of information about the Prophet, and they talked and engaged freely with the men around them. But they could also be controversial and attracted comment, gossip and even scandal. To make matters worse, the enemies of the Prophet had threatened him by declaring their intention to marry his wives after his death. And rumours and gossip were circulating about his wives.

Second, the specific occasion when 33:53 was revealed. The Prophet had just married Zaynab Bint Jahsh and had invited a number of guests to the wedding. Three of the guests had overstayed their welcome and were unwilling to leave when the wedding meal was over. The Prophet was keen to be alone with his new bride but the guests refused to take the hint. He left the unwilling guests a number of times only to find them still there on his return. When the guests finally left, the Prophet's attendant, Anas ibn Malik, insisted on talking and helping him. Finally, the Prophet let a curtain fall between himself and Anas to ensure some privacy. It is at that moment that the *hijab* verse descended.

When seen in this context, the verse becomes quite clear. Specifically, its meaning is that even prophets need privacy and time to themselves. Universal principles, respect for privacy and modesty, emphasised elsewhere in the Qur'an are applied in this verse to a very specific—and unrepeatable—instance, in the case of the Prophet and his wives. There never will be comparable cases because Muhammad is the last prophet, no other women therefore will be wives of a prophet. Generally, we can read 33:53 as a call from God for etiquette.

This, then, is the extent of the multifaceted use of the term *hijab* in the Qur'an. So the question is how does this term, used in such various contexts, come to be the universally recognised term for Muslim women's head covering?

There are many verses addressed to the Prophet that have universal significance. So the question is how we distinguish between the specific and the universal. Should behaviour required towards a unique individual and his unique household be the model for all Muslim households? Or does this verse extend a general principle to circumstances that can never arise again? A reasoned and proportionate answer, I think, is to see this verse as an exception that is particular, time-bound and distinct from the general rule.

To treat everyone, and especially every woman, according to what was especially deemed appropriate for the Prophet and his wives strikes me as a presumption too far. In practice, it has led to a vast and generalised injustice to women since it has been used to justify not only the seclusion of women but also a denial of education to women as well as other limitations. The social reality produced severely affects women's ability to be active agents in creating and working for just and equitable societies, a duty which the Qur'an specifically and repeatedly addresses to believing men and believing women. And still we have not come upon any reference to mode of dress!

A reference to mode of dress occurs in 33:59: 'O Prophet, tell your wives, your daughters and women believers to wrap their outer garments closely around them, for this makes it more likely that they be recognised and not be harassed. God is All-Forgiving, Compassionate to each.' Here we have clearly moved from the specific to the general by the inclusion of 'believing women'. However, it is not seclusion from society but specifically going out and about which is the context in which mode of dress is mentioned. And what is mentioned is 'outer garments'; the word used is *jalabib* (singular, *jilbab*), which can mean a mantle or cloak. We can be confident that the purpose of wrapping the outer garments closely around themselves is to be modest and to identify themselves to the rest of the community as modest women, since that is the subject of the entire passage in which the verse occurs. But to understand what it means in terms of type of apparel, we need to know more about the conventions in Medina at the time of the Prophet, which is where 24:31 comes in.

We get a clearer idea about the type of dress worn by the women of Medina and more generally the Arabia of the Prophet from verse 24:31, though much depends upon the translation one consults. Khalidi's translation makes self-evident what other translators usually confine to footnotes. Khalidi gives the verse as:

Tell believing women to avert their eyes, and safeguard their private parts, and not to expose their attractions except what is visible. And let them wrap their shawls around their breast lines, and reveal their attractions only before their husbands or fathers, or fathers-in-law, or sons, or sons of their husbands or brothers, or sons of brothers, or sons of sisters, or their womenfolk, or slaves, or male attendants with no sexual desire, or children with no intimate knowledge of the private parts of women. And let them not stamp their feet to reveal what they hide of their ornaments.

What is evident is that the style of dress prevalent in Medina exposed a good deal of the female body. The shawl mentioned in this verse, the term used being *khimar* (plural *khumur*), refers to a head covering at the time commonly worn mostly as an ornament that hung loosely down a woman's back. The dress worn by women of the time had a deep cleavage which exposed the breasts. A sensible reading of the verse, then, suggests that what it is seeking to achieve is a covering of nakedness, the 'charm' in question.

It seems to me that in both these verses, 24:31 and 33:59, the only ones in the Qur'an that specifically refer to matters of dress, the objective is to achieve modesty and public chastity by concealing nakedness and not sexualising one's appearance. Rather than specifics of how to dress, or designating a specific form of attire or uniform, it is the combination of lowering one's gaze along with seeking modesty within the dress conventions of the time that we are meant to understand. Modesty cannot be reduced to a piece of cloth, whatever form or fashion it might have, but rather consists of the sum total of behaviour and a distinctive moral outlook. And this is exactly the point made in verse 7:26: 'We have sent down upon you a garment to hide your shame, and as adornment. But the garment of piety—that is best' (Khalidi). In this instance I have to confess I prefer the translation of Yusuf Ali, who translates the crucial phrase as 'the raiment of righteousness'. This raiment of righteousness, counterposed to any actual garments one wears, is a moral condition, a state of mind and of being. It can and will be found within any and all styles, customs and fashions of dress by those intent on righteousness or God consciousness. And equally no style of dress will be sufficient if the moral intention of righteousness is not within the heart and mind of the person. So far as I am aware, pieces of cloth have no moral conscience in and of themselves.

In discussion of form of dress, the Qur'an speaks in general and vague terms rather than specifics. It provides a moral context in which judgements are to be made about how to dress and how to comport oneself however one is dressed. And none of the relevant verses we have considered explains the precise association that Muslim society has made between the term *hijab* and conventions of dress [28]. Those conventions are based on pre-existing social customs; the *niqab*, the *burqa* or the *chador* derive from the cultural traditions of regions beyond Arabia not anything the Qur'an itself says. Seclusion and veiling of women were prevalent practices of the Hellenic Middle East and Persian society, heartlands of the development of classical Muslim civilisation.

I can just about see the contorted route of reasoning by which extreme forms of the seclusion of women and obsessive covering have emerged [29]. But to me, they seem to owe more to misogyny than uplifting moral principle. 'Virtuous women' become vicarious custodians of social probity, responsible for men's weakness and proclivity for sexual lasciviousness. This is by no means a perversity exclusive to Muslim society, since such attitudes are depressingly common around the globe in so many societies and cultures. It is, however, explicitly at odds with the transformative vision that the Qur'an seeks to inculcate. Instead of achieving a concrete or specific material form of 'raiment of righteousness', what results is an entirely unbalanced onus placed upon women. Verse 24:31 has to be reintegrated into the whole passage in which it occurs, beginning with verse 24:30: 'Tell believing men to avert their eyes, and safeguard their private parts; this is more decent for them.' Modesty cannot become the raiment of righteousness of an entire society when it is the burden and obligation of only one half of the population. Traditional interpretation in fact performs an inversion of Qur'anic principle by making women responsible for the lack of moral probity and modesty, not to say the sexual obsession of men. Reading verses 24:30 and 31 together make it abundantly clear how perverse this habit is. In fact it is not so much perverse as potentially perverted, a licence for lechery which is exactly what the Qur'an's balanced approach seeks to end.

So where does that leave the vexed matter of *hijab* as a political issue in the here and now? I can see no Qur'anic warrant for *burqas*, *chadors*, *abayas* and *niqab*. There is no legal requirement, sanctioned by the Qur'an or the Prophet, that compels Muslim women to wear specific dress, to hide their faces in public, or to shroud themselves from top to bottom. Had this been the case, the injunction of the Qur'an for men and women to 'lower their gaze' would hardly make any sense. And I find the whole notion that certain men, in the guise of moral police, should go around telling women to cover themselves totally reprehensible. And there are just as many women prepared to serve as harridan scourges ready to tell other women that not even a strand of hair should be allowed on public view.

However, in the case of *hijab*, the convention of covering the head, it seems to me that Muslim women should be free to choose for themselves how they observe modesty. It has been made into a volatile political issue not only by Muslim society but increasingly in many Western nations with Muslim minorities. Campaigns and tirades against the *burqa* and *niqab* reveal more about the prejudice and suspicion of the host society than they do of insight into Muslim culture. Nevertheless, the unthinking resistance by which custom and tradition are upheld in the name of Islam by Muslim men does nothing to advance mutual understanding or increase the freedom of choice and empowerment of Muslim women. *Hijab* is, in my view, a private and personal matter for each woman; the choice will no doubt be conditioned by culture, circumstance and history, and the choice of each individual should be respected. To regard a woman's choice as solely a function of male dogmatism and imposition is to reduce the integrity, agency and conscience of Muslim women even further. It belittles and demeans the intelligence and commitment of the way in which some women have come to understand and express their religion. It can never be the case that covering or not covering is the beginning and end of the matter, however. Covering does not preclude immoral behaviour. There are millions of Muslim women who do not wear the *hijab* or cover their heads, yet are modestly dressed. Modesty is a judgement that must be made on the basis of more than what is worn; it is about behaviour, of men as well as women, about their attitude and outlook, it is a whole person project and must be understood as such by society.

Traditional exegesis of the Qur'an may have subverted the equality of women. But that does not mean we cannot reconcile our commitment to the Qur'an with equality for all—men and women.

48

FREEDOM OF EXPRESSION

We have seen the importance that the Qur'an gives to reason and rational enquiry. The believers are repeatedly asked to explore and investigate the world around them, study the laws governing nature, and discover the 'signs of God': 'God reveals to you the signs so that you may think' (2:266). But thinking and the associated activities of study and investigation are not possible without freedom of thought, opinion and enquiry. It would thus be logical for the Qur'an to promote freedom of expression.

Freedom of expression begins with total freedom of belief and conviction: we have already discussed the categorical injunction that 'there is no compulsion in religion' (2:256) in chapter 23. Men and women, of their own free will, decide to believe or not to believe in the 'unseen'. As a corollary, both those who choose to believe and those who choose not to believe are equally free to criticise and challenge each other's positions, air their disputes, and speak and listen freely and without impunity. There will, of course, be disputes on all sides. The believers are given specific advice on how to settle their differences: 'If you are in dispute over any matter, refer to God and the Messenger' (4:59). At the time of the Prophet Muhammad, the mosque was often the best place to settle such disputes. It was both a place of worship and an arena for debating, discussing and sorting out differences of opinion, thoughts, ideas and strategies openly and freely. The equivalent place for debating the differences between the believers and non-believers is the public space, where contesting truth claims can be properly debated and the goal of promoting ideas, enquiry and investigations achieved only in an atmosphere of total freedom of expression. As such, freedom of expression, I would argue, is as sacred as the mosque.

It was in the mosque in Medina that a woman (we know her to be Kholah, daughter of Thalaba and wife of Aws bin Thabit) complained to the Prophet about being insulted and abused by her husband. But this was not an ordinary complaint: she has a fierce argument with the Prophet, who by now was also the political leader of the community, and expressed her opinion openly and forcefully. Indeed, she was so outspoken that the Qur'an, in the opening verse of chapter 58, called 'The Dispute', refers to the incident: 'God has heard the words of the woman who disputed with you [Prophet] about her husband and complained to God' (58:1). The dispute in question concerned a pagan divorce practice by which a wife was not only deprived of her marital rights but also prevented from marrying someone else—effectively left in limbo, neither married nor unmarried. The second verse explains what this practice amounted to: 'Even if any of you say to their wives, "You are to me like my mother's back", they are not their mothers; their only mothers are those who gave them birth. What they say is certainly blameworthy and false, but God is pardoning and forgiving' (58:2). The Prophet's reply to the woman was 'you are unlawful to him now'. But the revelation takes the woman's side; the rules of divorce, as we saw in chapter 21, are changed to prevent such cruel treatment of wives. The purpose of the exercise is to show that forthright opinion, expressed openly and freely, can promote justice and lead to progress in law and knowledge.

Indeed, it is a sacred duty of the believers to stand up and speak truth to power. The Qur'an urges the Muslims to 'be a community that calls for what is good, urges what is right, and forbids what is wrong: those who do this are the successful ones' (3:104). This verse is often rendered differently to read, for example in Yusuf Ali's translation, as 'let there arise out of you a band of people inviting to all that is good...' But the verse refers, as Abdel Haleem rightly suggests, to 'the whole community, not just a part of it' [30]. So, every member of the whole community is asked to stand up for what is 'good' and what is 'right', or, in other words, truth and justice. Arriving at truth requires constant interrogation and criticism. Defending a just cause also necessitates criticising what is unjust. And one can only stop 'wrong' being committed by loudly condemning and even denigrating it. All this can only be done in an atmosphere where freedom of expression is respected, where there is no fear of penalty, persecution or intimidation. The sacred duty of 'inviting to all that is good' can only be performed when the instrument for its delivery, freedom of expression, is seen as equally sacred, respected and upheld.

While freedom of expression is sacred, the Qur'an does prescribe the etiquette for its exercise. Believers are asked to argue in the 'best way' (29:46) and 'most courteous way' (16:125). Making erroneous assumptions or speaking badly about other people without any reason is to be shunned: 'Believers, avoid making too many assumptions—some assumptions are sinful—and do not spy on one another or speak ill of people behind their backs: would any of you like to eat the flesh of your own dead brother?' (49:12). Moreover, one should not believe what one reads in a newspaper or hears through the grapevine, but should check the facts before opening one's mouth: 'Believers, if a trouble-maker brings you news, check it first, in case you wrong others unwittingly and later regret what you have done' (49:6). An honest opinion, 'a good word' based on evidence and facts, expressed courteously, says the Qur'an, is 'like a good tree whose root is firm and whose branches are high in the sky, yielding constant fruit by its Lord's leave...' (14:24–5).

The verse continues: 'but an evil word is like a rotten tree, uprooted from the surface of the earth, with no power to endure' (14:26). So freedom of expression can also be abused. Such abuse often comes in the form of slander, or 'false assertions', which can be uttered both in public and private places, for example against chaste women (24:4); or libel; or straightforward insult and abuse. The believers are asked not to 'revile those who invite others to profess faith in deities other than Allah, lest they, in their hostility and ignorance, revile God' (6:108). Furthermore, believers, men and women, are asked 'not to jeer at another, who may after all be better than them', or 'speak ill of one another', or to 'use offensive nicknames for one another' (49:11). So there are both legal and moral restraints on the freedom of expression.

But the moral restraints are addressed specifically to the believers. The Qur'an does not expect the non-believers to show similar restraint. Which brings us to blasphemy. In Islamic history, blasphemy was intrinsically linked with apostasy, heresy, and rejection of God and revelation. The juristic arguments for and against these, as Mohammad Hashim Kamali shows in his excellent book *Freedom of Expression in Islam* [31], are convoluted, sophistic and, frankly in my opinion, have little contemporary relevance. In general, opinions (*ra'y*) expressed in public were divided into three verities: praiseworthy, blameworthy or doubtful.

Praiseworthy opinions, as one would expect, were those that extolled the virtues of the Qur'an and the Prophet Muhammad. Blameworthy opinions were those seen as blasphemy, sedition, heresy and the like. Often political offences were given religious overtones. And jurist after jurist argued that capital punishment was the only way to deal with such opinions. For example, the jurist Ibn Taymiyya (1263–1328) went out of his way to deduce 'evidence' to prove that the punishment for using insulting language directed towards God and the Prophet (*Sabb Allah wa Sabb al-Rasul*) was death [32]. I think such juristic gymnastics and the rulings they produced should be left where they belong—in history. They serve no useful purpose for our times.

Classical juristic opinion is at odds, as it frequently seems to be, with the spirit and teachings of the Qur'an. I find the whole idea of blasphemy irrelevant to Islam. Either you are free to believe and not believe or you are not. If there is no compulsion in religion then all opinions can be expressed feely, including those which cause offence to religious people. The believers will show respect and use respectful language toward God and His Prophet simply because they are believers. Non-believers, by definition, take a rejectionist attitude to both. We should not be too surprised if non-believers resort to the use of what the believers would regard as unbecoming language towards sacred religious notions. The Qur'an expects this; and this is how the real world behaves.

God, 'the Self-Sufficient One', in His Majesty, is hardly going to be bothered if a few insults are hurled at him. He can certainly look after himself: 'the Most Excellent Names belong to God: use them to call on Him, and keep away from those who abuse them—they will be requited for what they do' (7:180). In other words, punishment or reward for those who abuse God lies with God; we have nothing to do with it and are required simply to stay away from such matters. As for the Prophet himself, he was constantly abused and blasphemed, in everyday words as well as poetry, during the period of his prophethood, particularly his time in Mecca. He took no action against those who ridiculed him. If the Prophet himself did not penalise those who uttered profanities against him, who are we to act on his behalf?

Of course, we, the believers, have the right to be offended. But we have no right to silence our critics. To do so would be to act against the clear injunctions of the Qur'an and the example set by the Prophet. In matters of blasphemy, unfair criticism or expression of serious differences, the Qur'an expects the believers to show moral restraint, and not to be unnecessarily oversensitive. When the differences become truly irreconcilable, the Qur'an asks the believers to live and let live:

> Say 'O unbelievers! I do not worship what you worship,
> Nor do you worship what I worship;
> Nor will I ever worship what you worship,
> Nor will you ever worship what I worship.
> You have your religion
> And I have mine.' (109:1–6)

The faith of the faithful cannot be damaged by ridicule or blasphemy, whether it comes in the form of fiction or non-fiction.

But the faithful do have the right to retort in equal measure. This is well illustrated by the Prophet, who instructed his followers: 'when the Jews greet you with the phrase "death be upon you (*al-sam 'alaykum*)", then you should simply say "and upon you (*wa 'alaykum*)"'. So words can be used against words. The Qur'an provides us with another illustration. An uncle of the Prophet Muhammad was fiercely opposed to him; he and his wife often ridiculed and insulted the Prophet by shouting 'may your hands be ruined'. He was a beautiful, glowing man who had acquired the nickname Abu Lahab, 'father of the flame'. His wife used to tie bunches of thorns with rope to throw at the Prophet. The Qur'an's retort to Abu Lahab and his wife comes in chapter 111, 'Palm Fibre' or 'Twisted Strand': 'May the hands of Abu Lahab be ruined! May he be ruined too! Neither his wealth nor his gains will help him: he will burn in the Flaming Fire—and so will his wife, the firewood carrier, with a palm-fibre rope around her neck' (111:1–5). In the verse Abu Lahab's name becomes a pun; his 'hand' is used as a metonym for 'power'. 'Carrier of firewood' is not only a literal description for his wife, but also has the literary connotation of someone who perpetuates slanderous and hateful fiction. The rope around her neck not only describes the twisted nature of her mind, but also alludes to the spiritual truth we read elsewhere in the Qur'an: 'we have bound each human being's destiny to his neck' (17:13). The overall message of the *sura* is clear: fight metaphor with metaphor, idea with idea, book with book. The believers are asked to express themselves as freely as anyone else.

It is, of course, one thing to have a right; quite another to be able to exercise it. There are very few places in the Muslim world where one is genuinely free to express oneself, where open criticism of power is actually tolerated, or where criticism of obnoxious religious practices is not seen simply as an attack on Islam itself. State power, particularly in countries that carry the appendage 'Islamic', where Ibn Taymiyya still rules, is total and absolute. Often, law, religion, morality, ethics and politics are one and the same thing, bound together in a totalitarian formula. Those who criticise such entities, stand up to demand justice, urge good and right actions, are indeed very brave for they are frequently persecuted, thrown in prison, tortured and even killed. The propensity for suppression and torture in most Muslim countries is truly harrowing. In such places, freedom of expression and the teachings of the Qur'an exist only as abstract ideals and play virtually no part in shaping the religious and political make-up of the state.

However, the problems of freedom of expression are not limited to the Muslim world. In the contemporary world, freedom of expression works as a one-way street: it works for Western writers, thinkers, intellectuals and journalists to say what they wish about the Qur'an, the Prophet, Islam and Muslims and to promote their agenda on a global level. The flow of thoughts and ideas is strictly from the West to the Muslim world. Hardly any cultural product from Muslim societies comes to the West, even in these days of globalisation. So we do not find the cultural products of Islam and Muslims in the bookshops of the Western democracies or at the airport lounges of the world. Only one kind of expression has the full freedom to express itself. Indeed, the notion of freedom of expression sometimes becomes an instrument of power to frame Islam and Muslims in images of violence, depravity, ignorance, stupidity and monstrosity. In the eighteenth and nineteenth centuries the notion of a civilizing mission was used to shove out the manure about the exotic orient, the beastly savages, and the noble white men taking up their burdens in tropical hell holes and getting no thanks for their pains. The notion of freedom of expression, it seems to me, has become the twenty-first-century equivalent of a civilizing mission. It is sometimes used to perpetuate a literary and media culture that serves as handmaiden to neo-colonialism, neo-conservatism and instrumental modernity with the sole aim of controlling and containing Muslim cultures. No wonder that Muslims as a whole have rather ambivalent attitudes to freedom of expression.

Western societies certainly claim to uphold freedom of expression. However, without equality of access to the public space that ensures balanced cultural flows of opinion, that enables word to answer word, book to answer book, freedom of expression is honoured in the abstract while injustice is the routine practice. Denial of access to the free expression of one's contrary opinion fuels dissension and division, a far from healthy recipe for a stable society. Indeed, freedom of expression, especially as the right to a free press, has been raised to the level of an absolute in Western discourse. It has become an irreducible concept that can have no limits. This is the Larry Flint argument for freedom of expression: even the most explicit pornography must be permitted, otherwise the jackboots of tyrants will march over the rights of all ordinary citizens. Where one right is raised to the level of an absolute it becomes impossible to reason between principle, context, substance and meaning. I would argue that there is a distinction to be made between robust open debate, even the kind which causes offence, and dissension. The Qur'an counsels against dissension, by which it indicates unsubstantiated opinion used to stimulate division and acrimony. I would suggest, for example, that 'hate speech', the intentional desire to demonise particular ideas or groups of people and incite injustice or violence towards them, would fall into this category. The essence of the limits of freedom of expression, without which the Qur'anic moral and ethical framework cannot operate, is to be found and guaranteed by establishing a society of mutual respect. In a society where all people feel assured in their rights to believe and live according to their beliefs and have equitable access to the public space, the etiquette of mutual tolerance can flourish and freedom of expression can operate as debate rather than the dynamics of dissension.

But in the end, the community that follows the Qur'an is defined by the fact that it is 'guided to good speech and to the path of the One Worthy of all Praise' (22:24). The Qur'an's general advice to believers is to ignore the opinions of those who hurl abuse at them, demonise them in their fiction, films and television shows, mock their Prophet in cartoons, and scorn and stereotype them in their media. Rather, Muslims are asked to concentrate on their own shortcomings and tackle their own problems. 'Now if you paid attention to the majority on earth, they would lead you away from the path of God. They follow nothing but speculation; they themselves do nothing but guess' (6:116). I guess that sums it up!

49

SUICIDE

(ASSISTED OR OTHERWISE)

Life is one the most precious gifts of God. The Qur'an makes it clear that life is sacred and human beings are sacrosanct. Each life is an integral part of the humanity as a whole: that is why 'if anyone kills a person—unless in retribution for murder or spreading corruption in the land—it is as if he kills all mankind; while if any saves a life it is as if he saves the lives of all mankind' (5:32). By equating an individual life with the rest of humanity, the Qur'an emphasises the overall importance of preserving and conserving life. We are thus asked to regard the lives of others as well as our own life as inviolable, a bequest from God that has to be cherished and lovingly maintained.

Life is sacred; but it is not ours. It does not belong to us. It is not our property or possession. The formula 'my life, my death, my choice', paraded in Western societies, is wrong on all three counts. It is not your life. Rather, it is an *amana*, a trust, from God. We are merely trustees of our own lives. We have the responsibility of looking after this trust, to make sure that we maintain the trust and live the best possible life. We cannot take our own life, simply because it is not ours to take. We have no choice. To commit suicide would be to violate the trust. It would be an act of monumental ungratefulness. It would be taking something that belongs to God. It would not just be killing oneself but like killing all of humanity. Hence, the unambiguous, categorical instruction in the Qur'an: 'Do not contribute to your destruction with your own hands' (2:195).

Life is sacred; but it is not meaningless. It has a purpose. 'Do you think we have created you in vain?' (23:115), God asks in the Qur'an. The purpose of life, as the Qur'an tells us again and again, is to seek justice and equity, to pur-

345

sue knowledge and virtue, to worship God; and to stay on this earth till the appointed time when God takes you back, and you return from whence you came. To commit suicide is to deny that life—*your* life—however meaningless it may appear, has a purpose. It is to infringe the right of the true author of life, who is the only One who can write an ending for your life. It is an act of usurpation, a vain attempt to acquire the attributes of God. This is why when you face God, after committing suicide, 'He will say: Begone! Do not speak to Me' (23:108).

Life is sacred; but it is also a journey, 'a passing delight and a play' (29:64). During a journey, we come across many wonders that delight us as well as many sights that upset us. We go up high on the mountains and go down into the valleys. We face happiness and we face grief. A play has its twists and turns, its struggles and battles, its moments of joy and triumphs and its instances of sorrow and deep tragedy. In life, we face all these things; and all come as a test from God. 'We will certainly test you with fear and hunger, and loss of property, lives and crops', we read in 2:155; and again, in 47:31: 'We shall test you to see which of you strive the hardest and are steadfast; we shall test the sincerity of your assertion.' We have no problem with the test, and hence life, when we are happy (although I would argue that the test here is just as severe); but in times of depression, despair and calamity, life becomes a burden and thoughts of suicide may enter the mind.

Despair is a powerful driver. It is not only unbearably painful but a state of total hopelessness and meaninglessness. It is absolute emptiness with awful pain. This is why despair is one of the major causes of suicide. But for believers, there is always hope. That, after all, is the prime function of faith. A true believer cannot descend into a state of despair, for that would be tantamount to denial of the mercy and beneficence of God. The Qur'an repeatedly asks the believers not to despair, but to 'be steadfast' (16:127) and say, 'when afflicted with calamity, "we belong to God and unto Him we shall return"' (2:156). Do not 'hope for death', the believers are told, 'before you encounter it' (3:142). The Qur'an, I would argue, does not look with favour at despair.

That there is always hope is well illustrated in the story of Prophet Job. First, he lost his wealth. But he was not grieved. Then his children were killed. Still he remained steadfast. Then he was struck with an unbearable illness that left him incapacitated. Indeed, his body was so afflicted that people felt disgusted when they looked at him. In excruciating pain, he cried to God: 'Suffering has truly afflicted me, but you are the Most Merciful of the merciful.' Eventually, Job received a reply to his cries for help: 'We answered him, removed his suffering, and restored his family to him, along with more like him, as an act of grace from Us and a reminder for all who serve Us' (21:83–4).

There are three lessons to be drawn from this story. First, suffering is a natural part of life: anyone can be inflicted with pain and sorrow, and no one, not even a prophet, has the right to escape pain. Of course, no one wants to suffer; and we must do all we can to alleviate pain and reduce suffering as much as possible. But there is no absolute right that states that we should not suffer. Second, suffering has a value. It is only through seeing the pain and agony of others that we learn what compassion is all about. People found it difficult to look at Job: but only by looking at him could they realise that they too can become victim of such affliction. It is through that connection, of seeing someone suffering, that one understands the true meaning of human compassion. Three, one should never give up. At each stage of the story, Job remains steadfast; he does not ask for death as an escape from his suffering, but prays for an end to suffering itself. It is his steadfastness that is ultimately rewarded. When it comes to suffering and death, mercy comes only from God; it is not a human prerogative.

Life is sacred; so it cannot be ranked. All life, whatever its quality, according to the Qur'an, is equally valid and valuable. The value of life does not lie in its alleged usefulness, however we may define and measure usefulness. It lies in the fact that it is a life: it has not been created as a 'pointless game' but has a 'true purpose' that not all of us can 'comprehend' (44:38–9). The idea that certain lives are not worth living violates the very notion of humanity that the Qur'an is arguing for. The lives of a terminally ill person, the person in a coma, the person in excruciating pain, the senile person confined to their bed, are all as valid and important as the lives of anyone else. The life of suffering has a purpose. It is still a journey that must reach its natural conclusion. The notion that it would be 'merciful' to end such lives is an obnoxious idea. 'Mercy killing' is in fact killing: with or without the consent of the person involved.

Life is sacred; therefore all possibilities for life must remain open. The underlying assumption of such notions as 'mercy killing' and 'assisted suicide' is that suffering is an objective and static phenomenon. It can be assessed and measured; and thus we can make a reasonable decision. But unbearable situations can change, suffering can be alleviated, if not today than sometime in the future. Who is to say that a cure is not around the corner? Who is to say that palliative care will not improve? This possibility is totally eliminated from the equation if we allow or aid someone pleading to die. It is equally possible that the person in question may change his or her mind: not necessarily because pain and agony has been reduced but because they have changed their own self-perception. People change their minds often; and their own perception about themselves and their experience changes just as frequently. Mercy and assisted killings also eliminate this possibility. As trustees of God, it is our responsibility to keep all the possibilities for life open, right up to the last breath. There is still hope when 'nothing further can be done': the hope of prayer and of God's mercy. Hence, the injunction in the Qur'an: 'Do not kill each other for God is merciful to you' (4:29).

There is another assumption in the arguments put forward for 'assisted suicide' that I find rather odd. 'Assisted suicide', it is suggested, allows a person to die with dignity. The assumption here is that a severely ill dying person loses dignity because of the way he or she is dying. This is an absurd notion of dignity. A dying person has innate dignity, a product of the simple fact that they are a human being. All human beings have a right to be treated with dignity; and just because they are dying of some incurable illness, or suffering from pain and agony, does not mean that their dignity has somehow evaporated. Surely, it is the duty and responsibility of those who surround the dying person to acknowledge the fact of their dignity and to treat them in a dignified manner. It is the height of folly, I would argue, to suggest that their dignity can only be preserved or restored by killing them.

This brings us to a contemporary phenomenon that has gained currency in certain Muslim circles: 'suicide bombing'. It is quite astonishing that such an abhorrent act is accepted and practised by those who, loudly and frequently, declare their love for Islam. I find the arguments of those who justify 'suicide bombings' to be both twisted and pathological. The 'suicide bombers', it is suggested, are in a position of such despair and helplessness that they have no option but to use their bodies as a weapon. Killing civilians is regrettable but is ultimately justified in the cause of a 'just war' against oppression, and, in any case, all innocent victims will go to paradise. This position undermines virtually every teaching of the Qur'an.

First, 'suicide bombing' involves a suicide, which, as I have shown, is strictly forbidden. There are always other victims of a suicide, with or without the bomb, than the individuals who kill themselves. These include their family, who suffer the effects of the suicide and have to live with its emotional, religious and other consequences for many years. Second, killing innocent civilians is nothing but mass murder; and, according to the Qur'anic formulation, even if a single person is killed it is in fact like killing all of humankind (5:32). So a suicide bomber simultaneously commits two cardinal sins. The notion that the bomber is heading straight for paradise is perverse, to say the least. Third, if the actual act of suicide bombing is an act of despair, then it signifies rejection of God's mercy and abandonment of hope. In other words, it undermines the very raison d'être of Islam: 'to be mindful of God'. Even in despair, the Qur'an asks the believers 'to do good in this world' and 'persevere patiently': 'God's earth is wide' (39:10). Finally, if suicide killing was a viable weapon of a just war, however conceived, then the Prophet Muhammad himself would have used it. He had ample opportunity to do so. During his days in Mecca, where he was severely persecuted and his life constantly threatened and his followers were tortured, murdered and driven out of the city, the Prophet remained steadfast. Even when he had to fight his enemies in Medina, he did not engage in suicide missions; his battles were well-planned and based on strategies designed to preserve life. Moreover, he forbade the taking of innocent lives, killing of non-combatants, civilians, women and children, and destroying plants and animals. During one of his battles, children of the enemy were killed by mistake. The Prophet was visibly pained and started to cry. One of his followers tried to console him; 'they were only the children of unbelievers', he said. The Prophet replied angrily: 'Aren't you the child of an unbeliever too?' To consider suicide bombing as a military tactic, or as a way of fighting, is to violate everything that the Qur'an and Islam stand for.

Life is sacred; that is why 'no human being can die except with God's permission at an appointed time' (3:145). Our humanity is most tested at times of severe despair and desperation, acute pain and agony, when life itself becomes horrendous. But it is precisely at these moments that respect for life needs to be reinforced.

50

SCIENCE AND TECHNOLOGY

We have already seen that the Qur'an gives immense importance to the pursuit of knowledge. The Qur'an tells us that the universe is full of the 'signs of God', and these signs can only be deciphered through rational and objective enquiry. Verses encouraging us to read the 'signs of God', or to systematically study nature, abound in the Sacred Text. The believers are repeatedly asked to think, ponder and reason; and pray: 'Lord, increase me in knowledge' (20:114). One of the most frequently cited verses of the Qur'an reads: 'Surely in the heavens and earth there are signs for the believers; and in your creation, and the crawling things He scatters abroad, there are signs for a people having sure faith, and in the alternation of night and day, and the provision God sends down from heaven, and therewith revives the earth after it is dead, and the turning about of the winds, there are signs for a people who understand' (45:3–5). Such verses indicate that the Qur'an places a high priority on scientific enquiry.

The Qur'an, however, does not simply suggest, in general terms, that science is important. It points towards methods for doing science. First, it urges the readers to appreciate the importance of observation: 'let man observe out of what he has been created' (86:5) and 'do the believers not observe how rain clouds are formed, how the heavens are lifted, how the mountains are raised high, how the earth is spread out?' (88:17). Second, it emphasises the significance of measurement and calculation: 'everything have We created in due measure and proportion' (54:49); 'We send it down only according to a well-defined measure' (15:21); and 'it is He who made the sun a shining radiance and the moon a light, determining phases for it so that you might know the number of years and how to calculate them' (10:5). Third, after observations, measurements and calculations have been made, we are asked to draw inferences: in all this, we are told, 'there are messages indeed for people who use their reason' (2:164), so 'will you not, then, use your reason?' (2:73). Finally, we are asked to proceed on the basis of evidence as 'God Himself proffers evidence' (3:18).

The notion of 'measure' used in the Qur'an has a number of connotations. Apart from the obvious idea of measurement, it also includes the suggestion of proportion or mathematical relationships. These relationships, it is said, can be insignificant, nothing more than froth; or deeply abiding, and hence have the force of the laws of nature. This is brought out in 13:17: 'Whenever He sends down water from the sky, and [once-dry] river-beds are running high according to their measure, the stream carries scum on its surface; and, likewise, from that [metal] which they smelt in the fire in order to make ornaments or utensils, [there rises] scum. In this way does God set forth the parable of truth and falsehood: for, as far as the scum is concerned, it passes away as [does all] dross; but that which is of benefit to man abides on earth.' What we are being told is that understanding the deep structures of the material universe would yield dividends for humanity. But these dividends are not freely available. The 'measure' also has the idea of extraction: we acquire our 'due measure' through our own efforts; that is, discoveries have to be made. 'If God were to grant abundant sustenance to all', says the Qur'an, we 'would behave on earth with wanton insolence.' Rather, we get 'due measure' according to the effort we put into understanding and using the laws of nature (42:27). In other words, nature does not yield its secrets without due and systematic effort.

It is worth noting that it is not just science that the Qur'an emphasises, but also technology. There is a chapter called 'Iron' where God tells us that He 'sent iron, with its mighty strength and many uses for mankind' (57:25). Iron, here, serves as a metaphor for technology, which can be developed as a 'means of protection' against nature and natural causes, from 'heat and cold', and as a form of military defence (16:81). Technology comes in the form of 'many coloured things' which can be developed to make jewellery as well as ships, agriculture and animal husbandry and instruments for navigation and exploration (16:10–16).

The Prophet Muhammad—who himself could not read or write—also emphasised that the material world can only be understood through scientific enquiry. Islamic culture, he insisted, was a knowledge-based culture. He valued science over extensive worship, and declared: 'An hour's study of nature is better than a year's prayer.' This is why he directed his followers to listen to the words of the scientist and instil in others the lessons of science and 'go even as far as China in the quest of knowledge'. The emphasis the Prophet gave to rationality is well illustrated by the incident of the death of his infant son, Ibrahim. The death of Ibrahim coincided with the eclipse of the sun. Some Muslims in Medina saw that as a miracle, a sign from God. A rumour spread throughout Medina that even the heavens are crying at the deep sorrow and loss of the Prophet. But Muhammad was not consoled; instead he was angry at this irrational gossip. 'The sun and the moon are signs of God', he announced. 'They are eclipsed neither for the death nor the birth of any man' [33].

But the study of nature and the use of reason have their limitations. The Qur'an suggests that not all knowledge is good and wholesome. Knowledge can become a temptation to do evil. In the verses that talk about Solomon, we read about harmful knowledge that can destroy societies: 'they learned what harmed them, not what benefited them, knowing full well that whosoever acquires this knowledge shall have no share in the good life to come' (2: 102). The knowledge in question here is described as 'witchcraft', but it applies equally to all forms of knowledge, including scientific and objective knowledge. It is specifically to avoid falling into this trap that the Qur'an suggests we see scientific enquiry as a way of contemplating the unity of God. The Qur'anic notion of *'ibada* or worship, as I noted in the chapter on 'Reason and Knowledge', is intimately linked to the concept of *'ilm*, or knowledge: both are a form of listening to God. This has two significances. First, scientific enquiry becomes an obligation for Muslim societies. Second, as contemplation, or form of worship, our scientific and technological endeavours cannot involve any form of violence, oppression or tyranny or be pursued for unworthy goals and end up as destructive 'harmful knowledge'. Science has to be the pursuit of goodness and truth on behalf of the public good and the promotion of social, economic and cultural justice. As human beings, scientists are not independent of God, but are responsible and accountable to God for their scientific and technological activities.

Moreover, as we saw in the chapter on 'Nature and Environment', as trustees or *khulafa'* of God on earth, all of us, scientists or not, are responsible for maintaining and conserving nature and the creations of God.

Given the emphasis in the Qur'an, and the Prophet's example in the support of science and technology, the conventional notion that science and religion are inimical does not hold water within an Islamic framework. No long and protracted war between science and religion took place in Islamic history. The 'war' between 'science' and 'religion' was—and is—a purely Western affair, and even there it is more of an illusory and self-serving argument.

The intimate connection between Islam and science is clearly demonstrated in the early history of Muslim civilisation. The initial drive for scientific knowledge was based on religious requirements. The need for determining an accurate time for daily prayers and the direction of Mecca from anywhere in the Muslim world, establishing the correct date for the start of the fasting month of Ramadan and the demands of the lunar Islamic calendar (which required seeing the new moon clearly) led to intense interest in celestial mechanics, optical and atmospheric physics and spherical trigonometry. Muslim laws of inheritance led to the development of algebra. The religious requirement of annual pilgrimage to Mecca generated intense interest in geography, map-making and navigational tools [34].

Given the special emphasis the Qur'an places on learning and enquiry, it was natural for classical Muslim societies to seek to master ancient knowledge. At the instigation of powerful patrons, teams of translators lovingly translated Greek thought and learning into Arabic. But Muslims were not content with slavishly copying Greek knowledge; they tried to assimilate its content and apply its principles to their own problems, in the process discovering new principles and methods. Scholars such as al-Kindi, al-Farabi, ibn Sina, ibn Tufayl and ibn Rushd subjected Greek philosophy to detailed critical scrutiny.

At the same time, serious attention was given to the empirical study of nature. Experimental science, as we understand it today, began within Muslim civilisation. 'Scientific method' evolved out of the work of such scientists as Jabir ibn Hayan (who was Christian), who laid the foundations of chemistry in the late eighth century, and ibn Al-Haytham, who established optics as an experimental science in the tenth century [35]. From astronomy to zoology, there was hardly a field of study that Muslim scientists did not pursue vigorously, or to which they did not make an original contribution. The nature and extent of this scientific enterprise can be illustrated by four institutions which are considered typical of 'the Golden Age of Islam': scientific libraries, universities, hospitals and instruments for scientific observation (particularly, astronomical instruments such as celestial globes, astrolabes, sundials and observatories).

The most famous library was the 'House of Wisdom' [36], founded in Baghdad by the Abbassid Caliph al-Mamun, which played a decisive role in spreading scientific knowledge throughout the Islamic empire. In Spain, the library of Caliph Hakam II of Cordoba had a stock of 400,000 volumes. Similar libraries existed from Cairo and Damascus to as far away as Samarkand and Bukhara. The first university in the world was established at the Al-Azhar mosque in Cairo in 970. It was followed by a host of other universities in such cities as Fez and Timbuktu. Like universities, hospitals too—where treatment was mostly provided free of charge—were institutions for training as well as theoretical and empirical research. The Abodi hospital in Baghdad and the Kabir an-Nuri hospital in Damascus acquired worldwide reputations for their research output. Doctors were entirely free to experiment and prescribe new drugs and treatment, and wrote up their experiments in special reports which were available for public scrutiny. The basic set of surgical instruments that would be familiar to surgeons today were first developed by Muslim doctors. Similarly, there were a string of observatories dotted throughout the Muslim world; the most influential one was established by the celebrated astronomer Nasir al-Din al-Tusi, working at Maragha in Azerbaijan, where he developed the 'Tusi couple' which helped Copernicus to formulate his heliocentric theory [37].

I reiterate this simply to bring out the stark contrast with the situation of science and technology in the contemporary Muslim world. Science is inconspicuous in Muslim countries, where, in general, research and development have a very low priority. The little research that is undertaken is usually associated with defence, and in particular with the development of nuclear or other weapons. Not a single university of international renown can be found in any Muslim country. So, whatever happened to what the historian of science George Sarton [38] described as 'the miracle of Arab culture'?

Numerous theories have been developed to explain the decline of science in Muslim civilisation. Blame has been placed on Islamic law, Muslim family relationships and lack of protestant ethics in Muslim culture. Even Islam itself, seen as 'anti-progressive' and 'anti-science', has been blamed [39]. I do not think that any of these theories are credible. I have my own theories which I have described elsewhere [40]. Here, suffice to state a single brutal fact: Muslims, consciously and deliberately, abandoned scientific enquiry in favour of religious obscurantism and blind imitation. The idea of knowledge, which included scientific and technological knowledge, was reduced, over centuries, to mean only religious knowledge.

A major driving force behind the scientific spirit of Muslim civilisation was the notion of *ijtihad* or systematic original thinking, based on the Qur'anic injunctions to think and reason, 'to use their minds' (2:164), which became a fundamental component of the classical worldview of Islam. The religious scholars, a dominant class in Muslim society, feared that continuous and perpetual *ijtihad* would undermine their power. They were also concerned that scientists and philosophers had a higher prestige in society than religious scholars. So they banded together and, over a number of centuries, managed to close

355

'the gates of *ijtihad*'; the way forward, they suggested, was *taqlid*, or imitation of the thought and work of earlier generation of scholars. Ostensibly, this was a religious move. But given the fact that the Qur'an propagates a highly integrated view of the world and emphasises that everything is connected to everything else, the reduction had a devastating impact on all forms of enquiry. The 'minds' were closed not just on religious but also on scientific and technological issues. The religious scholars thus buried scientific enquiry to preserve their hold on society.

Contemporary Muslim societies have deep emotional attachment to their scientific heritage. But this attachment often expresses itself as an inferiority complex. Nowadays, science in the Muslim world is not associated with laboratories and centres of excellence but with a totally different endeavor: the 'discovery' of 'scientific miracles in the Qur'an'. A whole body of literature has evolved, known as *ijaz*, designed to read scientific facts and theories into the Qur'an [41]. We have seen that the Qur'an contains many verses that point towards physical phenomena. But they are mostly poetic and allegorical in nature. Considerable mental gymnastics and distortion are required to read scientific discoveries in these verses. Yet, almost everything, from relativity, quantum mechanics, big bang theory, black holes and pulsars, genetics, embryology, modern geology, thermodynamics, subatomic physics, electricity, even the laser and the hydrogen fuel cells have been 'found' in the Qur'an. Indeed, some verses of the Qur'an have even been turned into equations that are combined like algebra to yield the value of the speed of light, the ages of the Universe and of the Earth, the distances between the 'seven heavens' [42], and other such bewildering feats.

This is a highly toxic combination of religious and scientific fundamentalism. Elsewhere I have dubbed it 'Bucaillism', as it began in the mid 1970s with the publication of *The Bible, the Qur'an and Science* by Maurice Bucaille [43], an eccentric and authoritarian French surgeon. Bucaille examines the Holy Scriptures in the light of modern science to discover what they have to say about astronomy, the earth, animal and vegetable kingdoms. He finds that the Bible does not meet the stringent criteria of modern knowledge. The Qur'an, on the other hand, does not contain a single proposition at variance with the most firmly established modern knowledge, nor does it contain any of the ideas current at the time on the subjects it describes. Furthermore, the Qur'an contains a large number of facts which were not discovered until modern times. The book has been translated into almost every Muslim language from the original French, and has spread the illusion that the Qur'an is a scientific treatise. In more recent times, the *ijaz* literature and movement have been turned into a global industry by the Turkish creationist Adnan Oktar, who writes under the pseudonym of Haroon Yahya. In his book *Miracles of the Qur'an* [44], Yahya claims to explain the verses of the Qur'an 'in such a way as to leave no room for doubt or question marks'. He suggests that the verse 'we have sent down iron in which there lies great force and which has many uses for mankind' (57:25) is a 'significant scientific miracle' because 'modern astronomical findings have disclosed that iron found in our world has come from the giant stars in outer space'. The verse 'glory be to Him Who created all the pairs of things that the earth produces' (36:36) is claimed to predict anti-matter. And the verse 'He has let loose the two seas, converging together, with a barrier between them they do not break through' (55:19–20) is said to be all about surface tension. But such inanities are not limited to crackpots and dogmatic puritans. These notions are widely accepted by so-called scientists and university professors in Muslim countries. Programmes to harness the energy of *jinn* and prove the superiority of flies have been devised. Geology in the Qur'an is on the curriculum of quite a few geology departments.

Bucaillism is a pathological tendency that does violence to the Qur'an and is an insult to any sensible notion of scientific enquiry. The people who propagate and lap up such toxic nonsense, in the words of the Qur'an, 'hear nothing but the sound of a voice and a cry: they are deaf, dumb, and blind, they understand nothing' (2:171).

To be faithful to their scientific heritage, Muslims need to do much more than simply preserve the ashes of its fire: they need to transmit its flame. It is the neglect of science that has plunged the contemporary Muslim world into poverty and underdevelopment. Just as the spirit of Islam in history was defined by its scientific enterprise, so the future of Muslim societies is dependent on their relationship with science and learning. Without science and technology, Muslim culture is, and will remain, truncated and unbalanced. Given that scientific knowledge is a form of worship, a way to understand God's creation and His will, and an obligation as important as prayer, I would argue that Muslim worship is incomplete without science.

Those who believe in the Qur'an are obliged to make a conscious effort to pursue science and technology. Science is all about empirical research, hard graft, viable models and testable theories; it is discovered not in the pages of scripture, but by rolling up one's sleeves and going back to the laboratory. There are no quick fixes in science and technology. 'What about someone who worships devoutly by night, bowing down, standing in prayer, ever mindful of life to come, hoping for his Lord's mercy?' the Qur'an asks. Then answers: 'how can those who know be equal to those who do not know?' (39:9). Prayer is prayer; it is not a substitute for knowing. Acquiring scientific knowledge too requires endless devotion, serious thought and constant effort. However, the pursuit of science must be a socially responsible activity; it needs a reasoned moral and ethical framework for its means and ends, as well as in setting its priorities for research and development, to make its fullest contribution to the transformative advancement of society and knowledge. To be true to their beliefs, Muslim societies need to put as much effort into science as they do on prayer; and place science where it belongs: at the very centre of Islamic culture.

51

EVOLUTION

Let me start by pointing out the obvious. The entire debate about faith and evolution has been constructed out of the history and concepts of Christian thought. The Creationists' arguments, including the idea of Intelligent Design, are shaped by a literalist reading of the Biblical text. We should be careful not to import attitudes and ideas from the familiar context of this debate into the very different context of the Qur'an. The Qur'an refers, as we have already seen, to narratives familiar from the Bible—including the creation, Prophet Nuh (Noah) and the flood—but it does so in its own distinctive ways. The narratives of the Qur'an are not meant to be 'creation myths' but allegories. As always, we must read and try to understand the Qur'an on its own terms.

We find frequent reference in the Qur'an to God as the Creator of all things. In 7:54 we read: 'Your Lord God is He Who created the heavens and the earth in six days.' What are we to make of these 'six days'? Should we take them literally? The word translated here as 'days' is *yawm*, which can signify both a day in the sense of 24 hours as we understand it or an indeterminate period of time, 'whether extremely long (aeon) or extremely short (moment)', to use the words of Muhammad Asad. That the word is not to be taken literally, and only has allegorical significance, is made clear elsewhere in the Qur'an. In 41:9, for example, we read: 'Would you indeed deny Him who has created the earth in two aeons?' The verse then goes on to present a clearly allegorical image of creation: 'Above the earth He erected towering mountains, and he blessed it, and appraised its provisions in four days, in equal measure to those who need them. Then he ascended to heaven, while yet smoke, and said to it and the earth: "Come forth, willing or unwilling!" And both responded: "We come willingly."

359

He then ordained the seven heavens in two days and inspired each heaven with its disposition...Such was the devising of the Almighty, All-knowing' (41:10–12). (I have used the rather poetic translation by Tarif Khaldi here.)

We also have to consider the use of the word *yawm* in relation to 32:5, which not only deals with creation but also our ultimate return to God for judgement in the Hereafter, when 'everything will ascend to Him in the end, on a day that will measure a thousand years in your reckoning'. Clearly, when we are dealing with things that are beyond direct human experience, we are not dealing with the kind of mundane days of our reckoning, but talking in metaphorical terms. This is made clear in the verse that follows, 32:6: 'Such is He who knows all that is beyond the reach of a created being's perception, as well as all that can be witnessed by a creature's senses of mind: the Almighty, the Dispenser of Grace who makes most excellent everything that He creates.'

So what we are dealing with is an allegory, a figurative vision of the awesome creation of the universe. It is not, nor is it meant to be, a precise manual of the processes of creation which occurred in time, and definitely not the kind of timescale we are familiar with in our daily life. It would be totally foolish to confuse the allegorical with the literal. The Qur'an leaves us to work out the precise details of how the universe came into being, what are the laws that determine its existence and expansion, and how it will evolve, using our own reason. There are, however, a few hints for us to ponder: 'Are the disbelievers not aware that the heavens and the earth used to be joined together and that We ripped them apart, that We made every living thing from water' (21:30); 'And it is We Who have constructed the sky (space) with might, and it is We Who are steadily expanding it' (51:47); 'We shall roll up the skies as a writer rolls up [his] scrolls. We shall reproduce creation just as We produced it the first time' (21:104). The hints whet our appetite and encourage us to venture forth and discover.

The creation of humankind is not directly related to the period of the creation of the heavens and the earth. But a connection is definitely made. On a number of occasions, the Qur'an tells us that humankind is created out of sounding clay, out of dark slime transmuted, or fetid mud. In other words, we are formed from the same substance as the earth.

The metaphor of being formed from clay is used repeatedly throughout the Qur'an. In 55:12 we are told: 'He has created man out of sounding clay, like pottery.' But this origin in the basic substance of the earth is distinct from the process by which each human being is generated as a living person, which is referred to in 23:12: 'Now, Indeed, We create man out of the essence of clay, and then We cause him to remain as a drop of sperm in [the womb's] firm keeping, and then We create out of the drop of sperm a germ cell, and then We create out of the germ cell an embryonic lump and then we create within the embryonic lump bones, and then we clothe the bones with flesh—and then we bring [all] this into being as a new creation, hallowed, therefore, is God, the best of artisans!'

How can we relate these two versions of human creation? It seems to me we have a metaphor of origins that concentrates on humanity as part of the common substance of the universe. But the metaphor of clay and mud also has the implication that the substance of the earth is malleable, that the creation of humankind was an intentional and purposeful process of shaping and making in which humanity acquired its specific characteristics, its abilities. Among the characteristics derived from this origin is the routine process by which each individual human being comes into existence, the human biological process of generation.

What I find most striking in the Qur'an's discussion of human creation is the sense of process, the repeated ongoing nature of creation which relates the newest newborn child to the conceptual beginning of human life in the clay and mud, the materials of earth from which we originate. And this view of human creation has to be related to the diversity of humankind, including the diversity of colour and language.

In all the various references to human creation in the Qur'an there is a sense of motion, of continuous action through time, of creation as constant becoming for each new generation of human beings. We are not presented with a static portrait of a once and for all event. Rather, creation is presented as a dynamic, ongoing phenomenon that is constantly evolving and changing. Indeed, in 71:14 we are specifically asked to reflect on the fact that 'He has created you stage by stage'.

This is why Creationism, as formulated by Christian fundamentalists, has never been a Muslim position in history. As early as the tenth century, Muhamad al-Nakshbandi, a teacher of religion from central Asia, wrote in *The Book of the Yield*: 'while man has sprung from sentient creatures, these have sprung from plants, and these in turn from combined substances' [45]. And in his philosophical novel *Life of Hayy*, the twelfth-century Andalusian philosopher ibn Tufayl had his protagonist Hayy 'spontaneously generated' from a mud slime to evolve through various stages into a rational man [46].

It is not surprising, then, that Muslim societies have not witnessed raging debates about Darwin and Creationism of the kind we have seen in the West.

When *The Origins of Species* first appeared in the Ottoman Empire during the 1870s, it was embraced by liberal thinkers. Novelist and publisher Ahmet Mithat (d.1912) promoted evolution in his works, lawyer Ahmed Suayib (d.1913) used evolutionary ideas to argue for the development of Turkish institutions, and philosopher Riza Tevfik (d.1949) declared himself an apprentice of Darwin. There were odd reactions to these intellectuals from conservative quarters, but they were based more on anti-Western sentiments than on a total rejection of evolution. Throughout most of the twentieth century, evolution was taken for granted in Muslim societies and was hardly discussed.

But Creationism as an idea reared its ugly head towards the end of the last century. Its driving force was the American Christian Creation movement, which built alliances with ultra conservatives in the Muslim world. 'Islamic creationism', as it is known, is also closely associated with the *ijaz* ('scientific miracles of the Qur'an') literature that I mentioned in the last chapter. Virtually all the Islamic creationist literature is produced by one man: the Turkish cult leader Adnan Oktar, aka Haroon Yahya, who has acquired a huge following in the more dogmatic circles of the Muslim world. Yahya's books, such as the lavishly illustrated 786 pages tome *Atlas of Creation* [47], blame everything from Nazism to terrorism on evolution; and are based on, and freely lifted from, the American creationist literature. They also promote conspiracy theories and religious paranoia.

However, given the emphasis that the Qur'an gives to systematic and demonstrative knowledge, dogmatic creationism has no place in Muslim societies. Indeed, as we have seen, the Qur'an's position is that science and revelation go hand in hand, both delineating different aspects of the truth. So, Muslims in general should have no problem with reconciling their belief in the Qur'an with evolution. It has not been a problem in history; and it should not be a problem today.

52

ART, MUSIC AND IMAGINATION

There are no direct references to art and music in the Qur'an. But given the fact that the Qur'an is the very foundation of Islam, it is not surprising that the creative spirit of Muslim societies emerges from and rests on the Sacred Text. Islamic arts, on the whole, are Qur'anic arts: aesthetic expressions that derive their basis and motivation, seek their goals and implementations, from the Qur'an.

In 42:11 and 6:103 we see that the Qur'an describes God as the unique, unchanging and eternal Creator: 'there is nothing like Him'; and 'no vision can take Him in' (6:103). As such, He is beyond representation, and humans are incapable of signifying him by any anthropomorphic image. So it makes sense to argue that the Qur'an does not permit figural representation of God; but to suggest, as some Muslims do, that this is a ban on all forms of human representation is an argument too far.

The Qur'an is clear that idols, images of deities, are the ultimate category mistake: human attempts to encapsulate the idea of God, to reduce the Infinite within the limitations of human consciousness, to appropriate, possess and control the idea of deity. The story of the golden calf is repeated a number of times in the Qur'an as the prime example (2:51; 4:153; 7:148; 20:88; 2:55). Idols turn people away from the One God and substitute veneration for aspects of God's powers and creation. Idols cannot be, and are not, representations of God; they are indications of a wrong relationship with religion. The Qur'an constantly reveals the nature of God through His attributes, which we must stretch our understanding to comprehend and endeavour to worship by approximating and applying in our lives. The purpose of religion is to expand human consciousness, to be fully and continually aware of what is beyond the limitations of our created nature. The existence of God is the imperative to stretch our imagination and understanding of the Infinite.

Not surprisingly, Islamic art traditionally shuns figural representation of God. Instead, focusing on the fact that God is Infinite, Islamic art tends to be abstract and aims to create the impression of infinity and transcendence. So in a variety of plastic arts we see the play of geometric outlines: lines transformed into patterns, patterns combined into modules, modules combined to produce larger motifs, and repeated endlessly to produce movement. Combination and repetition—which, as we have seen, are central to the structure of the Qur'an itself—go on ad infinitum to generate an intuition of infinity, that which is beyond space and time [48]. Such aesthetic expressions can be seen in arabesques, witnessed on carpets, walls and furniture, and are the inspiration for design elements of architecture from the conception of buildings to the decorative detail of their interior, such as architraves or ceramic wall tiles [49].

A logical consequence of the importance of the words of the Qur'an is the development of calligraphy: representation of words as an art form. Primarily calligraphy uses the verses of the Qur'an itself to communicate the feeling of reverence and awe through line, shape, colour and movement—and transform word into art. Various styles of writing Arabic developed, which were used in the calligraphy of verses, expressions such as *Bismillah ir-Rahman ir-Rahim* (in the name of God, the Beneficent, the Merciful) or even the word '*Allah*', and made into adornments for objects, as pictures and plaques and even worked into the decorative detail of buildings [50]. Calligraphy becomes an aesthetic which encourages Muslims to read their environment through the words of the Qur'an, to move from the line and form of the word to the observation of the world, and thus fulfil the frequently repeated exhortation in the Qur'an to open our eyes to appreciate the *ayat*, the signs, of God in nature and the operation of His creation.

The Qur'an has repeated metaphorical descriptions of paradise, vivid word pictures of a place replete with gardens, fountains and pavilions, the very epitome of beauty, which have played an important part in Islamic art. These descriptions and evocations have inspired paintings, miniatures and architecture. Paradise is invoked in the construction of the Alhambra in Granada. The art of making gardens was practised by the Moguls in the Indian subcontinent. The idea of a garden was internalised within the construction of traditional houses built around inner courtyard gardens with fountains, which can still be found in what is left of traditional cities such as Old Jeddah and Cairo. The notion of *khalifa* (trusteeship), a central theme of the Qur'an, also played an important part both in architecture and city planning. The emphasis on pres- ervation of nature is all too evident in traditional cities like Fez and Aleppo. In this way an aesthetic becomes practical art, interwoven in a way of living, from city planning down to the form and decoration of household utensils, a reflection of humanity's trusteeship of the natural world and responsibility for prudential guardianship [51]. Elegance and beauty, grace and design become not ends in themselves but means to live out and reflect in myriad ways upon the constant presence of the Infinite.

There are, however, some Muslim purists who reject all forms of art, and argue that the Qur'an bans any kind of representation—full stop. Since God 'gave everything its perfect form' (32:7), the argument goes, mortals should avoid trying to copy His perfection. But this nonsensical argument assumes that an artist is imitating God, rather than seeking to explore, understand and reflect on his creation. There are some Muslims who accept traditional abstract arts grudgingly; for them the totality of Islamic art must be abstract with no figurative representation. The puritans also argue that music is forbidden in Islam and should not be allowed in Muslim societies. I must admit I find such proclamations to be mad and inhuman. Such dumbfounding and absurd inter- pretations not only kill imagination but are life-denying and undermine what makes us truly human. The Qur'an provides us with the best description of such people, for they have 'hearts they do not use for comprehension, eyes they do not use for seeing, and ears they do not use for hearing. They are like cattle, no, even further astray: these are the ones who are entirely heedless' (7:179).

Fortunately, the 'heedless' ones had little effect on the artistic practices of Muslim societies in history. Figurative representations are dominant in Persian miniatures, often used in illustrations of books, both literary and scientific, and of course portraits not just of kings and sultans but also poets, writers and painters. All this, I think, has immensely enriched Islam's contribution to art, as well as shaping a distinctive Islamic aesthetic of figural representation.

Music too has played a distinctive role in Muslim history. Indeed, to be a Muslim, I would argue, is to have a natural love of music. It cannot be other- wise: as Muslims we constantly hear the Qur'an, whose aesthetic dimension is expressed through sound—by recitation. Both melody and vocal ornamenta- tion are beautifully presented in Qur'anic recitation; and, to a lesser form in the *adhan*, the call to prayer. So Muslims are constantly surrounded by sacred music. I must confess that a beautiful recitation, indeed a good *adhan*, has a deep emotional impact on me. That is why I cannot live without my music: 'music of the past, and music of the future' [52].

The Qur'an does not refer to music directly; but we do find indirect mention of music. When talking about Prophet David, God tells us he had 'been taught the speech of birds' (27:16). This melodious voice and ability to sing was a special 'favour' of God; and David used his gift to sing the praises of God. But he did not sing alone; for God said: 'You mountains, echo God's praises together with him, and you birds, too' (34:10). So when David sang, the valleys truly came alive with the sound of music, with mountains joining him in glorifying God 'at sunset and sunrise; and the birds, too, in flocks, all echoed his praise' (38:18). The Prophet Muhammad followed David and is known to have played music both at his own and his daughter's weddings.

Despite this, some classical scholars, particularly the legal-minded, sought to ban music. Then, as now, 31:6 and 17:64 are used to argue for the ban. In 31:6, which reads 'there is the sort of person who pays for distracting tales, intending, without any knowledge, to lead others from God's way, and to hold it up to ridicule', the words 'distracting tales' were interpreted to mean music. Similarly, 'voice' in the verse 'entice whichever you can with your voice' (17:64) was described as singing and music, and associated with the work of Satan. This interpretation is, of course, skating on very thin ice. The first verse refers to those who mock the Qur'an with word play. The second verse occurs in a passage where Iblis is refusing to submit to Adam—'Shall I submit to whom You have created out of dust' (17:61)—and refers to the voice of Satan. The 'voice' here signifies all kinds of desire and temptation and has no reference to music whatsoever. Perhaps this is why most anti-music arguments come from fabricated and dubious *Hadith*, or sayings of the Prophet.

But such absurd interpretations, and the condemnation of music associated with them, were and are rightly ignored by Muslim people. Indeed, the Sufi mystics gave a privileged position to music and placed it at the heart of all their ceremonies. Sufi music is in fact an integral part of Islam. Many great philosophers of Islam, including al-Kindi (d.866), al-Farabi (d.950) and ibn Sina (d.1037), wrote profusely on the theory of music and encouraged its performance. Al-Kindi, for example, argued that music can change our ethical qualities and turn anger into calm, grief into joy, depression into a state of relaxation, rage into friendliness, avarice into generosity and cowardice into bravery [53].

The other major Muslim art is poetry. Poetry was the traditional art form of the Arabs, and the Qur'an notes that Muhammad was seen by many people as a mad poet, rather than a messenger of God. Such slight references again explain why traditional purists condemn poetry as arrogant human presumption, motivated by the Qur'an's challenge to unbelievers of the impossibility of producing a text comparable to its poetry. Nevertheless, poetry, the search for concision in use of words to express emotion, ideas and feeling, has been a major creative force in Islamic history. Indeed, poetry has been a key instrument for unleashing the religious imagination, for going beyond reason in unveiling the truth and discovering what it means to be human. It remains a vibrant art form across the Muslim world, a popular oral art form enjoyed by the majority, rather than the preserve of the elite.

To read the Qur'an is to unleash one's imagination, to be surrounded by its sounds and imagery, to lose one's self in the Infinite. Inasmuch as God is 'within us', exploring the Infinite with our imagination is a part of our *fitra*, or innate nature. As such, imagination is in fact a form of knowing. It is knowing from being: what in Muslim tradition is sometimes called the 'expansion of the bosom', a way of connecting with your inner self, your *fitra*, and thus realising the beauty and grace of God. As al-Ghazali (d.1111), the celebrated Muslim philosopher and theologian, said, 'anyone who thinks that the unveiling of truth depends (only) on carefully formulated proofs has indeed placed the abundant mercy of God under restraint' [54]. Reason guides us to truth; but it is imagination that teaches us the appreciation of truth and how it touches and transforms us as human beings.

Each Muslim country has its own tradition of unleashing imagination, of music, poetry, literature, art, dance and theatre; and all take their inspiration, directly or indirectly, from the Qur'an. In creative arts, as in everything else, the Qur'an's overall message is of balance and moderation. The function of art in Islam is to provide objects of aesthetic contemplation that generate an intuition of the truth, give meaning and purpose to our lives and force us to think about ourselves and our society. Aesthetic, reflective beauty is not something that has to be confined to rarefied objects we call 'art'; it is something that can be transmitted equally through common objects such as plates, lamps, candlesticks, vases, doors and windows. A work of art is, in Islamic parlance, something to wonder about. It points the viewer not towards what God is not, but what God *is*.

Perhaps this is why the 'Verse of Light' (24:35), which describes God in a series of metaphors, is the most used verse in the Qur'an for unleashing the religious imagination. It has inspired great epic poems, calligraphy, artefacts and cultural products. Each metaphor in the verse has produced a trajectory of its own, leading the believers to explore new heights of imagination. The light that God casts in our bosom is the key to unleashing the full flight of our imagination:

God is the light of the heavens and the earth.
The simile of God's light is like a niche in which is a lamp,
The lamp in a glass,
The glass like a shimmering star,
Kindled from a blessed tree,
An olive, neither of the East nor of the West,
Its oil almost aglow, though untouched by fire.
Light upon light.

EPILOGUE

Reading the Qur'an is a demanding but a rewarding experience. As I said at the outset, it requires effort; although the endeavour has turned out to be a little more taxing than I expected. I must also admit to considerable intellectual pleasure along the way. So what have I discovered?

The Qur'an is a dynamic, interconnected text. It does not present a static view of society; but actively encourages change, evolution, progress, and asks us constantly to adjust to change. But to discover the underlying dynamics of the Qur'an one needs to do much more than simply read its verses in isolation and assume that what the verse says is all there is. One needs to connect one segment of the text to the next, and many other segments throughout the Sacred Text. Movement becomes visible when these connections are made, and a whole new dynamic of meaning emerges. The meaning evolves, develops and changes the more connections are made and the more we see the Qur'an as an integrated text.

We find some contradictions in the Qur'an but, as I have argued, they serve a special purpose. They point us toward directions and connections we are not used to considering. They tell us that the world itself and all that is in it, the creation of God, is complex, full of contradictions and not amenable to simplistic analyses of situations and problems. They suggest that choices we make always involve oppositions, and any moral choice requires us to think seriously about intended and unintended consequences. They express a general way of looking at the world, incorporating complexity and change as natural and essential.

Context is everything in the Qur'an. It is an eternal text; but it is also a text revealed in history, over 1,400 years ago, to a Prophet who lived in the Arabian society of the seventh century. In as far as it is a commentary on the life of the Prophet, a revelation that seeks to guide him through an eventful life, it

369

addresses and seeks to change the moral, social and cultural conditions of that period. But, of course, as a religious text the Qur'an is also a source of guidance for Muslims everywhere at all times. However, to understand the overall message of the Qur'an we must start by taking seriously the time and place of revelation, the days of Prophet Muhammad and his society and background. Learning as much as possible about the language, customs, circumstances and personalities at the time of revelation has heightened my sense of the distinction between what I think is specific and that which I find universal and timeless. Locating the time-bound detail, I have discovered, is essential for releasing the universal and timeless, which makes the Qur'an relevant and alive in my time and in relation to my problems. To understand the context of verses that I had read numerous times, and whose meaning I took for granted, is nothing short of enlightening.

To be a believer is to see the Qur'an as a living book. But this is not just a definition of a believer; it is also a statement about belief. What it means is that I, unlike those who see it as a fixed text, can never be certain about its meaning—which changes with changing circumstances. All I can do is interpret the Sacred Text, using my own reasoning and knowledge. But in the end I have to give the Qur'an the benefit of the doubt—my doubt that I have a complete grasp of what it is saying.

It is doubt and open-mindedness that keeps the text alive and capable of revealing its relevance through different situations and circumstances. The moment a reader thinks that he or she possesses the capacity for full comprehension and total judgement, the text of the Qur'an starts to shrink and conforms to prejudices and predilections. As the celebrated Muslim thinker al-Ghazali suggested, the best way to read the Qur'an is by freeing the mind of all dogma, interpretations and commentaries—these limit and condition our understanding of the Qur'an [1]. We may also sometimes have to reject the obvious, outward exegesis and literal meaning to get a deeper appreciation of what the Qur'an is trying to say to us. An open text, with an eternal message, demands an open mind, ready to engage with all possibilities.

However, open engaging minds are not the hallmark of the contemporary Muslim world. Indeed, a couple of observations stand out quite clearly. First, Muslim society in our time seems to bear no relationship to the eternal message of the Qur'an. The Qur'an's emphasis on justice and equity, truth and plurality, ethics and morality, humanity and diversity, reason and knowledge, rights and duties, and reading and writing—what I see as the main themes of the Sacred Text—are nowhere reflected in the contemporary Muslim world.

On the contrary, injustice and inequity, ignorance and illiteracy, oppression and inhumanity seem to be the norms. This is particularly evident in societies which claim most loudly that the Qur'an has a special place in their legal, political, social or cultural framework.

The second observation is related to the first. A great deal of what is justified nowadays on the basis of the Qur'an—from autocracy to theocracy, suppression of freedom of expression, obscene accumulation of wealth to gross inequity, oppression of women to the denial of rights to minorities, exclusive ownership of truth to suicide bombing—has no relationship to the Sacred Text whatsoever. The more that people use the Qur'an to justify their age-old customs and traditions, obnoxious behaviour and violent actions, it seems to me, the further they are from the spirit of the Sacred Text. For Muslims, the distinctive feature of contemporary times is the sheer abuse of all they supposedly believe to be sacred.

My reading of the Qur'an has not just brought these observations into sharper focus, but made me realise just how anchored Muslims are in unjust interpretations of history. While I emphasise the historical context of the Qur'an, in fact I read it without history—leaving out the time between the Prophet and myself. Indeed, I am open to the accusation that I have offered an ahistorical reading of the Qur'an. I have not tried to read the Qur'an through the traditions of interpretation in which I was raised, of which I am aware, and by which my day-to-day life as an ordinary Muslim has been and is shaped.

Unwittingly, this has turned out to be a good rather than a bad thing. Without the weight of tradition, I have encountered the Qur'an anew. Moreover, by reading the Qur'an on its own terms, by largely ignoring classical commentaries, I discovered that a great deal of historic interpretation has taken Muslim societies in the wrong direction. Muslim attitudes to women, apostasy, other religions, freedom of expression, democracy, morality and ethics, the delusion that the *Shari'a* is divine, are all firmly anchored in dim and distant history where great jurists supposedly gave unalterable opinions and interpretations. However relevant these interpretations may have been in history, they have little or no relevance today. Indeed, a contemporary reading of the Qur'an reveals many historic rulings and interpretations to be diametrically opposed to the actual teachings of the Qur'an. I always suspected this. But to see it unfold, as I read and interpreted various verses and passages for myself, has been nothing short of a revelation.

The Qur'an invites us not to look backwards but to see ahead. History in the Qur'an provides narratives of caution, seminal lessons in hubris and folly.

These serve as building blocks for the future. The Qur'an seeks to guide and change individual and social behaviour and transform society—things that can only be accomplished in the future.

There are three vital future lessons I have drawn from my reading. In interpreting the Qur'an, we must differentiate between legal requirements and moral injunctions. Muslim tradition sees the Qur'an as a book of law, rather than the source of principles for the making of laws. The Qur'an seeks to build a moral society, not a legalistic one. A legalistic society, as we see in countries where the *Shari'a* has been imposed, does not necessarily uphold moral virtues. And laws, even those supposedly derived from the Qur'an, need not be just, equitable and ethical. Only by specifically addressing the moral and ethical outlook of the Qur'an will Muslims be able to address the urgent issues of contemporary times, such as women's rights, freedom of expression and the development of civic society.

As we have seen, legal injunctions in the Qur'an are relatively few; and most of them are quite specific and specifically time-bound. Yet, behind each legal injunction is a principle which, as we have discovered, can be understood in its historic context and set in motion through time. It is the principle that is paramount. The specific legal injunction, or law, provides an example of how that principle was realised during the life of the Prophet Muhammad in the context of seventh-century Arabia. When the context changes or the law ceases to reflect the principle, the law must be changed. Indeed, if the law is not changed it will inevitably end by violating the principle. There are legal injunctions in the Qur'an—for example, those relating to crime and punishment and female witnesses—that are deeply rooted in the context of the time of revelation. These legal injunctions made sense within their context; they are specific and not eternal. We need to develop new laws based on the eternal principles behind these injunctions, which will actually promote their principles. It makes no sense, for example, to punish people on the basis of a seventh-century penal system when we have prisons and other correctional facilities; or for women to wait for four months before remarrying after the death of their husbands when we have tests to determine whether they are pregnant; or to assume that in the contemporary world women are less capable of handling business and financial matters than men. The challenge of understanding the Qur'an is to understand it in our own time, to relate the principles the Sacred Text exhorts to our own conditions.

It is also necessary, I think, to ask relevant questions. If you approach the Qur'an with the view that it has nothing to say to you, that it is an outdated historic text, then the questions you will ask will yield nothing of importance. If it is interrogated with a view to finding faults, then your questions echo your own prejudices. Believers are not immune, I would argue; they too need to ask questions of significance and value. It is not productive to ask what the Qur'an says about this or that specific subject; much more fruitful is to ask how one can draw moral guidance from the Sacred Text on particular issues that are of concern to us. To produce genuine insight, we need a higher order of questions: not what the Qur'an says about individual behaviour, but what can we learn from the Qur'an about combining individual fulfilment with individual acceptance of social responsibilities; to ask not just what the Qur'an says about justice, but rather what guidance it offers on reducing injustice; to ask not just what the Qur'an says about freedom of expression, but rather what it teaches about managing debate and dissent in a complex society, increasingly vulnerable to disruptions; to ask not just what the Qur'an says about establishing peace, but also what guidance it provides about peaceful social change. Simplistic questions generate simplistic answers; complex questions would lead to a more holistic and deeper understanding of the Sacred Text.

Reading the Qur'an, I have come to realise, is not a one-dimensional, reductive act. Rather, it is a process, involving synthesis, looking for interconnections, discovering context, wrestling with contradictions, and asking complex questions. And one should not limit oneself to traditional modes of exegesis. One needs to use any relevant method that enhances understanding. An eternal text, by definition, is open to all methods of reading.

So, with new determination, I say that we Muslims have to teach ourselves to read and think about the Qur'an, liberated from the weight of tradition and classical commentaries. Tradition has come to mean following what previous generations thought and have said about the Qur'an: a process perpetuated by religious scholars who claim sole authority to interpret the Qur'an. We need to read and think for ourselves, rather than simply repeat. Muslim scholars and experts should not be gatekeepers, permanently excluding the rest from using their own knowledge and insight to make sense of the Qur'an for themselves. Such power raises traditional scholars above the Sacred Text itself.

My fellow Muslims will raise an obvious question. If we liberate the Qur'an for personal interpretation, what happens to consensus? How do we, in the face of diverse personal readings, arrive at collective judgements? We do so not only by reading and thinking, but also by inclusive debate. Consensus is not something that can be imposed from above, by a select group of scholars. It emerges from below, through open discussion and debate about meaning and relevance. When we accept the Qur'an as nothing more than a given set of dos and don'ts there is no debate and we make our faith less and less relevant to the world in which we live.

Of course, there is a possibility, the inevitable nagging doubt, the self-critical reflection that I got everything wrong. In which case, I seek refuge in the words of the Qur'an itself: 'You will not be blamed if you make a mistake, only for what your hearts deliberately intend, God is most forgiving and merciful' (33: 5). I hope my intention is clear and I have made a small contribution to the permanent work in progress that is human engagement with the living Qur'an.

NOTES AND REFERENCES

PREFACE

1. Harold Bloom, *The Western Canon: The Books and Schools of the Ages*, Harcourt, Brace and Company, New York, 1994, p. 531.

PROLOGUE

1. Fazlur Rahman, *Major Themes of the Qur'an*, Bibliotheca Islamica, Chicago, 1980, p. xi.
2. Ziauddin Sardar, *The Future of Muslim Civilisation*, Croom Helm, London, 1979; second edition, Mansell, London, 1987.
3. Al-Ghazali, *The Jewels of the Qur'an*, edited by Laleh Bakhtiar, Great Books of the Islamic World, Chicago, 2009, p. 11.
4. Ibn Rushd concludes his monumental defence of rationality, and attack on al-Ghazali, with these words. *Averroes' Tahafut al-Tahafut (The Incoherence of the Incoherence)*, translated by Simon van den Berch, Luzac, London, 1978; one-volume edition of the original two-volume 1954 version, p. 363.

PART ONE

1. Our regular visits to Indian movies did have their virtues! See Ziauddin Sardar, 'Dilip Kumar Made Me Do It' in Ashis Nandy (editor), *The Secret Politics of Our Desires*, Oxford University Press, Delhi, 1998; Zed Press, London, 1998.
2. For a more detailed account, see my intellectual autobiography, *Desperately Seeking Paradise: Journeys of a Sceptical Muslim*, Granta Books, London, 2004.
3. Sayyid Qutb, *In the Shade of the Qur'an*, translated by M. Adil Salahi and Ashur A. Shamis, MWH London publishers, London, 1979, volume 30, p. 301.
4. Ebrahim Moosa, 'Inside the Madrasa', *Boston Review*, January/February 2007.
5. Mahir-ul-Qaderi, 'Lament of the Qur'an', translated from Urdu by Latif Choudry, *The Muslim*, December 1969, p. 58.
6. M. M. Al-Azami provides a detailed account of how the final text was produced in *The History of the Qur'anic Text from Revelation to Compilation*, UK Islamic Academy, Leicester, 2003.

7. This view is associated with P. Crone and M. Cook, *Hagarism: The Making of the Islamic World*, Cambridge University Press, Cambridge, 1977; and J. Wansbrough, *Qur'anic Studies: Sources and Method of Scriptural Interpretation*, Oxford University Press, Oxford, 1977.

8. See Mustansir Mir, *Coherence in the Qur'an*, American Trust Publications, Indianapolis, 1986.

9. Penguin, London, 1989.

10. See Neal Robinson, *Discovering the Qur'an: A Contemporary Approach to a Veiled Text*, SCM Press, London, 1996.

11. Students of science will appreciate this. I read physics at university and discovered that most of the physics I had learned during my schools days was so simplified that it was of little use in my undergraduate work.

12. Mona Siddiqui, *How to Read the Qur'an*, Granta Books, London, 2007, p. 103.

13. Farid Esack, *The Qur'an: A User's Guide*, Oneworld Publications, Oxford, 2005, pp. 1–10.

14. Mahmoud Ayoub, *The Qur'an and Its Interpreters*, State University of New York Press, Albany, 1984. I have used volume 1 quite extensively for this study.

15. Feras Hamza and Sajjad Rizvi with Farhana Mayer, *An Anthology of Qur'anic Commentaries*, Oxford University Press, Oxford, 2008, volume 1.

16. For a more detailed analysis of these films see Ziauddin Sardar, *Orientalism*, Open University Press, Milton Keynes, 1999, pp. 95–106.

17. See Bruce Lawrence (editor), *Messages to the World: The Statements of Osama bin Laden*, Verso, London, 2005.

18. Fazlur Rahman, 'Interpreting the Qur'an', *Inquiry*, May 1986, p. 45.

19. Ibid., p. 46.

20. Abdullah Saeed, *Interpreting the Qur'an*, Routledge, London, 2006.

21. See Ziauddin Sardar, 'Paper, Printing and Compact Discs: The Making and Unmaking of Islamic Culture', *Media, Culture, Society*, 15, 1992, pp. 43–59.

22. Sayyed Abdul Hasan Ali Nawdi, *Studying the Glorious Qur'an*, UK Islamic Academy, Leicester, 2003, p. 84. The Maulana is addressing the pious who are into 'hearing and obeying' and goes on to suggest that 'fear' and 'belief in the unseen' are essential for understanding the Qur'an.

23. Asma Barlas, 'Believing Women' in *Islam: Unreading Patriarchal Interpretations of the Qur'an*, University of Texas Press, Austin, 2002, p. xii.

24. Quoted by A. L. Tibawi, 'Is the Qur'an Translatable? Early Muslim Opinion' in *Arabic and Islamic Themes*, Luzac, London, 1976, pp. 78–9.

25. *Fatawa al-Imam Muhammad Rashid Rida*, Dar al-Kitab al-Jadid, Beirut, 1970, vol. 2, pp. 642–50.

26. M. M. Pickthall, *The Meaning of the Glorious Koran*, New American Library, New York, 1930, 'Translator's Foreword'.

27. A. J. Arberry, *The Koran Interpreted*, Oxford University Press, Oxford, 1964, p. x.

28. Tibawi, op. cit., p. 83.

29. Mahmoud Ayoub, 'Translating the Meaning of the Qur'an: Traditional Opinion and Modern Debates', *Inquiry*, May 1996, p. 38.

30. A recent example is the declaration of British author Sebastian Faulks: 'it is a depressing book. It really is. It's just the rantings of a schizophrenic. It's very one-dimensional, and people talk about the beauty of Arabic and so on, but the English translation I read was, from a literary point of view, very disappointing. There is also the barrenness of the message. I mean, there are some bits about diet...With the Qur'an there are no stories. And it has no ethical dimension like the New Testament, no new plan for life.' Cathy Galvin, 'The author of our misfortunes', *Sunday Times Magazine*, 23 August 2009, pp. 23–4.

31. See Mohammad Khalifa, *The Sublime Qur'an and Orientalism*, Longman, London, 1983.

32. The complete title of Ross's translation: *The Alcoran of Mahomet / Translated out of Arabique into French by the Sieur Du Ryer, Lord of Malezair, and resident for the King of France at Alexandria; and newly Englished [by Alexander Ross] for the satisfaction of all that desire to look into the Turkish vanities*, London, 1649.

33. George Sale, Koran, commonly called the Alcoran of Mohammed, translated into English immediately from the original Arabic; with explanatory notes, taken from the most approved commentators. To which is prefixed a preliminary discourse, London, 1734, p. vii.

34. Khalifa, op. cit., p. 44.

35. Constantin François Chasée-Beouf Volney, *Oeuvres Complètes*, Paris, 1860.

36. Charles M. Doughty, *Travels in Arabia Deserta*, Dover, New York, 1979; facsimile of original 1888 edition; volume 1, p. 142.

37. Thomas Carlyle, *On Heroes, Hero-worship and the Heroic in History*, Cassell, London, 1891, p. 42.

38. Ibid., p. 57.

39. Zaid Elmarsafy, *The Enlightenment Qur'an*, Oneworld Publications, Oxford, 2009, pp. 81–120.

40. Arberry, op. cit., p. xiii.

41. Pickthall states categorically: 'The Koran cannot be translated. That is the belief of old-fashioned Sheykhs and the view of the present writer', op. cit.

42. A moving account of his life is provided by M. A. Sherif, *Searching for Solace: A Biography of Abdullah Yusuf Ali Interpreter of the Qur'an*, Islamic Book Trust, Kuala Lumpur, 1994.

43. See, for example, the 'revised and edited in modern English' version of Pickthall's translations by Arafat K. El-Ashi, Amana, Beltsville, 1996.

44. Abdullah Yusuf Ali, *The Holy Qur'an: Text, Translation and Commentary*, Dar al Arabia, Beirut, 1968, p. v.

45. *The Holy Qur'an: English Translation of Meanings and Commentary*, Revised and Edited by the Presidency of Islamic Researches, IFTA, Call and Guidance, King

Fahd Holy Qur'an Printing Complex, Riyadh. The translation is not dated; but the Royal Decree, 'The Custodian of the two Holy Mosques King Fahd ibn Abdul Aziz Al-Saud, King of the Kingdom of Saudi Arabia, has the honour to order the printing of this Holy Qur'an and the translation of its meaning and commentary'), no. 12412, is dated 27/10/1405. The quote is from p. viii.

46. Muhammad Taqi-ud-Din Al-Hilali and Muhammad Muhsin Khan, *Interpretation of the Meanings of the Noble Qur'an*, Darussalam, Riyadh, 2007.

47. S. V. Ahmad Ali, *The Holy Qur'an with English Translation and Commentary according to the version of the Holy Ahlul Bait. With special notes from Ayatullah Agha Haji Mirza Mahdi Pooya Yazdi*, Karachi, 1964, p. 47.

48. *Qur'an: A Reformist Translation*, translated and annotated by Edip Yuksel, Layth Saleh al-Shaiban and Martha Schulte-Nafey, Brainbowpress.com, 2007.

49. Rashad Khalifa, *The Computer Speaks: God's Message to the World*, Islamic Productions International, Tucson, 1980.

50. Muhammad Asad, *Sahih al-Bukhari: The Early Years of Islam*, Dar Al-Andalus, Gibraltar, 1981; reprint of original 1938 edition.

51. Muhammad Asad, *The Road to Mecca*, Simon & Schuster, New York, 1954.

52. Muhammad Asad, *The Message of the Qur'an*, Dar Al-Andalus, Gibraltar, 1980, p. viii.

53. M. A. S. Abdel Haleem, *The Qur'an: A New Translation*, Oxford University Press, Oxford, 2004, p.ix.

54. Tarif Khalidi, *The Qur'an: A New Translation*, Penguin, London, 2008, pp. x–xi.

PART TWO

1. Shaykh Muhammad al-Ghazali, *A Thematic Commentary on the Qur'an*, translated by Ashore Shamis, International Institute of Islamic Thought, Herndon, 2000, p. 3.

2. Sayyid Abul Ala Mawdudi, *Towards Understanding the Qur'an*, translated by Zafar Ishaq Ansari, Islamic Foundation, Leicester, 1988, p. 37.

3. *Tafsir al-Qurtubi: Classical Commentary of the Holy Qur'an*, translated by Aisha Bewley, Dar al-Taqwa, London, 2003, p. 125.

4. Mahmoud Ayoub, *The Qur'an and Its Interpreters*, State University of New York Press, Albany, 1984, p. 49.

5. Ibid., p. 53.

6. All these characteristics are clearly evident in Richard Dawkins, *The God Delusion*, Black Swan, London, 2006 and Christopher Hitchens, *God is Not Great*, Atlantic Books, London, 2007. See also the elegant response of Karen Armstrong, *The Case for God*, Bodley Head, London, 2009 and Tina Beattie, *The New Atheists*, Darton, Longman and Todd, London, 2007.

7. Muhammad Asad, *The Message of the Qur'an*, Dar al-Andalus, Gibraltar, 1980, note 10, p. 5.

8. Sayyid Qutb, *In the Shade of the Qur'an*, translated by Adil Salahi and Ashur Shamis, Islamic Foundation, Leicester, 1999, p. 175.

9. Asad, op. Cit., pp. 34–5, note 137.

10. *Khuda Ke Liye*, directed by Shoaib Mansoor, released in 2007.

11. *Al-Khwarazni's Algebra*, Pakistan Hijra Council, Islamabad, 1989.

12. An interesting parallel is provided by Ashis Nandy, *The Intimate Enemy: Loss and Recovery of Self Under Colonialism*, Oxford University Press, Delhi, 1983, who argues that colonisation brutalised both the colonised and the colonisers.

13. Qutb, op. cit., p. 270.

14. Ibid., p. 273.

15. Mawdudi, op. cit., p. 153.

16. *The Autobiography of Malcolm X*, as told to Alex Haley, Penguin, London, 1965.

17. Merryl Wyn Davies, *Knowing One Another: Shaping an Islamic Anthropology*, Mansell, London, 1988, pp. 131–2.

18. Asad, op. cit., p. 50, note 216.

19. M. A. S. Abdel Haleem, *The Qur'an: A New Translation*, Oxford University Press, Oxford, 2004, p. 25.

20. See Janice Delaney, Mary Jane Lupton and Emily Toth, *The Curse: A Cultural History of Menstruation*, University of Illinois Press, Champaign, 1988; and Elissa Stein and Susan Kim, *Flow: The Cultural Story of Menstruation*, St. Martin's Griffin, New York, 2009.

21. This is a well-established point in science and development literature; I tried to show how technological aid increases dependency in *Science, Development and the Muslim World*, Croom Helm, London, 1977; see more recent studies, such as Paul Collier, *The Bottom Billion: Why the Poorest Countries are Failing and What Can Be Done About It*, Oxford University Press, Oxford, 2008; Dambisa Moyo, *Dead Aid: Why Aid is Not Working and How There is Another Way for Africa*, Penguin, London, 2010; and Amartya Sen, *Development as Freedom*, Oxford University Press, Oxford, 2001.

22. George Makdisi, *The Rise of Colleges*, Edinburgh University Press, Edinburgh, 1981.

23. Dante Alighieri, *The Divine Comedy*, translated by C. H. Sisson, Oxford University Press, Oxford, 2008.

24. Hans Wehr, *A Dictionary of Modern Written Arabic*, edited by J. M. Cowan, Otto Harrassowitz, Wiesbaden, 1979.

25. Asad, op. cit., p. 622, note 35.

26. Ibid.

27. See Ziauddin Sardar, 'The Language of Equality', Equality and Human Rights Commission, London, 2008.

28. After denigrating women in Western society, and singing the virtues of women in Islam, Muhammad Qutb asks: 'the demand for treating men and women as equals

in their function in life and the modes of their actual performance is concerned, can that ever be feasible?' And answers: 'that is simply impossible'. See Muhammad Qutb, *Islam: The Misunderstood Religion*, Barul Bayan, Kuwait, 1964, p. 190. Good examples of the traditional misogynist genre are Sayyid Abul Ala Mawdudi, *Purdah and the Status of Women in Islam*, Islamic Publications, Lahore, 1972; Mohammad Zafeeruddin Nadvi, *Modesty and Chastity in Islam*, Islamic Book Publishers, Kuwait, 1982; and the classic text, *Perfecting Women: Maulana Ashraf Ali Thanawis Bihishti Zewar*, translated by Barbara Daly Metcalf, Oxford University Press, Delhi, 1992.

PART THREE

1. For a more detailed account see Geoffrey Parrinder, *Jesus in the Qur'an*, Oneworld Publications, Oxford, 2003.
2. See the chapter on Eschatology in Fazlur Rahman, *Major Themes of the Qur'an*, Bibliotheca Islamica, Chicago, 1980.
3. Ibid., p. 81.
4. As for example in the case of *The Satanic Verses*, and more recently with the Danish cartoon affair. See Ziauddin Sardar and Merryl Wyn Davies, *Distorted Imagination: Lessons from the Rushdie Affair*, Grey Seal, London, 1990; and Jytte Klausen, *The Cartoon That Shook the World*, Yale University Press, London, 2009. Klausen argues that the affair was a political rather than a cultural conflict.
5. It is interesting to note how all the biographies of the Prophet are written in exactly the same way, emphasising the same aspects of his life. See 'Rewriting the Seerah' in Ziauddin Sardar, *Islamic Futures: The Shape of Ideas to Come*, Mansell, London, 1985.
6. A. Guillaume, *The Life of Muhammad: A Translation of Ibn Ishaq's Sirat Rasul Allah*, Oxford University Press, Oxford, 1955.
7. Although it is not surprising that early Muslim historians saw history in less dynamic ways. See Nisar Ahmed Faruqi, *Early Muslim Historiography*, Idarah-I Adabiyat-I Delli, Delhi, 1979.
8. See the excellent Richard Fletcher, *Moorish Spain*, Weidenfeld & Nicolson, London, 1992; and the more detailed two-volume survey, *The Legacy of Muslim Spain*, Brill, Leiden, edited by Salma Khadra Jayyusi, not dated.
9. Normal Daniel's classic studies provide an excellent account of the relationship between Christianity and Islam: *Islam, Europe and Empire*, Edinburgh University Press, Edinburgh, 1966; *Arabs and Medieval Europe*, Longman, London, 1979; *Heroes and Saracens*, Edinburgh University Press, Edinburgh, 1984; *Islam and the West*, Oneworld Publications, Oxford, 1993 (original edition, 1960); for a concise account see Ziauddin Sardar, *Orientalism*, Open University Press, Milton Keynes, 1999.

10. See Mahmood Ahmad Ghazi, *The Islamic Renaissance in South Asia (1707–1867): The role of Shah Waliullah and his successors*, Adam Publishers, 2004.

11. Merryl Wyn Davies used this verse to develop a model of Islamic anthropology; see her *Knowing One Another: Shaping an Islamic Anthropology*, Mansell, London, 1988.

12. For a contemporary perspective see Abdou Filali-Ansary and Sikeena Karmali Ahmed (editors), *The Challenge of Pluralism: Paradigms from Muslim Contexts*, Edinburgh University Press, Edinburgh, 2009.

13. The line occurs in Jean-Paul Sartre's 1944 play, *No Exit*.

14. Anwar Ibrahim argues that the *umma* now includes all the marginalised and oppressed people of the world. See his essay 'The Ummah and Tomorrow's World', *Futures* 23 (3), April 1991, pp. 302–10.

15. See Hammudah Abd al-Ati, *The Family Structure in Islam*, American Trust Publications, Indianapolis, 1997.

16. For a fascinating account of how reason, beyond simple logic, can be a source of values and morality and shaped the ethical tradition of Muslim societies, see George Hourani's collection of papers in *Reason and Tradition in Islamic Ethics*, Cambridge University Press, Cambridge, 1985.

17. See Jurgen Habermas, *The Theory of Communicative Action, Vol. 1: Reason and the Rationalization of Society*, translated by T. McCarthy, Beacon Press, Boston, 1984.

18. There were over 500 definitions of *'ilm* during the classical period of Muslim civilisation, most explained and explored by Franz Rosenthal, *Knowledge Triumphant: The Concept of Knowledge in Medieval Islam*, Brill, Leiden, 1970.

19. For the dire state of knowledge in Muslim societies, see *The Arab Human Development Report 2003: Building a Knowledge Society*, Cairo, 2003; for a more general exploration, see Ziauddin Sardar (editor), *An Early Crescent: The Future of Knowledge and the Environment in Islam*, Mansell, London, 1989.

20. M. A. S. Abdel Haleem, *The Qur'an: A New Translation*, Oxford University Press, Oxford, 2004, p. xviii.

21. See Tahir Wasti, *The Application of Islamic Criminal Law in Pakistan: Sharia in Practice*, Brill, Leiden, 2009.

22. Abdel Haleem, op. cit., p. 20. For an explanation of how *qisas* came to shape Islamic law see Yasin Datton, *The Origins of Islamic Law*, Routledge, London, 2002.

23. For an alternative view see Wael B. Hallaq, *An Introduction to Islamic Law*, Cambridge University Press, Cambridge, 2009.

24. This and subsequent citations are from the Universal Declaration of Human Rights: http://www.un.org/en/documents/udhr/index.shtml

25. For a general comparison see Masood A. Baderin, *International Human Rights and Islamic Law*, Oxford University Press, Oxford, 2005.

26. The details of the International Covenant on Economic, Social and Cultural Rights can be found at: http://www2.ohchr.org/english/law/cescr.htm

27. Ziauddin Sardar, *Postmodernism and the Other*, Pluto Press, London, 1998, Chapter 2, 'The joy of cynical power'.

28. For a more detailed discussion, see Ziauddin Sardar (editor), *The Touch of Midas: Science, Values and the Environment in Islam and the West*, Manchester University Press, Manchester, 1982.

29. St. Augustine, *The City of God*, Penguin Classic, London, 2003.

30. Francis Bacon, *Advancement of Learning*, with an Introduction by Stephen Jay Gould, Modern Library Classics, New York, 2001.

31. For an elaboration of this argument see Abdullah Naseef, 'Dawa: Planning Beyond Disasters' in Merryl Wyn Davies and Adnan Khalil Pasha, *Beyond Frontiers: Islam and Contemporary Needs*, Mansell, London, 1989.

32. 'Disputes Between Animals and Man' has been translated as *The Island of Animals* by Denys Johnson Davies, Quartet Books, London, 1994.

33. See the brilliant Titus Burckhardt, *Fez: The City of Islam*, Islamic Text Society, Cambridge, 1992.

34. There are numerous translations of Sadi, for example, *The Gulistan of Sadi*, translated by Edward B. Eastwick, Octagon Press, London, 1979; and *The Bustan*, translated by H. Wilberforce Clarke, Darf, London, 1985.

35. Farid al Din Attar, *Conference of the Birds*, Penguin Classic, London, 2005.

36. Kenneth Cragg, *Readings from the Qur'an*, Collins, London, 1988.

37. See the work of the fourteenth-century thinker, ibn Qayyim al-Jawzi'yah, *Patience and Gratitude*, translated by Nasiruddin al-Khattab, Taha, London, 1997.

38. For an interesting discussion see Muhammad Madani, *The Moderation of Islam*, Supreme Council of Islamic Affairs, Cairo, 1961.

39. Muhammad Hamidullah, *The First Written Constitution in the World: An Important Document of the Time of the Holy Prophet*, Ashraf, Lahore, 1975.

40. M. M. Al-Azami provides a list of sixty-eight companions who acted as scribes to the Prophet. *The History of the Qur'anic Text from Revelation to Compilation*, UK Islamic Academy, Leicester, 2003, p. 68.

41. See Roshdi Rashed (editor), *Encyclopaedia of the History of Arabic Science*, Routledge, London, 1996; Donald R. Hill, *Islamic Science and Engineering*, Edinburgh University Press, Edinburgh, 1993; George Makdisi, *The Rise of Colleges: Institutions of Learning in Islam and the West*, Edinburgh University Press, Edinburgh, 1981; Ehsan Masood, *Islam and Science*, Icon, London, 2009.

PART FOUR

1. For a background to the *Shari'a*, see Wael B. Hallaq, *The Origins and Evolution of Islamic Law*, Cambridge University Press, Cambridge, 2005; and *Sharia: Theory, Practice, Transformations*, Cambridge University Press, Cambridge, 2009.

2. A typical example of this suggestion comes from Abdur Rahman Doi, *Shari'ah: The Islamic Law*, Ta-ha Publishers, London, 1997.

3. *Muwatta' Imam Malik*, translated by Muhammad Rahimuddin, Kazi Publication, Chicago, 1994; see also Yasin Dutton, *The Origins of Islamic Law: The Qur'an, the Muwatta and Madinan Amal*, Routledge, London, 1999.

4. For various rules and regulations of *fiqh* and its role in the *Shari'a*, see Imran Ahsan Khan Nyazee, *Theories of Islamic Law*, Islamic Research Institute, Islamabad, 1994.

5. For the impact of the *Shari'a* on the Muslim world, see Rashid Ahmad Jalandhari, *Islamic Sharia and its Application with special reference to Pakistan*, Institute of Islamic Culture, Lahore, 2003; Mohammad Tawfiq Ladan, *Handbook on Sharia Implementation in Northern Nigeria*, League of Democratic Wormen, Kaduna, 2005; and Jorgen S. Nielson and Lisbet Christoffersen, *Sharia as Discourse*, Ashgate, Farnham, 2010.

6. For a more detailed analysis of this point see Chapter 5, 'Shariah as problem solving methodology', in Ziauddin Sardar, *Islamic Futures*, Mansell, London, 1985.

7. Hugh Kennedy, *The Early Abbasid Caliphate: A Political History*, Croom Helm, London, 1981.

8. On the whole notion of Islamic state, see S. A. A. Maudoodi, *First Principles of the Islamic State*, Islamic Publications, Lahore, 1967; Ishtiaq Ahmad, *The Concept of an Islamic State*, Pinter, London, 1987; and Asghar Ali Engineer, *The Islamic State*, Vikas, Delhi, 1994.

9. On the notion of *Vilat-e-Faqih* see Imam Khomeini, *Islamic Government*, translated by Hamid Algar, The Institute for Compilation and Publication of Imam Khomeini's Works, Tehran, n.d.

10. Qamaruddin Khan, *Political Concepts in the Qur'an*, Institute of Islamic Studies, Karachi, 1973, gives a similar argument, pp. 43–53.

11. Sir William Muir, *The Caliphate: Its Rise, Decline and Fall*, Edinburgh University Press, Edinburgh, 1915, pp. 4–5.

12. For an interesting democratic theory for Muslim societies, see Nader Hashemi, *Islam, Secularism and Liberal Democracy*, Oxford University Press, Oxford, 2009. Hashemi argues for both rethinking liberal democracy and Muslim political thought.

13. For various historical interpretation of this verse, see Mohamed Mahmoud, 'To Beat or Not to Beat: On the Exegetical Dilemmas Over Qur'an 4:34', *Journal of American Oriental Society*, 126 (4), 2006, pp. 537–50.

14. Laleh Bakhtiar, *The Sublime Qur'an*, www.sublimequran.org, Chicago, 2009.

15. Asma Barlas, *'Believing Women' in Islam: Unreading Patriarchal Interpretations of the Qur'an*, University of Texas Press, Austin, 2002.

16. Amina Wadud, *Women in the Qu'ran*, Oxford University Press, Oxford, 1999.

17. Leila Ahmed, *Women and Gender in Islam*, Yale University Press, New Haven, 1992.
18. Barlas, op. cit., p. 158.
19. Haleem, op. cit., p. 220.
20. For an excellent account and analysis of sexual problems and practices in Islam and Muslim societies, see Kecia Ali, *Sexual Ethics and Islam*, Oneworld Publications, Oxford, 2006.
21. On Pakistan's Hadood Ordinance, see Afiya Shehrbano Zia, *Sex Crime in the Islamic Context: Rape, Class and Gender in Pakistan*, ASR Publications, Lahore, 1994.
22. See Mohammad Hashim Kamali, *Punishment in Islamic Law: An Enquiry into the Hudud Bill of Kelantan*, Ilmiah Publishers, Kuala Lumpur, 2000.
23. Scott Siraj al-Haqq Kugle, *Homosexuality in Islam*, Oneworld Publications, Oxford, 2010, p. 2.
24. Scott Siraj al-Haqq Kugle, 'Sexuality, Diversity and Ethics' in *Progressive Muslims*, edited by Omid Safi, Oneworld Publications, Oxford, 2003, p. 217.
25. *Sahih Bukhari* translated by Muhammad Matraji, Islamic Book Service, Delhi, 2004 (9 volumes).
26. See Mohja Kahf, *Western Representations of the Muslim Women*, University of Texas Press, Austin, 1999.
27. Fatima Mernissi, *Women and Islam*, Blackwell, Oxford, 1991, provides an excellent account of the overall situation in Medina when 33:53 was revealed.
28. For a general discussion of how women appear in the Qur'an and how the Qur'anic verses have been interpreted in history and modern times, see Barbara Freyer Stowasser, *Women in the Qur'an, Traditions and Interpretations*, Oxford University Press, Oxford, 1994.
29. For truly extreme and obnoxious views, see S. A. A. Mawdudi, *Purdah and the Status of Women in Islam*, Islamic Publications, Lahore, 1972; and Mohammad Zafeerudding Nadvi, *Modesty and Chastity in Islam*, Islamic Book Publishers, Kuwait, 1982.
30. Haleem op. cit., footnote on p. 42.
31. Mohammad Hashim Kamali, *Freedom of Expression in Islam*, Berita Publishing, Kuala Lumpur, 1994
32. Ibid., pp. 218–19.
33. Muhammad Haykal, *The Life of Muhammad*, American Trust Publications, Indianapolis, 1976, p. 454.
34. I have explored the relationship between Islam and the emergence of science in the Muslim civilisation in *Explorations in Islamic Science*, Mansell, London, 1989; but for an alternative view see Ehsan Masood, *Islam and Science*, Icon Books, London, 2009.
35. For the latest research, see the excellent collection of papers in *The Enterprise of*

Science in Islam, edited by Jan Hogendijk and Abdelhamid Sabra, MIT Press, Cambridge, 2003.

36. See Jonathan Lyons, *The House of Wisdom*, Bloomsbury, London, 2009.

37. See George Saliba, *A History of Arabic Astronomy: Planetary Theories During the Golden Age of Islam*, New York University Press, New York, 1994.

38. George Sarton, *Introduction to the History of Science*, Baltimore, 1927.

39. Some of these theories have been put forward by Toby Huff, *The Rise of Early Modern Science: Islam, China and the West*, Cambridge University Press, Cambridge, 1993.

40. Ziauddin Sardar, 'Islamic Science: Beyond the Troubled Relationship', *Nature* 448, 12 July 2007, pp. 131–3.

41. Ziauddin Sardar, 'Weird Science', *New Statesman*, 21 August 2008.

42. Jamshed Akhtar, *The Ultimate Revelation*, Oriole International Books, Delhi, 1996.

43. Maurice Bucaille, *The Bible, The Qur'an and Science*, Paris, 1976; countless editions and translations.

44. Harun Yahya, *Miracles of the Qur'an*, Al-Attique Publishers, Scarborough, 2008.

45. Heinz Halm, *The Fatimids and their Traditions of Learning*, IB Tauris, London, 1997, p. 51.

46. L. E. Goodman, *Ibn Tufayl's Hayy Ibn Yaqzan: A Philosophical Tale*, Chicago University Press, Chicago, 2009.

47. Haroon Yayha, *Atlas of Creation*, Al-Attique Publishers, Scarborough, 2009.

48. See Keith Critchlow, *Islamic Patterns*, Thames & Hudson, London, 1976.

49. See Carel J. Du Ry, *Art of Islam*, Harry Abrams, New York, 1970; Markus Hattstein and Peter Delius, *Islam: Art and Architecture*, Konemann, Cologne, 2000; and *Treasures of Islam*, Sotheby's, London, 1985.

50. See Sheila S. Blair, *Islamic Calligraphy*, Edinburgh University Press, Edinburgh, 2008; and for contemporary revival of calligraphy see Venetia Porter, *World Into Art*, British Museum, London, 2006.

51. This is best demonstrated in Muslim Spain. See Titus Burckhardt, *Moorish Culture in Spain*, Allen & Unwin, London, 1970.

52. As Michael Ball says in his famous song, 'Music', from the 2000 album *Music*.

53. George Atiyeh, *Al-Kindi: The Philosopher of the Arabs*, Kitab Bahvan, Delhi, 1994.

54. Quoted by Ebrahim Moosa, *Al-Ghazali and the Poetics of Imagination*, University of North Carolina Press, Chapel Hill, 2005, p. 177.

EPILOGUE

1. Al-Ghazali, *Ihya Ulum al-Din*, translated by Muhammad Abdul Quasen, Kegan Paul International, London, 1982, Book 8, p. 71.

BIBLIOGRAPHY

Abdel Haleem, M. A. S., *The Qur'an: A New Translation*, Oxford University Press, Oxford, 2004.

Abdel Haleem, M. A. S., *Understanding the Qur'an*, IB Tauris, London, 1999.

Abdul-Rauf, H., *Qur'an Translation: Discourse, Texture, Exegesis*, Curzon, Richmond, 2001.

Afsaruddin, Asmaa, *The First Muslims: History and Memory*, Oneworld Publications, Oxford, 2008.

Ahmed, Leila, *Women and Gender in Islam*, Yale University Press, New Haven, 1992.

Al-Azami, M. M., *The History of the Qur'anic Text, from Revelation to Compilation*, UK Islamic Academy, Leicester, 2003.

Al-Ghazali, Sheikh Muhammad, *A Thematic Commentary on the Qur'an*, International Institute of Islamic Thought, Herndon, 2000.

Al-Ghazali, Sheikh Muhammad, *The Jewels of the Qur'an*, translated by M. Abul Quasem, Kegan Paul, London, 1983.

Al-Hilalai, Taquiuddin and Khan, Muhammad Muhsin, *Explanatory English Translation of the Meaning of the Holy Qur'an*, Chicago, 1977.

Ali, Abdullah Yusuf, *The Holy Qur'an: Translation and Commentary*, Lahore, 1934–7.

Ali, Kecia, *Sexual Ethics and Islam*, Oneworld Publications, Oxford, 2006.

Ali, Muhammad, *The Holy Qur'an: English Translation*, Lahore, 1917.

Ali, S.V. Ahmad, *The Holy Qur'an with English Translation and Commentary according to the version of the Holy Ahlul Bait. With special notes from Ayatullah Agha Haji Mirza Mahdi Pooya Yazdi*, Karachi, 1964.

Arberry, A. J., *The Koran Interpreted*, Oxford University Press, Oxford, 1964.

Arkoun, Mohammed, *The Unthought of Contemporary Islamic Thought*, Saqi Books, London, 2002.

Arkoun, Mohammed, *Rethinking Islam*, Westview Press, Boulder, 1994.

Asad, Muhammad, *The Message of the Qur'an*, Dar Al-Andalus, Gibraltar, 1980.

Ayoub, Mahmoud, *The Qur'an and Its Interpreters*, State University of New York Press, Albany, 1984.

387

Badawi, Elsaid M. and Haleem, Muhammad Abdel, *Arabic–English Dictionary of Qur'anic Usage*, Brill, Leiden, 2008.

Bakhtiar, Laleh, *The Sublime Qur'an*, www.sublimequran.org, Chicago, 2009.

Barlas, Asma, *'Believing Women' in Islam: Unreading Patriarchal Interpretations of the Qur'an*, University of Texas Press, Austin, 2002.

Bell, Richard, *The Qur'an translated with a crucial rearrangement of Surahs*, London, 1937.

Ben Nabi, Malik, *The Quranic Phenomenon*, American Trust Publications, Indianapolis, 1983.

Bewley, Aisha (translator), *Tafsir al-Qurtubi: Classical Commentary of the Holy Qur'an*, Dar Al-Taqwa, London, 2003, volume 1.

Brown, Daniel, *Rethinking Tradition in Modern Islamic Thought*, Cambridge University Press, Cambridge, 1966.

Campanini, Massimo, *The Qur'an: The Basics*, Routledge, London, 2007.

Cragg, Kenneth, *Readings in the Qur'an*, Collins, London, 1988.

Dar, Bahsir Ahgmad, *Quranic Ethics*, Institute of Islamic Culture, Lahore, 1960.

Daryabadi, Abdul Majid, *The Holy Qur'an with English Translation and Commentary*, Lahore, 1941–57.

Davies, Merryl Wyn, *Knowing One Another: Shaping An Islamic Anthropology*, Mansell, London, 1988.

Dawood, N. J., *The Koran*, Penguin, London, 1956.

Donnan, Hastings (ed.), *Interpreting Islam*, Sage, London, 2002.

Draz, M. A., *The Moral World of the Qur'an*, IB Tauris, London, 2008.

Draz, Muhammad Abdullah, *The Qur'an: An Eternal Challenge*, The Islamic Foundation, Leicester, 2001.

Elmarsafy, Zaid, *The Enlightenment Qur'an: The Politics of Translation and the Construction of Islam*, Oneworld Publications, Oxford, 2009.

Esack, Farid, *Qur'an, Liberation and Pluralism*, Oneworld Publications, Oxford, 1997.

Esack, Farid, *The Qur'an: A User's Guide*, Oneworld Publications, Oxford, 2005.

Fadel, Muhammad, 'Two Women, One Man: Knowledge, Power, and Gender in Medieval Sunni Legal Thought', *International Journal of Middle East Studies* 29 (2), May 1997, pp. 185–204.

Fakhry, Majid, *The Qur'an: A Modern English Version*, Garnet Publishing, Reading, 1997.

Filali-Ansary, Abdou and Ahmed, Sikeena Karmali (eds), *The Challenge of Pluralism: Paradigms from Muslim Context*, Edinburgh University Press, Edinburgh, 2009.

Goodman, Lenn, *Islamic Humanism*, Oxford University Press, Oxford, 2003.

Guillaume, A., *The Life of Muhammad: A Translation of Ibn Ishaq's Sirat Rasul Allah*, Oxford University Press, Oxford, 1955.

Hamid, Eltigani Abdelgadir, *The Qur'an and Politics*, International Institute of Islamic Thought, London, 2004.

Hamza, Feras, Rivzi, Sajjad and Mayer, Farhana, *An Anthology of Qur'anic Commentaries*, Oxford University Press, Oxford, 2008, volume 1.

Hashemi, Nader, *Islam, Secularism, and Liberal Democracy*, Oxford University Press, Oxford, 2009.

Hawting, R. and Shareef A., *Approaches to the Qur'an*, Routledge, London, 1993.

Ibn Rushd, *On the Harmony of Religion and Philosophy*, translated by G. Hourani, Luzac, London, 1971.

Irving, T. B., Ahmad, Khurshid and Ahsan, M. A., *The Qur'an: Basic Teachings*, The Islamic Foundation, Leicester, 1992.

Irving, T. B., *The Qur'an: The First American Version*, Vermont, 1985.

Izutsu, Toshihiko, *The Structure of the Ethical Terms in the Qur'an*, Keio University Institute of Philosophical Studies, Tokyo, 1959.

Jensen, J., *The Interpretation of the Koran in Modern Egypt*, Brill, Leiden, 1980.

Jullundri, Ali Ahmad Khan, *Translation of the Glorious Holy Qur'an with Commentary*, Lahore, 1962.

Kahf, Mohja, *Western Representations of the Muslim Woman*, University of Texas Press, Austin, 1999.

Kamali, Mohammad Hashi, *Islamic Law in Malaysia: Issues and Development*, Ilmiah Publishers, Kuala Lumpur, 2000.

Kamali, Mohammad Hashim, *Freedom of Expression in Islam*, Brita Publishing, Kuala Lumpur, 1994.

Khadduri, Majid, *The Islamic Concept of Justice*, John Hopkins University Press, Baltimore, 1984.

Khalidi, Tarif, *The Qur'an: A New Translation*, Penguin, London, 2008.

Khalifa, Mohammad, *The Sublime Qur'an and Orientalism*, Longman, London, 1983.

Khamenei, Sayyed Ali, *The General Pattern of Islamic Thought in the Qur'an*, Islamic Propagation Organisation, Tehran, 1985.

Khan, Muhammad Muhsin and Al-Hilali, Muhammad Taqi-ud-Din, *Interpretation of the Meanings of the Noble Qur'an*, Darussalam, Riyadh, 2007.

Khan, Qamaruddin, *Political Concepts in the Qur'an*, Institute of Islamic Studies, Karachi, 1973.

Khatib, M. M., *The Bounteous Koran: A Translation of Meaning and Commentary*, London, 1986.

Kidwai, A. R., *Bibliography of the Translations of the Meanings of the Glorious Qur'an into English 1649–2002: A Critical Study*, King Fahd Qur'an Printing Complex, Riyadh, 2007.

Kidwai, Abdur Raheem, *The Qur'an: Essential Teachings*, The Islamic Foundation, Leicester, 2005.

Kugle, Scott Siraj al-Haqq, *Homosexuality in Islam*, Oneworld Publications, Oxford, 2010.

Kymlicka, Will, *The Rights of Minority Cultures*, Oxford University Press, Oxford, 1995.

Lawrence, Bruce (ed.), *Messages to the World: The Statements of Osama bin Laden*, Verso, London, 2005.

Lawrence, Bruce, *The Qur'an: A Biography*, Atlantic Books, London, 2006.

Leaman, O. (ed.), *The Qur'an: An Encyclopaedia*, Routledge, London, 2005.

Madigan, D., *The Qur'an's Self-Image*, Princeton University Press, Princeton, 2001.

Mahmood, Tahir (ed.), *Human Rights in Islamic Law*, Institute of Objective Studies, Delhi, 1993.

Maitland, Sara, *A Big-Enough God*, Mowbray, London, 1995.

Mawdudi, Sayyid Abul Ala, *Towards Understanding the Qur'an*, The Islamic Foundation, Leicester, 1988–(6 volumes).

McAuliffe, J. D. (ed.), *Encyclopaedia of the Qur'an*, Brill, Leiden, 2001–5.

McAuliffe, Jane Dammen (ed.), *The Cambridge Companion to the Qur'an*, Cambridge University Press, Cambridge, 2006.

Mernissi, Fatima, *Women and Islam*, Blackwell, Oxford, 1991.

Mir, Mustansir, *Coherence in the Qur'an*, American Trust Publications, Indianapolis, 1986.

Mir, Mustansir, *Dictionary of Qur'anic Terms and Concepts*, Garland Publishing, London, 1987.

Moosa, Ebrahim, *Ghazali and the Poetics of Imagination*, University of North Carolina Press, Chapel Hill, 2005.

Nadvi, Syed Muzaffaruddin, *A Geographical History of the Qur'an*, Ashraf, Lahore, 1936.

Nadwi, Sayyed Abdul Hasan Ali, *Studying the Glorious Qur'an*, UK Islamic Academy, Leicester, 2003.

Nadwi, Sayyid Abul Hasan Ali, *Guidance from the Holy Qur'an*, The Islamic Foundation, Leicester, 2005.

Othman, Norani (ed.), *Shari'a Law and the Modern Nation-State*, Sisters in Islam, Kuala Lumpur, 1994.

Palmer, E. H., *The Koran*, London, 1880.

Parrinder, Geoffrey, *Jesus in the Qur'an*, Oneworld Publications, Oxford, 2003 (reprint of 1965 edition).

Penrice, John, *A Dictionary and Glossary of the Qur'an*, Curzon Press, London, 1976; original edition, 1873.

Pickthall, M. M., *The Meaning of the Glorious Koran*, London, 1930.

Presidency of Islamic Researches, IFTA, Call and Guidance, *The Holy Qur'an: English Translation of Meanings and Commentary*, King Fahd Holy Qur'an Printing Complex, Riyadh.

Presidency of Islamic Researches, *The Holy Qur'an: English Translation of the Meanings and Commentary*, King Fahd Holy Qur'an Printing Complex, Medina, 1990.

Qutb, Sayyid, *In the Shade of the Qur'an*, The Islamic Foundation, Leicester, 1999, volume 1.

Rahman, Fazlur, *Islamic Methodology in History*, Central Institute of Islamic Research, Karachi, 1965.

Rahman, Fazlur, *Major Themes of the Qur'an*, Bibliotheca Islamica, Chicago, 1980.

Rahman, Fazlur, *Revival and Reform in Islam*, Oneworld Publications, Oxford, 2000.

Rippen, A. (ed.), *The Qur'an and its Interpretative Tradition*, Ashgate, Farnham, 2001.

Robinson, Neal, *Discovering the Qur'an: A Contemporary Approach to a Veiled Text*, SCM Press, London, 1996.

Rodwell, J. M., *The Koran*, London, 1861.

Rosenthal, Franz, *The Classical Heritage of Islam*, University of California Press, Berkeley, 1965.

Ross, Alexander, *The Alcoran of Mahomet translated out of Arabique into French, by the Sieur Du Ryer... And newly Englished, for the satisfaction of all that desire to look into the Turkish vanities*, London, 1649.

Saeed, Abdullah, *Interpreting the Qur'an*, Routledge, London, 2006.

Safi, Omid (ed.), *Progressive Muslims*, Oneworld Publications, Oxford, 2003.

Sale, G., *The Koran: Commonly called the Alkoran of Mohammed*, London, 1734.

Sands, K. Z., *Sufi Commentaries on the Qur'an in Classical Islam*, Routledge, London, 2006.

Sardar, Ziauddin, *Desperately Seeking Paradise: Journeys of a Sceptical Muslim*, Granta Books, London, 2004.

Sardar, Ziauddin (ed.), *An Early Crescent: The Future of Knowledge and the Environment in Islam*, Mansell, London, 1989.

Sardar, Ziauddin, *Islamic Futures: The Shape of Ideas to Come*, Mansell, London, 1985.

Sardar, Ziauddin, *Orientalism*, Open University Press, Milton Keynes, 1999.

Sardar, Ziauddin, *The Future of Muslim Civilisation*, Croom Helm, London, 1979; second edition, Mansell, London, 1987.

Sarwar, Ghulam, *Translations of the Holy Qur'an*, Singapore, 1920.

Shakir, M. M., *Holy Qur'an*, New York, 1982.

Sherif, Faruq, *A Guide to the Contents of the Qur'an*, Garnet Publishing, Reading, 1995.

Sherif, M. A., *Searching for Solace: A Biography of Abdullah Yusuf Ali, Interpreter of the Qur'an*, Islamic Book Trust, Kuala Lumpur, 1994.

Siddiqui, Mona, *How to Read the Qur'an*, Granta Books, London, 2007.

Stowasser, Barbara Freyer, *Women in the Qur'an, Traditions and Interpretation*, Oxford University Press, Oxford, 1994.

Tabatabai, Sayyed Muhammad Husain, *The Qur'an in Islam*, Islamic Propagation Organisation, Tehran, 1984.

Taj-Farouki, S. (ed.), *Modern Muslim Intellectuals and the Qur'an*, Oxford University Press, Oxford, 2004.

Tibawi, A. L., 'Is the Qur'an Translatable? Early Muslim Opinion' in *Arabic and Islamic Themes*, Luzac, London, 1976.

Translation Committee, *The Majestic Qur'an: An English Rendition of Its Meaning*, Ibn Khaldun Foundation, Burr Ridge, Illinois, 2000.

Wadud, Amina, *Women in the Qur'an*, Oxford University Press, Oxford, 1999.

Wansbrough, J., *Qur'anic Studies: Sources and Method of Scriptural Interpretation*, Oxford University Press, Oxford, 1977.

Wasti, Tahir, *Sharia in Practice: The Application of Islamic Criminal Law in Pakistan*, Brill, Leiden, 2009.

Watson, Brenda, *Truth and Scripture*, Aureus, Glamorgan, 2004.

Watt, W. M. and Bell, R., *Introduction to the Qur'an*, Edinburgh University Press, Edinburgh, 1970.

Whittingham, Martin, *Al-Ghazali and the Qur'an: One Book, Many Meanings*, Routledge, London, 2007.

Yuksel, Edip, al-Shaiban, Layth Saleh and Schulte-Nafey, Martha, *Qur'an: A Reformist Translation*, Brainbowpress.com, 2007.

Zaman, Muhammad Qasim, *The Ulama in Contemporary Islam: Custodians of Change*, Oxford University Press, Oxford, 2002.

Zayid, Mahmud Y., *The Qur'an: An English Translation of the Meaning of the Qur'an*, Beirut, 1980.

INDEX

393

Halal: 300; as dietary arrangement, 236; concept of, 119–20

al-Halali, Muhammad Taqi al-Din: explanation of *fitna*, 48–9; explanation of *zalimun*, 49; Interpretation *of the Meaning of the Noble Qur'an in the English Language*, 48

Haleem, M. A. S. Abdel: 59, 338; background of, 51; description of *jalada*, 319; description of menstruation, 170–1; description of verses of Qur'an focusing on crime and punishment, 255; *The Qur'an: A New Translation*, 51–2, 54, 170, 200, 306–7; translation of term *'nashaza'*, 307

Hanafi School of Thought: founded by Imam Abu Hanifa, 39

Hanbal, Imam: 39; view of role of structure of Qur'an, 39

Hanifa, Imam Abu: background of, 39; development of *Al-Istihsan*, 286; founder of Hanafi School of Thought, 39

Haram: 300; as part of *Shari'a*, 270; concept and location of, 119, 270; established by Prophet Muhammad, 270

Hassan, Imam: grandson of Prophet Muhammad, 47

Hayan, Jabir ibn: role in foundations of chemistry, 354

Hayat: concept of, 184

Hell: denizens of, 329

Hijab: 335; as a political issue, 334; concept of, 329; occurrence in Qur'an, 329–30; origin of term, 331–2

Hijra: role in Indian and Pakistani culture, 327

Hinduism: Durganavami festival, 130; Krishna, 237; 'People of the Book', 237; Ram, 237; the Vedas, 237

Hima: as part of *Shari'a*, 270; concept and location of, 270; established by Prophet Muhammad, 270; in Saudi Arabia, 270

Hitchcock, Alfred: *The Birds*, 186

Homosexuality: as part of *fitra*, 324–5; Christian view of, 324; culture of, 327–8; Jewish view of, 324; Muslim view of, 324; lack of direct mention in Qur'an, 323, 327; use of term *'fahisha'* to designate in Muslim circles, 325–6

Hud: 217

Hussein, Imam: grandson of Prophet Muhammad, 47

Hyderabad: Nizam of, 45

Iblis: behaviour of, 106; refusal to submit to Adam, 366

ibn al-Arabi: mystical interpretation of Qur'an, 22

ibn Al-Haytham: establishment of optics as experimental science, 354

ibn Arabi: commentary of, xviii, 26, 70; followers of, 70

ibn Ishaq: *Life of Muhammad*, 225

ibn Kathir: commentary of, xviii, 26, 196

ibn Rushd: 354

ibn Sina: 354; writings on theory of music, 366

Ibn Taymiyya: aim to find evidence to justify death penalty for blasphemy, 339–40; influence of, 341

Ibn Tufayl: 354; *Life of Hayy*, 361

Ibrahim: story of attempted sacrifice of son of, 51

Ihram: 146

Ijma': concept of, 286

Ijaz: evolution of, 356

'Ilm: concept of, 253, 353

Imam: 58

In the Name of God: cast of, 119

India: 8, 49, 226, 237; contribution to First World War, 46; *Hijra*, 327; *ulama* of, 141

gay and lesbian community, 36; history of, 23, 28, 113, 120, 242, 284; literacy rates in societies of, 279–80; literal readings of Qur'an, 23; migration to Medina, 154, 159, 228, 306; modernists, 219; persecution of, 75, 136–7, 158, 342; poetry of, 366; political nature of, 302; prayer, 47, 57, 110, 113, 131, 207, 221, 225–6, 358, 365; preference to not depict Prophet Muhammad in images, 221; presence in Indonesia, 112; presence in Morocco, 112; progression of women in societies of, 201–2; prohibition of printing in societies of, 32–3; relations with other Arabian tribes, 139; relationship with Christians, 236; relationship with Jews, 235–6, 341; scholarship, 93, 113, 220; significance of Qur'an for, 5, 10, 14, 17, 60, 197, 363, 370–2; traditions of, 128, 204; view of homosexuality, 324–5; view of *mushaf*, 16; view of *ulama*, 32; worldview of, 66, 253, 288, 341, 367, 370

Muslim Brotherhood: and Sayyid Qutb, xviii, 7, 139
Muzdalifah: role of in *Hajj*, 146

Nabi: Adam as first, 217; role as category of Prophet, 216–17
Nadwi, Abdul Hasan Ali: commentary of, 35
Naskh: principle of, 225
Nigeria: prevalence of polygamy in, 305; religious tension in, 8; school system of, 9
Nimrod: and Abraham, 185; family of, 185
Niqab: opposition to, 334; origin of, 333
Noah (Nuh): xvi, 20, 217; parable of, 359; people of, 294

Oktar, Adnan: as Haroon Yahya, 357, 362; *Atlas of Creation*, 362; following of, 362; *Miracles of the Qur'an*, 357
Orientalism: 43: presence in translations, 45
Othman: establishment of committee of twelve companions of the Prophet, 15–16; *mushaf*, 16; Rightly Guided Caliph, 15, 298
Ottoman Empire: collapse of (1923), 47; liberal thinkers in, 362

Pakistan: 7, 17, 22, 27; and Jamaat-e-Islami, 139; capital punishment, 257; *Hijra*, 327; Hudud Ordinance, 256, 320; media of, 119; territory of, 3
Palestine: 51; history of, 293; occupied by Canaanites, 175
Persia: 39; culture of, 316, 333; Empire of, 288; expansion of Islam in, 23
Pharaoh: 294; family of, 310; in parable of Moses, 220, 231; oppression under, 159
Pickthall, Mohammad Marmaduke: background of, 45; *The Meaning of the Glorious Koran*, 45–6, 48; suggestion of menstruation as 'illness', 170; translation of term 'Qawwam', 309; view on translation of Qur'an, 40
Pompeii: ruins of, 185
Prophecy: as one community, 217; concept of, 215; humanity of, 347; Qur'an presentation of, 215; revelation, 216

Qawwam: concept of, 310; translation issues surrounding, 309
Qisas: concept of, 257–8; effect on conventional Muslim thought, 257–8; translation of, 257
Qiyas: concept of, 286
Qur'an: xiii–xxii, 4–11, 15–16, 19–24, 28–9, 31, 36–7, 41–2, 44–5, 57–9,

68–70, 72–3, 93, 107, 112, 119, 121,
123, 135, 141, 145, 149, 164, 171,
180, 184–6, 199, 201, 208, 265, 284,
289–90, 295, 309–10, 316, 339,
342, 351, 369, 371–4; aims for social
change in, 203, 245, 253, 275–6,
293, 334; *al-Fatiha*, xx; *al-Baqara*,
xx; and Bible xiii-xiv, xvi, 14; and
Prophecy, 215; and Torah, 14; and
ulama, 32; argumentative nature of,
26; avocation of chastity, 315; call
for self-defence when under
persecution in, 136–8, 141; care of
orphans in, 166, 168, 306; chapters
of, 57, 60, 63–4, 66, 71, 76; concept
of prophets in, 176; concept of risk
in, 269; concept of *shura* in, 176–7;
condemnation of corruption in, 132;
condemnation of *Riba*, 196;
confessional interpretations of, 22;
contradictions in, 227, 305, 308;
continuity in, 174; creation of
humanity in, 360–1; critical
interpretation of, 22; depiction of
Hereafter, 74; deviation of *Shari'a*
from, 288; difference between trade
and usury, 194, 197, 200; dynamic
nature of, 212; emphasis on justice
in, 269, 306; emphasis on need for
humility in, 92; emphasis on
plurality of creation in, 64; equality
of humanity in, 124, 241–4, 261,
263, 269, 274, 345, 347–8; feminist
interpretation of, 36, 204, 310; focus
on governance in, 293–4; gender-
based reading of, 172, 203, 307, 335;
goals of, 283; guidelines for religious
harmony in, 238; guidelines for
witnessing usury in, 200–1; *Hijab* in,
329–30; history as a guide in,
231–3; idea of patience, 275;
importance of science in, 362;
institution of fasting as form of
worship, 130; Jesus in, 217–18;
language used in, xvi, 15, 34–5, 40,

51–3, 60–1, 64, 84, 86–7, 110;
literal readings of, 23; memorisation
of, 279; migration as beneficial
exercise in, 159; morality of, xx, 343;
mystical interpretation of, 22, 211;
natural phenomena in, 266–7;
nature of charity in, 191–2, 274;
notion of measure in, 352; notion of
reason, 251–3; oral form of, 279;
parable of Adam and Eve in, 171;
parable of David and Goliath, 175,
177; parable of Talut/Saul, 175, 177;
perceived aggression in, 48;
perceived as scientific treatise,
355–7; perceived necessary caveat
when reading, 157; perceived sexism
in, 43; portrayal of homosexuality,
327; portrayal of sex in, 313, 315,
317, 321; power within framework
of as an *amana*, 297, 302–3;
prescription of fasting during
Ramadan in, 132; principles of, 25;
prohibition of alcohol in, xviii-xix,
225–6; prohibition of printing of in
Muslim societies, 32–3; property
rights in, 127; punishment for crime
in, 124–6; recitation of, 365;
revelation of (AD 610—632),
xv-xvii, xix, 4–5, 13–16, 23–4, 45,
50, 52, 63, 71, 74, 85, 90, 102–3,
136, 140, 195, 201, 218, 221, 256,
277, 317, 323, 330, 369–70; role in
the Enlightenment, 44; sexuality-
based reading of, 36; significance of
for Muslims, 5, 10, 14, 17, 60, 197;
socially rational interpretation of
verses of, 212–13; story of Hager,
117; structure of, 40, 51; *suras* of, 14,
16–17, 19, 22–4, 50, 52, 60, 68,
72–3, 80, 85, 91, 103–6, 124, 130,
138, 153, 156–8, 165, 168, 175,
192–3, 195–7, 201, 205, 207, 217,
221, 225, 229–30, 232, 247, 262,
266, 271, 274, 278, 303, 305–6,
313–14, 318, 323–4, 331, 341, 346;

The servants of the Lord of Mercy are those who walk humbly on the earth, and who, when the foolish address them, reply, 'Peace'! (25:63)